WITHDRAWN

HARVARD LIBRARY

WITHDRAWN

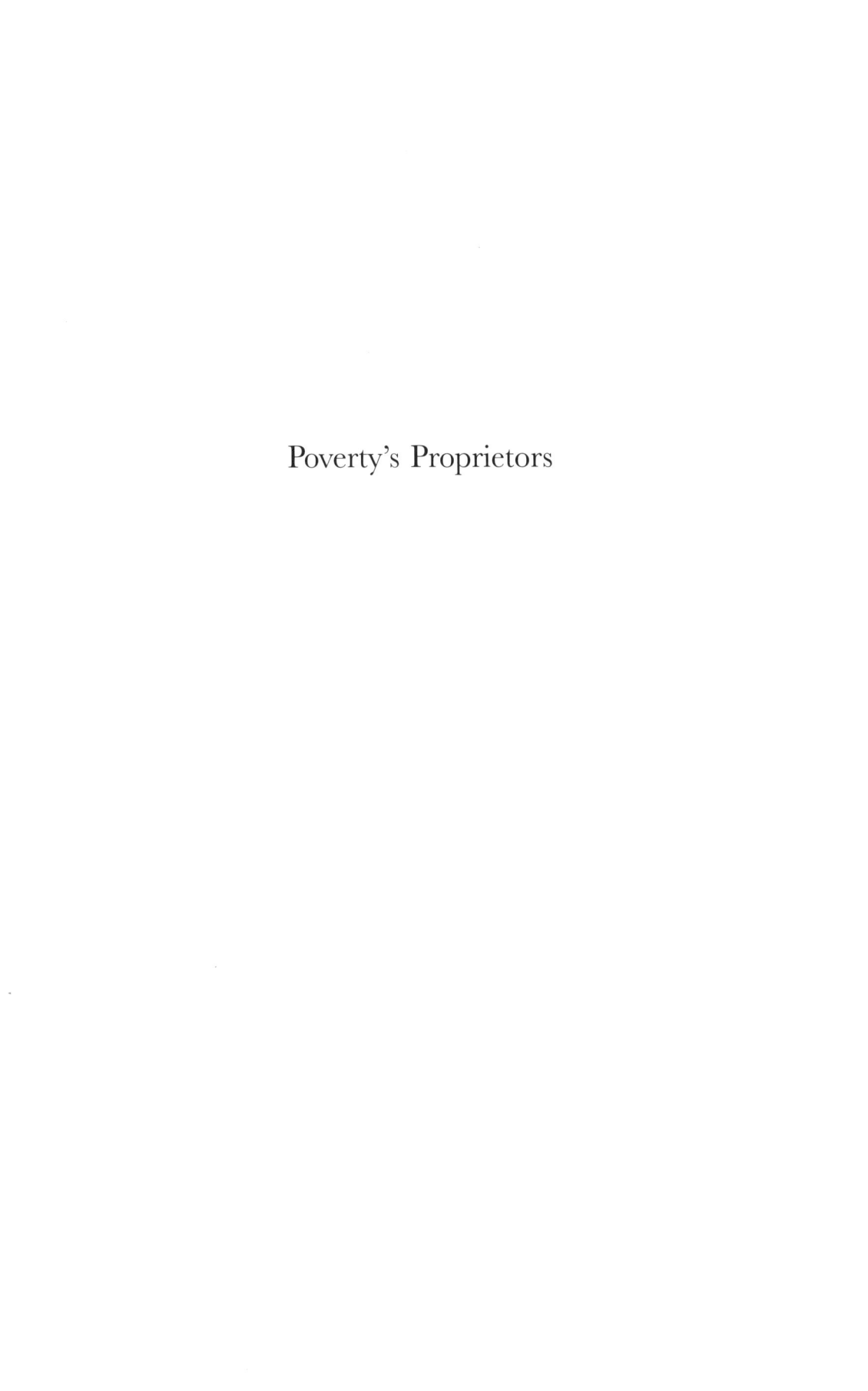

Poverty's Proprietors

Studies in the History of Christian Traditions

Founding Editor
Heiko A. Oberman †

General Editor
Robert J. Bast
Knoxville, Tennessee

In cooperation with
Henry Chadwick, Cambridge
Scott H. Hendrix, Princeton, New Jersey
Paul C.H. Lim, Nashville, Tennessee
Eric Saak, Indianapolis, Indiana
Brian Tierney, Ithaca, New York
Arjo Vanderjagt, Groningen
John Van Engen, Notre Dame, Indiana

VOLUME 143

Poverty's Proprietors

Ownership and Mortal Sin
at the Origins of the Observant Movement

By
James D. Mixson

BRILL

LEIDEN • BOSTON
2009

Cover illustration: Detail of manuscript Melk CM 737, fol. 100r.

This book is printed on acid-free paper.

Library of Congress Cataloging-in-Publication Data

Mixson, James D.
  Poverty's proprietors : ownership and mortal sin at the origins of the Observant Movement / by James D. Mixson.
    p. cm. — (Studies in the history of Christian traditions ; v. 143)
  Includes bibliographical references and index.
  ISBN 978-90-04-17405-4 (hardback : alk. paper) 1. Poverty, Vow of—History of doctrines—Middle Ages, 600–1500. 2. Property—Religious aspects—Catholic Church—History of doctrines—Middle Ages, 600–1500. 3. Church renewal—Catholic Church—History of doctrines—Middle Ages, 600–1500. 4. Monasticism and religious orders—Germany—Bavaria—History—Middle Ages, 600–1500. 5. Monasticism and religious orders—Austria—History—Middle Ages, 600–1500. 6. Bavaria (Germany)—Church history. 7. Austria—Church history. I. Title.
  BX2435.M557 2009
  271.00943'0902—dc22

2008053384

ISSN 1573-5664
ISBN 978 90 04 17405 4

Copyright 2009 by Koninklijke Brill NV, Leiden, The Netherlands.
Koninklijke Brill NV incorporates the imprints Brill, Hotei Publishing,
IDC Publishers, Martinus Nijhoff Publishers and VSP.

All rights reserved. No part of this publication may be reproduced, translated, stored in a retrieval system, or transmitted in any form or by any means, electronic, mechanical, photocopying, recording or otherwise, without prior written permission from the publisher.

Authorization to photocopy items for internal or personal use is granted by Koninklijke Brill NV provided that the appropriate fees are paid directly to The Copyright Clearance Center, 222 Rosewood Drive, Suite 910, Danvers, MA 01923, USA.
Fees are subject to change.

PRINTED IN THE NETHERLANDS

For Ashley

"Therefore take up the whole armor of God,
that you may be able to withstand in the evil day,
and having done all, to stand."

Ephesians 6:13

CONTENTS

List of Maps and Illustrations ix
Acknowledgements xi
Abbreviations xv

Introduction 1

Chapter One   Cultures of Property between Cloister and
   World 25

PART I

Chapter Two   Calls from Without 67

Chapter Three   Revolt from Within 97

PART II

Chapter Four   Property and Community between Principle
   and Practice 135

Chapter Five   Property and Community between Penance
   and Perfection 175

Conclusion 217

Appendix: An Inventory of Works "On Property" and
   Their Manuscripts 223

Bibliography 235
Index 255

LIST OF MAP AND ILLUSTRATIONS

Map

1. Religious Houses Referred to in Chapters Four and Five 133

Illustrations

1. Melk CM 737, fol. 96v 188
2. Melk CM 737, fol. 100r 189

ACKNOWLEDGEMENTS

Twenty years ago the University of Georgia history department welcomed me to its summer program at Oriel College, Oxford. After many days in a centuries-old community of learning that had been home to the Oxford Movement, and after many pints in a pub that claimed to have been in business for over seven hundred years, I became increasingly drawn to the study of the history of the church and of the Middle Ages. I have since cultivated a more complex sense of church history and the legacies of medievalism, and I have developed a healthy skepticism toward claims about medieval origins. But I could not have begun to do so without those UGA teachers who introduced me to the professional study of ancient and medieval history. I owe my first debts of gratitude to them—Joseph Berrigan, Stewart Brown, Judith Shaw, James Alexander, Richard LaFleur, Edward Best and their colleagues. I owe a similar debt to the Rotary Foundation and to my teachers at University of Edinburgh, Alan Hood and Roy Pinkerton, for helping me prepare for the rigors of graduate work in my field.

The current project began when John Van Engen kindly threw in my lap dozens and dozens of pages of microfilm photocopies. They were a reproduction of a sprawling, scarcely legible manuscript of John Nider on the reform of the religious orders. John had faith in me that I would soon make sense of it all, and he helped me use the manuscript to formulate and refine ideas about a new project on Observant reform. In the years to come he also taught me, through both word and example, how to meet the challenges of scholarship and life with charity, patience and perseverance. Kent Emery, Jr. taught me similar virtues. He helped me engage the challenges of text editing and codicology, and he helped me take command of all of the material my early research on the Observants uncovered. Professor Emery was also generous with his praise of my best ideas, and always honest with me about my worst.

During the early stages of my research and writing in Munich I enjoyed the hospitality of Professor Rudolf Schieffer, Herbert Schneider and Christian Lohmer at the Monumenta Germaniae Historica and Professors Stephan Weinfurter, Walter Ziegler and their students and colleagues at the Ludwig-Maximilian University in Munich, especially

Werner Bomm and his kind circle. I also received kind attention and encouragement from Kaspar Elm and his student Wilhelm Ernst Winterhager during a visit to Berlin, as well as Alexander Patschovsky, Bernhard Neidiger and Sabine von Heusinger during a brief visit to Constance. As my early research became a finished dissertation, Caroline Walker Bynum, William Courtenay, Johannes Fried, Patrick Geary and Robert Lerner provided me with challenging questions and encouragement at key points along the way. Olivia Remie Constable and Thomas Noble were also keen critics of the dissertation manuscript, and their insights proved to be of lasting importance in helping the project move from dissertation to book.

I have incurred other debts of gratitude as I have worked craft a publishable manuscript. From our first hilariously awkward conversation about John Nider in the halls of the MGH, Michael Bailey has been a close friend and valued colleague. A kindred scholarly and comedic spirit, he has endured all of this project's scholarly and personal trials. He has also patiently read (and re-read), in one form or another, almost all of what follows. Thomas Luongo was a keen critic of an early draft of the Introduction. Howard Kaminsky's criticism and advice helped ground the first chapter's arguments more firmly in the cultural and conceptual complexities of *status*. John Freed provided many helpful comments on the visitations outlined in the fourth chapter. Mark DuPuy, Julie Hotchin and Warren Lewis were similarly keen critics of the book's later chapters. Ulrich Horst has also read my work and advised me in ways that have helped refine my overall argument.

Other friends and colleagues have also helped me time and again professionally and personally over the years. I acknowledge with special fondness the friendship and intellectual companionship of Christine Caldwell Ames, David Bachrach, Daniel Hobbins, Lezlie Knox, Rachel Koopmans, Jonathan Lyon, David Mengel and Justin Poché. Michael Waddell, too, has been a cherished friend and colleague ever since that first-day graduate school joke about all of the "old books" in Notre Dame's collection. Still other scholars at other institutions have proven to be valuable colleagues and critics as well: Dave Collins, Sean Field, Valerie Garver, Jennifer Kolpacoff Deanne, June Mecham, Thomas Prügl, David Scheffler, Steven Stofferan, Michael Vargas, Anne Winston-Allen and Matthew Wranovix. I am also grateful to my colleagues and students at the University of Alabama for their professional and personal support in recent years.

Generous funding from many sources has supported this project at every stage. The Fulbright Commission, the Bavarian Cultural Ministry and the University of Notre Dame supported my early research and writing. The support of the German Academic Exchange Service; the Heckman scholars program of the Hill Monastic Manuscript Library; and the Research Advisory Council of the University of Alabama all supported the research and revision required to transform a dissertation project into a book. More important still has been the professional assistance of staff members at a several institutions: Roberta Baranowski, Margaret Cinninger, Linda Major and Marina Smyth at the University of Notre Dame; the librarians and staff of the Monumenta Germaniae Historica and the Bavarian State Library in Munich; the kind community of the Hill Monastic Manuscript Library in Collegeville, Minnesota, especially Columba Stewart, Matthew Heintzelman and Jennifer Cahoy; the librarians and staff of the Gorgas Library at the University of Alabama, especially Lou Pitschman, Brett Spencer, Millie Jackson and their colleagues in Interlibrary Loan. I am also grateful to Craig Remington and the staff of the Cartographic Research Laboratory at the University of Alabama for their care in preparing the map for Part II.

Through the long process of submission, revision and publication of a manuscript, my editor, Robert Bast, has been a kind voice of scholarly reason and insight. I am also grateful to the anonymous readers of the manuscript, who challenged me to contextualize, nuance and clarify my work in crucial ways. The tireless work of Deborah Johnson and Gera van Bedaf, has also saved me from all manner of errors and infelicities. Any that remain, of course, are my responsibility alone.

Certain passages in Chapter Three have appeared in portions of my essay, "The Setting and Resonance of John Nider's *De reformatione religiosorum*," in *Kirchenbild und Spiritualität. Dominikanische Beiträge zur Ekklesiologie und zum Kirchlichen Leben im Mittelalter. Festscrhift für Ulrich Horst OP zum 75. Geburtstag*, ed. Thomas Prügl and Marianne Schlosser (Schöningh, 2006), 319–38. I am grateful for permission to reproduce these passages here. I am also grateful to Professor Gottfried Glassner and the community of Melk for permission to reproduce the images in Chapter Five.

Three who shared in the unfolding of this project did not live long enough to see its conclusion. My cousin Debra Overholt was always enthusiastically curious about these strange sources and their stories.

My uncle, Professor William J. Hatcher, gently challenged me to be less of a perfectionist and to get the writing done, and helped me and my project mature in ways he never realized. His wife Kay Hatcher led the way in helping us become a part of faculty and community life in Tuscaloosa, showering us with a hospitality that turned junior-faculty life into a joyful Southern carnival. We miss all three of these loved ones still, and the completion of this project is a tribute to their memory.

The completion of this book is also a tribute to many other friends and family. Vin Moscardelli and his brothers have been lifelong friends and fellow travelers through a world of beer, bands and football games good and bad. Penn and Karin Müller-Osten welcomed me into their home in Germany too many times to recall, just as Bob and Joan Comas have done in Tuscaloosa. To Judge Brad Almond and the Tuesday Morning Knuckleheads, I owe far more than I can express here. I am also thankful for all the Bateman clan, who have shown us so much love and support in so many ways. To John, Lyn, Meredith and Drayton, thank you for always thinking the very best of the family medievalist. To my parents, thank you for teaching me how to work, to think, to laugh, and never to quit. And to my wife, Ashley, I owe my deepest expressions of gratitude. I dedicate this book to her, a companion who has taught me so much about courage and honesty, faith and forgiveness, hope and love.

ABBREVIATIONS

ACC	Acta Concilii Constanciensis. Edited by Heinrich Finke. 4 vols. Münster: Regensbergsche Buchhandlung, 1896–1928.
AFH	Archivum Franciscanum Historicum
AFP	Archivum Fratrum Praedicatorum
Amort	Vetus Disciplina Canonicorum Regularium et Secularium. Edited by Eusebius Amort. 5 vols. Venice, 1747. Reprint Farnborough: Gregg, 1971.
BBKL	Biographisch-Bibliographisch Kirchenlexicon
BHSTAM	Bayerisches Hauptstaatsarchiv München
BSB	Bayerische Staatsbibliothek
Canivez	Statuta capitulorum generalium ordinis Cisterciensis: ab anno 1116 ad annum 1786. Edited by J.-M. Canivez. 8 vols. Louvain: Bureaux de la Revue, 1933–41.
CCCM	Corpus Christianorum, Continuatio Medievalis
CIC	Corpus Iuris Canonici. Edited by Emil Friedberg. 2 vols. Leipzig, 1879–81. Reprint Union, NJ: Lawbook Exchange, 2000.
Clm	Codex Latinus Monacensis
CM	Codex Mellicensis
FRA	Fontes Rerum Austriacarum
Früwirth	Acta capitulorum generalium Ordinis Praedicatorum. Edited by A. Frühwirth. 3 vols. Rome, 1898–1900.
Mansi	Sacrorum conciliorum nova et amplissima collectio. Edited by Johannes Dominicus Mansi. 31 vols. Florence/Venice, 1758–98. Reprint Paris: H. Welter, 1901–27, 1960–61.
MGH	Monumenta Gemaniae Historica
ÖNB	Österreichische Nationalbibliothek
PL	Patrologia Latina
SC	Sources Chrétiennes
StLA-U	Steiermärkisches Landesarchiv—Urkunden
VL	Die deutsche Literatur des Mittelalters: Verfasserlexikon. Edited by Kurt Ruh et al. 11 vols. Berlin: De Gruyter, 1977–.

INTRODUCTION

A millennium ago monks, nuns and canons held a virtual monopoly on Christian ideals in Western Europe. They alone were "the religious" (*religiosi*)—those who had turned from the world and whose sacred vows had bound them back to Christian perfection. Their obligations were many, but one of the most essential was to renounce ownership (*proprium*) and to embrace the common life of the apostles. To do so was to uphold the commandment of Christ: "If you would be perfect go and sell all that you have, and follow me"; to echo Peter's words to Christ: "Behold, we have left all and followed you"; and to return to the ideal of the early church, when all lived "with one heart and one soul," all "had everything in common," and "it was given to each as any had need."[1] In pursuit of these ideals some religious bound themselves to the *Rule* authored by St. Augustine. "Do not call anything your own," he had commanded. "Possess everything in common. Your superior ought to provide each of you with food and clothing, not on an equal basis to all... but to each one in proportion to his need."[2] Others were bound to the precepts of Benedict of Nursia, who in the thirty-third chapter of his *Rule* denounced what he called the "vice" of ownership—it was "to be cut out of the monastery by the roots." No monk was to presume to give or receive anything without his abbot's permission, or to have anything as his own—"anything whatever, whether book or tablets or pen or whatever it may be. Let all things be common to all, as it is written, and let no one say or assume that anything is his own."[3]

For centuries religious men and women lived out these ideals in communities that had become centers of great wealth, social and spiritual power.[4] In the twelfth century, wave after wave of religious experiments then exposed that irony with vigor. New orders of Cistercians and regular canons recommitted to the common life, to austerity

---

[1] Mt 19:21 and 27; Acts 4:32–35.
[2] George Lawless, *Augustine of Hippo and his Monastic Rule* (Oxford, 1987), 81.
[3] Timothy Fry, ed., *RB 1980: The Rule of St. Benedict in Latin and English with Notes* (Collegeville, MN, 1982), c. 33.
[4] For broader context see Ulrich Meyer, *Soziales Handeln im Zeichen des 'Hauses.' Zur Ökonomik in der Spätantike und im früheren Mittelalter* (Göttingen, 1998).

and simplicity. They also fashioned a reforming spirituality centered on inward reflection, self-knowledge and imitation of the life and suffering of Christ. As Giles Constable's work has shown, the religious reforms of the twelfth century were a "Reformation" in their own right, a turning point that would shape European religious thought for centuries.[5] And the reform of monastic life, in turn, was but one part of a much wider embrace of apostolic poverty. In his *Religious Movements in the Middle Ages*, the German historian Herbert Grundmann showed how that ideal inspired Waldensians and Humiliati, the Franciscans and Dominicans, Beguines and Cathars to challenge monasticism's ancient monopoly. Grundmann's arguments remain foundational seven decades and more after their original publication, and the field his seminal work established continues to inspire an inexhaustible scholarly fascination.[6]

After the twelfth century, many surveys have suggested, religious life in the great landed houses began to settle in to a certain mediocrity. In most narratives the inertia of older institutions yields to the energy of the new mendicant orders, whose histories dominate most accounts of thirteenth century.[7] For the fourteenth century, debates over Franciscan poverty become central, along with all of the wider issues of property and political power they raised.[8] Yet even the friars seem eventually to

---

[5] Giles Constable, *The Reformation of the Twelfth Century* (Cambridge, 1996). See also his *Three Studies in Medieval Religious and Social Thought* (Cambridge, 1995).

[6] Herbert Grundmann, *Religiöse Bewegungen im Mittelalter. Untersuchungen über die geschichtlichen Zusammenhänge zwischen der Ketzerei, den Bettelorden und der religiösen Frauenbewegung im 12. und 13. Jahrhundert und über die geschichtlichen Grundlagen der deutschen Mystik*, 2nd ed. (Darmstadt, 1961). For general context and a discussion of the work's broader significance see Robert Lerner's excellent introduction to the English translation by Steven Rowan, *Religious Movements in the Middle Ages* (Notre Dame, IN, 1995). Standard as well is Lester K. Little, *Religious Poverty and the Profit Economy in Medieval Europe* (Ithaca, 1978). See also the more recent study of Lutz Kaelber, *Schools of Asceticism: Ideology and Organization in Medieval Religious Communities* (Universtiy Park, PA, 1998).

[7] Cf. André Vauchez, "The Religious Orders," in *The New Cambridge Medieval History*, ed. Cristopher Allmand (Cambridge, 1998), vol. 6, 220–54 and C. H. Lawrence's surveys: *Medieval Monasticism. Forms of Religious Life in Western Europe in the Middle Ages*, 3rd ed. (New York, 2001) and *The Friars: The Impact of the Early Mendicant Movement on Western Society* (New York, 1994).

[8] David Burr, *Olivi and Franciscan Poverty: The Origins of the usus pauper Controversy* (Philadelphia, 1989), and *The Spiritual Franciscans. From Protest to Persecution in the Century after Saint Francis* (University Park, PA, 2001); Malcom Lambert, *Franciscan Poverty: The Doctrine of the Absolute Poverty of Christ and the Apostles in the Franciscan Order, 1210–1323*, 2nd ed. (New York, 1998); Ulrich Horst, *Evangelische Armut und Kirche. Thomas von Aquin und die Armutskontroversen des 13. und beginnenden 14. Jahrhunderts* (Berlin, 1992); idem, *Evangelische Armut und päpstliches Lehramt. Minoritentheologen im Konflikt mit Papst Johannes XXII. (1316–34)* (Stuttgart, 1996).

lose their original energy. In an age of crisis marked by famine, war and plague, institutional religious life yields the stage to mystics, prophets, beguines and heretics. And the story turns to these more compelling figures, seemingly, with good reason. As the portraits of Boccaccio, Chaucer and so many "antifraternal" writers suggest, ordinary friars, monks, canons and nuns seem somehow to have become spectacularly incapable of upholding their own ideals.[9]

Religious life's ideals had by no means lost their vitality, however. Many continued to embrace them, ironically, beyond the ranks of the religious orders themselves. In England, as Stephen Lahey's work has most recently shown, John Wyclif's theology of dominion shaped a new vision of poverty, charity and community grounded in God's grace.[10] The same vision had sharp implications for the religious orders: for Wyclif and the Lollards, the avaricious appropriations of Christendom's "private sects" of "possessioner" monks and friars convicted them all of mortal sin. Less divisively, but in an analogous mood, the secular cleric and preacher Geert Groote and his followers embraced the apostolic ideal in the Low Countries. The Brothers and Sisters of the Common Life appropriated for themselves many of the hallmarks of traditional religious life. They shared their incomes and goods in common, adhered to routines of prayer and reading built on all of the texts of the monastic tradition, yet they firmly refused formal profession of religious vows.[11]

The ideals of the Gospels and of Acts were perhaps nowhere more visible in the fourteenth and fifteenth centuries, however, than within the orders' own ranks. In a variety of experiments now known collectively as the Observant Movement, religious themselves sought to return to their founding ideals and to strict observance of their obligations. The result was one of the most remarkable religious movements Western Europe had seen in centuries. A survey of only the most visible efforts in Italy and the Empire begins to suggest its scope. In the 1330s in Bohemia, Bishop John of Draschitz established a reformed house of Augustinian canons in Raudnitz. In Foligno by the 1360s, Paolucci

---

[9] Penn R. Szittya, *The Antifraternal Tradition in Medieval Literature* (Princeton, 1986).
[10] Stephen Lahey, *Philosophy and Politics in the Thought of John Wyclif* (Cambridge, 2003).
[11] See now John Van Engen, *Sisters and Brothers of the Common Life: The Devotio Moderna and the World of the Later Middle Ages* (Philadelphia, 2008), as well as *Devotio Moderna. Basic Writings* (New York, 1988).

Trinci had embraced a return to strict observance among the Franciscans, an effort that would win hundreds of houses in Italy and beyond within a century. By the 1380s Benedictine reform had taken root in the community of Kastl in the Palatinate under the patronage of Count Rupert. In 1388, Master General Raymond of Capua sanctioned the establishment of at least one Dominican house for friars seeking a more strict observance. Within a year, reformed Dominicans had established a priory at Colmar, and made their way across the Empire from there. In 1408 in Padua, the young patrician and canon lawyer Ludowico Barbo established a reformed Benedictine congregation with strong ties to humanists. The Benedictine community of Melk was reformed in 1418, and by the 1420s the Augustinian canons of Windesheim had established strong links with the Modern Devotion. By century's end Observant circles had produced some of the most remarkable religious figures in all of European history: the visionary Bridget of Sweden; the reformed Windesheim canon Thomas of Kempen, whose *Imitation of Christ* remains one of the most widely read works in Western history; the crusading Franciscan John of Capistrano; the Dominican prophet and preacher Savonarola; and even the young Martin Luther himself, who was an Observant Augustinian friar before becoming a reformer of another stripe.

Since the late 1970s the leading historian of late-medieval religious life and Observant reform has been one of Herbert Grundmann's last students, Kaspar Elm. Grundmann himself never fully pursued the later history of apostolic poverty as it became settled within established orders of monks, nuns, canons and friars other "semi-religious" groups.[12] But Elm recognized how important that line of inquiry could be for late-medieval scholarship, and he first explored it in a masterful essay on the "decline and renewal" of the religious orders in the fourteenth and fifteenth centuries.[13] The orders themselves, Elm noted, had sponsored much of the writing of their own histories, and in doing so they tended to perpetuate older moralizing generalizations about late-medieval decline. Institutional rivalries also tended to prevent a broader view

---

[12] Van Engen, "The Christian Middle Ages as an Historiographical Problem," *American Historical Review* 91 (1986): 519–52, here 524.
[13] Kaspar Elm, "Verfall und Erneuerung des Spätmittelalterlichen Ordenswesens: Forschungen und Forschungsaufgaben," in *Untersuchungen zu Kloster und Stift*, ed. J. Fleckenstein (Göttingen, 1980), 189–238.

of the orders' common circumstance. Elm thus called for patient work that grounded fourteenth- and fifteenth-century religious observance and its renewal in both local particulars and wider contexts. That work began in earnest with an impressive conference held in 1979. Its essays, unfortunately not published until a decade later, still provide one of the best starting points for model studies of the Observant Movement. They surveyed reform in the ranks of monks, canons, mendicants and the military orders, and linked reform to the councils, to the interests of territorial princes and the cities, and to the early days of the Reformation.[14] Elm's students soon authored studies of the orders in Basel, Barcelona, Strasbourg and other locales.[15] Gert Melville, Klaus Schreiner and many others also came to focus on the late-medieval orders in ways complementary to Elm's original program.[16]

---

[14] Kaspar Elm, ed., *Reformbemühungen und Observanzbestrebungen im spätmittelalterlichen Ordenswesen* (Berlin, 1989). See also Dieter Mertens, "Monastische Reformbewegungen des 15. Jahrhunderts: Ideen—Ziele—Resultate," in *Reform von Kirche und Reich: zur Zeit der Konzilien von Konstanz (1414–1418) und Basel (1431–1449). Konstanz-Prager historisches Kolloquium (11.–17. Oktober 1993)*, ed. Ivan Hlaváček and Alexander Patschovsky (Constance, 1996), 157–82. Older but still useful is the brief survey provided in E. Delaruelle, E.-R. Labande, and Paul Ourliac, *L'Église au temps du Grand Schisme et de la crise conciliaire (1378–1449)* (Paris, 1964).

[15] Bernhard Neidiger, *Mendikanten zwischen Ordensideal und städtischer Realität: Untersuchungen zum wirtschaftlichen Verhalten der Bettelorden in Basel* (Berlin, 1981); Andreas Rüther, *Bettelorden in Stadt und Land: Die Strassburger Mendikantenkonvente und das Elsaß im Spätmittelalter* (Berlin, 1997); Nikolas Jaspert, *Stift und Stadt: das Heiliggrabpriorat von Santa Anna und das Regularkanonikerstift Santa Eulàlia del Camp im mittelalterlichen Barcelona (1145–1423)* (Berlin, 1996).

[16] Gert Melville, ed., *De ordine vitae: zu Normvorstellungen, Organisationsformen und Schriftgebrauch im mittelalterlichen Ordenswesen* (Münster, 1996); idem, ed., *Institutionen und Geschichte* (Cologne, 1992); Gert Melville and Jörg Oberste, eds., *Die Bettelorden im Aufbau: Beiträge zu Institutionalisierungsprozessen im mittelalterlichen Religiosentum* (Münster, 1999). Among Klaus Schreiner's many works, see especially *Mönchsein in der Adelsgesellschaft des hohen und späten Mittelalters. Klösterliche Gemeinschaftsbildung zwischen spiritueller Selbstbehauptung und sozialer Anpassung* (Munich, 1989); idem, "Benediktinische Klosterreform als zeitgebundene Auslegung der Regel. Geistige, religiöse und soziale Erneuerung in spätmittelalterlichen Klöstern Südwestdeutschlands im Zeichen der Kastler, Melker und Bursfelder Reform," *Blätter für württembergische Kirchengeschichte* 86 (1986): 105–95; and idem, *Sozial und standesgeschichtliche Untersuchungen zu den Benediktinerkonventen im östlichen Schwarzwald* (Stuttgart, 1964). See also Jürgen Miethke, "Kirchenreform auf den Konzilien des 15. Jahrhunderts. Motive—Methoden—Wirkungen," in *Studien zum 15. Jahrhundert. Festschrift für Erich Meuthen*, ed. Johannes Helmrath und Heribert Müller (Munich, 1994), 13–42. A magnificent festschrift for Elm, a volume of nearly a thousand pages from some fifty authors, now stands as a testament to these collective efforts: Franz J. Felten and Nikolas Jaspert, eds., *Vita Religiosa im Mittelalter. Festschrift für Kaspar Elm zum 70. Geburtstag* (Berlin, 1999).

Most of this German scholarship, along with the study of medieval Germany in general, has found only limited reception among Anglophone scholars. Most of their work in the last generation, with few exceptions, has tended to focus on England and France before 1300.[17] But Anglophone scholars of religious life have now begun to turn to the later Middle Ages in more focused ways.[18] And in doing so they have also increasingly turned to the Observant Movement, whose history is perhaps best known through its fiery Italian preachers and penitent women; Catherine and Bernardino of Siena, and Savonarola and his women followers, for example, have received focused scholarly attention in recent years.[19] Scholars of early modern Catholic reform have also pointed to the Observant Franciscans in Italy, France and the New World as important cultural agents alongside the more famous Jesuits.[20] A few Anglophone medievalists are also now focused religious life and its reform in the Empire. Michael Bailey has placed Observant reform ideology at the heart of the German Dominican John Nider's enormously influential thought on witchcraft. Anne Winston-Allen has argued for the importance of women's reform in shaping vernacular

---

[17] On medieval German history generally, see Edward Peters, "More Trouble With Henry: The Historiography of Medieval Germany in the Angloliterate World," *Central European History* 28 (1995): 47–72 and Patrick Geary, *Medieval Germany in America* (Washington, D.C., 1996). For a fine general orientation to monastic history see Barbara Rosenwein, "Views from Afar: American Perspectives on Medieval Monasticism," in *Dove va la storiographia monastica in Europa? Temi e metodi di ricerca per lo studia della vita monastica e regolare in età medievale alle soglie del terzo millennio. Atti del Convegno internazionale Brescia-Rodengo, 23–25 marzo 2000*, ed. Giancarlo Andenna (Milan, 2001), 67–84. For an exemplary recent study see also Constance Berman, *The Cistercian Evolution. The Invention of a Religious Order in Twelfth-Century Europe* (Philadelphia, 2000).

[18] So, for example, recent studies of religious life in England: Joseph A. Gribbin, *The Premonstratensian Order in Late Medieval England* (Woodbridge, 2001); Nancy Bradley Warren, *Spiritual Economies. Female Monasticism in Later Medieval England* (Philadelphia, 2001); Marilyn Oliva, *The Convent and the Community in Late Medieval England: Female Monasteries in the Diocese of Norwich, 1350–1540* (Rochester, 1998); and James G. Clark, ed., *Religious Orders in Pre-Reformation England* (New York, 2002).

[19] F. Thomas Luongo, *The Saintly Politics of Catherine of Siena* (Ithaca, 2006); Franco Mormondo, *The Preacher's Demons. Bernardino of Siena and the Social Underworld of Early Renaissance Italy* (Chicago, 1999); Donald Weinstein, *Savonarola and Florence. Prophecy and Patriotism in the Renaissance* (Princeton, 1970); Tamar Herzig, *Savonarola's Women: Visions and Reform in Renaissance Italy* (Chicago, 2007).

[20] Megan C. Armstrong, *The Politics of Piety: Franciscan Preachers during the Wars of Religion, 1560–1600* (New York, 2004). See also P. Renée Baernstein, *A Convent Tale: A Century of Sisterhood in Spanish Milan* (New York, 2002).

chronicles, and Jeffrey Hamburger and June Mecham have shown the importance of reform for women's visual and devotional culture.[21]

This book contributes to these efforts to understand Observant reform within the fifteenth-century German landscape. Its theme—the tensions of religious reform, poverty, property and community—has long shaped our accounts of religious life in the twelfth and thirteenth centuries.[22] The theme took on other shapes in other late-medieval settings, however, in ways that deserve more careful attention. By 1400, a vigorous culture of personal property had become integral to the daily life of the cloister. Abbots and other prelates lived in splendor and comfort. They also issued licenses and dispensations for the enjoyment of a variety of personal cash incomes among the rank and file—corporate funds appropriated for personal use, endowed stipends in cash and kind, and cash payments for masses and other spiritual services. Moralists and legislators reacted sharply against the seemingly rising tide of excess—apostasy, drinking, gambling, debt, fashionable clothing and more, all were repeatedly condemned in sermon and statute. But too often the preaching and legislation seemed stunningly ineffective. Lordly prelates and their propertied religious remained unavoidably, at times infuriatingly, visible to ordinary people in every locale. Monks in fine wool rode on horseback; friars walked the streets clutching bags filled with spices and coins; nuns adorned themselves with jeweled crowns, silken veils and silver rings; men and women across the orders ate, drank, and prayed in intimate cells adorned with tapestries, paintings and sculptures. By 1400, Observants across the orders had begun the struggle to renounce these propertied patterns of life, and to bind their orders back to the observance of community as it was enshrined in their rules. Struggles over poverty, property and observance are familiar to most scholars as a Franciscan story, but it is important to recognize

---

[21] Michael D. Bailey, *Battling Demons. Witchcraft, Heresy and Reform in the Later Middle Ages* (University Park, PA, 2003); Anne Winston-Allen, *Convent Chronicles. Women Writing About Women and Reform in the Late Middle Ages* (University Park, PA, 2004); Jeffrey Hamburger, *The Visual and the Visionary. Art and Female Spirituality in Late-Medieval Germany* (New York, 1998); idem, *Nuns as Artists. The Visual Culture of a Medieval Convent* (Berkeley, 1997); June Mecham, "A Northern Jerusalem. Transforming the Spatial Geography of the Covent of Wienhausen," in *Defining the Holy: Sacred Space in Medieval and Early Modern Europe*, ed. Sarah Hamilton and Andrew Spicer (Aldershot, 2005), 139–60. See also Mecham's "Reading Between the Lines: Compilation, Variation, and the Recovery of an Authentic Female Voice in the Dornenkron Prayer Books from Wienhausen," *Journal of Medieval History* 29 (2003): 109–28.

[22] See notes 5–7 above.

that struggle's much broader fifteenth-century horizons. After 1400, Benedictines and Cistercians, Augustinian canons, Dominicans, Augustinian Hermits and others all sought a return to the obligation to live in community. As they did so, they reflected their era's enthusiasm for what they imagined to be the simplicity of Christian antiquity—the modest food and drink of the common table, the stern simplicity of a common dormitory, and so on. They also clothed their return to rules and community in the penitential devotion and the language of law that characterized reform discourse in their era. And to achieve their ends reformers fully embraced the power of their kings and princes, whom they often served as advisers and confessors.

The book offers a detailed account of one inflection of this wider reforming contest over property and community. It begins that account with an overview of the cloister's culture of personal property as fifteenth-century reformers inherited it. Turning to the southern territories of the Empire, it then races the emergence of a distinct reforming discourse that sought to uproot that culture. At the Council of Constance and beyond, a generation of theologians and lawyers trained in Germany's new universities sharply and publicly condemned the "vice of property" among religious, and they denounced monks, nuns, canons and friars alike as mortally sinful "proprietors" (*proprietarii*). The slur word was rather clumsy, but it soon became one of the most effective slogans of the age. Reforming monks, friars and other religious then made the slogan their own, and revolted from within. What other than "pestiferous property," one reforming friar asked, led so many laymen to denounce propertied religious as "false monks," criminals worse than robbers and whores? And as the fierce rhetoric developed, there emerged a focused effort to establish reform in practice. Across the Empire after Constance, alliances of princes and bishops, theologians, lawyers and recent converts to religious life fought to uproot the "vice of property" and to enforce strict observance of the common life. This study traces that effort primarily from within reforming circles centered on the Benedictine communities of Melk and Tegernsee, among others, and on a constellation of Augustinian canonries reformed according to the statutes of Raudnitz in Bohemia.[23] By 1450 monks and canons from

---

[23] For general overviews see Ulrich Faust and Walter Krassnig, eds., *Die benediktinischen Mönchs- und Nonnenklöster in Österreich und Südtirol*, 2 vols. (St. Ottilien, 2000–2001); Ulrich Faust and Franz Quarthal, eds., *Die Reformverbände und Kongregationen der Benediktiner im deutschen Sprachraum* (St. Ottilien, 1999); Josef Hemmerle, *Die Benediktinerklöster in Bayern*

these communities had become the leaders of reform in the region, and they had composed, copied and circulated the corpus of texts that allow this study access to their efforts.

The reforming discourse of property and community at the heart of this study is given focused scholarly attention here for the first time. The contexts and points of origin of the discourse; the composition, compilation and circulation of key texts; the translation of reforming ideas into practice all appear here as an empirical contribution to the wider history of the Observant Movement in the Empire. At the same time, all of the fresh evidence is also allowed to speak here to our wider efforts to rethink the history of reform, church and society in the fourteenth and fifteenth centuries.

* * *

Historians of fourteenth- and fifteenth-century church and society have long framed their story within a general dialectic of crisis and reform. Thirty years ago intense debate raged over precisely which factors best explained what was presumed to be a general crisis of the later

---

(Augsburg, 1970); and Romuald Bauerreiss, *Kirchengeshcichte Bayerns 5: Das Fünfzehnte Jahrhundert* (St. Ottilien, 1955). For the Melk reforms see Joachim Angerer, "Reform von Melk," in *Die Reformverbände*, ed. Faust and Quarthal; Albert Groiß, *Spätmittelalterliche Lebensformen der Benediktiner von der Melker Observanz vor dem Hintergrund ihrer Bräuche. Ein darstellender Kommentar zum Caeremoniale Mellicense des Jahres 1460* (Münster, 1999); Meta Niederkorn-Bruck, *Die Melker Reform im Spiegel der Visitationen* (Vienna, 1994); Klaus Schreiner, "Benediktinische Klosterreform als zeitgebundene Auslegung der Regel" (above, n. 16); and Joachim Angerer, *Die Bräuche der Abtei Tegernsee unter Abt Kaspar Aindorffer (1426–1461), verbunden mit einer kritischen Edition der Consuetudines Tegernseensis* (Augsburg, 1968). The reform of the Augustinian canons in the region, and for the later Middle Ages generally, has not received as much scholarly attention. Provisionally one may consult the literature cited in Elm, "Verfall und Erneuerung," 211–12 and n. 38, especially Franz Machilek, "Reformorden und Ordensreformen in den böhmischen Ländern vom 10. bis 18. Jahrhundert," in *Bohemia Sacra: das Christentum in Böhmen 973–1973*, ed. Ferdinand Seibt (Düsseldorf, 1974), 63–80; C. Giroud, *L'Ordre des chanoines réguliers de Saint Augustin et ses diverses formes de régime interne. Essai de synthèse historicojuridique* (Martigny, 1961); E. van Ette, *Les chanoines réguliers de Saint-Augustin. Aperçu historique* (Cholet, 1953); and H. Vissers, *Vie canoniale* (Bruges, 1953). For a brief overview see also Ludo Milis, "Reformatory Attempts within the Ordo Canonicus in the Late Middle Ages," in *Reformbemühungen*, ed. Elm (Berlin, 1989), 3–19. For the communities of Bavaria see N. Backmund, *Die Stifte der Chorherren in Bayern* (Passau, 1972), and for their reform Ignaz Zibermayr, "Zur Geschichte der Raudnitzer Reform," *Mitteilungen des Instituts für Österreichische Geschichtsforschung 11. Ergänzungsband* (1929): 323–53, especially 336–38; A. Angerpointer, "Das Kloster Indersdorf und die Raudnitzer Reform im 15. Jahrhundert," *Amperland* 5 (1969); J. N. A. Zeschick, *Das Augustinerchorherrenstift Rohr und die Reformen in bairischen Stiften vom 15. bis 17. Jahrhundert* (Passau, 1969).

Middle Ages.[24] Some argued that overpopulation brought diminishing returns on overused land, falling standards of living and rising mortality. Others argued for a general "agrarian crisis" characterized by falling revenues and abandoned properties. Historians inspired by Marx countered that population pressures and an ailing agrarian economy were secondary to a deeper "crisis of feudalism," a growing conflict between lords and peasants that "prepared the ground" for the transformation to capitalism. Still others invoked crisis to explain religious and cultural change: František Graus, most notably, placed the horrors of the plague, mass murder of Jews and the flagellants at the heart of a sophisticated argument for a general crisis of the fourteenth century. Institutional and spiritual crisis, in turn, often served as the backdrop for discussions of fifteenth-century reform. Steven Ozment's influential "age of reform," for example, traced the origins of the Reformation to fourteenth-century institutional crisis, the rise of mysticism and so on.[25] Berndt Hamm later placed fourteenth-century crisis at the origins of a new interpretive model. Drawing on the works of both Graus and Jean Delumeau, Hamm presumed a general crisis mentality to have pervaded the fourteenth and fifteenth centuries. For Hamm, an overall perception of crisis inspired a quest for certainty and assurance, and fuelled the "alignment of both religion and society towards a standardizing, authoritative, regulating and legitimizing focal point"—a complex process Hamm has called "normative centering."[26]

---

[24] For an introduction to a vast literature see Howard Kaminsky, "From Lateness to Waning to Crisis. The Burden of the Later Middle Ages," *Journal of Early Modern History* 4 (2000): 85–125 and Peter Schuster, "Die Krise des Spätmittelalters. Zur Evidenz eines sozial- und wirtschaftsgeschichtlichen Paradigmas in der Geschichtsschreibung des 20. Jahrhunderts," *Historische Zeitschrift* 269 (1999): 19–55. To note only some of the most accessible works: František Graus, *Pest, Geißler, Judenmorde: Das 14. Jahrhundert als Krisenzeit* (Göttingen, 1987); idem, "The Church and its Critics in Time of Crisis," in *Anticlericalism in Late-Medieval and Early Modern Europe*, ed. Peter A. Dykema and Heiko A. Obernann (Leiden, 1993), 65–81; Rodney Hilton, *Class Conflict and the Crisis of Feudalism: Essays in Medieval Social History* (London, 1990); T. H. Aston and C. H. E. Philpin, eds., *The Brenner Debate: Agrarian Class Structure and Economic Development in Pre-Industrial Europe* (Cambridge, 1985); Ferdinand Seibt and Winfred Eberhard, eds., *Europa 1400: Die Krise des Spätmittelalters* (Stuttgart, 1984).

[25] Steven Ozment, *The Age of Reform 1250–1550: An Intellectual and Religious History of Late Medieval and Reformation Europe* (New Haven, 1980). For a view looking forward from the Middle Ages see Francis Oakley, *The Western Church in the Later Middle Ages* (Ithaca, 1979).

[26] Berndt Hamm, "Normative Centering in the Fifteenth and Sixteenth Centuries: Observations on Religiosity, Theology and Iconology," *Journal of Early Modern History* 3 (1999): 307–54, here 311–15. For a collection that offers an overall view of Hamm's

Histories of the religious orders have long reflected this larger dialectic of crisis and reform. Drawing from a long tradition of scholarship, Kaspar Elm's early essay highlighted the impact of several fourteenth-century calamities. From 1315 to 1322 an unprecedented famine devastated northern Europe, and in its grip, northern European religious communities often struggled to maintain solvency. The campaigns of the Hundred Years' War devastated the religious communities of France. The arrival of the Black Death in 1347 only worsened the general circumstance. The orders lost three of ten, five of ten, even six of every ten in the initial years of the epidemic, and long after it had passed the orders struggled to keep up their numbers and their revenues.[27] By the end of the century, years of papal schism had exacted further tolls—divided loyalties, administrative disarray, fiscal burdens and exhausted treasuries.[28] Elm and others naturally placed the origins of Observant reform in dialogue with these manifestations of crisis. For Berndt Hamm, the Observant reformers' recovery of monastic theology, and especially their commitment to penance and the passion of Christ, provided one of the best manifestations of the wider process of "normative centering." Driven by crisis and uncertainty, reformed religious cultivated penance and the imitation of Christ's sufferings through both inward and outward discipline. Like "rays of light passing through a magnifying glass," so Hamm eloquently put it, Observant cloisters concentrated the reforming energies of the day—and that intensity, in turn, attracted the protection and patronage of secular princes, who sought to establish reformed discipline and order in the churches and communities of their domains.[29]

Larger models of crisis and reform have thus helped free late-medieval religious life from older moralizing generalizations about decline, and to integrate the history of the orders into our discussions of fourteenth- and fifteenth-century history. Yet recent critiques of the larger models themselves merit careful attention. As Peter Schuster, Howard Kaminsky and others have shown, scholars have invoked crisis so loosely and frequently as to deprive the concept of much of its explanatory

---

thought see Berndt Hamm and Robert J. Bast, *The Reformation of Faith in the Context of Late Medieval Theology and Piety: Essays by Berndt Hamm* (Leiden, 2004).

[27] Bernd Zaddach, *Die Folgen des Schwarzen Todes (1347–51) für den Klerus Mitteleuropas* (Stuttgart, 1971).
[28] Elm, "Verfall und Erneuerung," 204 (above, n. 13).
[29] Hamm, "Normative Centering," 323.

force.[30] Local studies have now relativized models of demographic and agrarian crisis almost to the breaking point. Models for a crisis of feudalism fail to account for the fact that the social order of land and lordship survived, albeit transformed, deep into the early modern era. The plague, though an unprecedented catastrophe, opened up new horizons of comfort and consumption for those who survived. Models of a "crisis of the age" and of "crisis mentalities" reach their limits as well, to the extent that they fail to account for the perceptions of those who did not experience crisis, or who successfully negotiated its difficulties.

Historians are also increasingly aware of the limits of our larger narratives of reform and pre-Reformation. While a generation of scholarship has begun to trace continuities between the medieval and Reformation eras, a preoccupation with the drama, the questions and categories of the sixteenth century still tends to distort or to simplify the religious history of the fourteenth and fifteenth. In a wealth of texts, images and archives we are only beginning to explore, historians of fifteenth-century religion and church life are now finding evidence that resists synthesis and refuses to anticipate later events. And the call to reform in particular, now seen as multivalent and multidirectional, is increasingly well-grounded in regional and local specifics, in careful review of new works and manuscripts, in new figure studies, and so on.[31]

The theme of property and community as it is explored in this study offers another opportunity to work beyond the limits of inherited models

---

[30] See the detailed critiques offered in Schuster, "Krise" and Kaminsky, "Lateness" (above, n. 24). See also James L. Goldsmith, "The Crisis of the Late Middle Ages: The Case of France," *French History* 9 (1995): 417–50.

[31] For an overview of the issues see Howard Kaminsky, "The Problematics of 'Heresy' and 'The Reformation'," in *Häresie und vorzeitige Reformation im Spätmittelalter*, ed. František Šmahel (Munich, 1998) 1–22; John Van Engen, "The Church in the Fifteenth Century," in *Handbook of European History 1400–1600*, ed. Thomas Brady, Heiko Oberman and James Tracy, (Leiden, 1994), 305–30; idem, "The Future of Medieval Church History," *Church History* 71 (2002): 492–522; and idem, "Multiple Options: The World of the Fifteenth-Century Church," *Church History* 77 (2008), 257–84. For an example of the possibilities see now the magisterial work of Caroline Walker Bynum, *Wonderful Blood. Theology and Practice in Late Medieval Northern Germany and Beyond* (Philadelphia, 2007). For a well-grounded approach to reform, and one keenly attentive to the manuscript evidence, see Phillip H. Stump, *The Reforms of the Council of Constance* (Leiden, 1994). For new biographies see, among many others, Brian Patrick McGuire, *Jean Gerson and the Last Medieval Reformation* (University Park, PA, 2005) and now Daniel Hobbins, *Authorship and Publicity before Print. Jean Gerson and the Transformation of Late Medieval Learning* (Philadelphia, 2009).

of crisis and reform. The appearance of propertied men and women in the cloister has long served as proof that things somehow went wrong for the religious orders in the fourteenth century, as they did for Europe generally.[32] Reform of community, in turn, has long been assumed a largely self-evident reaction to that circumstance. In recent years, however, scholars have begun, piecemeal, to complicate the picture. Kaspar Elm and his student Bernhard Neidiger, for example, have shown that a decline in the observance of poverty is best judged in relation to a range of variables: the guidelines established by papal privilege and statute, contemporary norms and attitudes toward poverty, wealth and work; and evolving standards of living, all within the social, economic and institutional particulars of a given locale or region.[33] And David Burr has shown how the Franciscans, for all of their explosive debates over poverty, took seriously the institutional and social circumstance of the ordinary friar.[34] Even in this recent work, however, propertied men and women still often appear only in passing, too often as two-dimensional figures, too often victims or villains whose way of life confirms prior assumptions about the moral consequences of crisis.[35] This study moves toward a more complex account of their circumstance. It seeks what might be called a more complex genealogy of propertied morality and its discontents. Without denying that professed religious often faced difficult circumstances and choices in the fourteenth century, this study seeks to recover the daily presence of propertied religious among their contemporaries, to put a more human face on their daily lives, and to give them back a certain cultural agency and possibility that larger models of crisis have long displaced or ignored.

An introductory chapter, "Cultures of Property Between Cloister and World," begins that work by grounding fourteenth- and fifteenth-century religious life within a longer chronological view and a wider

---

[32] So, for example, one historian of the Franciscan Observants locates "violations of individual poverty" at the "core of Conventualism," describing them as a "new phenomenon" for the fourteenth century that was "against every principle of the regular life." Duncan Nimmo, "The Franciscan Regular Observance," in *Reformbemühungen*, ed. Elm, 189–205, here 192.

[33] Bernhard Neidiger, *Mendikanten zwischen Ordensideal und städtischer Realität* and Andreas Rüther, *Bettelorden in Stadt und Land* (above, n. 15).

[34] Burr, *Franciscan Spirituals* (above, n. 8) especially chs. 5 and 6.

[35] So, for example, speculation about the moral consequences of plague: a flood of bequests after the Black Death may have so enriched the orders that it fostered moral laxity in the cloister and resentment among the laity. See Elm, "Verfall und Erneuerung," 207 and n. 29.

contemporary context than most traditional approaches have provided. The chapter surveys an ancient nexus of custom, prayer and provision that continued, in ways scholarship has often missed, to sustain religious households deep into the Middle Ages. It grounds its account of propertied life first in the conceptual frameworks of custom and status. Historians of the early Middle Ages have long known the legal and cultural importance of good custom and status, and they have often stressed that importance through studies of monastic life—in the study of monastic customaries, for example, the study of liturgical memory, or of kinship networks and property.[36] This chapter suggests some of the ways in which custom and status lived on in the thirteenth and fourteenth centuries, and in particular how they continued to shape the sensibility of the cloister's culture of property in important ways. As Daniel Wickberg has noted, the concept of sensibility helps capture a composite of "emotional, intellectual, aesthetic, and moral dispositions" across a wide range of human action.[37] Here and in later chapters the notion of sensibility is invoked from time to time in this sense, as an interpretive shorthand that helps the cloister's patterns of life escape prejudices of lateness, waning and crisis. To that same end Chapter One also reads its evidence within the wider context of an explosive fourteenth-century culture of property. The phenomenon is perhaps most visible and well known in its Italian settings. There historians have read a "celebration of the urge to own," an enthusiasm for marking status through luxury and the cultivation of intimate domestic space as hallmarks of the Renaissance.[38] They have also traced the same emer-

---

[36] Among many works see Megan McLaughlin, *Consorting with Saints: Prayer for the Dead in Early Medieval France* (Ithaca, 1994); Barbara H. Rosenwein, *To be the Neighbor of Saint Peter: The Social Meaning of Cluny's Property, 909–1049* (Ithaca, 1989); and Stephen D. White, *Custom, Kinship and Gifts to Saints. The Laudatio Parentum in Western France 1050–1150* (Chapel Hill, NC, 1988).

[37] Daniel Wickberg, "What is the History of Sensibilities? On Cultural Histories, Old and New," *American Historical Review* 112 (2007): 661–84.

[38] Susan Mosher Stuard, *Gilding the Market. Luxury and Fashion in Fourteenth-Century Italy* (Philadelphia, 2006); Richard Goldthwaite, "The Empire of Things: Consumer Demand in Renaissance Italy," in *Patronage, Art and Society in Renaissance Italy*, ed. F. W. Kent, Patricia Simons and J. C. Eade (Oxford, 1987), 153–75, and idem, *Wealth and the Demand for Art in Italy 1300–1600* (Baltimore, 1993); Dora Thornton, *The Scholar in His Study. Ownership and Experience in Renaissance Italy* (New Haven, 1998); Peter Thornton, *The Italian Renaissance Interior, 1400–1600* (New York, 1991); and Lisa Jardine, *Worldly Goods: A New History of the Renaissance* (New York, 1998). Most are now aware of the dangers of teleology latent in an overly-strong "Renaissance" reading of the evidence. For an overview see Paula Findlen, "Possessing the Past: the Material World of the Italian Renaissance," *American Historical Review* 103 (1998): 83–114.

gent culture of property in the flood of Italian sumptuary legislation that becomes visible after 1300, legislation whose very failures attest to the power of the cultural forces the laws sought to curtail.[39] Other scholars have traced how a culture of cash, clothing, domestic comfort and status (and analogous failures to regulate that culture) shaped daily life beyond Italy as well.[40] Chapter One allows the men and women of the religious orders to appear in these contexts as something other than victims of crisis. Without denying all of the challenges of falling incomes and rising expenses, the impact of the plague, war and so on, it also accepts that monks, nuns, canons and friars could fully participate in a culture that in other settings has been read as a marker of vitality and renewal. Religious, too, marked their status through clothing, food, drink, and intimate spaces, and they struggled to reign in excesses that were as frustrating as they were intractable. At the same time, religious also disposed of cash and other goods in ways consistent with the demands of their profession.

A number of studies have at least touched on how Observant reformers worked to contest and reform the culture of property surveyed in Chapter One. Most have done so only in passing, however, or in ways that limit the analysis to one particular order, to a leading figure, to a particular text or to one locale. Parts I and II of this study instead offer a thematic analysis of the reform of community by turning to one of its most well-documented microclimates. Across the southern territories of the Empire after 1400, preachers, teachers and confessors trained at the University of Vienna promoted a brand of pastoral piety that had analogues in the Modern Devotion of the Netherlands and in similar

---

[39] Catherine Kovesi Killerby, "Practical Problems in the Enforcement of Italian Sumptuary Law 1200–1500," in *Crime, Society and the Law in Renaissance Italy*, ed. Trevor Dean and K. J. P. Lowe (Cambridge, 1995), 99–120; idem, *Sumptuary Law in Italy, 1200–1500* (Oxford, 2002).

[40] Ulf Dirlmeier, *Untersuchungen zu Einkommensverhältnissen und Lebenshaltungskosten in oberdeutschen Städten des Spätmittelalters* (Heidelberg, 1978); Cristopher Dyer, *Standards of Living in the Later Middle Ages. Social Change in England 1200–1500* (Cambridge, 1989). For discussions of sumptuary law see Neithard Bulst, "Feste und Feiern unter Auflagen. Mittelalterliche Tauf-, Hochzeits- und Begräbnisordnungen in Deutschland und Frankreich," in *Feste und Feiern im Mittelalter*, ed. Detlef Altenburg, Jörg Jarnut, and Hans-Hugo Steinhoff (Sigmaringen, 1991), 39–51; idem, "Les ordonnances somptuaires en Allemagne: expression de l'ordre social urbain (XIVe–XVIe siècle)," *Académie des inscriptions et belles-lettres. Comptes-rendus des séances* 3 (1993): 771–83; idem, "Zum problem städtischer und territorialer Kleider- Aufwands- und Luxusgesetzgebung in Deutschland (13.–Mitte 16. Jahrhundert)," in *Reniassance du puvoir législatif et genèse de l'état*, ed. André Gouron and Albert Rigaudiere (Montpellier, 1988), 29–57.

movements elsewhere.[41] Its hallmarks were affective piety, penitence and the pursuit of personal holiness, all grounded in an intense textuality and an impulse to translate popular pastoral and devotional works for a wider audience. Among the most important members of that audience were the circles of pious laymen gathered around the courts of the region's princes, especially the Hapsburg Duke Albert V, whose family had helped establish Vienna's university, and who took a keen interest in the proper ordering of the church life of his domain. The councils of Constance and Basel provided a further regional catalyst. Their sessions not only worked through all of the issues of papal authority and church property that Phillip Stump and others have studied in detail. As Jürgen Miethke, Johannes Helmrath and others have shown, the councils also provided an unprecedented forum for airing public opinion and a thriving market for the exchange of texts, books and ideas. In the universities and at the councils, the region's leading "public intellectuals" debated and struggled to apply their learning to concrete problems within the church and society.[42] The energy of the schools, courts and councils in turn both reflected and fostered an explosion of books and texts.[43] After 1400, reforming monks, priests, students and professors across southern Germany became remarkably active textual entrepreneurs. They bought, sold, traded and copied Bibles and liturgical texts; treatises on the virtues and vices; and all of the legal, devotional and pastoral tracts their region produced. In doing so they provided unprecedented local access to the wider reforming debates of the day, some of the most volatile of which turned on the property and privileges of the church and the religious orders.

---

[41] For these developments see especially the works of Van Engen noted above (n. 11). See also now *Die Neue Frömmigkeit in Europa im Spätmittelalter*, ed. Marek Derwich and Martial Staub (Göttingen, 2004), especially the essay of Gisela Drossbach, "Die sogenannte Devotio moderna in Wien und ihre geistigen Träger zwischen Tradition und Innovation," at 267–81.

[42] Johannes Helmrath, "Kommunikation auf den spätmittelalterlichen Konzilien," in *Die Bedeutung der Kommunikation für Wirtschaft und Gesellschaft*, ed. Hans Pöhl (Stuttgart, 1989), 116–72; Jürgen Miethke, "Die Konzilien as Forum der öffentlichen Meinung," *Deutsches Archiv* 37 (1981): 736–73. See also Stump, *Reforms of the Council of Constance* (above, n. 31) and now Daniel Hobbins, "The Schoolman as Public Intellectual: Jean Gerson and the Late Medieval Tract," *American Historical Review* 108 (2003): 1308–37.

[43] Matthew Wranovix, "Parish Priests and their Books in the Fifteenth-Century Diocese of Eichstätt" (Ph.D. Diss, Yale, 2007). For context generally see Uwe Neddermeyer, *Von der Handschrift zum gedruckten Buch: Schriftlichkeit und Leseinteresse im Mittelalter und in der frühen Neuzeit. Quantitative und Qualitative Aspekte* (Wiesbaden, 1998).

Parts I and II explore, within this general context, what might be called a "cultural mechanics" of Observant reform. Part I traces the formation of the reformers' attack on the "vice of property" and the *proprietarii*. Against an older tendency to see reforming calls to the common life as transparent or straightforward, its chapters reveal how reformers crafted, argued out and applied their ideology, from multiple positions, often against determined resistance. Chapter Two, "Calls from Without," highlights the works of three authors whose works became some of the most influential and revealing treatments of the theme for the coming reforms: a sermon of the exiled Parisian theologian Henry of Langenstein to the canons of Klosterneuburg near Vienna; the Cologne theologian Dietrich Kerkering's consultation with the nuns of St. Giles in Münster; and a treatise composed by the civil and canon lawyer Job Vener at the Council of Constance. Recent histories have highlighted the ways in which the reform of the orders owed much of its energy, inspiration and success to those who worked beyond the ranks for the orders themselves.[44] In keeping with that insight, this chapter shows how three outsiders framed some of the earliest reforming discussions of religious life's core ideals. Two devout university theologians explored the social and psychological tensions of the cloister's culture of property, and called for an inward embrace of the common life. The sessions of the Council of Constance then allowed a renowned jurist to air a sweeping legal condemnation of the *proprietarii*. Analysis of these sources reveals how much these figures were reacting, in part, to the real and frustrating proportions of unrepentant propertied life. Read carefully in light of the first chapter, however, these texts also reveal how easily the reformers' call to embrace the common life might be contested, and how sharply reformers themselves, as unsympathetic outsiders, dismissed the arguments that made sense of the inherited ways. Careful reading also reveals how easily reformers polemically distorted the excesses of propertied life to suit their own perspectives and purposes. In these sources, religious crisis was, as Robert Bast has suggested in another context, "part perception, part topos, part strategy," here deployed in a contest over the shape religious community should take.[45]

---

[44] See, for example, the remarks of Elm, "Verfall und Erneuerung," 224–25.
[45] Robert J. Bast, *Honor Your Fathers. Catechisms and the Emergence of a Patriarchal Ideology in Germany, 1400–1600* (Leiden, 1997), especially the Introduction (quoted here at ix) and Chapter One, 32–42. See also the reflections of Oakley, *Western Church* (above, n. 25), especially 113–14.

Chapter Three, "Revolt from Within," shows how those within the orders came to engage that same contest within their own ranks. The chapter begins, however, with those professed religious who actively defended inherited custom in the face of reforming attack. The witnesses are few and often indirect, and must bear much interpretive weight. But they provide a crucial reminder of the degree to which Observant calls to reformed community remained, for years after they were first articulated, a matter of conflict, debate and confusion. The chapter then turns to the reformers themselves. In ways that reflected the sensibilities of the new piety and its affective spirituality, a minority within the orders tapped into the textual and intellectual energies of the Constance era to craft a vigorous publicist campaign against the *proprietarii* of every order. In pamphlets they published for a broad monastic audience, reformers sought to denounce and expose propertied life, and to return religious life to thirteenth-century foundations of penitential theology and church law. The chapter concludes with an analysis of a reforming treatise in which one author tried to reach beyond all of the slogans and rhetoric, and to address to the core complexities of property and community that his movement confronted. Taken together, these readings reveal something of the agency of reformers, both the many who sought to reduce the complexity of inherited circumstance to pithy slogans, and the few who took on the deeper conceptual issues at stake. These sources also reveal the agency of the reformers' antagonists, who sought to defend inherited customs. The result was a new and explosive set of arguments and counterarguments, all of which charged the cloister's culture of property with a new moral urgency.

Scholarly accounts of poverty and property in the later Middle Ages almost always find their way to the legacy of Francis and to the debates between John XXII and the Spirituals, as well as the debates among the seculars and the mendicants, and all that those debates inspired.[46] Part I explores a range of new sources that touch on many of the same issues: tensions between spirit and institution; competing models of ownership and use; competing ideas about the power to dispense with vows; the proper strictness in matters of religious poverty. In one sense, much of the material surveyed in Part I may thus seem

---

[46] Janet Coleman, "Property and Poverty," in *The Cambridge History of Medieval Political Thought c. 350–c. 1450*, ed. J. H. Burns (Cambridge, 1991), 607–52. For the longer view see also Peter Garnsey, *Thinking about Property: From Antiquity to the Age of Revolution* (Cambridge, 2007).

at first glance familiar, even tired and predictable—still more critiques of the world in the name of the poverty, still more calls to conversion and to the embrace of the common life, all reflecting a long tradition of spiritual commonplaces. Yet these sources refuse to adhere to the boundaries of our well-known narratives of poverty and property, and they offer much that is fresh, surprising, even troubling. The authors explored in Part I seldom mentioned Francis at all, and they shaped their material in ways that turned sharply away from the old rivalries between seculars and mendicants. These authors called for renewal in a way that cut across the boundaries of the orders, and in a way that located religious life at the intersection of public morality, obedience to the law and personal holiness. They also clothed their call to reform in a striking rhetoric whose tone recalls what in other settings is often described as "anticlerical" sentiment, heresy or dissent.

Richard Newhauser and others have highlighted the importance of moral discourse for the cultural history of the later Middle Ages, and the importance of locating moral discourse within its specific and changing historical circumstance.[47] In a related line of inquiry, scholars have stressed the centrality of law to late-medieval culture, not only in secular matters, but also in matters of religious life.[48] These insights are central to understanding the story of property, community and observance that begins to unfold in Part I. Reform of the orders is framed there, in a general way, as a return to both moral discipline and obedience to the law of the church. It is also framed as the product of particular intellectual, political and textual networks that took shape in the southern Empire after 1400. Moreover, the sources repeatedly betray the presence, in that setting, of men and women who resisted reform in a variety of ways, whether through principled argument, double-talk, smug indifference, or open hostility. To recover these many particulars helps this study restore a certain normative confusion, contingency and possibility to the origins of Observant reform. It is, to recall Hans Freyer's epigraph to Grundmann's *Religious Movements*, "to restore history to the complex situation which prevailed when it was still in the course

---

[47] Richard Newhauser, *The Treatise on Vices and Virtues in Latin and in the Vernacular*. Typologie des Sources du Moyen Âge Occidental 68 (Turnhout, 1993). See also the introduction and the essays in Newhauser's edited volume, *In the Garden of Evil: The Vices and Culture in the Middle Ages* (Toronto, 2005).

[48] Ruth Mazo Karras, Joel Kaye, and E. Ann Matter, eds., *Law and the Illicit in Medieval Europe* (Philadelphia, 2008).

of being decided." It is to "dissolve" the hindsight that makes Observant reform seem predictable, to restore "living power of decision" to fifteenth-century reform, to make it all "happen again."[49]

Part II traces that same "power of decision" as it translated (or failed to translate) into practice. It focuses on the reforms of the Benedictines and Augustinian men and women across a region that encompassed the archdiocese of Salzburg and the domains of the dukes of Austria and Bavaria-Munich. The leaders of these reform circles, many of them prolific authors and industrious copyists, left behind abundant records of their ideas, arguments and practices. These sources allow access to a reform of community whose drama and details have often escaped scholarly attention.

Chapter Four, "Property and Community between Principle and Practice," shows how alliances of politicians, princes and university-trained Observant converts sought to uproot the "vice of property" through visitation and inquest. The chapter reveals how they preached against property in their visitation sermons, and how they interrogated a community's men and women about their everyday enjoyment of personal property. The chapter then gives detailed attention to the strategies reformers adopted when faced with superiors who refused to yield. It concludes with a consideration of the reformers' attempts to establish their new regime through charter and statue. All of these considerations reveal again how reformers advanced their agenda as outsiders within their own ranks, zealous converts who sought to break into established communities, and to uproot the established ways of their seemingly somnolent peers. Close reading of the sources also reveals something of the human dimensions of reforming practice, and thought about practice—the strategies that advanced reform of community, the ambiguities, uncertainties and dilemmas, the resistance and compromises that reform of community inspired.

Chapter Five, "Property and Community Between Penance and Perfection," turns to the inner life and devotional practice. Here the focus remains on the Observant monasteries of Austria and Bavaria-Munich first reformed in the visitations after Constance, and especially on the texts and codices found in the libraries of reform's leading communities, including the Augustinian canonry of Indersdorf and the monastic communities of Melk and Tegernsee. From those sources the chapter

---

[49] The phrases are taken from Steven Rowan's translation (above, n. 6).

traces how reformers copied and compiled the most popular treatises on the "vice of property" authored in the Constance years, and applied their calls to conversion and repentance locally in devotion and daily life. The chapter then turns to the resonance in wider circles of that same call to conversion and penance. Far from trapping themselves in an intramural discussion, reformers translated their penitential call into the vernacular and extended it beyond their own ranks to women and lay brothers as well as to lay audiences. In doing so religious and their wider audiences cultivated a common devotional ground, one that gave broad access to the reform cloister's culture of penance and moral progress. The chapter then returns to the cloister, where devotion and scrupulosity shaped the observance of common life in daily practice. The analysis here again reveals the particular strategies that established lasting reform, again within and across the boundaries of the orders.

Jean Leclercq long ago pointed to the importance for the fifteenth and sixteenth centuries of twelfth-century monastic theology, and Giles Constable done the same through bibliographical and thematic studies.[50] More recently, Berndt Hamm, Denis Martin and others have made clear that the broader enthusiasm for the spiritual classics of the twelfth century was perhaps nowhere more concentrated than within the reformed religious orders.[51] The evidence presented in these final chapters establishes in still more detail the religious and cultural affinities between twelfth-century spirituality and the reforms of the fifteenth. At the same time, the sources reveal particulars that begin to disrupt those affinities in fruitful ways. Again, the theme of resistance is key: Chapters Four and Five highlight how reform in practice often cut deeply against the grain of inherited ways and assumptions; how it had to be crafted and argued out textually and conceptually; and how it had to be shrewdly enforced, often against steady resistance. Similarly, these chapters reinforce what Kaspar Elm noted long ago: that reforming

---

[50] Ulrich Köpf, "Monastische Theologie im 15. Jahrhundert," *Rottenburger Jahrbuch für Kirchengeschichte* 11 (1992): 117–35; Jean Leclercq, "Monastic and Scholastic Theology in the Reformers of the Fourteenth to the Sixteenth Century," in *From Cloister to Classroom: Monastic and Scholastic Approaches to Truth*, ed. E. Rozanne Elder (Kalamazoo, 1986), 178–201; Giles Constable, "The Popularity of Twelfth-Century Spiritual Writers in the Late Middle Ages," in *Renaissance Studies in Honor of Hans Baron*, ed. Anthony Molho and John A. Tedeschi (Florence and DeKalb, 1971), 5–28; idem, "Twelfth Century Spirituality and the Late Middle Ages," in *Medieval and Renaissance Studies 5*, ed. O. B. Hardison, Jr. (Chapel Hill, 1971), 27–60.

[51] Hamm, "Normative Centering" (above, n. 26) and Denis Martin, *Fifteenth-Century Carthusian Reform: The World of Nicholas Kempf* (Leiden, 1992), especially 63–65.

spirituality was always something other than a straightforward return to an earlier age.[52] Reformers crafted much of their spiritual program from twelfth-century precedents, to be sure, but they did so within the context of a culture of texts, learning and books particular to their own era. They also built on the foundations theology and mysticism first established in the thirteenth and fourteenth century. Moreover, as noted above, these texts were grounded in a meticulous attention to law and statute that can rest uneasily alongside modern categories of "reform spirituality." Reforming practice, whether enforced legally and physically from without or cultivated devotionally from within, recovered and applied the spirit of an earlier age within its own fifteenth-century horizons.

* * *

The propertied men and women who appear in these pages seem at times hopelessly compromised, and their attempts to articulate some sense of their way of life can seem like feeble rationalization. In arguing for the cultural logic of that way of life and in exploring its sensibilities, this book may seem at times too willing to make the best of it all, or to offer a whimsically, even perversely partisan defense of the indefensible. The book's purpose, however, is merely to follow the scholarly lead of those who have begun to historicize some of the more surprising or challenging aspects of late-medieval religion, whether the Eucharistic piety of its religious women or the world view of its inquisitors.[53] Friars with salaries and monks with comfortable apartments, too, can seem shocking in their own way, and they deserve a more bold and thorough historical reading than they have often received. To offer that reading is not somehow to excuse or defend all manner of gluttony and lust and excess among those solemnly professed to follow Christ and the apostles. Rather, it is to begin to recover religious medieval life's place within what Peter Brown has called, in another setting, the religious

---

[52] Elm, "Verfall und Erneuerung," 233: "In the fourteenth and fifteenth centuries, for all of the conscious and programmatic efforts to return to beginnings, for all of the pedantic precision with which the observance of rule, constitutions and liturgical *ordines* were renewed or promoted, a new spiritual landscape developed across the orders, one that was not simply identical with that of the high or the early Middle Ages."

[53] See the concluding remarks of Christine Caldwell Ames, "Does Inquisition Belong to Religious History?," *American Historical Review* 110 (2005), 11–37, here at n. 89, following Caroline Walker Bynum.

"common sense" of the age, and to begin to accept the full range of the resulting possibilities.[54]

In the same spirit, this book searches for a competing Observant "common sense" that itself can trouble modern assumptions about religious reform. Here the interpretive challenge is inverted. Modern minds tend to understand the Observants more easily than their propertied antagonists, just as we gravitate more easily toward the humanists of the era than to the supposedly "late" scholastic minds of the universities. Thus the interpretation here tends to pay close attention to and highlight those aspects of Observant thought and practice that seem at odds with our expectations: its often polemical, at times almost heretical tone; its meticulous attention to the minutiae of law and statute; and the way its principles could be shrewdly, even ruthlessly applied. To do so will at times seem to press the darkness, the strangeness, and violence of the Observant effort to reform the *proprietarii*. But this too is merely an attempt to historicize that reform more fully, and to highlight more of what makes Observant reform distinct, interpretively challenging and rewarding.

---

[54] Peter Brown, *The Rise of Western Christendom. Triumph and Diversity, A.D. 200–1000*, 2nd ed. (Oxford, 2003), 18–19.

CHAPTER ONE

CULTURES OF PROPERTY
BETWEEN CLOISTER AND WORLD

In 1202 Pope Innocent III arrived at the monastery of Subiaco in Italy. There, in the community St. Benedict himself had founded more than six centuries before, Innocent learned of monks who had presumed to claim the community's goods as their own. The monks had embraced the one vice that Benedict had said should be "cut out from the monastery by the roots." Innocent wrote a letter condemning the circumstance in the strongest terms: "We strictly prohibit, by virtue of holy obedience and under pain of divine judgment, that henceforth any monk possess anything of his own in any way; but if someone should have something of his own, let him resign all of it immediately. And if, after this, someone will have been found to have property, let him be expelled from the monastery with the regular warning, and let him not be received again unless he do penance according to monastic discipline." To underline his seriousness, the pope invoked an ancient story from one of Benedict's greatest followers: "And if *proprietas* should be found among anyone who is near death, let it be buried with him outside the monastery in a dung heap, as a sign of his damnation, as Gregory tells us in the *Dialogues*."[1]

Innocent's letter looked back on a centuries-old monastic tradition that had condemned personal ownership (*proprium*) as among the worst of monastic sins. Innocent's own contemporaries then embraced the ideal of religious poverty in new ways—most famously in the new orders of Franciscans and Dominicans that Innocent himself helped establish. And for the friars as much as for the older orders of monks and canons,

---

[1] The letter is cited here from the *Decretals*: X 3, 35, 6 (CIC II: 599): "Prohibemus quoque districte in virtute obedientiae sub obtestatione divini iudicii, ne quis de cetero monachorum proprium aliquo modo possideat; sed, si quis aliquid habeat proprii, totum in continenti resignet. Si vero post hoc proprietatem aliquam fuerit deprehensus habere, regulari monitione praemissa de monasterio expellatur, nec recipiatur ulterius, nisi poeniteat secundum monasticam disciplinam. Quodsi proprietas apud quemquam inventa fuerit in morte, ipsa cum eo in signum perditionis extra monasterium in sterquilinio subterretur, secundum quod beatus Gregorius narrat in dialogo se fecisse."

the renunciation of ownership remained one of the core principles of religious life. The Dominican William Peraldus soon upheld it again in his *Summa on Vices*, written about 1250. Peraldus' work reflected the best of his young order's marriage of scholarship and pastoral care. The *Summa* provided preachers and confessors with a broad synthesis of teachings on sin, one so useful that it became one of the most widely read works of its kind for centuries. In Peraldus' general discussion of avarice, readers encountered a treatment of what Peraldus called the "vice of property" (*vitium proprietatis*)—the sin of avarice among those professed to religious poverty. Drawing from Genesis to Revelation and from Anthony to Gregory the Great, Peraldus cited twelve exempla that condemned the "proprietors" (*proprietarii*), those who committed the sin. He then surveyed their twelvefold "foolishness," and all of the crimes it entailed. The *proprietarii* were thieves who stole from the poor; apostates who threw away voluntary poverty; murderers whose greed deprived the poor of their bread; hypocrites who were outwardly pious in habit and gesture but inwardly foul in spirit.[2]

Throughout the later Middle Ages, the religious orders upheld the condemnation of the "vice of property" evident in these texts. Yet at every turn the condemnations remained in tension with daily patterns of religious life as most lived or encountered them so to speak, in the streets. This chapter seeks a better understanding of that tension, both on its own terms and as a foil for the story of reform that unfolds in later chapters.

Foundations and Legacies: Custom, Prayer and Provision

Pope Innocent's letter to Subiaco recalled a story that had been known in Western monastic communities for generations. In Book Four of his *Dialogues*, Gregory the Great related the fate of his physician Justus, a monk of the small aristocratic community of St. Andrew's. On his death bed, Justus had revealed how he had kept for himself, hidden away among his medicines, three gold pieces. Wanting both to save Justus from sin and to teach other monks a stern lesson about strict observance of the common life, Gregory decreed that Justus was to be cut off from any consolation during his illness. His isolation in the hour

---

[2] Peraldus, *Summa aurea de virtutibus et vitiis* II (*De avaritia*), Part II, c. xiii. I have consulted a Cologne edition of 1546, here 2: 301–14.

of death was to serve as a penitential trial that would purify him of sin. After his death, Justus' body was to be thrown on a dung heap. When Justus died, the monks did as Gregory commanded, for good measure casting the gold pieces onto the dung heap and calling after their dead brother in the words of Peter to Simon Magus (Acts 8:20): "May your money perish with you!" Gregory's discipline worked. Terrified by Justus' fate, the monks began to bring forth all the little things they had kept for themselves, even things Gregory had normally allowed. And after thirty days of intercessory prayer, Justus came to his brother in a vision to tell of his fate: after a time of miserable suffering, he had finally been cleansed.[3]

Gregory's story reinforced a moral dichotomy between property and community, the letter of the *Rule* and its violation. But his contemporaries and heirs also knew that a more complex conceptual and cultural framework governed daily life. They knew ownership (*proprietas*) not only as the full and free disposition of things, as it appeared in Roman law, but also as a concept shaped by a wider culture of lordship.[4] Roman law had accorded lordship (*dominium*) to the *paterfamilias*, who held absolute power and authority over spouse and children, kinsmen, slaves and others in his household. Emperors later governed, in an analogous way, as lords of the extended imperial household, and down to the millennium the concept of lordship governed a wide range of relationships among kings, princes and local strongmen. Property and its rights, within that setting, were in turn constitutive of those relationships. Held of privilege and confirmed by a variety of rituals, property marked ties of friendship, kinship and dependence among lords, subjects and their extended households.

---

[3] Gregory the Great, *Dialogues*, 4: 57. SC 265 (Paris, 1978).

[4] For general orientation see Dietmar Willoweit, "Dominium und Proprietas. Zur Entwicklung des Eigentumsbegriffs in der mittelalterlichen und neuzeitlichen Rechtswissenschaft," *Historisches Jahrbuch* 94 (1974): 131–56; *Handwörterbuch zur deutschen Rechtsgeschichte* (Berlin, 1971), 1: 754–57 (*dominium*) and 3: 2035–36 (*proprietas*), each with further literature. See also Thomas Bisson, "Medieval Lordship," *Speculum* 70 (1995): 743–59; John Van Engen, "Sacred Sanctions for Lordship," in *Cultures of Power*, ed. Thomas Bisson (Philadelphia, 1995), 203–30; Coleman, "Property and Poverty," (above, 18 and n. 46). See also *Property and Power in the Early Middle Ages*, ed. Wendy Davies and Paul Fouracre (Cambridge, 1995), especialy Timothy Reuter, "Property Transactions and Social Relations between Rulers, Bishops and Nobles in Early Eleventh-Century Saxony: the Evidence of the *Vita Meinwerci*," 165–99, esp. 172, and David Ganz, "The Ideology of Sharing: Apostolic Community and Ecclesiastical Property in the Early Middle Ages," 17–30.

Shaping the relationships among lords and their property, in turn, were normative forces of custom and status. For the Romans, the ancient world's local routines—the agricultural routines of household and farm; the municipal rituals of the city; the particular ways of every people and province—had a distinct legal presence. Roman law used a variety of terms to capture that presence: *mos, mores* or *mos maiorum; consuetudo*; and *ius non scriptum*. But all of these phrases collectively described "custom," a normative guide in the interstices of written law (*lex*) that under the right circumstances could become legally binding.[5] Custom maintained its presence to the millennium and beyond, intertwined with lordship and embodied in ways that reflected status. Custom graced great Frankish men and women with a crowd of kin and vassals, friends and followers, whose presence brought appropriate honor and allowed lords to live "honorably."[6] On grand occasions, custom and status governed a complex calculus of giving and receiving, gestures and ceremonies that marked relationships among the powerful. Custom also shaped more mundane routines, such as the lord's provision of bread, beans and wine, clothing, cash and other necessities to his household and dependents. Churchmen, too, embodied status as custom dictated. Surrounded by retinues of dependents and followers, bishops lived like lords. They gave and received costly clothing, spices and other gifts, both to mark bonds of friendship and trust and to help negotiate complex circumstances. They received guests lavishly, and entertained in courts complete with chamberlains, stewards, seneschals and cellarers.[7] And all the while, a churchman's worldly social bonds could have a sacred resonance. Household drinking festivals in honor of the saints, for example, blended the sensibilities of a Roman funerary meal and the Last Supper, and marked bonds of charity, community and ritual memory.[8]

These cultural frameworks of property and lordship, custom and status, shaped daily life in religious houses from Gregory the Great's day forward. Gregory's story about Justus presumed and underscored the power of lordly abbots, who used their discretion to govern their

---

[5] For an overview here see John Gilissen, *La Coutume*, Typologie des Sources du Moyen Âge Occidental 41 (Turnhout, 1982).
[6] Heinrich Fichtenau, *Living in the Tenth Century*, trans. Patrick Geary (Chicago, 1991), especially chs. 1–3, here 56.
[7] Ibid., 197–201.
[8] Ibid., 58–60.

households and estates, and to police the disposition of property that was, in principle, common to all. The story also showed how the abbot's lordly power extended to govern the bonds between the living and the dead—at Gregory's word, the chants of his monks had liberated Justus from damnation.[9] And in religious houses, too, the affairs of property and prayer alike were governed by the force of good custom. Most religious communities presumed more than they recorded about custom, but they encountered it every day in their liturgies; in the presence of their superior, whose will was law and whose temperate discretion provided a "living exegesis" of their obligations; and in their "customaries," texts that recorded the particulars of local traditions and offered guidance where written rules were unclear or silent. In all these ways custom remained a ubiquitous, normative presence, a *ratio vivendi* whose authority helped interpret, supplement and even supplant written rules.[10]

Custom, status and the lordship of the household superior in turn shaped religious life's durable bonds of intercessory prayer and provision. The arrangements varied widely across time and locale, but all were rooted in the notion of sacrifice of self and goods at the moment of profession. In return for that sacrifice—and often in return for a customary "gift"—those who entered a local religious household enjoyed a "prebend," a regular portion of food, drink, clothing and other necessities.[11] Typical prebends might also include cash to supplement provision in kind. As an expression of their gratitude for diligent intercession, patrons could also arrange for prebends in connection with the

---

[9] Conrad Leyser, *Authority and Asceticism from Augustine to Gregory the Great* (Oxford, 2000), 154. For general context and a discussion of the transformation of monasteries into "powerhouses of prayer," see Peter Brown, *Rise of Western Christendom*, ch. 9.

[10] Kassius Hallinger, "Consuetudo. Begriff, Formen, Forschungsgeschichte, Inhalt," in *Untersuchungen zu Kloster und Stift*, ed. J. Fleckenstein (Göttingen, 1980), 140–66, esp. 144. See also Albert Groiß, *Spätmittelalterliche Lebensformen der Benediktiner von der Melker Observanz vor dem Hintergrund ihrer Bräuche. Ein darstellender Kommentar zum Caeremoniale Mellicense des Jahres 1460* (Münster, 1999), 14–17. For broader context see Meyer, *Soziales Handeln im Zeichen des 'Hauses'* (above, 1 n. 4), 242–315, especially 280–300.

[11] For the following, and for orientation generally, see Werner Ogris, "Die Konventualenpfründe im Mittelalterlichen Kloster," *Österreichisches Archiv für Kirchenrecht* 13 (1962): 104–42 and Helga Schuller, "*Dos-Praebenda-Peculium*," in *Festschrift Friedrich Hausmann*, ed. Herwig Ebner (Graz, 1977), 453–87. See also the relevant articles in *Handwörterbuch zur deutschen Rechtsgeschichte* (Berlin, 1971), e.g. "Laienpfründe," 2: 1353–55. For attempts to reform the practice, see the foundational treatment of Joseph H. Lynch, *Simoniacal Entry into the Religious Life from 1000 to 1260: A Social, Economic, and Legal Study* (Columbus, 1976).

household's cult of remembrance. For all who enjoyed them, prebends were a key marker of membership in a community's extended social and spiritual household. They also marked the wider world's hierarchies of status. Abbots, abbesses and other notables enjoyed generous and multiple prebends in grand style; priests and important officers enjoyed more modest portions; novices and lay brothers, servants and other more humble household members had to be content with more modest shares still.

In many ways synonymous with the prebend, and sometimes hard to distinguish from it in practice, was the "pittance" (*pictantia*)—typically an occasional improvement of regular household provision, most often an extra portion of food, drink or clothing.[12] Magnanimous household superiors and patrons showered monks and nuns with pittances as a sign of largesse and mercy. At Cluny, abbots arranged pittances to ameliorate the harshness of fasting. Elsewhere testators provided their intercessors with pittances of chicken, fish and eggs; spiced bread or fine wine; costly servings of game; new shoes or clothing—all expressions of charity from beyond the grave. Pittances were often shared among the community as a whole, but patrons also arranged for their charity to fall to individuals—especially to professed priests, who enjoyed special meals or other gifts on the days they were to sing intercessory masses. Abbots and other patrons also provided pittances in cash, both as token amounts dispersed among the community and as fixed sums to individuals. In these and in other instances, the sources sometimes describe the cash payments as *peculium*. To the Romans, the word had denoted a variety of payments to slaves, soldiers and others.[13] Those uses soon disappeared, but the general concept of *peculium* remained a useful way to describe the disposition of cash among those who, like slaves, were forbidden to have anything of their own.

---

[12] For an overview of pittances, see Gerd Zimmermann, *Ordensleben und Lebensstandard. Die Cura Corporis in den Ordensvorschriften des abendländischen Hochmittelalters* (Münster, 1973), 48 ff. with source citations and further literature. See also Hans Lentze, "Pitanz und Pfründe im Mittelalterlichen Wilten," in *Veröffentlichungen aus dem Stadtarchiv Innsbruck*, ed. Karl Schadelbauer (Innsbruck, 1954), 5–15; Hermann Watzl, "Über Pitanzen und Reichnisse für den Konvent des Klosters Heiligenkreuz," *Analecta Cisterciensia* 47 (1978): 40–147; and Reinhard Schneider, "Lebensverhältnisse bei den Zisterziensern im Spätmittelalter," in *Klösterliche Sachkultur des Spätmittelalters* (Vienna, 1982), 43–72.

[13] For a brief survey of the terms see Barry Nicholas, *An Introduction to Roman Law* (Oxford, 1962), 68–69.

Beyond arrangements for prayer and provision, custom shaped a broader sensibility of spiritual status and hierarchy. The abbot of Fulda, along with superiors of other venerable communities such as Fleury and Montecassino, enjoyed a host of ritual honors and privileges that underscored his preeminence.[14] The same sensibility shaped the lives of household officers who administered the corporate wealth of their communities.[15] Known as "obedientiaries" in monastic houses, in principle these figures held their positions at the pleasure of the household superior and carried out their duties in the name of the community and its saints. But in practice, especially in greater households, they could be encountered as powerful lords who governed complex bundles of rights, estates and incomes with virtual independence. They also enjoyed the comforts and privileges of their office in personal ways that reflected status—special lodgings, discretionary enjoyment of substantial incomes, a staff of servants and so on.

In none of the circumstances surveyed thus far did contemporaries necessarily discern any violation of solemn religious profession. On the contrary, many clothed their arrangements in the language of charity. At Fulda, zealous monastic obedientiaries engaged in a kind of competition, both sacred and social, to see who could earn and spend most wisely and piously, bringing honor to God and St. Boniface and blessing their community with prosperity.[16] In the same community, one monk's foundation of a special meal in memory of an abbot was described as *caritas*. At St. Gall the provision of a prebend was given as a "consolation," the provision of lodging for a lay patron granted "through mercy and charity."[17] At Cluny and many other places, the provision of pittances and other portions of food, drink or clothing was also synonymous with charity, as was the monks' customary gathering for a festive social drink, enjoyed from special cups (here another inflection of the broader culture of memorial drinks among bishops

---

[14] Fichtenau, *Living in the Tenth Century*, 16–18.
[15] Jacques Hourlier, *L'âge classique, 1140–1378: Les religieux* (Paris, 1973), 307 ff., with further literature.
[16] K. Lübeck, "Der Privatbesitz der Fuldaer Mönche im Mittelalter," *Archiv für Katholisches Kirchenrecht* 119 (1939): 52–99. For these examples see 63–70.
[17] Emile Lesne, "Une source de la fortune monastique: les donations à charge de pension alimentaire du VIIIe au Xe siècle." *Mélanges de philologie et d'histoire, publiés à l'occasion du cinquantenaire de la Faculté des lettres de l'Université catholique de Lille. Mémoires et travaux publiés par des professeurs de Facultés Catholiques de Lille* 32 (1927): 33–45, here 39.

and other churchmen noted above).[18] The religious habit, too, could be laden with symbolism that marked both spiritual ideals and status. The deep black of the Cluniac monk denoted abjection, contempt, death, penance, adversity, sin and sadness. The nun's veil symbolized her virginity and purity as a bride of Christ, just as the white Cistercian habit later symbolized transfiguration, purity, glory, victory, innocence, happiness, goodness.[19]

Yet the same cultural frameworks of custom and status allowed for more worldly expressions as well. Abbots spoke of "my monk" or "my professed" and governed their extended households in ways that reflected ties between lords and vassals.[20] Ordinary monks and nuns might also appear in ways that made it hard to distinguish them from their peers in the world. Adalbero of Laon, for example, lamented a Cluniac monk who adorned himself in a fur cap, fashionable coat and belt, and who carried weapons.[21] And at every turn the personal enjoyment of what was supposed to be community property could be suddenly condemned as *proprium*. Monks at Fulda complained in the language of Galatians about the anger and strife, dissension and drunkenness that arose from the monks' love of "private business" and worldly revenues.[22] And in 1179, after decades of calls for reform, the Third Lateran Council declared that monks were not to be accepted into any community for a price, and that they were not to enjoy *peculium*. Moreover, echoing Gregory's *Dialogues*, the council decreed that those found on their deathbeds to have concealed their *peculium* were to be denied burial among their brethren.[23] It was in the same reforming climate that Innocent III wrote his stern letter to the monks of

---

[18] Zimmermann, *Ordensleben und Lebensstandard*, 42, with sources and further literature.

[19] Giles Constable, "The Ceremonies and Symbolism of Entering Religious Life and Taking the Monastic Habit, from the Fourth to the Twelfth Century," *Segni e riti nella chiesa altomedievale occidentale: Settimane di Studio del centro italiano di studi sull'alto medioevo* 33 (1987): 771–834, here 829 and nn. 190 and 192. See also *Krone und Schleier. Kunst aus Mittelalterlichen Frauenklöstern* (Munich, 2005).

[20] Constable, "Ceremonies," 788–89.

[21] Fichtenau, *Living in the Tenth Century*, 68.

[22] MGH Ep. 4: 550, no. 15; Cf. Galatians 5.20–2.

[23] X 3, 35, 2 (CIC II: 596–97): "Monachi non pretio recipiantur in monasterio, nec peculium permittantur habere.... Si quis autem exactus pro sua receptione aliquid dederit, ad sacros ordines non ascendat. His vero, qui eum receperit, officii sui suspensione mulctetur. Qui vero peculium habuerit, nisi ab abbate fuerit ei pro iniuncta administratione permissum, a communione removeatur altaris, et qui in extremis cum peculio inventus fuerit, et digne non poenituerit, nec oblatio pro eo fiat, nec inter fratres accipiat sepulturum; quod etiam de universis religiosis praecipimus observari."

Subiaco, condemning *proprium* and reminding them again of Gregory the Great's ancient warning against the vice.

Property and the Religious Estate after 1200

After 1200, building on the older traditions outlined above, Western Christians came increasingly to articulate models of church and society grounded in the concept of "estate" (*status*).[24] Every rank and every "condition," in heaven or on earth, from the angels and other "estates of heaven" to the pope and the king down to the humble farmer, came to be seen as a distinct way of life, each with its proper place in the established order. And for each earthly estate, clergymen provided detailed moral instructions. In their sermons *ad status*, in treatises on virtues and vices, in confession and so on, they reminded knights to be merciful, married men and women to be faithful, merchants to be honest in their business dealings. *Status* was more, however, than a system of social classification or a set of moral prescriptions. In Aristotelian terms it was also something akin to a "substance," a metasocial reality embodied in the property and social circumstance of countless particular men and women. The local lord, the noble widow, the bishop and the merchant each held their particular bundles of lands and goods, rights and revenues, offices and so on as representatives of their particular way of life. And the nobility in particular, as representatives of their estate, not only held their property by right, but also had a right to be maintained in their position atop society in an appropriate fashion, "according to their estate."

Within this broader framework of estates, institutional religious life occupied a central place. Monks, nuns and canons, many of their houses centuries old by 1200, were the embodiment of an entire way of life, a distinct *status* whose men and women, property and privileges remained, along with the other estates, constitutive of the social order. Foundational for most discussions of that estate in the later Middle Ages was the *Decretals*, a massive collection of papal decrees in five books commissioned by Gregory IX. Historians of religious poverty perhaps know Gregory best as the author of *Quo Elongati*, one of the earliest in a series of papal bulls that wrestled with the tensions of spirit

---

[24] For the following see Howard Kaminsky, "Estate, Nobility and the Exhibition of Estate in the Later Middle Ages," *Speculum* 68 (1993): 684–709.

and institution so central to Franciscan history. But his *Decretals* were also influential for wider discussions of religious life. In the thirty-fifth title of its third book, Gregory's collection gathered together a corpus of decrees, "On the Estate of Monks and Regular Canons" (*De statu monachorum et canonicorum regularium*). Its precedents, along with those of similar compilations commissioned by later popes, provided generations of students and commentators an opportunity to reflect on a range of issues related to religious life.

Among the earliest medieval schoolmen to engage in those reflections was the influential canonist Henry of Segusio, or Hostiensis. He served as a church prelate in many capacities, attaining the rank of cardinal bishop of Ostia prior to his death in 1271, and over the course of his long career he authored several foundational commentaries on papal law.[25] As he turned to the *Decretals'* precedents on the religious estate, Hostiensis confronted the matter of individual property (*proprium*) in two key texts. The first (X 3, 35, 2) was the decree of Lateran III noted above. It declared that monks were not to be accepted into any community at a price, and not to enjoy *peculium*. Those found to enjoy property without legitimate administrative purpose were to be excommunicated. The canon also declared that those found on their deathbeds to have concealed their property or who were unrepentant were to be denied burial. The second text (X 3, 35, 6) was Innocent III's stern condemnation of *proprium* among the monks of Subiaco.[26]

Hostiensis approached these texts with care. The Lateran prohibition of *proprietas*, as he read it, concerned only monks without administrative duties.[27] Cellarers and almoners and other officers, of course, had to receive and spend money in a variety of ways, and they could do so with proper license. Hostiensis then qualified his position: it was perhaps more fitting to say that the "administrative capacity" in itself, rather than the individual monk, governed the money and goods.[28] Turning to Innocent's condemnation of *proprium* at Subiaco, Hostiensis worked to maintain a similar balance. As he read it, the condemnation applied only

---

[25] For an overview see Kenneth Pennington, *The Prince and the Law, 1200–1600: Sovereignty and Rights in the Western Legal Tradition* (Berkeley, 1993), 48–9.

[26] For X 3, 35, 2 (CIC II: 596–97) see above, n. 23. For X 3, 35, 6 (CIC II: 599), see above, n. 1.

[27] Hostiensis, *Decretalium Commentaria* (Turin, 1965), 133: "[Qui vero] id est nisi abbas administrationem sibi commiserit, et sic per consequens proprium habere licebit."

[28] Ibid.: "[Administratione].... Talis enim ratione administrationis potest habere proprium, ut hic dicit, sed vere loquendo potius habet ipsum proprium administratio...."

to "cloister monks" who had no official duties.[29] Hostiensis also defined individual property (*proprietas*) simply as whatever was "concealed from the abbot." The negative construction recognized the unquestioned authority of the household superior, and allowed individual monks to dispose of money and goods held in his name. A monk was simply to be "prepared to surrender" his property whenever his superior wished. The construction thus allowed individuals to dispose of money as long as they did not spend it for their own purposes (*in propriis usibus*) or give it away without permission.[30] It even allowed individual monks, with license, to accept direct cash donations.[31] Hostiensis quickly balanced his concessions, however, with firm reminders: any arrangement not sanctioned by the abbot was illicit, and monks risked violation of their vows, as Benedict himself had taught, by appropriating even the smallest thing without permission.[32]

Later in his letter to Subiaco, Innocent had issued a stern and absolute warning to the abbot of the community: neither he nor anyone else should presume to grant dispensations against the vow of poverty. Even here Hostiensis worked to maintain a balance. No administrator was to be licensed to dispose of money and goods with total freedom (*uti ad libitum*). And even with proper license, Hostiensis admitted, monks who disposed of money were in a dangerous circumstance. Without doubt, he stressed, it was always better to avoid spending cash. At the same time, for Hostiensis the abbot's discretion and authority still remained. As long as a monk disposed of his money in the name of his abbot and community, and as long as he remained "prepared to surrender" to the will of his superior, he did no wrong. Hostiensis concluded by hedging his bets one final time: it was all a dangerous matter, he noted, and

---

[29] Ibid., "[Monachorum] Claustralis simplex, qui nullam obedientiam, nullam administrationem habet."

[30] Ibid.: "[Quod si proprietas] Dicitur autem proprietas, quidquid concelatur abbati. Nam de permissione abbatis videtur quod possit habere pecuniam, dum tamen ipsam non expendat in propriis usibus, nec alicui det sine abbatis conscientia. Sed nomine abbatis tenet, paratus resignare quandocunque volet."

[31] X 3, 35, 6 (CIC II: 599): "Unde, si quicquam alicui fuerit specialiter destinatum, non praesumat illud accipere, sed abbati vel priori vel cellerario assignetur."

[32] Hostiensis, *Decretalium Commentaria*, 133: "[Non praesumat] scilicet monachus q. d. sine licentia abbatis. Si ergo habet abbatis licentiam non est praesumptio, dummodo illud sibi non appropriet....[Assignetur]...Et hoc intelligitur non solum de magnis, sed etiam de minimis, etiam si graphium sit, secundum regulam xxxiii et liiii c. Immo nec licet monacho occulte, id est sine licentia abbatis litteras sibi etiam missas, vel aliquod munus quantumcumque etiam minimum ab aliquo accipere, xii q. i Non dicatis in principio."

potentially set a very bad example. He therefore cautioned superiors not to grant their license "without great, evident and urgent cause."[33]

Hostiensis' intricate commentary helped make sense of a way of life dominated by abbots and obedientiaries in Christendom's great landed households. In many locales it was not uncommon for nearly half of a given community to hold at least one office.[34] There were second, third and, on occasion, fourth priors; chamberlains; sacristans; administrators of forests and hunting rights, of ponds and fishing rights; gardeners and porters; officers to care for the provision of bread, wine and vegetables of proper quality.[35] In ways that were often hard to distinguish from their secular peers, these figures held land, rights and cash revenues in the name of their corporation, and they did so often with only minimal supervision; most were required to render proper accounts to their superiors only a few times a year.[36] Yet officers ran afoul of their renunciation of *proprium* only if they spent money in ways not licensed by their superior. Moreover, with that license they often disposed of their corporate incomes in ways only loosely related, if at all, to the "official" functions of their offices. English account books record personal expenses for medicine or entertainment, and donations of alms and gifts to other community members or to laymen. They also suggest how an *ad hoc* arrangement could evolve into a virtual patrimony: in 1335, for example, a fund was created for rebuilding Westminster after a fire in 1298. An officer, the *custos novi operis*, was put in charge of the revenues. The building of the nave was not completed until 1528, however, and the administrators of its funds had long since come to dispose of their incomes in ways wholly unrelated to the construction

---

[33] Ibid.: "[Super habenda proprietate] ut ea possit uti ad libitum, alias autem de voluntate abbatis potest monachus pecuniam recipere et habere.... Sed nec potest dici proprietas dummodo nihil de quantitate vel qualitate concelet abbati, nec sine eiusdem conscientia quid recipiat vel expendat. Et quandocumque sibi placuerit, paratus sit totum reddere nec intendat aliquid nomine proprio sed tantum abbatis et monasterii possidere. Est tamen res periculosa.... Unde et consulo abbati quod nisi magna et evidens, urgens vel utilis causa subsit, caveat a tali licentia concedenda."

[34] David Knowles, *The Religious Orders in England*, 3 vols. (Cambridge, 1948–1959), 1: 49–64; R. H. Snape, *English Monastic Finances in the Later Middle Ages* (Cambridge, 1926), 32–53.

[35] Hourlier, *L'âge classique*, (above, n. 15) 308–35, with further literature, e.g. G. L. Dubar, *Recherches sur les offices du monastère de Corbie jusqu'à la fin du XIIIe siècle* (Paris, 1951); P. Tisset, *L'abbaye de Gellone au diocèse de Lodève des origines au XIIIe siècle* (Troyes, 1992); G. Valous, *Le monachisme clunisien des origines au XVe siècle: vie intérieure des monastères et organisation de l'ordre* (Ligugé, 1935).

[36] Snape, *Finances*, 36–49, 64–65 and 111–13.

of any building—paying the pensions of older monks, giving presents to other monks for a first mass, and the like.[37] Women who served as administrators disposed of their communities' incomes and goods with similarly broad latitude. As Marilyn Oliva has shown, the nuns of the diocese of Norwich served as officers in ways that mirrored male monastic administration, as well as administration in secular households. Second prioresses, sacrists, almoners and other officers who served their convents could be encountered in a variety of ways—out in the world on official trips; collecting rents, fines and other revenues; paying servants; giving alms; and so on.[38] Across the landscape, these men and women were figures whose temporal, spiritual and social power visibly embodied and represented the religious estate.

Yet Hostiensis' model also stood in uneasy tension with new realities of cash and commerce that were reshaping daily life in lordly households generally.[39] By the later thirteenth century, passersby must have encountered seemingly ever greater numbers of monks, canons and nuns who, as representatives of their estate, disposed of personal cash incomes in new and more visible ways. In part the changes reflected the wider economy. By 1300 lords increasingly met the demands of status, administration and provision through pensions, stipends and other endowed cash incomes, often arranged in elaborate written contracts.[40] In an analogous way, the customary provision of prebends and pittances was increasingly arranged under written contract, paid either in cash and in kind, or in cash alone as an endowed stipend.

Closely related to these changes, often almost inseparable from them, was the emergence of a more vigorous, diverse and efficient market for intercessory masses.[41] At the center of the business was the salaried

---

[37] Ibid., 65.

[38] Marilyn Oliva, *The Convent and the Community in Late Medieval England: Female Monasteries in the Diocese of Norwich, 1350–1540* (Rochester, 1998), 83–90, esp. 84–86 and n. 63.

[39] For general context see Peter Spufford, "Trade in Fourteenth-Century Europe," *New Cambridge Medieval History*, vol. 6 (1300–1415), 155–208 and R. H. Britnell, *The Commercialisation of English Society* (Cambridge, 1993).

[40] In England, for example, hundreds of thirteenth-century contracts survive through which household lords provided food and drink, robes and other colorful clothing, cash or other incomes for their dependents. See Britnell, *Commercialisation*, 131.

[41] Jaques Chiffoleau, *La comptabilité de l'au-delà: les hommes, la mort et la religion dans la région d'Avignon à la fin du Moyen Âge (vers 1320–vers 1480)* (Rome, 1980); idem, "Sur l'usage obsessionnel de la messe pour les morts à la fin du moyen âge," in *Faire croire. Modalités de la diffusion et de la réception des messages religieux du XIIe au XVe siècle* (Rome, 1981), 236–56.

priest, who was often a monk, a canon or friar. In meticulous contracts, patrons stipulated the particular masses a given priest (or team of priests) was to perform, how many and when, the income to be received and under what conditions. By the end of the fourteenth century, some of these spiritual business deals could reach striking proportions. Contracts for one hundred to one thousand masses were not uncommon, with a small number of foundations established for two and even four thousand.[42] Most arrangements were more modest, but they too brought more and more cash into the hands of individual religious. Numerous German and Austrian charters suggest typical payments for that region: in return for anniversary masses, monks and canons enjoyed not only extra portions of bread, wine, fish and other food, but also cash sums of 2–7d, paid to individuals or to the community as a whole.[43]

Similar trends were at work in households of nuns and canonesses. From before 1300, parents and friends arranged individually endowed stipends for their religious women, most often to provide for clothing, spending cash, or the improvement of standard household provision. In 1297, "for the healing of our soul," dukes Otto and Steven of Bavaria donated forty pounds of incomes to the Cistercian nuns of Seligenthal. The donation was intended "especially," however, for their sister Elizabeth, who was to enjoy the endowment's modest revenues for life.[44] In 1327, when another nun was taken into the community of Seligenthal, her patrons arranged for her to receive (along with another sister who was also a nun in the community) an annual income of one pound in Regensburger *pfennig*.[45] Women in the same community, and in communities across the region, enjoyed similar individual subventions "for the improvement of their prebends" down to the end of the fourteenth century. And among women, as among men, arrangements for cash incomes such as these were often tied in with intercessory work. At the Cistercian nunnery of Heiligenkreuztal, nearly every purchase of a nuns' prebend in the late fourteenth century was arranged in conjunction with intercessory prayers.[46] At Göttweig (1308, 1309 and 1326), Seligenthal (1320) and Admont (1329), patrons who endowed prebends,

---

[42] Hans Lentze, "Begräbnis und Jahrtag in mittelalterlichen Wien," *Zeitschrift für Rechtsgeschichte, Kanonische Abteilung* 67 (1950): 328–64, here 346.
[43] Cf. FRA II/18, no. 167 (pp. 191–92).
[44] *Landshuter Urkundenbuch*, ed. Theo Herzog (Neustadt an der Aisch, 1963) 1: 169. Cf. Schuller, "Dos, Praebenda, Peculium" (above, n. 11), 468.
[45] Schuller, "Dos," 312.
[46] Ibid., 477–78.

pittances and other incomes for their daughters similarly arranged for male chaplains to sing anniversary masses.[47]

By the mid-thirteenth century the ideal of apostolic poverty and the new mendicant orders posed a fundamental challenge to the *status* of nuns, monks and canons. The followers of Dominic and Francis had in principle renounced the world in the name of apostolic poverty.[48] Yet in the name of the active life, they also claimed the right to teach in the schools, to preach and to hear confessions in the parishes. In doing so the mendicants cut deeply into the established privileges and revenues of the secular clergy, and inspired endless debate over the legitimacy of the mendicant way of life.[49] In the middle of the early debates, Aquinas crafted some of the most compelling arguments for the place of the mendicants within the established order. In a society of estates, Aquinas argued, there were those who were fully devoted to the pursuit of charity, and so merited inclusion in what he called the "estate of perfection" (*status perfectionis*). The bishops were members by virtue of their ministry. So too were religious of every order, the mendicants included, by virtue of their vows of poverty, chastity and obedience. Through their vows religious had set themselves apart, binding themselves perpetually to those things which removed obstacles to charity and freed them to "tend to perfection."[50]

As these debates over religious life and status evolved, all sides reaffirmed their commitment to individual poverty. Yet toward 1300 that commitment stood in uneasy tension with the same realities of cash and commerce that were transforming daily life for the *status* of monks and canons. Individual friars, too, disposed of ostensibly corporate incomes and goods in a range of visible and personal ways. They disposed of cash as students, preachers and inquisitors. They received stipends as mass priests.[51] Friars also disposed of cash and personal property as

---

[47] FRA II/ 51, nos. 245, 248 and 338. Schuller, "Dos," 473–4 (cf. *Landshuter Urkundenbuch* 1: 270 and StLA-U 1986e).

[48] See here the excellent overview of Neidiger, *Mendikanten*, (above, 5 and n. 15), especially Chapter Two.

[49] Standard now are the works of Ulrich Horst (above, 2 and n. 8).

[50] Horst, *Evangelische Armut*, ch. 3, provides a close reading of Aquinas' arguments in the *Summa* and places them thoroughly in the context of his earlier works.

[51] So, for example, Dominican inquisitors were required to render accounts of their personal goods to their conventual prior, and an account of their "official" goods to their provincial prior. The provincial prior, in turn, was to render an account of both his official and personal goods: Frühwirth 2:130: "...superiores, ad quos spectat talem recipere racionem, ipsam ab inferioribus requirant et audiant cum effectu; imponentes

"limitors" (*terminarii*)—the administrators of a mendicant household's preaching territories. In that capacity they preached, ran indulgence campaigns, provided pastoral care for parishioners and rest for their traveling brothers. They also accepted and guarded donations of cash and valuables on behalf of their communities, bought and sold land and incomes, and received sometimes handsome gifts of cash.[52]

Mendicant nuns, too, appeared as modestly propertied figures in most locales. Their houses served as holding companies for much of the real estate and revenue the men could not technically own.[53] But as individuals, mendicant women also enjoyed endowed personal incomes, most arranged in ways similar to their peers in older, landed convents. To choose only a few of the numerous examples provided in one study of women's religious houses in Austria: In 1296, as sisters Agnes and Gertrude entered the Dominican nunnery of Mahrenberg, for example, their mother endowed each of them with a two-mark income.[54] In 1327, the parents of Elspeth Lobming, a Clare in the community of Judenburg, donated a one-mark income to provide for her clothing.[55] And again, arrangements like these often linked material provision with spiritual intercession. In 1306, for example, the Clares in Munich arranged to pray for the souls of the father and mother of one of their sisters, Katarina Egling. In return, Katarina was to receive either a yearly payment in kind or a one-pound cash pension.[56] In 1318, the abbess of the same community provided her women extra portions of bread, wine, fish and cash in return for their intercessory prayers on behalf of Adelheid Kramer. Adelheid's daughter was also to enjoy an annual income of three pounds until her death.[57]

It is tempting to associate the patterns of life outlined here in some way with an emergent crisis of economy and society, one in which declining revenues and other pressures pushed religious men and

---

singulis prioribus conventualibus, quod semel in anno per preceptum a quolibet fratre subdito requirant in scriptis, quantum debet et cui, quantum ei debetur et a quo, et quantum habeant et ubi in pecunia et rebus aliis preciosis...."

[52] Kaspar Elm has explored their circumstance among the Augustinian Hermits: "Termineien und Hospize der westfälischen Augustiner-Eremitenklöster Osnabrück, Lippstadt und Herford," *Jahrbuch für Westfälische Kirchengeschichte* 70 (1977): 11–40. See especially 12–13; 15; 31; 38–39 and n. 137.

[53] Neidiger, *Mendikanten*, 75 ff.

[54] StLA-U 1501a; cf. Schuller, "Dos," 469.

[55] StLA-U 1963c; cf. Schuller, "Dos," 470.

[56] *Monumenta Boica* 18: 46. cf. Schuller, "Dos," 475.

[57] *Monumenta Boica* 18: 98–9; cf. Schuller, "Dos," 481.

women to rely on personal incomes rather than the common life to meet their needs. There is some measure of truth here, and in fact contemporaries themselves occasionally remarked that their incomes helped them negotiate difficult circumstances. At the same time, no model of crisis has yet fully accounted for the durable conceptual and cultural frameworks that helped reconcile religious profession with the enjoyment of personal incomes. To take that reconciliation seriously is to see how contemporaries, quite apart from whatever crises they endured, continued to adapt to and make sense of their circumstance.

One of the oldest conceptual touchstones was good custom. Fourteenth-century monks and nuns in Austria, for example, repeatedly stressed that their enjoyment of pittances had been arranged "according to honorable custom." They also clothed complex unwritten arrangements surrounding burial and intercession, the sharing of cash incomes for anniversary masses and so on in similarly terse but legally forceful phrases: "according to the custom of their order," or "as is their custom."[58] Similar language appears in charters from women's houses. The provision of endowed cash incomes for the Dominican sisters Agnes and Gertrude Vinkelstein at Mahrenberg, noted above, was described explicitly as having been arranged "according to the custom of the Preachers."[59] The Clares of Judenburg used the same language. In the fall of 1304, four brothers endowed a three-mark stipend to provide for their sisters' needs, "as it has come down through custom in the same cloister."[60]

The concept of "use" (*usus*) also allowed for the personal disposition of cash incomes. Though best known for its importance among the Franciscans, *usus* had a wider resonance that should not be missed. In lay and ecclesiastical contexts alike, *usus* denoted the disposition of things as a means of preserving the common good, or of meeting

---

[58] Cf. FRA II/11, nos. 67 and 68 (pp. 60–63). See also nos. 78 (1322), 82 (1322); 136 (1331); 139 (1331); 158 (1337); 170 (1338); 229 (1358). The monks of Benedictine houses like Göttweig similarly enjoyed their pittances as pious "consolations" in accordance with the "observed custom of their order," and described their intercessory arrangements as in accordance with "what has been customary in our house." Cf. FRA II/51, no. 666. For the sharing of anniversary masses, see FRA II/18, no. 226 (pp. 256–57).

[59] StLA-U 1501a: "nach der prediger gewonheit." Cf. Schuller, "Dos," 469. See also StLA-U 1926b: "Nach der prediger geownheit mit zwanzig march silbers..." Cf. Schuller, "Dos," 472.

[60] StLA-U 1667c: "...als es von aller gewonhait in dem selben kloster herkoemen ist...." Cf. Schuller, "Dos," 469.

manifest necessity. Hence, the same conceptual framework that allowed the laity to "turn" objects and incomes to their use in a variety of settings also allowed nuns to "turn" corporate revenues to their own uses, "in consultation with the abbess."[61] Other charters drew a distinction between the outright ownership (*dominium*) of a nun's endowment, which was retained by her household, and the woman's "administration and governance" (*administratio et gubernatio*) of the proceeds—concepts that were in turn part of a wider discourse of ministry, oversight and custody in the name of the common good.[62] It is possible to dismiss these frameworks as legal fictions, euphemisms and so on. But to do so is to miss their importance for making sense of daily life and complex circumstance. These constructions helped make sense of the way that individual religious, men and women alike, lived from day to day—in the interstices of ownership, as it were, obedient to their superiors, yet free to meet their personal needs and the obligations of their estate without scandal or violation of their vow to live *sine proprio*.

As religious drew up their charters locally, schoolmen crafted models that made sense of that same circumstance. Writing just before 1300, the Parisian theologian Godfrey of Fontaines asked in his tenth quodlibet whether professed religious might live on fixed incomes (*certos redditus*), and even defend their enjoyment in court.[63] Godfrey had weighed in frequently in the academic battles against the privileges of the mendicant orders in the 1280s, and he was no friend of the friars. But in this quodlibet he advanced a careful, nuanced argument that fully presumed the local realities religious faced in every order. He built his case around the concepts of licensed use (*usus*), proportion and *status*. Godfrey argued that a vow to live *sine proprio* did not prevent the use of

---

[61] Gabriel LePointe, "Réflexions sur des textes concernant la propriété individuelle des religieuses cisterciennes dans la région Lilloise," *Revue d'histoire ecclésiastique* 49 (1954): 743–69. Cf. *Deutsches Rechtswörterbuch* (Weimar, 1914 ff.), 10: 39–40, eg.: "...in sinen nûtz zû kerin" and "an keynen andern nutz uber keren noch belegen."

[62] Schuller, "Dos," 454. Du Cange, *Glossarium* 1: 83 notes that *administratio* was often synonymous with *praebenda*. Terms synonymous with *gubernatio* included *servare*, *providere*, *curare*, and *ministrare*. Cf. *Glossarium* 4–5: 127.

[63] J. Hoffmans, ed., *Le dixième Quodlibet de Godefroid de Fontaines* (texte inédit) (Louvain, 1931), 388–91: "Utrum aliquis religiosus salvo voto paupertatis possit sibi procurare certos redditus sic quod ad solvendum illos sibi possit agere de iure, alius tamen de iure ei illos tribuere teneatur." For Godfrey's biography see Maurice De Wulf, *Un Théologien-Philosophe du XIIIe Siècle. Étude sur la vie, les oevres et l'influence de Godefroid de Fontaines* (Brussels, 1904).

money and goods "in fitting proportion" to others in one's community.[64] As long as religious did not claim any *ius proprium* and enjoyed their incomes and goods with proper license, they in no way violated their vows. A prelate's license, as Godfrey saw it, "transferred" ownership (*ius et dominium*) of things from the individual monk, nun, canon or friar directly to the community as a whole.[65] The enjoyment of personal cash incomes then fit easily within Godfrey's framework: just as one might give a one-time donation of alms to a religious, he reasoned, one might just as easily donate the same "for a long, continuous period of time" by "assigning" a corporate cash income to one individual.[66]

Godfrey also explicitly linked his model, it should be emphasized, to the concept of *status*. Religious were to enjoy their corporately owned, licensed incomes in ways "fitting" for their order and "according to their condition and estate."[67] It is unclear precisely what Godfrey thought this should look like, but his remark is consistent with what most must have encountered from day to day—a differentiated hierarchy of communities of monks, nuns, canons and friars, with all of their discrepancies of wealth, sacred and social power, whose members disposed of their individual incomes accordingly. Again, it is tempting to read most of Godfrey's argument as rationalization, which it could doubtless become in any given circumstance. But it remains important to see in Godfrey's work a genuine attempt to reconcile the demands of religious community with both the social and cultural imperatives of *status*, and the complexities of a modern economy. Here again was

---

[64] *Quodlibet* X, ed. Hoffmans, 388–89: "Dicendum quod in voto paupertatis duo includuntur, videlicet primo et principaliter, nihil habere in proprio, ut dictum est; et ex consequenti etiam nihil habere de his quae in communi veniunt quantum ad usum nisi secundum convenientem proportionem et habitudinem quam habet unus de communitate ad alios qui sunt pars eiusdem communitatis."

[65] Ibid: "...et quia [religiosus] non est capax ut singularis persona secundum se et absolute, sed ut pars communitatis, ideo ius et dominium in talibus per se et directe transit in ipsam communitatem; prout dicitur quod illud quod monachus acquirit acquiritur monasterio. Propter quod etiam talis persona non potest agere ad habendum talia, sed ipsa communitas vel talis persona nomine communitatis."

[66] Ibid.: "Unde sicut potest aliquis per modum eleemosynae statim vel in proximo consumendae dare aliquid alicui personae determinatae in collegio, et singularis persona hoc potest procurare et recipere secundum modum suae regulae convenientem, ita etiam potest fieri de eleemosyna per longa tempora duratura secundum assignationem alicuius redditus determinati."

[67] Ibid.: "...uti secundum conditionem sui status et suae perfectionis, quantum ad haec duo non peccat nec agit contra votum paupertatis. Sed illa non debet talia recipere nisi de licentia eius ad quem hoc pertinet; et etiam illis non debet uti nisi secundum dictam proportionem."

a model that allowed individual religious to meet their needs and to appear as representatives of their way of life without running afoul of their vow to live *sine proprio*.

Soon after Godfrey wrote, another schoolman tried again to reconcile the enjoyment of cash incomes with the demands of both religious community and *status*. Reflecting on Innocent III's letter to Subiaco, the influential legal scholar John Andreae reiterated the general principles others had outlined before him: no personal cash income could be called *proprietas* as long as that income was properly licensed, accounted for and disposed toward its proper ends. Andreae then offered a more revealing observation: in his day, he noted, the Roman Curia itself openly allowed individual religious to pay for their clothing and other needs through personal endowments. In fact, Andreae pointed out, the popes themselves had allowed their chaplains—many of them members of the religious orders—to receive such payments from papal revenues. The popes had also long approved the custom that allowed nuns throughout Christendom to pay for their clothing either from cash donations, from incomes endowed by their parents, or from their own earnings—here a reference to precisely the kinds of arrangements outlined in the charters noted above.[68]

Andreae's reflections are also a reminder of how much papal power and papal law had helped, at times boldly, to reconcile tensions of cash and community. In the thirteenth century, canonists began to reflect extensively on the divine origins of the "positive law" that popes created through their decrees.[69] In that climate, one throwaway line at the end of Innocent's famous letter to Subiaco took on a strong intellectual attraction. Innocent had admonished the abbot of Subiaco not to abuse his authority by allowing his monks to enjoy personal property illicitly.

---

[68] Johannes Andreae, *In sextum decretalium librum nouella commentaria* (Venice, 1581), 179: "Nec videtur dici proprietas, quando de qualitate et quantitate nil celat abbati, nec sine ipsius conscientia aliquid recipit vel expendit, paratus totum reddere et dimittere ad iussum abbatis...." Ibid.: "Romana curia scit et tolerat quod regularibus taxetur aliquid pro vestimentis, vel dentur ad id certe possessiones, unde et regulares capellani papae de servitiis ita recipiunt portionem, sicut alii. Testari tamen de his non possunt quasi proprietarii.... Et idem de monialibus, quae a monasterio habent solum victum, et a parentibus, vel de suo lucro habent indumenta."

[69] Pennington, *Prince and the Law*, here, 56–75. For context generally see Ludwig Buisson, *Potestas und Caritas: Die Päpstliche Gewalt im Mittelalter* (Cologne, 1959). For the religious orders, see Andreas Fieback, "*Necessitas non est legi subiecta, maxime positivae*. Über den Zusammenhang von Rechtswandel und Schriftgebrauch bei Humbert de Romanis O. P.," in *De ordine vitae: zu Normvorstellungen, Organisationsformen und Schriftgebrauch im mittelalterlichen Ordenswesen*, ed. Gert Melville (Münster, 1996), 125–51.

The pope then explained why: "The renunciation of ownership, along with the preservation of chastity, is so joined (*annexa*) to the monastic rule that not even the highest pontiff may grant a license against it."[70] The stance seems clear: Innocent was insisting that no abbot had the authority to license whatever he pleased among his monks. Lotario de Segni's successors, however, interpreted his phrase in a way the pope may have found surprising: To say that the renunciation of property was joined to religious life was to say that it was, in fact, a matter of positive law, and therefore subject to papal dispensation.[71] What the proper conditions of dispensation might be, and how precisely an all-powerful pope might use such dispensation for the common good, remained unclear. But the principle of papal power remained, and it could have a direct impact on daily cloister life. In July 1245, Innocent IV (who had been one of the earliest to argue that the pope's absolute power extended to dispensation of religious vows) issued a privilege allowing the nuns of Marquette in Normandy to dispose of inherited wealth "as if they were in the world."[72] A similar privilege of Clement IV later granted the monks at Heiligenkreuz in Austria the same privilege, in the same language.[73] Future archival work will trace the scope and impact of these kinds of privileges in more detail. But the power of the papacy to sanction the enjoyment of personal property and incomes could clearly prove decisive in any given circumstance.

The religious orders themselves also turned to positive law to help govern the tensions of property and community in their ranks. Cluniacs and Cistercians, the mendicant orders, and soon even older Benedictine houses increasingly regulated their affairs through statutory legislation.[74] In doing so they left behind glimpses of how fully religious life

---

[70] X 3, 35, 6: "Nec aestimet abbas, quod super habenda proprietate possit cum aliquo monacho dispensare; quia abdicatio proprietatis, sicut et custodia castitatis, adeo est annexa regulae monachali, ut contra eam nec summus Pontifex possit licentiam indulgere."

[71] Pennington, *Prince and the Law*, 70–75, analyzes these passages in in eloquent detail.

[72] LePointe, "Réflexions sur des textes concernant la propriété individuelle," (above, n. 61), 743.

[73] FRA II/11, no. 192 (p. 196): "…indulgemus, ut possessiones et bona alia mobilia et immobilia, que liberas personas vestrorum fratrum ad monasterium vestrum mundi vanitate relicta convolantium et professionem facientium eodem iure successionis vel alio iusto titulo, si remansissent in seculo contigissent, et que ipsi, existentes in seculo, potuissent aliis libere elargire, petere, recipere ac etiam retinere valeatis sine iuris preiudicio alieni."

[74] Essential here are volumes edited by Melville (above, 5 and n. 16).

participated in an economy of personal incomes and worldly goods. In 1328, for example, the Dominican order condemned brothers who held cash, gold, silver, precious stones and other goods in places beyond their community, and those who loaned money and collected on loans outside the order, all without license.[75] In 1334 and 1335, Dominicans accused one another of illicit appropriation of community goods. In many convents, the brothers noted, their prelates had "carried off" books and other liturgical items. They demanded that none of their goods be sold, pawned or otherwise taken away without the consent of the convent, and demanded prelates not use the money they had acquired for anything other than pressing community needs.[76] The prelates then complained in 1344 about the "the reservation and dispensation to the brothers of appropriated goods." This, they said, seemed "to smack of the vice of property." It had also given rise to "excessive expense, useless and pointless redundancies, and scandals," and they ordered brothers not to dispense with their appropriated goods without proper license.[77]

A series of Cistercian statutes from the 1330s captures similar tensions among the white monks. In 1332 the Cistercian general chapter condemned monks and *conversi* who "held and possessed" goods and rents "under their use," and who claimed that they had documents (*litteras et instrumenta*) from previous abbots granting that privilege without the strictures of license.[78] The same written documents conferred upon the monks the right to invoke the secular arm to protect their privileged

---

[75] Frühwirth 2: 129.

[76] Ibid., 224: "...omni districtione qua possumus inhibemus ne predicta in conventu quocumque vendi vel impignorari vel quomodolibet aliter distrahi valeant nisi de consensu maioris partis conventus hoc etiam observato quod omnis pecunia ex premissis habita in usus notorios et conventui necessarios et non aliter expendatur; adiicientes quod mutuum quodcumque notabile non contrahatur ab aliquo priore, nisi de maioris partis sui conventus beneplacito et assensu...."

[77] Ibid., 297: "Cum bonorum fratribus appropriatorum reservatio et dispensatio per eosdem fratres facta sine scitu et licentia suorum conventualium prelatorum proprietatis vitium sapere videtur, insuper et ad hoc compertum sit subsequi expensarum excessus, combinationes inutiles et discursus, unde finaliter scandala et pericula statui nostro graviter adversantia generantur, imponimus prioribus provincialibus universis ut ipsi super hoc sedule vigilent et attente et observari faciant per priores quod videlicet fratres omnes bona ad ipsos pertinentia sine presidentium suorum speciali licentia non dispensent."

[78] Canivez, 3: 428: "...quamplures monachi et conversi...terras, possessiones, bona et redditus monasterii tenent et possident sub usibus...applicant, asserentes se super hoc ab abbatibus predecessoribus litteras et instrumenta habere, quibus eis conceditur quod eas tenere valeant et suis absque licentia cuiuscumque usibus applicare...."

arrangements. Again in 1334 the Cistercians complained of monks who bought unlicensed annual pensions (*pensiones ad vitam*) from other abbots and converted them to personal use. The protesting Cistercians demanded that abbots who illicitly accepted the purchase price of a pension should restore the cash within a month.[79] The following year, Jacques Fournier, himself a Cistercian and now Pope Benedict XII, condemned those who bought and sold capital, rights, lands, revenues, animals and other things "like merchants."[80] These monks had "held and illicitly detained" their property at the cost of their souls, and those who obstinately refused to render a full account to their abbots were to be deprived of any office they held within the order.[81]

Here again is an opportunity to read the evidence in a way that resists older models of institutional decline or crisis. Whatever the broader economic and other challenges facing the orders in the fourteenth century (none of them to be discounted), these statutes provide glimpses of a vigorous culture of property, legal and licensed or otherwise. They also reveal how that culture remained caught between distant legislation and local discretion. On the one hand, legislators and prelates consistently condemned the "vice of property" at every turn. Yet the boundary between licensed corporate use and illicit personal seizure could be difficult to discern in the best of circumstances, and it could be all but impossible to police from a distance. For all of its seriousness of purpose, the legislation faced too many competing forces: the power

---

[79] Ibid., 406: "...ne aliquis monachus aut conversus absque proprii abbatis licentia, pensiones ad vitam a quocumque abbate ordinis vell aliis quibuscumque emere audeat vel praesumat...Abbas autem ordinis qui ob huiusmodi receperit pecuniam ab eodem, ipsam pecuniam abbati cuius professionis exisitit, infra mensem restituere teneatur, monasterii usibus necessariis applicandam...."

[80] Ibid., 428: "...pecunia congregata, iura, possessiones, redditus, pensiones, animalia et alia bona emerunt et emunt seu emi fecerunt et faciunt aliquando proprio et saepe nomine alieno multis super his figmentis adhibitis...tamquam negotiatores exercent, nec non appetentes lucra turpia et sectantes peculium occultant et illicte detinent in suarum periculo animarum...." For context see Franz J. Felten, "Die Ordensreformen Benedikts XII. unter institutionengeschichtlichem Aspekt," in *Institutionen und Geschichte*, ed. Melville (above, 5, n. 16), 369–436; Bernhard Schimmelpfennig, "Das Papstum und die Reform des Zisterzienserordens im späten Mittelalter," in *Reformbemühungen und Observanzbestrebungen*, ed. Elm (above, 5, n. 14), 399–410, and idem, "Zisterzienserideal und Kirchenreform: Benedikt XII (1334–42) als Reformpapst," *Zisterzienser-Studien* 3 (1976): 11–43.

[81] Canivez, 3: 428: "...peculium predictum non revelantes et reddentes abbatibus...sint eo ipso inhabiles ad quodcumque officium, administrationem, regimen et gubernationem quamlibet in eodem ordine obtinenda...."

of local custom; the authority of local prelates; clever local strategies; and entrenched local interests. The power of these to determine just what counted as law, just which statutes were enforced, dispensed with, evaded or simply ignored, should never be underestimated, even for the later Middle Ages.

Even the Franciscan order, in the wake of all of their debates over poverty and poor use, managed itself from day to day in ways that reflected these tensions. In 1341, for example, a provincial chapter in Germany drew directly from the language of the *Decretals* to condemn the *proprietarii* within their ranks: those discovered after death to have concealed money or goods were to be denied proper burial, or exhumed, and denied intercession as well. The statute also condemned as *proprietarii* all who disposed of corporate goods without a license that was "explicit and obtained."[82] Later statutes condemned brothers who deposited or saved up any amount of money via a third party without specific license, and condemned as *proprietarii* all who refused to render an account of alms, who touched money personally, who deposited books or other goods outside of the order without knowledge of the guardian, or who contracted excessive debts. The Franciscans also warned the administrators of their preaching stations twice a year to render an account to their communities. Those who refused were to be deposed from their offices and punished as *proprietarii*.[83] Those who properly rendered accounts, however, presumably otherwise disposed of the money and goods they received with virtual independence. The Franciscans, along with the other orders, condemned the vice of property. But they, too, presumed the principles of license and discretion, and they too appeared on the local scene, disposing of cash and other goods they obtained and enjoyed, legally or otherwise, in the name of their corporation.

Status and Sensibility Toward 1400

Fourteenth- and fifteenth-century society organized itself conceptually as a society of estates, but the estates themselves were embodied and

---

[82] G. Fusseneger, ed., "Statuta provinciae Alemaniae superioris annis 1303, 1309 et 1341 condita," *Archivum Franciscanum Historicum* 53 (1960), 262–3.

[83] M. Bihl, "Statuta Generalia ordinis edita in capitulo generali an. 1354 Assisi celebrato communiter Farneriana appelata," *Archivum Franciscanum Historicum* 35 (1942): 35–112; 177–253, here 90–91.

encountered in the particular routines, behaviors and customs that rendered each *status* distinct. Most visibly, the estate of the nobility asserted itself through a self-consciously extravagant and refined way of life. As Howard Kaminsky has shown, the material culture of the nobility was the outward manifestation of a deeply meaningful cultural game. Those of noble status were to represent and prove their nobility, publicly and vividly, on every appropriate occasion.[84] They did so not only by claiming their property, rights and revenues. They also did so through a grand style and sensibility, one manifest above all, perhaps, through fashionable clothing. Carefully tailored outfits of every cut and color set off the beauty of the body, and each ensemble was adorned with its indispensable "accents"—stripes, pleats and tailored sleeves; silk borders; intricate brocades of gold thread and pearls; linings of ermine, sable and other luxury furs; the finest belts, boots and shoes; clasps, rings and jewelry of every kind.[85] Even the nobleman's horse was fashionably adorned—silk caparisons with heraldic patterns, brass bells for bridles and reins.[86] Just as visibly and publicly, nobles embodied their estate through feast and festival. At great gatherings noble hosts and their guests exchanged gifts and enjoyed carefully orchestrated meals at tables laden with gold and silver, meat and bread and wine, fruits and nuts and spices.[87]

Informing these outward manifestations of status was a multifaceted sensibility of refinement and power. On the one hand, by 1200 the personal power of lords had been refined through *curialitas*, "courtliness" or "courtesy." The ideal demanded of secular elites that they show inward greatness and virtue through refined outward manner and bearing. The courtier was to be honest and generous, tactful and elegant in speech, composed and graceful in gesture and bearing, refined and restrained in the enjoyment of food and drink.[88] At the same time, refined courtly sensibilities remained intertwined with a

---

[84] For the conceptual and cultural framework here see Kaminsky, "Estate," (above, 33 n. 24) especially 695–709.

[85] Joachim Bumke, *Courtly Culture. Literature and Society in the High Middle Ages*, trans. Thomas Dunlap (Berkeley, 1991), chs. 1, 3 and 4, especially 132–36. See also Stella Mary Newton, *Fashion in the Age of the Black Prince. A Study of the Years 1340–1365* (Woodbridge, 1980).

[86] Ulf Dirlmeier, Gerhard Fouquet, and Bernd Fuhrmann, *Europa im Spätmittelalter 1215–1378* (Munich, 2003), 39.

[87] Bumke, *Courtly Culture*, 178–96, especially 178–79.

[88] C. Stephen Jaeger, *The Origins of Courtliness. Civilizing Trends and the Formation of Courtly Ideals 939–1210* (Philadelphia, 1985), especially chs. 7 and 8.

culture of power that could be bloody and brutal, and whose materiality sent sharp messages about social hierarchy. It was only for nobles to wear brightly colored clothing; the farmer, the laborer and other "rustics" were to be content with their drab grays and browns. And only the nobility were to enjoy refined white bread and fine wine, or spiced meat and fish drawn from jealously protected forests and ponds. Rustics were to be content to gobble down their coarse bread, their beets, beans and cabbage.[89]

These cultural imperatives and sensibilities also shaped the lives of many beyond the courts and the ranks of the nobility. In the plazas and markets of Italy's cities and towns, as Susan Stuard has shown, new urban elites manifested their *status* through their fine and often astronomically expensive clothing, which became an "urban citizen's projection of a stately, almost regal persona through dress."[90] To meet the demand, merchants offered dozens of different kinds of textiles that could be cut and dyed according to taste and fashion. One account book from the 1340s listed some twenty different shades of red alone, including one offering that featured a variety of wine-colored spots.[91] Often with the advice of tailors, Italian men chose their combinations of cut and color, and accentuated their ensembles with ready-made linings and borders—furs of every kind, silk bands covered in plaques studded with gems, brocades of gilt thread, intricate weaves of pearls. They also adorned themselves with all manner of ready-made "dress accessories"—buttons of brass or bone, gilded or enameled or adorned with jewels; buckles and other fasteners; belts made of long and thin chains of enamel plaques, or of broad and sturdy links; daggers and knives with jeweled hilts; chains, medallions and bracelets; purses, hats and hoods.[92]

As reflections of a divinely established social order, these outward representations of *status* in the public sphere were a matter of intense legal and moral regulation. From the mid-twelfth century, Italian com-

---

[89] Klaus Schreiner, "Religiöse, historische und rechtliche Legitimation spätmittelalterlicher Adelsherrschaft," in *Nobilitas. Funktion und Repräsentation des Adels in Alteuropa*, ed. Otto Gerhard Oexle and Werner Paravicini (Göttingen, 1997), 376–430. See also Cristopher Dyer, *Standards of Living in the Later Middle Ages. Social Change in England 1200–1500* (Cambridge, 1989), ch. 3 and Bumke, *Courtly Culture*, ch. 3.
[90] Susan Mosher Stuard, *Gilding the Market. Luxury and Fashion in Fourteenth-Century Italy* (Philadelphia, 2006), 60.
[91] Ibid., 41.
[92] Ibid., 23–29 and 42–55.

munes regulated all of the most sensitive markers, especially luxury clothing, along with the display and expense of weddings and funerals. After 1300 the legislation became longer and more detailed, and it was issued with more frequency. Even smaller towns and villages passed legislation condemning pomp and superfluity at weddings and funerals, regulating the excesses of gambling and more, in ways that paralleled the legislation of larger cities.[93] And though the impulse to regulate the exhibition of estate was most visible in Italy, it also shaped similar projects across northern Europe from before 1300.[94] Already in 1244 statutes in Bavaria prohibited farmers from wearing expensive or colorful clothing, and after 1300, Nuremberg, Zurich and other major cities across the Empire passed legislation regulating a vibrant culture of fashionable clothing, gambling and other excesses in the name of the common good.[95] Yet in almost every instance the enforcement through fines and other measures was too weak, and the laws were easily evaded.[96] The bond between status and its exhibition proved more powerful than written legislation, and sumptuary law remained a grudging tribute to the power of the cultural forces it sought to curtail.

Churchmen took the lead in denouncing all of the pomp and pride that characterized this wider culture of property. But for all of their denunciations of the excesses, the clergy, too, presumed a world of hierarchies and estates that were manifested materially and publically.

---

[93] P. Toubert, "Les statuts communeaux et l'histoire des campagnes lombardes au XIVe siècle," *Mélanges d'archéologie et d'histoire de l'École française de Rome* 72 (1960): 397–508.

[94] Here note the many works of Neithard Bulst, e.g. "Les ordonnances somptuaires en Allemagne: expression de l'ordre social urbain (XIVe–XVIe siécle)," *Académie des inscriptions et belles-lettres. Comptes-rendus des séances* 3 (1993): 771–83; idem, "Feste und Feiern unter Auflagen. Mittelalterliche Tauf-, Hochzeits- und Begräbnisordnungen in Deutschland und Frankreich," in *Feste und Feiern im Mittelalter*, ed. Detlef Altenburg, Jörg Jarnut, and Hans-Hugo Steinhoff (Sigmaringen, 1991), 39–51; and idem, "Zum problem städtischer und territorialer Kleider- Aufwands- und Luxusgesetzgebung in Deutschland (13.– Mitte 16. Jahrhundert)," in *Reniassance du puvoir législatif et genèse de l'état*, ed. André Gouron and Albert Rigaudiere (Montpellier, 1988), 45–67. See also Gerhard Jaritz, "Kelidung und Prestige-Konkurrenz. Unterschiedliche Identitäten in der städtischen Gesellschaft unter Normierungszwängen," *Saeculum* 44 (1993): 9–31; and W. Jannssen, "'...na gesetze unser lande...' Zur territorialen Gesetzgebung im späten Mittelalter," in *Gesetzgebung als Faktor der Staatsentwicklung*, ed. Dietmar Willoweit (Berlin, 1984), 7–40.

[95] Eberhard Isenmann, "Norms and Values in the European City, 1300–1800," in *Resistance, Representation, and Community*, ed. Peter Blickle (Oxford, 1997), 185–215.

[96] Catherine Kovesi Killerby, "Practical Problems," and idem, *Sumptuary Law in Italy, 1200–1500* (above, 15 n. 39).

And they, too, embodied their own clerical estate in the appropriate ways. Their splendor, though its social and spiritual sensibilities reached back centuries, now helped affirm and constitute ever-more elaborate theories of papal power and clerical dominion. At the same time, clerical magnificence and power could be creatively interwoven with the more refined language of courtliness. Contemporaries praised Innocent III, as Vicar of Christ, for his "most courtly" and "most liberal" spiritual and pastoral diligence.[97] And as spiritual lords and princes, Innocent's successors held court, judicially and socially, in ways that often mirrored that of their secular peers—most famously at court in Avignon, but also in the courts of archbishops, bishops and other prelates across Europe.[98]

By virtue of their vows, the men and women of the orders had in principle renounced the magnificence and refinement of the courts and their world. But religious, too, could embody their estate in ways that reflected their contemporary culture of property. Again modern scholars have tended to read the resulting patterns of life as symptoms of fourteenth-century moral decline, but the longer view suggests something more complex. Long before 1300, English bishops legislated against nuns' silken wimples and monks who wore striped or fitted habits. German Benedictines complained of monks who wore long hair, silk belts decorated with gold and silver, linen shirts, colorful clothing with flowing sleeves, and fashionable hats and shoes.[99] German bishops condemned monks and nuns who sported fine mantels with luxurious fur linings; and nuns who wore habits with tight sleeves, necklaces, clasps, rings and belts.[100] Here were the same halting legislative projects that had so long tried, and so often failed, to regulate the links between property and status in the secular sphere, and they continued after 1300. Some measures tried desperately to police the boundaries between noble and religious status: hence the Council of Vienne's condemnation of religious who engaged in the noble pastimes of hunting, falconry and the like; who wore secular belts, knives and boots; and who were excessively

---

[97] Jaeger, *Origins of Courtliness*, 157.
[98] See for example Stefan Weiß, *Die Versorgung des päpstlichen Hofes in Avignon mit Lebensmitteln (1316–1378). Studien zur Sozial- und Wirtschaftsgeschichte eines mittelalterlichen Hofes* (Berlin, 2002).
[99] Harry Kühnel, "Beiträge der Orden zur materiellen Kultur des Mittelalters und weltliche Einflüsse auf die klösterliche Sachkultur," in *Klösterliche Sachkultur des Spätmittelalters* (Vienna, 1982), 9–30.
[100] Bumke, *Courtly Culture*, 153.

pompous in outfitting their horses.[101] A Dominican statute from 1332 also condemned brothers who wore their hair like knights (*ad modum equitantium*) and who wore gauntlets (*cirotecas*). Notably, however, the penalty for those who refused to refrain from such things was merely a one-day fast of bread and water—a penalty that, as the Dominicans grudgingly recognized, might be waived through dispensation.[102] Other legislation seems to have been aimed at luxury and fashion generally. At Vienne, a series of measures condemned religious who betrayed modesty by purchasing expensive, "subtle" material for their habits; who wore excessively long or short habits and sleeves; and those who wore habits with slits or buttoned sleeves. In 1328, 1334 and 1341, the Dominicans issued similar measures: brothers were to refrain from excessively long capes or hoods.[103] In 1335, Benedict XII legislated against all "curiosity" and superfluity in use of silver vessels, tapestries and other ornaments.[104] It is impossible to discern from these sources how widespread such excesses might have been. But statutes like these, issued repeatedly through the fourteenth century, attest to the longevity of the inherited cultural game of status, one that professed religious themselves continued to play well enough, and visibly enough, to inspire legislation at the highest level.

The arrival of the Black Death only raised the stakes of the old game. Scattered sources and studies suggest that, overall, some six in ten religious died of the disease.[105] But the statistical abstractions and averages can easily hide the human face of what was, in the short term, a cataclysm—houses left with only one or two members, even none at all; the death of cherished kin and companions; the loss of talented teachers and administrators and some of the orders' best leaders. Just as severe were the economic consequences. The chronicler Gilles Li Muisis expressed some of the common frustrations: abandoned properties, fewer laborers and renters; wealthy survivors who either refused to

---

[101] CIC I: 1166–7.
[102] Frühwirth, 2: 221.
[103] Ibid., 179. Cf. later legilsation at 2: 225 (1334) and 271 (1341).
[104] Canivez 3: 423.
[105] Bernd Zaddach, *Die Folgen des Schwarzen Todes (1347–51) für den Klerus Mitteleuropas* (above, 11 n. 27), 34, counts some 1327 deaths out of 1924 known members of the religious orders. For context see Jean-Noël Biraben, *Les hommes et la peste en France et dans les pays européens et méditerranéens*, 2 vols. (Paris, 1975) and now, among a growing number of works, the challenging arguments of Samuel Cohn, Jr., *The Black Death Transformed: Disease and Culture in Early Renaissance Europe* (London, 2002).

work or insisted on higher wages. Scattered local and regional studies have grounded the contemporary laments more firmly. One study of the estates of the Abbey of Tegernsee reveals that by 1380, after three outbreaks of the plague, some one-fourth of the estate's properties had been abandoned, and its cash incomes dramatically reduced.[106]

Precisely how these challenges shaped the cloister's culture of property is, given the current state of research, difficult to determine. On the one hand there are glimpses of a vigorous enjoyment of cash incomes after 1350. In Cologne, for example, fourteenth- and fifteenth-century Dominican friars resigned their rights as heirs in return for cash, most often paid as a generous annuity.[107] And in Basel in 1392, a Dominican named (fittingly) John "of the Golden Ring" drew up a magnificent will and testament in which he showered his brothers with hundreds of florins from inherited rents. Some of the incomes funded an array of anniversary masses. Others provided direct cash payments to his brothers on various occasions.[108] Yet from another perspective, as we have seen, these striking arrangements were broadly consistent with evolving customs of administration, prayer and provision. By 1350, households and corporations had long allowed individual religious to provide for themselves from endowed cash incomes, in proper proportion and with proper license, in keeping with status and the demands of a booming market in spiritual services. The same strategies must have only made more sense thereafter, to the extent that they relieved pressure on strained household finances or allowed the freedom and flexibility to adapt to circumstance. There was a constant concern to guard against abuse and excess, but the orders themselves seem to have worried little about the dangers of properly licensed cash incomes. A comparison of the statutes of four major religious orders suggests little overall change in condemnations of the "vice of property" between 1330 and 1370.[109]

---

[106] Heinrich Rubner, "Die Landwirtschaft der Münchener Ebene und ihre Notlage im 14. Jahrhundert," *Vierteljahrschrift für Sozial- und Wirtschaftsgeschichte* 51 (1964): 433–53.

[107] Gabriel Maria Löhr, *Beiträge zur Geschichte des Kölner Dominikanerklosters im Mittelalter. T. 1: Darstellung* (Leipzig, 1920) and *T. 2: Quellen* (Leipzig, 1922). Cf. vol. 2, nos. 748; 750–52; 754–55 and 757.

[108] Georg Boner, "Das Predigerkloster in Basel von der Gründung bis zur Klosterreform 1233–1429," *Basler Zeitschrift für Geschichte und Altertumskunde* 33 (1934): 195–303, here 271–76.

[109] Zaddach, *Folgen des Schwarzen Todes*, 94 ff. and especially the tables on 104–7. The number of condemnations among the Dominicans, notably, showed an increase from one to six across the two periods. On the other hand, other orders seemed relatively

A more difficult set of challenges centered on regulating inherited tensions of status and consumption. In the wake of the Black Death, ever-wider circles of ordinary Europeans enjoyed, on balance, somewhat improved standards of living—higher wages; a more diversified diet; and more diversified local markets that provided a range of affordable goods.[110] In England, as John Hatcher's work has shown, the post-plague economy afforded everyday people more disposable income, more independence and choice, and more access to goods that marked status through conspicuous display.[111] Artifacts from late-medieval London suggest something of the possibilities—garments that once shimmered with checkered patterns of black and pink or with bold stripes; shirts adorned with strips of cloth hanging from the sleeves, slashes to reveal the complementary colors of an inner lining, or decorative buttons from cuff to shoulder.[112] Local markets also made more available all of the appropriate accessories—buckles, clasps, pins and so on, often made of affordable lead, tin or pewter.[113]

After 1350 religious continued to participate fully in these broadening horizons of material culture. In 1354, the Franciscans condemned mantles made of cloth that had been "spattered" (*guttatim*) with various colors, or adorned with pleated (*rugatos*) or curled (*crispos*) collars.[114] In 1365, the bishop of Anjou legislated against monks who wore short shirts with buttons, as well as regular canons who wore multicolored, striped cloaks and cloaks fixed to the shoulders.[115] Again it is impossible to discern from these lines how often ordinary folk might have encountered fashionable friars sporting cloaks spattered with dye or styled with pleats and curls, monks or canons wearing buttoned shirts

---

unconcerned about legislating against the vice. The number of their condemnations either remained the same (three among the Cistercians for both periods), increased only slightly (one among the Augustinian canons from 1330 to 1348, two from 1350 to 1370), or even dropped (two among the English Benedictines from 1330 to 1348, one from 1350 to 1370). Moreover, it is important to note the sense in which these measures are, overall, negligible in number. In a flood of statutes on all sorts of issues across four decades, these orders collectively condemned the "vice of property" only eighteen times. Episcopal synods condemned the vice not even once.

[110] Cf. Britnell, *Commercialisation*, 168–69.
[111] John Hatcher, "England in the Aftermath of the Black Death," *Past and Present* 144 (1994): 3–35, especially 19 and 31.
[112] Cristopher Dyer, *An Age of Transition? Economy and Society in England in the Later Middle Ages* (Oxford, 2005), 144–45.
[113] Ibid.
[114] "Farneriana," ed. Bihl (above, 48 n. 83), 87–88.
[115] Mansi 26: 434.

and striped cloaks. But such figures were visible enough to inspire the ongoing legislation, and to give meaning to the work of the satirists. Hence Boccaccio's satire of the friars' luxurious habits: "They go about in those long, flowing robes of theirs," Pampinea lamented, "and when they are asking for alms, they deliberately put on a forlorn expression and are all humility and sweetness; but when they are reproaching you...they positively deafen you with their loud and arrogant voices."[116] Chaucer's tales, too, famously seized on the religious habits of a fashionable monk, who wore sleeves lined with fine gray fur, a "curious pin" in the shape of a "love knot" to fasten his hood, and "supple" boots; a friar, who wore a double-worsted cloak; and a prioress, who wore a pleated veil and an elegant cloak.[117]

Yet if the evidence of statute and satire signal something other than the observance of ascetic ideals, it is important also to discern all of the subtle ways in which the religious habit, for both men and women, also continued to embody spiritual ideals and sensibilities. Consider the famous story of the Carmelites who came to Paris with Louis IX in the summer of 1254. A crowd of commoners mocked the friars as the "barred brothers." The insult, echoed elsewhere in the "antifraternal" satire of Rutebeuf, reflected a general suspicion of stripes as markers of evil and illegitimacy.[118] But for the Carmelite brothers themselves, as Michel Pastoureau points out, the habit's stripes had a spiritual significance. Most often white and brown or white and black, the stripes for some recalled the cloak of Elijah, seared by the flames of the chariot that took him to heaven. For others, the habit's white stripes recalled the cardinal virtues, the brown stripes the theological virtues. In a similar way, the "love knot" on the "curious" pin of Chaucer's monk, as Laura Hodges has noted, in other settings symbolized the ideals of charity and spiritual grace. Hodges also notes how strongly Chaucer's portrait of the prioress signals a blending of courtly and spiritual refinement and status. The prioress' fair forehead and pleated wimple, her physical beauty and grace, all embodied her spiritual nobility. Contemporary

---

[116] Boccaccio, *Decameron*, trans. G. H. McWilliam (New York, 2005), 343.

[117] On these portraits from the prologue to the *Canterbury Tales* see Jill Mann, *Chaucer and Medieval Estates Satire. The Literature of Social Classes and the General Prologue to the Canterbury Tales* (Cambridge, 1973) as well as Laura F. Hodges, *Chaucer and Clothing. Clerical and Academic Costume in the General Prologue to the Canterbury Tales* (Cambridge, 2005).

[118] Michel Pastoureau, *The Devil's Cloth. A History of Stripes and Striped Fabric*, trans. Jody Gladding (New York, 2001), 7–10. For the broader tradition see Penn R. Szittya, *The Antifraternal Tradition in Medieval Literature* (Princeton, 1986).

nuns, as Chaucer and his readers knew well, signaled their status in countless analogous ways. Their jeweled crowns and silken veils, their altar hangings and tapestries, reliquaries and artwork, rosaries of coral and emerald were laden with spiritual significance and power. All of the materiality signaled the nuns' status as brides of Christ and courtiers of Mary, the Queen of Heaven.[119]

A Cistercian statute from 1357 captures succinctly how these same tensions of status and sensibility also shaped customs of provision. In that year, the general chapter complained of the many monks who asserted themselves "quite indiscreetly against their own abbots" in search of better food and drink. In "congregations and secret gatherings" the monks had schemed over "how they might extort from their abbots greater or better provision." They had then come before their abbots in an "unrestrained" and "lordly" way, asserting "insolently" that they receive better fare.[120] Threatened with violence and uprisings, the statute lamented, the fearful and embattled abbots could only concede what they might in normal circumstances have reasonably denied.[121] A Dominican statute from four decades later suggests similar tensions at work in that order. A 1396 measure, which had appeared in some form throughout most of the fourteenth century, offered a lengthy censure of priors who allowed the Dominicans to eat meat in ways contrary to their constitutions, and who seldom ate together in the refectory with the brothers. The 1396 measure then offered a revealing addendum: no brother, whatever his social station, was to "triple or multiply" his ordinary pittance of food or wine. The statute also seems to have

---

[119] Hodges, *Chaucer and Clothing*, ch. 2. For broader context see Klaus Schreiner, "*Nobilitas Mariae*. Die edelgeborene Gottesmutter und ihre adeligen verehrer. Soziale Prägungen und politische Funktionen mittelalterlicher Adelsfrömmigkeit," in *Maria in der Welt. Marienverehrung im Kontext der Sozialgeschichte 10.–18. Jarhundert*, ed. Claudia Opitz (Zurich, 1993), 213–42 and idem, *Maria: Jungfrau, Mutter, Herrscherin* (Munich, 1994). See also *Krone und Schleier. Kunst aus Mittelalterlichen Frauenklöstern* (above, 32 n. 19).

[120] Canivez, 3: 533: "Item. Propter detestabile gastrimargiae vitium in laborintum vitiorum descendatur, et in plerisque ordinis monasteriis nonnulli monachorum super cibis et potibus minus discrete abbates proprios inquietent, adeo quod super hoc faciant congregationes et conventicula, inter se tractantes qualiter ab abbatibus suis maiora vel meliora cibaria valeant extorquere, ad ipsosque abbates accedant fronte infrenabili et indomita ac in multitudine copiosa, petentes victualia eis procaciter ampliari."

[121] Ibid.: "…ipsique abbates, visa tali multitudine, perterriti sibi metuentes, ne in eos desurgant de facto manusque in eos incitant violentias, concedunt eis aliqua, que cessante tali metu denegarent et deberent rationabiliter denegari…."

condemned those who took their portions of food and drink from the refectory in order to sell them.[122]

A variety of post-plague difficulties could have prompted laments like these, but from the longer view, these statutes reflect the same older set of tensions traced thus far. Fourteenth-century Cistercians who enjoyed meat, for example, could cite against reforming legislators not only the license of their superiors, but the privileges of the Apostolic See itself, as well as ancient "customs and statutes."[123] Moreover, it is important to recall how bonds between food, drink and status continued to express ideals of refinement and charity. Consider the reflections of the Franciscan friar Salimbene de Adam. Just after 1280 Salimbene remembered fondly Tancred of Pellavicini, an abbot of Parma who proved himself "courteous" (*curialis*) and "generous" (*liberalis*) above all by providing a fine meal. When Salimbene had entered the Franciscan order, Abbot Tancred had sent a courtesy gift (*excenium*) of chickens to be had for a celebratory dinner—a "rustic" had arrived bearing a stick laden with them on both ends.[124] Salimbene joked that he would eat cabbage for the rest of his days as a Franciscan, but in reality he would be no stranger to the refined sensibilities of a courtly meal.[125] At Sens in 1248 he and his fellow Franciscans enjoyed a Lenten feast of fine white

---

[122] Frühwirth 3: 59: "...nulli fratres, cuiuscumque gradus aut conditionis existant, triplicent vel multiplicent ordinariam pitantiam conventus sive vinum...nec volumus quod illi qui carnes comedunt pitantiam recipiant refectorii, vel qui extra conventum comederint pro illa refectione panem et vinum et pictantiam refectorii ex iniquo fine quod pressisse alioquin allegatur, si vendidissent ullo modo...." As Frühwirth notes, the text here is unclear and may be corrupt, but the passage seems nontheless to refer to some sort of sale.

[123] Canivez, 3: 424: "Et quoniam aliqui monachi in nonnullis monasteriis et studiis sibi temere vendicare praesumunt quod certis diebus qualibet septimana iuxta observantias seu consuetudines vel statuta quae super hoc allegant (minus tamen rationabilia), eis carnes debeant ministrari: Nos huiusmodi abusum, observantias, consuetudines, seu statuta huiusmodi...penitus reprobantes, auctoritate eadem ordinamus quod nullus abbas, provisor, prior, cellerarius, vel alius deinceps haec aliquatenus observare presumat, ne etiam observari permittat, aut ministrare vel ministrari facere occasione observantiarum, consuetudinum, seu statutorum praedictorum carnes alicui predicti ordinis, praeterquam in aliis casibus licitis et permissis."

[124] *Salimbene de Adam Cronica. I A. 1168–1249* ed. Giuseppe Scalia, CCCM 125 (Turnhout, 1998) 1: 144: "...Tancredus de Pellavicinis, homo curialis et liberalis et bone fame et sancte et honeste vite, abbas Sancti Iohannis de Parma, misit exenium fratri Helye generali ministro, unum rusticum caponibus oneratum...."

[125] Ibid.: "...et illo sero post cenam fui receptus; et splendide cenaveram in domo patris mei, et nichilominus duxerunt me fratres illo sero ad infirmitorium et dederunt michi iterum optime comedere; processu vero temporis dederunt michi caules, quibus oportuit me uti omnibus diebus vite mee...."

bread and fine wine; fish, eels and crabs; and fine sauces and cakes, all "served properly and in abundance."[126] Among kings and abbots alike, *curialitas*, expressed through refined feasting and noble generosity, was the sister of Christian charity.[127] It was all the more unbearable for Salimbene, then, that so many religious superiors showed themselves to be avaricious "Lombards" who refused to share with others. While lordly prelates dined on fine wine and white bread, their subjects ate only coarse bread and beans. Salimbene denounced those greedy and grasping lords as "rustics," and he grounded his attack in Scripture: indeed the words of Nehemiah commanded prelates to "send a share to them that have not prepared for themselves."[128] It was this deeper sensibility of charity and generosity that lived on in countless settings. In St. Florian in Austria, for example, a fourteenth-century prior drew up elaborate contracts confirming the generous festival meals he was to enjoy with his canons. At Westminster, monks enjoyed meals that, though carefully regulated to observe the strictures of the *Rule*, provided both abundant daily portions and occasional fine pittances, some of which cost far more than any regular fare.[129]

Approaching 1400, these older expressions of status were also visible in a new way, through an ever-more vigorous enjoyment of appropriated space. The Italian evidence again provides the best starting point for a sense of a trend that eventually swept through Europe.[130] The fourteenth-century household was often conceived as a series of ever-more-open and public spaces that radiated outward from the lord's "privy" chamber, where he kept his most prized possessions.[131] Most rooms of the household were sparsely furnished. But in their inner chambers, fourteenth-century

---

[126] Ibid.: 1:322; quoted here in translation from Bumke, *Courtly Culture*, 181 and n. 22

[127] Ibid., 1: 165: "A curialitate humana etiam habetur quod proximus diligi debet. Caritas enim et curialitas sorores sunt."

[128] Ibid., 1: 166: "Sed prelati nostri temporis, qui Lombardi sunt, libenter volunt sibi que gula et appetitus requirit, et aliis dare nolunt; que maxima rusticitas reputatur...." cf. Nehemiah 8:10.

[129] Barbara F. Harvey, *Living and Dying in England, 1100–1540: The Monastic Experience* (New York, 1993), 43; Gerhard Jaritz, "Zur Sachkultur österreichischer Klöster des Spätmittelalters," in *Klösterliche Sachkultur des Spätmittelalters* (Vienna, 1982), 151.

[130] For general orientation to the Italian evidence see Dora Thornton, *The Scholar in his Study. Ownership and Experience in Renaissance Italy* (New Haven, 1998) and Peter Thornton, *The Italian Renaissance Interior, 1400–1600* (New York, 1991).

[131] David Austin, "Private and Public: An Archaeological Consideration of Things," in *Die Vielvalt der Dinge. Neue Wege zur Analyse mittelalterlicher Sachkultur. Internationaler Kongress Krems an der Donau 4. Bis 7. Oktober 1994* (Vienna, 1998), 163–206.

Italians began to blend intimacy, ownership and material culture in new ways. In the bedchamber, rich textiles suspended from bars or hooks provided both privacy and an opportunity for display—captured famously, for example, in Giotto's images of the bedchamber of the dreaming Pope Gregory. As the fourteenth century wore on, Italy's elites used their bedrooms and other intimate spaces to gather together a variety of "worldly goods"—clothing and tapestries, benches and other furniture, sculptures and paintings. Italy's "incipient consumerism" extended to a range of spiritually inspired objects as well—devotional images, reliquaries, liturgical instruments and the like.[132] Together these trends, as Dora Thornton has noted, helped fashion the domestic ideal of *commodità*—"a fusion of convenience and elegance perfectly adapted to one's needs."[133] The new domestic configurations allowed the refined conviviality of the court—a meal, musical entertainment and the like—to take root in more urban settings. They also shaped intellectual life. As Thornton has shown, the scholar's study became an important new kind of domestic space, one that blended ownership, intellect and identity. The scholar's study was a "place set apart for the use of a single owner," a place with a "secret identity of its own, which might persist long after the owner's death."[134] By 1400 aristocrats to the north, too, were retreating from the great halls of their drafty castles to the apartments of new urban residences. There they deployed a variety of improved technologies—glazed windows and wainscoting, ceramic-tile stoves with their even, flowing warmth, candles that provided longer-burning, cleaner light—all of which made for a more comfortable daily life. Elites also worked to export their urban domesticity back into the countryside. Their military fortifications soon had windows and niches cut into their walls to bring in the sun, and their great halls were soon subdivided or extended to accommodate more apartments.[135]

There is no comprehensive history of appropriated space in religious households. But scholars have begun to explore the intersections of domestic and sacred space generally, and scattered references suggest

---

[132] See Richard Goldthwaite, *Wealth and the Demand for Art in Italy 1300–1600* (Baltimore, 1993), 72 ff. for a discussion of "liturgical apparatus" and consumption, as well as 129 ff. for the "material culture of the Church and incipient consumerism."
[133] Thornton, *Scholar in his Study*, 176.
[134] Ibid., 1.
[135] Ulf Dirlmeier, *Geschichte des Wohnens 2, 500–1800: Hausen, Wohnen, Residieren* (Stuttgart, 1998), 240, 247–48.

how the broader trends noted here found parallels in the cloister.[136] Some of the earliest evidence from the Empire dates to the thirteenth century. At Gunterstal in southwest Germany in 1287, a man named Burkhard Turner financed for his two daughters their own house (*domus*) within the nunnery's walls.[137] In Basel soon after, nuns who paid the right price could enjoy a room with a view of the Rhine.[138] In Wienhausen, dowry chests sit even today outside the nuns' individual cells in a well-preserved dormitory—a visible reminder of the links between appropriated wealth and space.[139] In England the trend comes into view by the middle of the fourteenth century at the latest. By 1360, about half of the monks at Westminster lived in their own quarters, and others used curtains of blue muslin, likely hung from iron bars and rings, to separate their beds in the common dormitory. More sumptuous tapestries between beds preserved privacy for the inhabitants of the infirmary.[140] Roberta Gilchrist has noted how the nuns of Godstow in Oxfordshire divided up their cloister into communal halls in which *familiae* of nuns lived separately.[141] The Franciscan Eudes Rigaud legislated against similar practices among the nuns of France in the late thirteenth century.[142]

For all of the fourteenth century the orders fought a losing battle against the appropriation of community space.[143] The trend was widespread enough by the 1330s to frustrate Benedict XII, who in his general legislation issued stern condemnations of the many "unseemly things" (*dissolutiones*) that had occurred both in private cells built within community dormitories, and in private living arrangements beyond community walls. Benedict demanded that no private cells be constructed in the future, and that existing cells be torn down. But the pope also took strong opposition for granted. He excommunicated those who

---

[136] See now the essays collected in Sarah Hamilton and Andrew Spicer, eds., *Defining the Holy: Sacred Space in Medieval and Early Modern Europe* (Aldershot, 2005).

[137] Ogris, "Konventualenpfründe" (above, 29 n. 11), citing *Freiburger Urkundenbuch* II, 60.

[138] Jeffrey Hamburger, *The Visual and the Visionary. Art and Female Spirituality in Late-Medieval Germany* (New York, 1998), 40.

[139] Ibid., 75. Cf. *Krone und Schleier* (above, 32 n. 19), 437, noting the survival of dowry chests from Ebstorf.

[140] Harvey, *Living and Dying in England*, 130.

[141] Roberta Gilchrist, *Gender and Material Culture. The Archaeology of Religious Women* (London, 1994), 123–24.

[142] Adam J. Davis, *The Holy Bureaucrat. Eudes Rigaud and Religious Reform in Thirteenth-Century Normandy* (Ithaca, 2006), 75.

[143] Thomas Lentes, "*Vita perfecta* zwischen *Vita Communis* und *Vita Privata*. Eine Skizze zur klösterlichen Einzelzelle," in *Das Öffentliche und Private in der Vormoderne*, ed. Gert Melville and Peter von Moos (Cologne, 1998), 125–64.

obstructed the measure's enforcement, as well as anyone who allied with the resistance.[144] A decade later, in 1346, the Cistercian general chapter complained of brothers who appropriated rooms in which priors, cellarers and other monks ate, drank and entertained without license.[145] Revealingly, however, the Cistercians who lived this way had argued against both the chapter and their superiors that the practices were licit on the authority of custom (*consuetudo usitata*).[146]

The same tensions are in evidence among the Dominicans. In 1331 the Dominican general chapter prohibited any brother without administrative duties from enjoying private quarters, but the trend continued, and the Dominicans began slowly to accept the new reality. They soon commanded provincial priors simply to reign in the "excesses" of cells that seemed out of proportion to all others. Yet even here the legislators had to insist that the measure be enforced "with effect."[147] The reluctance to enforce the legislation was in part due to competing claims of status. When, for example, the general chapter tried to forbid that rooms should be conceded to brothers indiscriminately (*passim*), the legislation notably made exceptions for "distinguished bothers, to whom this might not easily be denied."[148] The remark is revealing. It may refer to the needs of officers, theologians and other officials, or it may instead reflect the local reality of brothers whose social station demanded they take for themselves the comforts of their own spaces. In any case, the link between status and space was presumed.

The Dominican evidence also makes clear what must have been true in other orders and houses—the appropriation of money and personal goods was often inseparable from the emergent bond between space and status. In 1359 the Dominicans condemned brothers who had private,

---

[144] Canivez 3: 426.
[145] Ibid., 504: "...quod in aliquibus monasteriis contra papalia statuta, priores, cellerarios et aliquos monachos extra infirmitorium cameras appropriatas habere, in quibus comedunt, pernoctant et invitant, quod [!] volunt, ad esum carnium sine proprii abbatis licentia...."
[146] Ibid., "dicentes sibi hoc licere de consuetudine usitata...."
[147] Frühwirth, 2: 209: "Item. Omni districtione, qua possumus, inhibemus, ne camere quibuscumque fratribus concedantur, nisi forte illis, quibus ratione officii vel status ordo hactenus concedere consuevit, vel nisi evidens neccessitas hoc requirat, imponentes prioribus provincialibus, ut excessum quarundam camerarum uniformitatem nostram in communi dormitorio deformantium ad uniformitatem studeant reducere cum effectu...."
[148] Ibid., 165: "Districte inhibemus, ne camere passim fratribus concedantur, nisi forte fratribus insignibus, quibus convenienter negari non possint. In ipsis autem cameris nullus frater comedat, nisi forte actu esset decumbens...."

locked rooms outside of the common dormitory, many of them funded by "appropriated wealth" (*ex appropriatis sibi sumptibus*). Yet status again made for important exceptions: provincial priors, masters of theology, seniors who had been in the order fifty years, inquisitors—indeed anyone deemed worthy by the provincial prior—all were excluded from the prohibition.[149] In 1365 the chapter had to revoke all exemptions for inheriting goods and enjoying rooms beyond the common dormitory. But realities that were controversial only decades before seem quietly to have become taken for granted. In 1370, the Dominicans expressed their wish that no brother should have two dwellings in the dormitory—thus conceding the reality that many enjoyed at least one. Moreover, in 1376, though the chapter revoked all exemptions and privileges allowing individual cells (as it often had before), it allowed exceptions not only for status, but for any who had made cells "from their appropriated wealth."[150] The link between resourceful appropriation of wealth and domestic space, forbidden a generation before, had received official sanction.

Religious who enjoyed comfortable cells again paid a heavy price at the hands of satirists. Several of the stories of Boccaccio's *Decameron*, for example, build themselves around the intimacy that individual cells afforded in the monastery. The third tale of the first day tells of a monk who seduces a farm girl in his private chamber. The young monk escapes punishment because he catches the abbot seducing the girl himself. In the second novella of the ninth day, a group of nuns sets a trap for their sister Isabetta, whom they knew to be sleeping with a young man in her cell. Catching Isabetta in the act, they run to alert the abbess in her own cell. The abbess is herself then caught in the act with her own lover (or more precisely after the act, when in her haste she has donned his undergarments instead of her veil).

Again, however, both statute and satire distort what contemporaries knew could be far more refined spiritual sensibilities. Again the Dominican evidence provides an accessible glimpse of assumptions that must have shaped life across the orders. Henry Suso described the

---

[149] Ibid., 386: "Item. Omni districtione, qua possumus, inhibemus, ne frater aliquis extra commune dormitorium sanus existens cameram habeat aut clavem ipsius teneat, etaim si ipsam ex appropriatis sibi sumptibus fabricasset...."

[150] Ibid., 433: "Quascumque autem gratias exemptorias et concessiones camerarum quarumcumque extra commune dormitorium...revocamus, exceptis dumtaxat gratiis de cameris factis magistris et baccalariis in theologia, et concessionibus camerarum factis illis fratribus, qui eas construi fecerunt propriis sumptibus et expensis."

ways in which a "privy space" of his own sheltered and nurtured his spiritual life, and he did so in ways that mirrored his contemporaries' conceptualizations of domestic space generally. Radiating out from Suso's "secret" cell were concentric circles of increasing insecurity and danger—the chapel and the choir of his community; the cloister as a whole; its gate; and the world beyond. Out in that world Suso felt like a hunted animal. But safe within, he was free to pursue his heroic experiments in asceticism and "detachment." Geoffrey Hamburger, Thomas Lentes and others have grounded Suso's writing in both a wider visual culture and in patterns of devotional space.[151] In the window of the cell Suso placed his famous image of "eternal wisdom" and on its walls were images of the "ancient fathers" whose spiritual power, as Suso saw it, enabled him to heal the diseased eyes of the artist he had hired to paint them. These links between visual and spiritual culture had their parallels in women's houses, where nuns painted images and crafted or commissioned objects for devotional use in intimate cells of their own.[152]

The propertied men and women who have appeared here remain in need of much more sustained scholarly attention. The foregoing has only begun to reconstruct something of the complexity of their circumstance, and to suggest that they are more interesting and accessible figures than their historiographical reputation has often allowed. They were heirs of an ancient conceptual and cultural legacy of custom, prayer and provision that had sustained their institutions for centuries until 1400. Within those institutions, they lived in ways that intertwined spiritual and material culture, social and spiritual status along a rich continuum. They negotiated the challenges of income and expense, unrepentant consumption and excess, and they did what they could, through discretion and legislation, to manage the inevitable tensions. The following chapters trace how those tensions came to be contested after 1400. General calls to reform religious life were to be heard across Europe by 1400, but some of their most audible, divisive and effective inflections emerged across the southern regions of the Empire.

---

[151] Cf. Lentes, "*Vita perfecta*" (above, n. 143).
[152] Hamburger, *Visual and the Visionary*, as well as his study *Nuns as Artists. The Visual Culture of a Medieval Convent* (Berkeley, 1997). See also Winston-Allen, *Convent Chronicles* (above, 7 n. 21), 50–55 and n. 136.

PART I

CHAPTER TWO

CALLS FROM WITHOUT

In 1386, soon after he arrived at the University of Vienna, Henry of Langenstein composed a sermon addressed to the Augustinian canons of nearby Klosterneuburg.[1] The Babenberger foundation for both men and women was by then some two centuries old, and it embodied all of the traditions of custom, status and lordship outlined above.[2] The canons, who in their everyday speech called themselves "choir-lords" (*Chorherren*), enjoyed their daily provision as a "lord's prebend," with its regular servings of the "lord's bread" and the "lord's wine." They also received supplements to their lordly provision in return for spiritual work. Throughout the fourteenth century, patrons who arranged for anniversary masses at Klosterneuburg graced the men and women there with extra servings of bread and wine and other gifts, with many of

---

[1] For Henry of Langenstein see BBKL II: 679–81 and VL II: 292 ff.; Michael Shank, *Unless You Believe, You Shall Not Understand: Logic, University, and Society in Late Medieval Vienna* (Princeton, 1988) and Paul Justin Lang, *Die Christologie bei Heinrich von Langenstein* (Freiburg i. Br., 1966). H. Heimpel dates the unedited sermon studied here to 1386, though with little explanation: H. Heimpel, *Die Vener von Gmünd und Strassburg 1162–1447: Studien und Texte zur Geschichte einer Familie sowie des gelehrten Beamtentums in der Zeit der abendländischen Kirchenspaltung und der Konzilien von Pisa, Konstanz und Basel* (Göttingen, 1982), 2: 934. The manuscript work for the current project has been unable either to confirm or refute that date, but it seems reasonable. I have drawn my readings from a manuscript from the Benedictine community of Mondsee, now MS Vienna, ÖNB Cod. 3700, fols. 173–85, collated against Munich, Bayerische Staatsbibliothek, Clm 7720, fols. 14r–29r and Klosterneuburg, Stiftsbibliothek, Cod. 384, fols. 180–87. For the Mondsee manuscript, see *Tabulae codicum manu scriptorum praeter graecos et orientales in Bibliotheca Palatina Vindobonensi asservatorum* (Vienna 1864–99). For dating see: Franz Unterkircher, *Die datierten Handschriften der Österreichischen Nationalbibliothek von 1451 bis 1500. 1–2 (Katalog der datierten Handschriften in lateinischer Schrift in Österreich)* III/1, 90 and III/2, 362. For other manuscripts see the Appendix no. 4, as well as Thomas Hohmann, "Initienregister der Werke Heinrichs von Langenstein," *Traditio* 32 (1976), 399–426; Kreuzer, *Heinrich von Langenstein*, 147–8, n. 680; and Lang, *Christologie*, 54–5 and n. 148.

[2] For Klosterneuburg see Floridus Röhrig, "Die materielle Kultur des Chorherrenstiftes Klosterneuburg unter besonderer Berücksichtigung der Aussage von Rechnungsbüchern," in *Klösterliche Sachkultur des Spätmittelalters* (Vienna, 1982), 214–24 and idem, *Klosterneuburg* (Vienna, 1972). For charters and other sources, see FRA II/10 and 28.

the arrangements clothed explicitly in the language of good custom.[3] Henry now upheld the stern simplicity of the Gospel against that way of life. He chose as his scriptural passage Peter's words to Christ in the Gospel of Matthew: "Behold, we have left all and followed you" (Mt. 19:27). Through that text Henry reminded the canons of Klosterneuburg of their moral responsibility to renounce their cash and comfort. He reminded his audience that Christ had commanded them to not be troubled over food or clothing, that his way of life freed its imitators from the strife and division of temporal wealth, and that the "law of Christ" offered them the spiritual blessings of peace, unity and concord.[4] Henry also reminded the canons how faithfully Christ had fulfilled the promises of apostolic poverty for those who had been bold enough to embrace it.[5]

Henry was heir to a long tradition of prophetic critics and reformers who had denounced laxity and abuse in established religious institutions, most famously among the Franciscans and their sympathizers. He was also heir to a full range of related debates over religious poverty and church property, from Fitzralph's attacks on the mendicants to Wyclif's more recent attacks against "possessioner" monks and "private religions." But at Klosterneuburg Henry pursued the familiar themes from a new angle, and sought a new purchase on the old patterns. His concern was to expose a culture of cash, consumption and status that had made a mockery of the common life. "At the common table one eats this, another that," Henry lamented, "one lacks while another has more than enough, one spends prudently the money he received, another has wasted it, one saves up money from the sum, another plays

---

[3] See, among many examples, FRA II/10, 293 (p. 281): "...und schol der Oblaymeister und die Chorherren zwen Jahrtegen einem igleichen herren geben ein semel, di dreier pfennig werd ist, und ein Stauf weins dezselben Weingarten und als vil Junchherren und den Prudern, als ez von alter gewonhait herchommen ist..."

[4] MS Vienna, ÖNB, Cod. 3700, fol. 173v: "...lex Christi non sit lex promissionis temporalium, sed spiritualium, et magis expediat spiritualiter vivere degentibus temporalium inopia quam optata divitiarum copia."

[5] Ibid.: "Ecce ergo quanta fidelitas impleta fuit olim in primis discipulis et impletur hodie in novissimis illa Christi promissio apostolice consolatoria paupertatis, de qua quidem paupertate scriptum est: 'multitudinis autem credentium erat cor unum et anima una, nec quisque eorum que possidebant aliquid suum esse dicebant, sed istis erant omnia communia.' Ecce ubi non erat diversitas rerum, vigebat unitas voluntatum. Nimirum ubi non est divisio census, ibi in unione caritatis plurimarum mentium conflatur affectus. Illic enim mens a mente dividitur, ubi facultatium communia non tenetur. Et ubi possessionum est diversa proprietas, ibi mens possidentium non est una."

games, another celebrates, another damnably does more secret things."[6] So foolishly did the canons spend their money that "at one table one has plenty of food, and choice food at that, but another doesn't even have any beans." So differently were they clothed, Henry quipped, that one looked like a prelate, the other his humble servant.[7] And what of the prior, who lived surrounded by a crowd of servants; who rode fine horses with golden reins; who enjoyed precious cloth and glorious dwellings; who gave magnanimous gifts of gold, silver and gems? In the Low Countries, Geert Groote had denounced the avarice of the clergy and the orders in similarly rousing sermons, and his followers had begun to appropriate the observance of common property for themselves. Independently of those events, but in a similar mood, Henry now exposed the moral scandal of those who professed the common life, but who failed to live up to their own ideal.

As Henry himself made clear, his concern was not to single out the abuses of propertied life at Klosterneuburg alone. The scandal of personal property, he pointed out explicitly, was well known in religious houses throughout Christendom. And for decades after he wrote, other reformers across the Empire, both beyond and within the ranks of the orders, attacked the same scandal in similar ways. The next two chapters trace the particulars of the reforming discourse they fashioned—its distinct points of origin beyond and within the orders; its rhetorical and textual strategies, internal tensions and ambiguities; its patterns of transmission; the resistance and confusion it fostered; and how all of these both drew from and reflected a wider intellectual and cultural landscape.

---

[6] Ibid., fol. 179ra: "Pensate ergo iam fratres, his et aliis superius inductis, monitionibus cordis intime attenti, si vestre professioni congruum non sit, si secundum regulam patris Augustini sit, singulis portionibus pecuniarum a praeposito receptis curam victus pro libito gerere, ita ut in communi mensa unus hoc edat, alius aliud, unus deficit, alter superfluat, unus receptas pecunias prudenter, alter fatue conservat, alius alia que ocultiora sunt dampnabiliter exerceat."

[7] Ibid., fol. 180vb: "Hinc et accedit eiusdem professionis monstrosa fratrum dissimilitudo in cibo et vestitu. In cibo quidem dum in una mensa unus cibariis habundat et electis, alter vero etiam leguminium patitur defectum. In vestitu etiam quando ita dissimiliter vestiuntur quod unus praelatus videri possit, alter vero alterius humilis minister."

"Christians of timid spirit."
Henry of Langenstein and the Canons of Klosterneuburg

In the fifth book of his *Horologium Sapientiae*, the Dominican Henry Suso recounted a vision.[8] A pilgrim showed him a once-magnificent city that had fallen into ruins because of the "neglect of those within." Wisdom then explained the meaning of the vision. The city was the "Christian religion, once fervent and devout." In that city, in the early days, many had shared "one mind and one heart." They had led a life of zeal, of fervor, simplicity and sincerity, one whose "exercises of piety" and "customs" had been "full of devotion." The leaders of the religion had been those who lived in monasteries, who had once fought against vice and the "spirits of wickedness." But in Suso's own day they had fallen away from their original glory. Under the guise of their spiritual work they had abandoned voluntary poverty and embraced greed. They seemed outwardly pious, but under their habits they hid worldly hearts and carnal desires. Through his *Horologium*, and through several other works in Latin and the vernacular, Suso hoped to wake his readers from their spiritual slumber. With a simple yet fervid narrative style, he called them to turn away from the outside world and turn inward toward repentance, moral progress and spiritual renewal.[9]

In the years leading up to 1400, ever-greater numbers of men and women, both within and beyond the ranks of the orders, made Suso's call to conversion and repentance their own. The patterns are first visible and best known in the Low Countries, in the circles associated with Geert Groote and his followers. Heeding Suso's call, they turned away from the ambitions of the world and toward a new way of life grounded in moral discipline and progress in the virtues. The "modern" brand of devotion they fostered is justly famous. But scholars now recognize that the New Devout offered only one of many similar experiments. Across the Empire after 1400, university schoolmen, monks

---

[8] Alois M. Haas, "Civitatis Ruinae. Heinrich Seuse's Kirchenkritik," in *Festschrift Walter Haug und Burghart Wachinger*, ed. Johannes Janota et al. (Tübingen, 1992), 389–406, here 400–402. For Suso's *Horologium*, see P. Künzle, *Heinrich Seuses Horologium Sapientiae. Erste kritische Ausgabe unter Benützung der Vorarbeiten von Dominikus Planzer O.P.* (Freibourg, 1977) and the translation by Edmund Colledge, *Wisdom's Watch Upon the Hours* (Washington, 1994), here 100–104.

[9] Nikolaus Staubach, "Von der persönlichen Erfahrung zur Gemeinschaftsliteratur. Entstehungs und Rezeptionsbedingungen geistlicher Reformtexte im Spätmittelalter," *Ons geestelijk erf* 68 (1994): 200–28.

and canons, nuns and friars collaborated with lay women and men to cultivate what has come to be called the "new piety." Its distinct mood and points of emphasis—inward conversion, a penitential turn away from the world and toward moral discipline and spiritual progress, an intense cultivation of devotional reading and writing, often in the vernacular—soon emerged in a variety of settings, some in dialogue with the Low Countries, others independently.[10]

The lasting success of the "new piety" in the Empire was in many ways conditioned by a thickening network of schools and scholars.[11] From the fourteenth century, princes in the region had begun to sponsor new universities, whose faculties and graduates helped them consolidate power and cultivate prestige. They continued to do so with particular energy in the wake of the Great Schism, as the Empire's courts and schools flooded with scholars exiled from Paris. One of the most successful efforts took root in Vienna, where Duke Albert III persuaded Pope Urban VI to crown his faltering *studium* in Vienna with a faculty of theology. The pope granted that privilege in 1384, and Vienna soon rivaled Prague for the intellectual leadership of the region.[12] Similar episodes played out across the Empire in the coming years. In 1387, Heidelberg won its final privilege from the Roman obedience. Its patron Rupert drew Marsilius of Inghen and other renowned theologians to his foundation. In the following year, the city of Cologne established a *studium* of its own.

As these new schools came into their own they became home to a new generation of "public intellectuals," scholars who sought not merely to win abstract academic debates in the classroom, but to apply their learning to concrete problems facing church and society.[13] To that end

---

[10] Marek Derwich and Martial Staub, eds., *Die Neue Frömmigkeit in Europa* (above, 16 and n. 41). Especially useful is the introduction offered by Kaspar Elm, "Die 'Devotio moderna' und die neue Frömmigkeit zwischen Spätmittelalter und früher Neuzeit," 13–30, and its extensive bibliography.

[11] For general context here see the brief synthesis offered in Erich Meuthen, *Das 15. Jahrhundert*, 3rd ed. (Munich, 1996), 175–80, with further literature, e.g. Frank Rexroth, *Deutsche Universitätsstiftungen von Prag bis Köln. Die Intentionen des Stifters und die Wege und Chancen ihrer Verwirklichung im spätmittelalterlichen deutschen Territorialstaat* (Cologne, 1991). For new approaches to the history of universities see the essays collected in William J. Courtenay, Jürgen Miethke, and David B. Priest, eds., *Universities and Schooling in Medieval Society* (Leiden, 2000), especially the introduction and Part I. Most relevant for current purposes is Shank, *Unless You Believe* (above, 67 n. 1).

[12] Shank, *Unless You Believe*, 11–14.

[13] Hobbins, "Schoolman as Public Intellectual," (above, 16 n. 42).

they turned away from traditional academic genres, such as the disputed question or the *summa*. They turned more frequently to composing "treatises" or "tracts" focused on particular questions or problems. In the wake of the Black Death, for example, physicians began to compose new treatises on how to diagnose and treat a disease that had been entirely unknown. In a similar way, jurists moved from commentary to consultation, seeking to apply precedent and legal reasoning to real world circumstance. To that end they composed practical treatises, called *consilia*, that focused on the particulars of individual cases. The new trend came into its own perhaps most forcefully, however, among university theologians. In ways resonant with Suso's call, many turned away from the vanity of the scholastic debate to embrace a more practical pursuit of virtue and moral progress. Their new treatises, accordingly, moved away from the intricacies of doctrine and toward practical discussions of vice and virtue, morality and society—and not least among their concerns was to expose the moral failures of so many complacent and unrepentant churchmen.

Exiled from Paris in the wake of the Great Schism, Henry of Langenstein made his way to the Empire, and there he became a full participant in these broader trends. By the 1380s he had begun in earnest to help fashion what came to be known as the "Vienna School" of devotional theology.[14] At its origins was an "Augustinian" turn from logic to faith, from a theology of disputation and debate toward a theology centered on pastoral care and piety in practice. The shift was under way before his arrival in Vienna, in the wake of his stay at the Cistercian monastery of Eberbach between 1382 and 1384. In Vienna, Henry retreated further still from a commitment to logic in matters of faith and apologetics, and began to emphasize inward penance, affective devotion, and moral discipline in ways generally characteristic of the new piety.[15] Henry's devout stance also inspired much of his best work as one of the Empire's most prolific public scholars—his treatise on contracts, for example, was consistent with wider concerns over debt, usury and avarice, and the social and economic injustices they inflicted on the downtrodden.[16]

---

[14] For an overview Drossbach, "Die sogenannte Devotio moderna in Wien," (above, 16 n. 41).
[15] Shank, *Unless You Believe*, 170.
[16] Ibid., 142 and n. 2. Kreuzer, *Heinrich von Langenstein*, 67, 64–88.

Life at an ancient canonry like Klosterneuburg stood out in bold contrast to the devout mood that Henry and his followers had begun to cultivate at Vienna. In head and members, the community crystallized the irony of a religious estate whose spiritual ideals were often embodied in splendor and financial security. Consider the prior himself, who in 1373 paid twenty-five and a half talents for three pieces of cloth.[17] By contemporary standards of living, that was a striking amount of money—the equivalent of the annual income of an arts faculty member of a university or a skilled artisan. In 1377 the account books recorded the purchase of six ells of cloth for "my lord the prior" at just over five talents, roughly the equivalent of ten florins—double the annual income of a cook or common servant.[18] In the same year the prior spent over eight talents for four lengths of black cloth for the caps of his servants. In 1385 he paid seven talents in the money of account (some fourteen florins) for four lengths of cloth "for his household"[19] and another sum, roughly the equivalent of fourteen florins, for a single pelt.[20] Customs that marked hierarchy and status materially also shaped the community's interactions with the world beyond the cloister. The canons offered gifts to notable visitors commensurate with status—a pelt costing nearly two talents for the duke's marshal in 1374; three pelts costing three and one-half talents each to ministerials in 1377;[21] and in the same year, three talents for a single cap for a court chaplain in Vienna.[22] Grand occasions also offered an opportunity to express charity in other ways. On the feast of St. Augustine in 1377, the canons paid six talents to a group of wandering scholars and entertainers for their performances.[23] At a wedding in the following year a juggler (*fistulator*) received two florins, the "jokers" (*joculatores*) of the bishop of Passau a half-talent.[24] On the feast days of St. Augustine and Michael in the same year, a second group of entertainers received three talents.[25]

---

[17] FRA II/28, 276.
[18] Ibid., 282. Compare the estimates of incomes provided in Dirlmeier, *Untersuchungen zu Einkommensverhältnissen* (above, 15 n. 40), 84, 98 and 428.
[19] FRA II/28, 283.
[20] Ibid.
[21] Ibid. These values are slightly to well above the 6s paid for the pelts for domestic servants and the prebendaries.
[22] Ibid.
[23] Ibid., 279.
[24] Ibid., 282.
[25] Ibid.

Klosterneuburg's account books also reveal that by the 1350s at the latest the canons and canonesses of the community enjoyed a variety of personal cash incomes. In 1353, for example, the prior arranged for a daily stipend to be paid to the priest who served the community's famous "beautiful chapel." In the same document the prior promised each ordained canon four ells of good white cloth or, if the cloth could not be found, a cash payment of equivalent value. The prior himself and his deacon were to receive 12s cash annually, "and no less," for their clothing. The canon celebrating mass at the community's altars of the Holy Trinity and the Crown of Thorns was to receive 4d daily for his services, and on the feast day of the virgin martyr Barbara, a 12s payment was to be distributed among the brothers.[26] A generation later, in the 1370s, the canons recorded their prebends in the community's account books as lump sums of cash.[27] By 1385—within a year of Henry's address to the canons of Klosterneuburg—they had begun to account for those cash amounts more precisely: each choir-lord was to receive 11s 14d for winter clothing; subdeacons, *conversi*, acolytes and nuns were to receive 70d. For summer clothing, the lords received 84d; acolytes, nuns and lesser clerics were given 54d.[28] In subsequent years the canons itemized the payments more precisely still: the 11s 14d for the choir-lords' winter clothing, they noted in 1392, was to substitute for the provision of furs, boots, stockings and some forty ells of linen cloth—a generous allowance by the standards of the day, and many times what the nuns, subdeacons and other clerics of the community received.[29] And all of these patterns, it should be noted, are in evidence in various ways in religious communities across the region. At the Praemonstratensian canonry of Wilten, for example, the community's fourteenth-century priests received not only the generous provision of a "lord's prebend" (*Herrenpfründ*), but also incomes in cash or in kind (described as *peculium*) from donated or inherited property. Other canonries described the provision of petty cash in similar terms—"prebend pennies" (*Pfründpfennige*), beer money, cheese money, shoe money and so on. All of the arrangements reflected both inherited custom and

---

[26] Ibid., 341.
[27] Ibid., 277.
[28] Ibid., 283.
[29] Ibid., 285. Cf. Dirlmeier, *Untersuchungen zu Einkommensverhältnissen*, 265. Dirlmeier estimates that ten ells of cloth was typical for festal attire, five to seven ells sufficient for daily wear.

discrepancies of status that most took for granted. One contract at Wilten even stipulated, revealingly, that the incomes it provided were to pay for shoes for the four poorest canons in the community.[30]

As we have seen, theologians and lawyers had long made some attempt to accommodate the reality that professed religious, with proper license, in proper proportion and in ways appropriate to their estate, could enjoy individual cash incomes. Generations of influential schoolmen, from Hostiensis and Godfrey of Fontaines to John Andreae and others, had long recognized that the money good custom brought to individual religious was, in itself, morally neutral. Money was a means to an end, an instrument that helped measure value and mark status, but it did not, of necessity, cause moral decline. Henry of Langenstein now rudely dismissed all of the attempts at reconciliation. Whatever the obligations of custom and estate, the discretion of superiors and practical circumstance, the canons of Klosterneuburg were nothing but "Christians of timid spirit." Why else did their ardent love for little courtesy gifts (*munuscula*), and even for their most humble of possessions, drive them to strife?[31] How could those who claimed to follow Christ—especially those called to be united in fraternal charity and to be poor in spirit—strive to appropriate the things of the world as their own?[32] And above all, how could they struggle so mightily over such abundant cash incomes?[33]

And yet Henry was aware enough of the practical, human dimensions of the challenge he issued, and he confronted the inevitable objections. In passages resonant with the many pastoral dialogues of his day, Henry engaged an imaginary interlocutor. Together they explored matters of psychology and conscience amid the dilemmas of daily life. Henry's

---

[30] Hans Lentze, "Pitanz und Pfründe im Mittelalterlichen Wilten," in *Veröffentlichungen aus dem Stadtarchiv Innsbruck*, ed. Karl Schadelbauer (Innsbruck, 1954), 5–15.

[31] MS Vienna, ÖNB, Cod. 3700, fol. 177ra: "Amant munuscula, delectantur in propriis et sepe ex vilissimis rebus sic inardescunt, quod concordia fratrum conturbatur, quod dyabolica persuasione fieri dubium non est."

[32] Ibid., fol. 175rb: "Quommodo ergo rite ibi abnegata est propria voluntas ubi remansit mundana et carnalis cupiditas? Nonne abnegari vult Christianus voluntatem carnis ut uniatur in communione fraterne caritatis? Et unde alias divisio hominum et dissimilitudo inter eos? Unde lites et discordie nisi quod unus hoc et alter illud sibi appropriando dicit suum esse? Estote pauperes, karissimi, quia ille vere pacem habet qui nihil appetit in seculo possidere."

[33] Ibid., fol. 175ra: "Cuius ergo regule queso sunt qui...de superflua praebendarum magnitudine contendunt? Non utique Basili, non Benedicti, non Francisci. Dicantur forsan Augustini, et quod magnas appettunt praebendas ut de residuo pauperibus habeant erogare."

accusations were preposterous, an interlocutor suggested, because as professed religious the canons were legally "dead," and therefore incapable of true ownership.[34] The canons simply received and used their cash and goods according to the will of their superior. What then was the difference between being given food and clothing and being given money, with good reason, to buy such things?[35] It was a crucial point, and one in keeping with complex scholastic theories about the nature and utility of money as a "medium and measure" of both social justice and the common good.[36] Other key objections followed: Whatever the abuses, they were not universal, and the canons themselves lamented moral failure wherever and whenever it might occur. But in the end, cash prebends were worth the moral risks, not least because they were an efficient way to do business. Here was the echo of the shrewd business sense of a progressive clerical "modernity," now helping to maintain financial stability in an ancient religious foundation: Cash incomes reduced the "lavish costs" of providing for the infirm, who could not provide for themselves; they freed busy prelates to spend their time worrying about more pressing matters; they spared the community's expenses because brothers could entertain their own guests from their own resources; and they eased the canons' concern about future shortfalls. The canons' defensive retorts were stylized, but it is important to bear in mind the all-too-human concern with security and stability that may have inspired them. The 1380s were a particularly difficult decade in Vienna. An epidemic, a series of bad wine harvests and a sharp coin debasement—all must have made the security, flexibility and cost-efficiency of cash incomes all the more attractive in houses like Klosterneuburg.[37]

---

[34] Ibid., fol. 179ra–b: "Si dixeris 'Dummodo essentialibus religiosis que sunt proprium non habere, prelato obedire et caste vivere, non obviat modus vivendi noster, salvi esse possumus. Utique videtur quod proprietarius inde argui non possum, cum enim sum civiliter mortuus et ex natura religionis incapax. Nullius rei utilis dominium aut proprietaria possesio in me transferri potest.'"

[35] Ibid., fol. 179vb: "Si dicas, 'Numquid ergo non licet mihi habere utiles res aut pecunias sciente et indulgente praelato meo? Quomodo est etiam contra regularem seu communem vitam si praelatus qui tenetur mihi de victu et vestitu providere facit hoc, certa ratione motus, distribuendo pro his pecuniarum portiones competentes. Numquid non idem iudicium est de his et de illis?'"

[36] Cf. Joel Kaye, *Economy and Nature in the Fourteenth Century: Money, Market Exchange, and the Emergence of Scientific Thought* (Cambridge, 1998). Also see below, 82 and n. 51.

[37] Cf. Shank, *Unless You Believe*, 17–18.

In England John Wyclif had recently heard similar arguments. To his dismay, those in the religious orders had justified their enjoyment of endowed pensions, "perpetual alms" and appropriated parishes as, in part, due to economic necessity. Financial straits, they argued, had forced them to adopt all of those strategies to maintain solvency. For Wyclif it was all mortal sin, "which man should not commit even for the salvation of the whole world."[38] Henry, too, scoffed at the same counterarguments and refused to compromise: no difficult circumstance could excuse the canons' appropriations, and no legal technicality could protect them. If the canons were not guilty of ownership in the strict sense (*dominium rei utilis*), they still desired inwardly to usurp things that were not theirs, and so committed mortal sin.[39] And in a mood similar to Wyclif's, Henry, too, sought to dissolve unjust and mortally sinful *dominium* through the embrace of charity and apostolic community. The apostles had renounced worldly ownership (*dominium*) "promptly," as Henry put it, "willingly," and "from the heart" to follow Christ. Henry called for the canons to do the same, returning promptly and willingly to the letter of their rule and allowing their prior to provide for their food and clothing and other needs in common. Only then could they be free to serve others, as was their calling, through both contemplation and action. Only then would they be true to their profession, following Christ in penitence, in trials and labors, in fasting and vigils, in poverty, purity and charity.[40] It was far from Henry's concern to advance a radical critique of church property in general. His concern instead reflected the more modest aims of the new piety that he and others had begun to cultivate in Vienna. His aim was to awaken the conscience of those under religious vows, to call them to repent and to uphold their own ideals. Hence Henry's invitation to the canons to judge for themselves how easily they might fall into mortal sin, even in

---

[38] Cf. John Wyclif, *On Simony*, trans. Terrence A. McVeigh (Fordham, 1992), 134–35. See also 140–44.

[39] MS Vienna, ÖNB, Cod. 3700, fol. 179rb: "...proprietarius non iudicaberis quasi in te transferratur dominium rei utilis, sed quia appropriative possidere vis que tua non sunt, et taliter tibi vindicas et usurpas res utiles, ut eas tenendo et eis utendo in nullo differas ab his qui pecuniarum simile usum et rerum proprietatem habent."

[40] Ibid., fol. 173rb: "Reliquimus equidem prompte, reliquimus voluntarie, reliquimus ex corde, nihil tenentes, reliquimus rerum dominium non reversuri, reliquimus omne quo ante viximus negotium, reliquimus mundum cui ante servivimus et secuti sumus te in penitentia, in tribulationibus, in laboribus, in ieiuniis, in vigiliis, in obedientia, in paupertate, in castitate, in caritate, discentes a te non prophetare, non super mare ambulare...."

the slightest desire to have the most humble thing.[41] It did not matter what any prelate might license, what any custom, however long-held and approved, might sanction, or what any hard times, however difficult, might bring. Henry looked only to the choir-lords' innermost intentions and desires, and there he found only the vice of an "appropriating intent" that destroyed the common good.[42]

And yet the old ambiguities and difficult questions of license and discretion, the proper proportions of use and so on remained unresolved. Cash prebends in themselves, as Henry himself no doubt recognized, were sanctioned by a prelate's discretion, good custom and the imperatives of status. His only leverage to bring about any real change in the daily life of the community he critiqued was thus to win the battle of conscience. To that end he fashioned vivid passages in which he held up religious life's best and most ancient ideals against a grotesque caricature of their worst modern realities. Yes, Henry admitted, the choir-lords enjoyed their prebends with the license of their superior. No, he conceded, the canons could not be accused of ownership in the strict sense, and there was good that might come from the proper use of money. But what of their actual way of life? The canons never once offered any account of income or expense. After ten or twenty years of buying and selling for their bread, wine, clothing and other daily needs, how could a prelate know how much each canon had saved or spent, won or lost?[43] Nor did the canons ever return any of their residual funds, and their prior never asked them to. Instead, the canons kept the money for themselves, some saving up for the future, others saving to entertain guests or notable visitors, still others saving up in the name of ambition, to live beyond the proper measure of their

---

[41] Ibid., fol. fol. 179va: "...iudicate fratres quantum peccatur et quam facile incurritur vitium proprietatis in rerum approbatione vilissimarum...."

[42] Ibid., fol. 180ra: "Esto quod prelatus tuus sciat te residuare de pecuniis quas tibi distribuit. Nihilominus intentio tua faciet te proprietarium, quia sic vel quomodolibet aliter ad tuam privatam utilitatem thezaurizas et non ad bonum commune collegii. Nec praelatus potest tecum dispensare ut pecunias congreges ad providendum tibi in casu depauperationis monasterii aut constitutionis indiscreti...nec aliqua intentione simili tendente ad bonum privatum, quia omnis talis intentio appropriativa est."

[43] Ibid.: "Esto ut sciat te pecuniam aliquam tenuisse. Quomodo etiam prelatus tuus scire potest quid et quantum pecunie residuande habeas qui forte cottidie quasi mercaris, iam panem et vinum vendendo, iam hoc iam illud reemendo, numquam praelato rationem faciens de expositis et receptis? Quommodo ergo sciet quantum negotiando cum recepta pecunia decem vel viginti annis lucratus es?"

estate.[44] Did not their enjoyment of cash "give pressing occasion for vagrancy, secret gatherings within and outside the monastery, apostasy paid for by money unaccounted for?" The questioning of conscience continued:

> Did not that prodigal son, having received his money, leave his father's house and consume his substance with whores? What more? Here drunkenness rages, here chastity is violated, here fasting is broken, here indulgence chatters, here no reading resounds, here no devotion cries out. Who doubts that from this poison root grow up dice games, contempt of brothers, blasphemies, fights, perjury, theft and things of this sort? For when one either wastes all that he has or loses it in a game, he is shaken by the shame of need, and strives through whatever means he can to seize another's goods.[45]

And what of the splendor of the choir-lords' prelates, who tolerated such excess? What of their many servants; their fine horses with golden reins; their precious cloths; their glorious dwellings; their magnanimous gifts (*enceniis*) of gold, silver and gems? The scandalous pomp only aggravated a community's indigence, both at Klosterneuburg and in religious houses throughout Christendom.[46]

Older models of late-medieval religious decline and renewal have long helped make sense of passages like these, and from within those models it makes sense to see Henry as yet another prophetic critic, one who offered here a more or less straightforward account of a way of life that was falling apart. Without question, Henry was in some way

---

[44] Ibid.: "...si de portionibus pecuniarum tibi pro victu et vestitu tue religioni congrua exponendum residues ad commodum tuum privatum, videlicet ut habeas quid expendere pro te in casibus fortuitis seu adversis aut pro quibus vis hospitibus aut notis tibi venientibus, vel ut lautius quam tue religionis mensura requirit vivas...."

[45] Ibid., fol. 180va: "Nonne illa portionum receptio peculialium praecipue religiosis inpellentem occasionem ministrat circumnavigandi, convivia intus et extra monasterium secreta faciendi, pecuniis residuis a religione apostandi? Nonne filius ille prodigus recepta portione pecuniaria a domo patris recessit, substantiam suam cum meretricibus devoratus? Quid plus? Ibi furit ebrietas, ibi violatur castitas, ibi solvitur ieiunium, ibi frangitur silentium, ibi dissolutio garrulat, ibi lectio nulla sonat, ibi nulla suspirat devotio. Quis etiam ambigitur ex hac radice venenata pullulare ludos taxillorum, contemptiones fratrum, blasphemias, percussiones, periuria, furta et huiusmodi, quia cum alter totum quod habet aut prodige exposuit aut ludendo perdidit, egestatis indignatione agitatus, quocumque modo potest aliena rapere studet?"

[46] Ibid., fol. 183ra: "Ecce ergo tam temporalis inopie regularium et generaliter religiosorum, videlicet defectus spiritualium, quam aggravat non parum maiorum pompa qui eius praesunt in mensa splendida, in multa familia, in equis magnis, in frenis aureis, in pannis pretiosis, in habitaculis gloriosis, in enceniis variis ex auro et argento et coruscantibus gemmis."

reacting to widely recognized excesses. But it remains possible to see how Henry's commitments drove him to embrace a rhetoric, one at times resonant with other forms of "estates satire" in his day, that polemically distorted the complexity of the canons' inherited circumstance. Customs of prayer and provision and ideals of status, as we have seen, had made room for cash prebends and other incomes for some time—in many houses from before 1300, and at Klosterneuburg from at least the 1350s. Most in the orders had shared a certain tolerance, remarkably high by modern standards, for the inevitable discrepancies of wealth and the occasional excesses. But whatever those excesses, good custom and status remained vital cultural principles, and they continued to sustain religious life in a way that could not simply be dismissed out of hand. As scholars have noted in other settings, fifteenth-century reformers often deliberately deployed a certain rhetoric of moral crisis to heighten the sense of urgency for spiritual renewal.[47] At Klosterneuburg another schoolman crafted claims about religious life that, while they in part reflected daily experience, also helped raise to the level of moral crisis what had long been understood to be part of daily life.

Henry knew, however, that for all his rhetoric, most did not see the renunciation of cash and the return to community he demanded as essential to salvation. As his imaginary interlocutor pointed out, echoing the gospel itself, who could otherwise be saved? Surely a charitable inward disposition mattered more than the technicalities of ownership. Henry responded, flatly, with the words of Hosea: "Destruction is thy own, O Israel; I alone am your help."[48] For Henry the choir-lords ignored at their peril the choice he had put before them. Would they renounce dominion, embrace charity and walk on to salvation? Or would they cling to their dominion, renounce charity, and go down to perdition? It was a passionate appeal, but only one among many claims on what in the end remained uncertain moral ground. A generation later another outsider sought to claim that ground yet again, this time at the request of a community of women far from the banks of the Danube.

---

[47] Cf. Bast, *Honor Your Fathers* (above, 17 n. 45), especially Ch. 1.
[48] Ibid., fol. 183vb: "Quid igitur dicam nisi illud dictum propheticum 'Perditio tua Israel ex te in me auxilium tuum.'"

"I am terribly afraid to cast into damnation such a multitude of religious souls."
Dietrich Kerkering and the Nuns of Münster

Around 1412, a troubled collective conscience prompted the Benedictine nuns of St. Giles in Münster to write to Dietrich Kerkering, renowned theologian of Cologne, regarding a stinging accusation. Could it be true, the women asked pressingly (*instanter*), that their customary enjoyment of personal incomes and goods had cast them all into mortal sin? The women had sought the advice of another of the Empire's leading public scholars, a theologian who shared the intellectual and institutional commitments of Henry of Langenstein and so many other pastoral theologians and devotional authors. A native of Münster and a student at Prague in the 1380s, Dietrich had come to Cologne by 1389, where he was one of the twenty-one masters who founded the new university there.[49] For the next thirty years, until his death in 1422, he composed tracts on more than a dozen topics, including papal and conciliar power; the Brothers and Sisters of the Common Life; the roles of alms, rents, usury and contracts; and matters of moral theology.

Dietrich's treatise to the nuns of Münster soon numbered among the most popular of these many works.[50] It began with a dispassionate description of the nuns' way of life:

> Each of you as she pleases, with the license of the abbess, takes the annual rents that fall to the monastery, and spends or consumes them for her personal utility and for her comfort, and even gives, if she wishes, certain alms from them or converts them to pious uses. Also, each of you receives, with the license of the abbess, the donations or gifts that are given by relatives or other friends, whether these are precious items, money, food or drink, and, when these things are given, uses them as she pleases with the license of the superior. Also, one who earns some money by manual labor makes use of it as she pleases with the license of the abbess; also, each of you as she pleases gives gifts or treasures, bread and beer to relatives and friends, and a sum to maidservants, and

---

[49] Scholars have noted Kerkering's career and works in passing, but there is no modern biography. For basic orientation see VL 4: 1129–32. A doctor of Theology by 1400, Kerkering served as rector of the University of Cologne three times (1400, 1406 and 1408/1409), dean of the faculty theology three times (1400, 1403 and 1406) and as vice-chancellor from 1410.

[50] The treatise survives in at least ten manuscripts (cf. VL 4: 1131). There is no critical edition. I take my readings from MS Melk, Stiftsbibliothek, CM 900, fols. 56r–62r, collated against Frankfurt, Stadt- und Universitätsbibliothek, MS Barth. 141, fols. 190r–197v.

all of this with the license of the abbess. Also, those on their deathbed seek to have certain gifts and treasures assigned to their friends, and the abbess customarily approves this.[51]

Each nun, Kerkering continued, was careful to confirm the authority and jurisdiction of her abbess over her use of goods by once a year turning in the keys to the chests and boxes in which each kept her things, thereby "recognizing that these are not her own property, but that they belong to the whole convent, of which the abbess is the head. And then the abbess customarily concedes to each the use of these things for utility, necessity and comfort."[52]

Kerkering's detailed description suggests he may have known a great deal of the actual circumstances of the nuns in his native Münster. In any event, his narrative accurately described patterns of life that, as we have seen, might have been encountered in any number of women's communities across the Empire. For at least a century by 1400, most religious women had enjoyed endowed cash prebends and other payments with the license of their superiors and in a way appropriate to their *status*. Now Kerkering, like Henry of Langenstein before him, sought to reduce the matter to a much simpler moral equation, one that again made immorality the necessary consequence of cash and comfort for religious men and women alike, in every order. For Kerkering, the incomes and goods religious women and men enjoyed were the source of a poisonous river of disobedience and pride, lying, lust and other vices.[53] Propertied nuns, like their male counterparts, were abusive

---

[51] MS Melk, Stiftsbibliothek, CM 900, fol. 56: "Modus vivendi quem tenetis est iste: Quaelibet ex vobis cui placet de licentia abbatisse tollit redditus annuos...et expendit seu consumit illos pro sua personali utilitate et pro suo commoditate, et dat etiam si vult de illis aliquas elemosinas, vel alias convertit in pios usus. Similiter quaelibet ex vobis recepit de licentia abbatisse donaria seu munera quae dantur sibi a consanguineis vel aliis amicis, sive consistant in clenodiis sive in pecuniis, sive in cibis sive in potibus, et illis sic datis utitur ad sui beneplacitum de licentia abbatisse. Item illa quae manibus operando aliud lucrat, illo utitur ad beneplacitum de licentia abatisse. Item quaelibet vestrum cui placet dat consanguineis vel aliis amicis donaria aut clenodia, panem vel cervisiam et ancillis servientibus pretium, et hoc totum de licentia abatisse. Item decumbentes ad mortem petunt aliquam donariam vel clenodiam suis amicis assignari, et hoc solet abbatissa ratificare."

[52] Ibid.: "Et ut iste usus rerum temporalium sit manifeste et comperte de licentia abbatisse, solet quilibet vestrum singulis annis permutare claves cistarum et scrineorum in quibus ille res temporales quibus utitur reponuntur, per hoc recognoscens quod ille res non sunt sue proprie, sed quod pertinent ad totum conventum cuius abatissa est caput. Et tunc solet abatissa illi concedere usum pro utilitate, necessitate et commodo suo."

[53] Ibid., fol. 56v: "...inobedientia, contumacia, superbia, contempnio, partialitas, avaritia, invidia, vana gloria, gulositas et circa cibos curiositas, mendacium, luxuria

rebels who were contemptuous of those who enjoyed less. Nuns who lived from cash prebends became divisive manipulators who used their money to promote factions in the household.[54] Their money led them to be more concerned with food and friends than with their liturgy and the spiritual exercises that helped them progress in virtue.[55] Instead of a life of contemplation, meditation and prayer, these women bought and sold and traded in the streets, where they became ensnared in all of the lying, swearing and other sins that stained the purity of their profession.[56] The result, as Kerkering saw it, was the same culture of property and its monstrous discrepancies that Henry of Langenstein had lamented at Klosterneuburg: One nun ate this, another that, another something else, one drank beer and another wine; one woman received two, three or even four times the portion of another, each according to her station.[57]

Like Henry of Langenstein before him, Dietrich Kerkering framed the matter of religious poverty and property differently than most of

---

et occupatio infructuosa ac multiplex dissolutio atque mentis evagatio circa illicita, et sic de aliis."

[54] Ibid.: "...magis contumeliose ac animate ad rebellandum seu ad resistendum superioribus suis, egre ferentes disciplinarem correctionem et inclinati ad despiciendum confratres suos ac consorores minus habentes de peculio. Etiam ille persone de facili possunt alias personas per munera ad se allicere et sic facere partialitates, quasdam personas exaltando, alias minus iuste opprimendo."

[55] Ibid.: "Quis etiam hoc non videt, quod sepe huiusmodi peculium seu proprietas est causa commessationum et ebrietatum...ita quod ratione peculii persone conventus possunt de facili excedere in cibo et potu et delicatius vivere quam exigit mensura religiose vite. Ex quo consequenter venit negligentia et remissio in divino cultu dum singule persone sollicite sunt circa coquinam et mensam et hospites quam circa exercitia spiritualia."

[56] Ibid.: "...proprietas et peculium sunt distractiones a contemplationibus, a meditationibus, ab orationibus et ab aliis exercitiis spiritualibus. Nam habentes proprietates seu peculia sepe occupantur circa illa et sepe etiam distrahuntur ab huiusmodi spiritualibus exercitiis per cibos delicatos, per vinum et...amicorum frequentationes. Occupantur etiam sepe circa emptiones et venditiones, in quibus vel ex parte vendentis vel ex parte ementis multiloquia, in quibus non deest peccatum nec non mendacia et sepe iuramenta et conversationes cum personis secularibus...per quae omnia puritas monastice vite perturbatur."

[57] Ibid.: "...ex ista proprietate seu peculio oritur plerumque dissimilitudo in cibo et potu atque vestitu dum unus vult uti isto cibo, alius alio cibo, unus vino alter cervisia, quae dissimilitudo detestanda est in illis personis que debent esse confratres vel consorores. Que quidem persone, de quanto magis sunt conformes in cibis et potibus atque vestitu, de tanto melius sunt concordes et pacifice. Nam similitudo in omnibus istis magis fovet et conservat amicitiam, quia naturale est quod simile applaudat suo simili." Ibid.: "...ibi plerumque inequaliter conceduntur, ita quod quandoque uni persone conceditur aliquando in duplo, triplo vel quadruplo plus quam alteri...."

his fourteenth-century predecessors. Kerkering was no radical prophet of poverty or disendowment. He never denied the nuns moderate enjoyment of food, clothing and other necessities, according to their circumstance. His focus, like Henry's, reflected a new pastoral, practical and pious mood. Kerkering's concern was the moral consequence of what he saw as the excessive freedom that cash prebends afforded, and what he saw as the pastoral negligence of the abbesses who licensed them.[58] Dietrich made the point with vivid rhetoric. Lady abbesses seemed far too liberal with their license. Whether wise or foolish, upright or scandalous, sober or drunken, chaste or lustful, religious of all stripes seemed to receive license to do whatever they wished with their assigned incomes.[59] All this Kerkering denounced, revealingly, as "evil custom." But he admitted that it would remain deeply rooted, both because of the lukewarm disposition of most ordinary religious, and because of the scandal that would erupt in trying to enforce reform.[60] Yet why else had the laity become so hostile to institutional religion, if not because those professed to live the common life of the apostles lived individually from "assigned portions"?[61] Again echoing Henry's style from years before, Kerkering made the point with remarkable rhetorical flourish:

---

[58] Ibid., fol. 57v: "Nemo credat quod proprium habere sit in se malum; sed est malum per sequelam, quae est uti illo proprio ad suum beneplacitum...." Ibid., "...non loquor hec contra usum cotidianum victus et amictus.... quae solet concedi personis monasticis a superioribus suis, sed loquor contra usum pecuniarum principaliter et aliarum rerum quae solent in pecunias converti, ut sunt balda, vina, pecora et consimilia."

[59] Ibid.: "...unde igitur hoc queso provenit quod moderni prelati et prelate religionum ita generaliter et ita faciliter singulis suis subditis, sive sunt prudentes sive insipientes, sive solide sive dissolute vite, sive sobrie sive ebriose, sive caste sive libidiose, sive liberales sive prodige, assignant certas portiones de bonis communibus, dantes eis libertatem utendi illis, propter quam libertatem excludendam et praecavendam illi sancti patres noluerunt suos subditos habere proprietatem, in quo utique videtur facere contra intentionem sanctorum patrum et eorum ordinationes violare?"

[60] Ibid.: "Certe illud provenit ex duobus: Primo ex hoc, quod ille antiquae sanctae observationes per malam consuetudinem sunt abolite, et mala consuetudo habituata non potest tolli sine grandi permutatione. Secundo non est hodie neque in superioribus neque in inferioribus ille zelus et ille fervor ad profectum spiritualem qui olim fuit."

[61] Ibid., fol. 58r: "Utinam moderni prelati et moderne prelate considerarent quam multi religiosissimi conventus diversorum ordinium miserabiliter defecerunt et cotidie magis et magis deficiunt in monastica disciplina, in regularibus observantiis, in divino cultu et communiter in favore quem ad eos habuit totus populus Christianus et sic in temporalibus profecerunt.... Quare non considerant quod hec mala veniunt per assignationem portionum cuilibet persone de bonis communibus...."

One for lust, another for debauchery, another for dice, another for pompous clothing or other treasures, another for pomp in horses, another for entertaining guests, according to that which each is inclined, through which they become dissolute, disobedient, contentious, rebellious, refusing monastic discipline, despising divine worship, with evil and deceitful intrigues persecuting those good people who displease them. And so they shamefully and sinfully pervert the good and ordered condition of their monastery, and a fall in spiritual matters, without fail, brings a fall in temporal matters.[62]

Faced with another compelling portrait of religious life seemingly in decline, it remains important to recover the original tension and ambiguity at the heart of Kerkering's rhetoric. As we have seen, women religious around 1400 need not have been portrayed in such harsh, moralizing tones. Like their male counterparts, they could be seen as heirs of good custom who, with the license of their superiors, could live from their cash incomes virtuously and in good conscience, not least because to do so gave them the flexibility they needed to negotiate life in the modern world. Kerkering's own description of the nuns' convenience and comfort (*commodum*) also perhaps reflected something of a wider sense of a new domestic sensibility.[63] In a way that recalled both Peraldus the estates satire of his own day, Kerkering abandoned these complexities in favor of highly charged, universalizing moral claims and vivid social critique. To see that agency helps highlight how another reforming schoolman sought to contest an established way of life—and in doing so, again helped move a long-accepted cultural equilibrium toward moral crisis.

Like Henry before him, however, Kerkering knew that a more complex circumstance lay behind his satire and polemic. Yet unlike Henry, Dietrich took up an extended consideration of that circumstance. In a series of thorny cases he tried to sort through the real dilemmas his call to the common life might have raised at Münster and elsewhere.

---

[62] Ibid.: "....qua portione assignata unus [!]utitur ad luxuriam, alius ad crapulam, alius ad ludos taxillorum, alius ad pompas vestitum vel aliorum clenodiorum, alius ad pompas equorum, alius ad hospitalitatem consanguineorum secundum quod quilibet est inclinatus, per que iste persone fiunt dissolute, inobedientes, contumeliose, superioribus rebelles, monasticam disciplinam declinantes, divinum cultum contempnentes, bonas personas quibus ista displicent dure persequentes malis et mendosis machinationibus, et sic bonum et ordinatum statum suorum monasteriorum pervertentes turpiter et inique, quem casum in spiritualibus infallibiliter concomitatur casus in temporalibus."

[63] See the discussions of *commodità* above, 60 and n. 133.

What of a struggling and indigent community, for example, in which no woman knew any lucrative skill, and every woman had to rely on the support of relatives and friends? The response here was that each woman might enjoy what she received individually, though with an "exhortation" that all should provide to those who had less from whatever they enjoyed beyond their basic needs.[64] Another case explored the dilemma of an abbess who demanded each woman render a complete account of her goods and then pay a tax proportional to her income for relief of great community debts. In this case, only those who refused to pay the fee would be judged *proprietariae*.[65]

Still another line of inquiry explored the possibility that an abbess—papal law to the contrary notwithstanding—might allow personal incomes through what Kerkering called "dispensation through interpretation." In certain special cases abbesses might "imagine" that the pope, were he either informed of local circumstance or actually present, would reasonably allow the nuns' cash incomes.[66] One case concerned a community reduced to indigence through fire, plunder or other misfortune, such that its members were forced to support themselves through manual labor. Should some be eager to go to work for their needs while others remained lazy and dissolute, content to live in leisure on the labor of others, a superior might allow those who worked to retain their wages, as long as they contributed to the support of the infirm. All dispensations allowing money under such circumstances, Kerkering cautioned, were only valid under "great, evident and urgent cause" (an echo of Hostiensis' standard legal commentary on the *Decretals*)[67] and they were to end as soon as circumstances changed for the better. Kerkering then admitted that since he did not know fully the

---

[64] Ibid., fol. 59v: "...fortassis nolunt eis mittere cibum, potum aut vestimentum si omnia quae miserint debeant cedere communitati, forte dicentes: 'Quid hec inter tantos?' In isto casu videtur similiter dispensare potest super eo quod quaelibet persona utatur pro se illis quae recipit ex favore amicorum, cum exhortatione eiusdem persone quod de illis quae recipit ultra necessitatem subveniat non habenti."

[65] Ibid., fol. 59r: "...absque dubio in vitio proprietatis declaratur et proprietaria est censenda, quia non vult suo conventui sucurrere in sua necessitate per illa quae sunt conventus, et sic probatur plus diligere proprietatem quam suum conventum."

[66] Ibid., fol. 59v: "Tertia conclusio: Non obstante statuto pape de non distribuendo personis conventualibus peculium, si tamen ocurrat casus specialis de quo verisimiliter praesumit superior quod si papa, cum praevidisset in illo casu, aliter ordinasset, vel si actu esset praesens papa in illo casu aliter ordinaret, et pro dispensatione habenda non potest commode papa consuli nec alius a quo valeat dispensatio obtineri, in hoc casu non peccat superior concedendo peculium."

[67] See above, 36.

circumstances within any one cloister, he could not decide whether one community or another enjoyed their property with proper cause.[68]

The women of St. Giles themselves recognized the pastoral dilemma that emerged from these considerations, and they had apparently pointed it out: Could it really be true, they had asked, that so many "noble religious" could be eternally damned for incomes and goods they enjoyed by virtue of custom, license and circumstance? Did not most professed women live uprightly, humbly, obediently and in charity? What of those who concealed nothing of their property and who lived their lives obediently, "prepared to surrender" their goods, as Hostiensis had put it explicitly, to their superiors? Henry of Langenstein had reacted sternly to this counterargument, offering a sharp choice between renunciation of the inherited ways of life or damnation. Dietrich Kerkering was more openly uncertain. He could not deny that it was possible for monks and nuns to dispose of their cash endowments in good faith. With remarkable candor the theologian wondered, revealingly, about the genuine uncertainty both he and the women faced.

> I am terribly afraid to cast into damnation such a multitude of religious souls, who are from the more noble portion of the Lord's flock, because both in your convent, and in so many others, there are indeed people who live an excellent way of life—according to human judgment—who do not wish to live against their vows or lead their lives down into mortal sin on account of their worldly goods. For some time this difficulty has terrified me indeed, and it continues to terrify me, such that I would rather put my finger over my mouth and stay silent than to judge harshly in such a great matter.[69]

These passages help ground and enrich our scholarly accounts of fifteenth century crisis and reform. Discussions of social and economic

---

[68] Ibid., fol. 60v: "Si autem illa causa cessavit, tunc etiam cessare debet effectus, quia deficiente causa deficit et effectus. Et quia nescio causam incohationis istius modi vestri, sicut nec vos scitis ut credo, nescio diffinire an causa fuerit rationabilis an non, nec possum dicere an illa adhuc duret an non, et per consequens non possum discutere an ex illa causa modus vester sit licitus vel non."

[69] Ibid., fol. 60r: "Modo tantam multitudinem religosarum personarum quae sunt de nobiliore portione dominici gregis ponere in statu dampnationis valde pertimesco, quoniam tam in vestro conventu quam in pluribus aliis modum vestrum tenentibus utique inveniuntur persone valde excellentis vite secundum humanum iudicium, que persone pro quibusdam bonis temporalibus nollent deducere vitam suam in peccato mortali seu vivere contra votum. Que quidem difficultas diu terruit me, et adhuc terret, ut potius vellem supponere digitum ori meo et silere quam in tam grandi materia aliquid temere diffinire."

crisis long tended to focus on the long view, on large-scale structural changes in society and economy, or on dramatic expressions of various "crisis mentalities." These passages, in contrast, restore a kind of sturdy, local humanity to what we have long called crisis. They suggest how women and men of the orders could face the fearful possibilities of fire, warfare, debt and so on in their day—tough circumstances that religious corporations might have faced at any time in the premodern era—with creativity and resolve, in ways consistent with the rugged framework of custom, license and so on that had long sustained religious life. Similarly, against narratives of an "age of reform" that tend to move quickly from the fourteenth century to the sixteenth, these passages provide a sense of the local uncertainty of the historical moment, and of an all-too-human ambivalence that haunted calls to reform.

In the end, Kerkering, again revealingly, could not condemn the women. For all of the rhetoric, even outsiders suspicious of compromise had to acknowledge the difficulties and leave matters of property and community where they long had been, in the hands of local superiors. For the nuns of St. Giles, Kerkering could only conclude his treatise with an extended exhortation to the common life, one consistent with the new piety he and others cultivated across the region. One key remark helps restore something of the exhortation's original resonance: In Cologne and in many other places, Kerkering noted—here almost certainly a reference to the New Devout, whom he himself defended in another treatise—there were "congregations of people who were not solemnly professed, who lived in common without individual property, yet who worked diligently for the support of the community." The common life had triumphed over self-love not among the professed, but among ordinary parishioners.[70] Shamefully for the nuns of Münster, charity had grown cold precisely where it should have been most fervent—in the households of professed religious.[71] Hence the sharp challenge at

---

[70] Ibid., fol. 61r: "Nam cum dicitur quod aliquae persone non ita diligenter laborarent manibus sicut modo faciunt, hoc certe arguit defectum caritatis et ad proximum et ad commune bonum, quod debet praeferri bono particulari, et arguit inordinatum amorem sui ipsius. Et nos videmus multas congregationes personarum non professarum in Colonia et extra, quae persone vivunt de communi non habentes peculium, et tamen singule persone diligenter laborant pro sustentatione sue communitatis."

[71] Ibid.: "Et certe dolendum est quod caritas magis refriguit in personis religiosis quam in personis sine religione convivientibus, quoniam in professis religionum deberet relucere maior caritas et maior perfectio quam in aliis."

the end of the treatise: As a marker of their charity, would the women renounce their claims to personal property and free themselves to work for spiritual perfection? Would they trust in their abbess and her officers to provide for each according to need?[72] Even here Kerkering rehearsed the obvious practical objections: The nuns' corporate resources were not nearly enough to sustain the entire community, and if the women were to share their incomes and other goods, surely many would be tempted not to work as diligently for the community as they had for themselves. For ordinary nuns in places like St. Giles, these must have been legitimate concerns. But for the university theologian, who knew nothing of religious life personally, the nuns' retorts only revealed their lack of Christian love of neighbor and love of the common good. Not to worry if some of their number had more to contribute than others (here a keen awareness of the daily tensions of the common life): Those able to earn more through their labors and their circumstance were simply to rejoice in their opportunity to embody charity more perfectly.[73] And not to worry (here another revealing comment) if disgruntled patrons might refuse to support such a strange communal experiment. Perhaps it would be better, after all, if these noble ladies were no longer troubled with all the little courtesy gifts offered by their family and friends! Those were things that, as Kerkering saw it, only incited envy, jealousy, curiosity and vanity among those who were to be "humble and devout."[74]

Soon after Kerkering composed his treatise for the nuns of Münster, he made his way to the Council of Constance, where he would serve as a representative of the University of Cologne. In November 1414 the Pisan antipope John XXIII, at the insistence of King Sigismund, called the council to heal decades of schism, to reform the church,

---

[72] Ibid., fol. 60v: "...prudenter et bene faceritis si quidquid proveniret...sive de redditibus perpetuis aut annuis sive de laboribus sive de amicorum donationibus, totum praesentaretur abbatisse vestre et per illam et per alias personas vestri conventus.... distribuetur prout cuicue opus esset, secundum modum illum quem sacntissimus Jeronimus scribit in regula Eustochii."

[73] Ibid.: "Et revera si vos vixeritis de communi, tunc ille persone quae sciunt labores lucrosos gaudere deberent quod per labores suos possent suo conventui succurere. In hoc enim haberent speciale meritum apud deum, quia esset opus magne pietatis pauperi conventui succurere."

[74] Ibid.: "Et fortassis non expedit pro devota et religiosa persona quod sic cottidie expectet aliquid delicatum accipere ab amicis, quoniam illa expectatio facit appetitum hominis nimis curiosum, et alie persone per hoc fortassis titillantur, temptantur vel egre ferunt si non recipiantur consimilia...."

and to defend the faith against heresy. In response, over the next three years, thousands made their way to the modest city in the southwestern corner of the Empire. The sheer numbers and diversity of the participants impressed contemporary chroniclers, who struggled to describe the scene. The estimates varied, sometimes widely, but one chronicler's attempt is representative: across the months and years of the council there had come to Constance some thirty-two of the highest prelates (popes, cardinals and patriarchs), twenty-seven archbishops, over a hundred bishops and abbots, and hundreds of schoolmen and other clerics, to say nothing of countless others—scribes, simple clerics, actors, musicians, heralds and prostitutes. It seemed, he noted, that one simply encountered "all the world" at Constance.[75] And at the great gathering, one of its most renowned leaders would take up again the concerns of property and community that had been aired in Vienna and Münster.

"Worse than thieves, whores or murderers."
Job Vener at Constance

The royal protonotary and lawyer Job Vener quickly emerged as a leader of the Council of Constance.[76] Vener is well known to only a handful of modern scholars.[77] But by the close of the council his work there had made him one of the most towering and celebrated figures in all of the Empire, if not in all of Christendom. Vener was of such renown that contemporaries simply called him "Lord Job." He even

---

[75] Stump, *The Reforms of the Council of Constance* (above, 12 and n. 31), xiii and n. 3, following Jürgen Miethke, "Die Konzilien as Forum der öffentlichen Meinung," *Deutsches Archiv* 37 (1981): 736–73. See also for general context, Van Engen, "Church in the Fifteenth Century," 312–18.

[76] For overall context, among many relevant works, see Walter Brandmüller, *Das Konzil von Konstanz* (Paderbron, 1991); Stump, *Reforms*; Ivan Hlaváček and Alexander Patschovsky, eds., *Reform von Kirche und Reich: zur Zeit der Konzilien von Konstanz (1414–1418) und Basel (1431–1449): Konstanz-Prager historisches Kolloquium (11.–17. Oktober 1993)* (Constance, 1996), especially Patschovsky's essay, "Der Reformbegriff zur Zeit der Konzilien von Konstanz und Basel," 7–28; Johannes Helmrath, "Reform als Thema der Konzilien des Spätmittelalters," in *Christian Unity. The Council of Ferrara-Florence 1438/9–1989* (Louvain, 1991), 75–153.

[77] Heimpel's *Vener von Gmünd und Strassburg* (above, 67 n. 1) is the only substantial modern study. For general context, see Hartmut Boockmann, "Zur Mentalität spätmittelalterlicher gelehrter Räte," *Historische Zeitschrift* 233 (1981): 295–316.

received four symbolic votes for pope in 1417.[78] A stellar student in the German Nation at Padua, Job had earned highest honors for his "very strong" exams in civil law in 1395. In 1402, after entering the service of King Rupert, he earned a doctorate in canon law. His schooling and service soon propelled him to the leadership of Rupert's court jurists, and upon Rupert's death in 1410, Job remained an advisor to his successor, Ludwig III. Job continued to serve in that capacity until early 1415, when he took up residence at Constance. There he worked as a representative of both Ludwig and the University of Heidelberg. He also served as one of the two presidents of the German Nation at the council. In these roles Job soon found himself a central figure in some of the most crucial and dramatic moments of the era: On July 4, 1415, as King Sigismund sat before the council's fourteenth session, with Carl Malatesta and a host of princes and prelates before him, Vener read aloud the series of official acts that accomplished some of the council's most pressing early tasks: to accept the resignation of Gregory XII through his representatives, and to officially convene the council. Two days later, Vener stood by the scaffold as Jan Hus burned.[79]

Sometime in the same year, Vener composed a treatise on the "vice of property" in the cloister.[80] It was only one of dozens of issues its tireless author had taken up, and only one of countless reform treatises the Constance years produced. But it is a testament to the issue's abiding importance. Years after Henry of Langenstein's sermon at Vienna, and independently of Kerkering's recent work at Münster, the unresolved issues had emerged yet again, this time as the concern of one of the most visible public figures of his generation. Vener's treatise was distinct from its predecessors, however, in important ways. The lawyer avoided all of the theologians' satire and social critique. He would have nothing of Henry's pastoral appeals to the common life, nothing of Dietrich Kerkering's exploration of concrete cases, and nothing at all of Kerkering's open ambivalence. At Constance, all of that seemed somehow hopelessly out of place. Vener instead turned

---

[78] Heimpel, *Vener von Gmünd und Strassburg*, 2: 359 and 374.
[79] For a vivid and detailed description of the events, and of Vener's role in them, see Ibid., 2: 341–44.
[80] The remarkably popular treatise survives in at least sixty-five manuscripts. See the appendix below, no. 21. The treatise is edited in Heimpel, *Vener von Gmünd und Strassburg*, 3: 1269–87.

vigorously to the law, and called for the religious orders to be bound back to the letter of the decrees that governed their estate.

Vener turned first to the decree of Lateran III as it appeared in the *Decretals* (X 3, 35, 2).[81] That text had excommunicated any monk found with *proprium*. It had also denied proper burial and intercession to any monk discovered after death to have concealed property. Vener knew how easily both the legal force of long-held custom and the power of local superiors could tame the force of these laws, so he began by refuting the obvious objections. It was perverse to argue, as so many did, that an abbot could license whatever he wanted to whomever he wanted, or that whatever the abbot licensed was not *proprium* simply because the abbot licensed it.[82] Vener then turned to his next precedent, Innocent III's letter to the monks of Subiaco (X 3, 35, 6). In that text, as noted above, Innocent had said that the vow of poverty was so essential to religious life (*annexa*) that not even the pope himself could dispense with it.[83] And as noted above, in his commentary on the letter, Hostiensis had used Innocent's turn of phrase to reflect on papal power, positive law and dispensation. The jurist's teaching, in effect, had turned Innocent's letter on its head. For Hostiensis, that a vow was joined to religious life (*annexa*) meant that the pope in fact had the absolute power to dispense with it as a matter of positive law. Vener now returned to the pope's original point, making it within a context neither Innocent nor Hostiensis could have imagined. At a great gathering that presumed to pronounce on the disputes of a divided papacy, Vener reminded his fellow reformers of the original meaning of Innocent's letter: Not even the pope could dispense with the vow of poverty. Still less were modern abbots justified in licensing monks across Christendom to enjoy so many cash stipends and worldly goods.

The sermons of theologians such as Henry of Langenstein and Dietrich Kerkering reflected a wider culture of the new piety, one that emphasized inward conversion and penance. Vener's polemic is a reminder, however, of the need to hold reform's spiritual dimensions in

---

[81] See above, 25.
[82] Heimpel, *Vener von Gmünd und Strassburg*, 3: 1269–70.: "Hic apparet, quod abbas nulli monacho poterit aliquid permittere peculii nisi officiali ratione officii sui dispensandi. Quo fallunt, qui dicunt, quod abbas poterit permittere quibus voluerit. Item fallunt, qui dicunt, quod quidquid abbas permiserit, hoc non sit proprium, quia, nisi incaute et male permittere posset proprium, de facto quamvis non de iure utique papa non prohiberet."
[83] See above, 45 ff.

tension with matters of law and estate, of legal and moral order. Only a few years before, Vener himself may have helped Duke Amadeus VIII of Savoy (later elected antipope Felix V in 1439) craft a series of laws restricting excess consumption, along with a range of other moral matters—blasphemy, strict observance of holidays and sabbaths and so on.[84] In a similar mood, Vener and his contemporaries now fought to bind the *proprietarii* of Christendom's cloisters back to the simplicity and modesty that was to govern their estate. The responses varied widely. Wyclif and others had spoken of returning the established order to the "law of Christ," charity and community. Vener's contemporaries in Bohemia vigorously condemned avarice, concubinage and other mortal sins, as "public sins," in the name of a return to strict moral law, and they too placed the ideal of common property at the center of their project. At Constance, where a commission on matters of faith confronted Wyclif's attacks on the religious orders, friars such as Matthew Grabow sought to undermine the legal foundations of the Modern Devotion. To appropriate the common life of the apostles without the binding legal vows of religion, Grabow argued, was both illegal and mortally sinful.[85] The jurist Vener now approached the whole matter of religious vows and common property for himself, this time from the opposite angle—to swear the vows of religion, and then not to uphold them, was also a broken law and a mortal sin. And although that position was in one sense traditional, Vener articulated it with an ostentatious breadth and severity that had few parallels in orthodox reforming discussions of religious life. All propertied monks in Christendom, he argued, were disobedient and recalcitrant violators of their vows, unworthy of even a proper burial. How then could they

---

[84] In 1403, likely inspired by the Observant Dominican preacher Vincent Ferrer, the duke had issued a series of laws restricting excess consumption, along with a range of laws on other moral matters—blasphemy, strict observance of holidays and sabbaths and so on. The laws also regulated the affairs of of Jews in the duke's territory. See the collection of essays *Amédée VIII—Félix V: Premier duc de Savoie et pape (1383–1451). Colloque international, Ripaille-Lausanne, 23–26 octobre 1990*, ed. Bernard Andenmatten and Augusto Paravicini Bagliani (Lausanne, 1992), especially Neithard Bulst, "La législation somptuaire d'Amédée VIII," 191–200 and Rinaldo Comba, "Les *Decreta Sabaudiae* d'Amédée VIII: un projet de société," 179–90. See also Heimpel, *Vener von Gmünd und Strassburg* 2: 694, where it is noted that excerpts from later editions of the statutes are to be found in Vener's personal papers. Heimpel also suggests that that Job may have had a hand in drawing up the original statutes.

[85] John Van Engen, "Illicit Religion: The Case of Friar Matthew Grabow O.P.," in *Law and the Illicit in Medieval Europe*, ed. Ruth Mazo Karras, Joel Kaye, and E. Ann Matter (Philadelphia, 2008), 103–16.

be tolerated among the living? The *proprietarii* were eternally damned, alive or dead, and no offering for their souls could ever be valid.[86] Vener fumed, echoing but also sharpening Peraldus, that the *proprietarii* were worse than thieves, whores or even murderers. At least those mortal sinners might at some time acknowledge their sin, or somehow find themselves not engaged in mortally sinful acts. Of all sinners, only the *proprietarii* were the very embodiment of their sin, and only they blindly and obstinately refused to repent.[87]

Yet beyond the rhetoric, Vener also knew all of the arguments that could be arrayed against his position, and he had to take them seriously. He recognized, for example, the generous and flexible models of community that so many had presumed consistent with canon law. He noted that John Andreae had defined *proprietas* broadly (*largo modo*) as "whatever was concealed from the abbot." Yet that broad definition had allowed abbots and other superiors, through their discretion, to license the enjoyment of all manner of incomes and goods. Vener recast the definition in a way that shifted the debate away from the principle of license toward the intentions of the user. He contended that *proprietas* was simply a "substance that one possesses, by himself or through another, yet in spirit having the thing for himself or defending it as his own insofar as he is able."[88] That stance, as Vener saw it, made better sense of the daily reality: whatever the principles of license and

---

[86] Heimpel, *Vener von Gmünd und Strassburg*, 3: 1270: "Si iustus vir salvabitur, proprietarii ecclesie inobedientes, deo recalcitrantes, propriam professionem violantes et conculcantes, ubi manebunt? Estimo, quod indigni sunt celo, qui propter ecclesiam privantur etiam eo, quod minus est, scilicet cimiterio. Quomodo illum suscipiet terra viventium, cui denegatur terra et sepulchrum mortuorum? Notandum, quod tali denegatur oblatio fidelium et ideo, quia non valeret, si fuerit pro eo exhibita. Et ostendendum, quod totum erit irritum, quidquid fuerit pro eo impensum. Et etiam declarat quod illi in tali statu fuit vita inutilis, mors dampnabilis. Ve illi, quod natus est, quia sive vivat sive moriatur, dampnatus est."

[87] Ibid., 3: 1271: "Hec omnia mala insunt proprietario et ideo proprietarius periclulosissimus est sibi, quia nec luxuriosus nec homicida nec quicumque alius ita malus est, quin aliquando confiteatur peccatum suum vel conteratur ab intra vel proponit aliquando velle cessare vel ad ultimum compellatur eciam cessare propter infirmitatem vel aliqua impedimenta...ergo melius habebunt suspensores, latrones et meretrices quam proprietarius."

[88] Ibid., 3: 1272: "Sed si aliquis interrogat: Quid est proprietas? Respondeo, quod largo modo sumpta per Iohannem Andree diffinitur sic: Proprietas est, ubi quidquid habetur sine licentia. Sed etiam potest haberi cum licentia mala et tamen esse proprium, sicut manifeste colligitur ex subsequentibus.... Ergo secundum alios diffinitur sic et melius: Proprietas est substantia, quam quis possidet per se vel per alium animo tamen pro se habendi vel quantum in ipso est tamquam suum defendendi, sive de licentia hanc habet sive non."

dispensation, most people encountered monks and other religious as figures whose licenses, privileges and attitudes made them unrepentant proprietors of the things they enjoyed. Vener's definition also allowed him to expose the hollow objections that might have been heard in any cloister across the region: "I am not a proprietor," Vener had an interlocutor object, "because I possess nothing, nor have anything in my power (*potestas*), but rather, under the power of the abbot, I have given them to a common reserve."[89] Money and other goods were held by the license of the superior, his opponents countered, and those licensed goods were still community property, to be used virtuously and in accord with good custom. But Vener dismissed even the principles, to say nothing of the practice, as an "abusive custom" that had allowed propertied life to take on grotesque proportions. Indeed, Vener fumed, amid all of these excuses it seemed a monk might have a thousand florins and not be accused of *proprietas*.[90] The essence of the religious life, as Vener saw it, was true community and true "poverty of spirit" that, if transgressed through even the slightest desire for gain or the slightest superfluity, brought mortal sin.

Vener's uncompromising stance was just as evident in the concluding sections of his treatise, where he offered his reading of the thirty-third chapter of the *Rule* of Benedict. There Benedict had said that the monk was to have nothing at all (*nihil omnino*) of his own, but was to "hope for all necessary things from the father of the monastery." Drawing from the language and principles of the canon law passages with which he began, Vener now read Benedict's texts as the *forma vitae* of every religious order.[91] Whether monk, canon or mendicant, male or female, all religious were bound by the obligation to live *sine proprio*, and they were to appropriate for themselves "nothing at all." Similarly, religious prelates and other officials across the orders were to provide only those things necessary for survival or for proper execution of administrative duties. To do otherwise would endanger the souls of their subjects. Not even abbots and other superiors, he argued boldly, could claim anything as their own. They, too, were professed to live *sine*

---

[89] Ibid., 1273: "Quomodo ergo illi excusantur, qui secundum consuetudinem abusivam monasteriorum aliquorum tradunt substantiam, quam possident, ad custodiendum et repetunt, quando volunt, et dicunt: 'non enim sum proprietarius, quia nichil possideo nec in potestate mea habeo quidquam, sed de potestate abbatis dedi ad reservatorium commune.'"

[90] Ibid.: "Nam si huiusmodi traditio valeret et sufficeret, tunc monachus posset habere mille florenos et non esse proprietarius."

[91] Ibid.

proprio, and they therefore had the right only to administer the goods of the church, not the right of ownership or alienation. Even they, their discretion and their powers to license were all subject to the letter of the law, which so clearly prohibited *proprium* among the professed. If not even the pope could allow a monk to have *proprium*, how could a lowly abbot presume to allow himself or his monks to do the same? "But alas today so many allow it," Vener lamented, "and for that, monks, along with their abbots, are all eternally damned."[92]

* * *

The texts explored here have begun to enrich our understanding of a distinct reforming attack on inherited customs of personal property. The emphasis here has been on those "public intellectuals" who attacked that culture from hostile positions outside the ranks of the orders. In part reacting to obvious excesses, in part rejecting a way of life they knew nothing of personally, these authors perceived and represented propertied religious life's circumstance in ways that reflected their own devout vision. In a similar way, a renowned lawyer on an international stage called for a reduction of inherited circumstance to strict obedience to the law, and did so with remarkable breadth and sharpness. The next chapter turns to explore how similar calls to reform took root within the orders themselves. In part, religious remarkably appropriated the outsiders' calls to reform—in their circles the texts surveyed here would remain some of the most widely read treatises of their kind for the remainder of the fifteenth century. But reformers within the orders also independently crafted attacks of their own that were of equal vehemence.

---

[92] Ibid., 1277–78.

CHAPTER THREE

REVOLT FROM WITHIN

By the time Job Vener rose to prominence at the Council of Constance, reformers within the orders had worked for decades to establish key enclaves of reform in central Europe.[1] Already in 1368, in the mountainous lands around his home of Foligno, the Franciscan Paoluccio dei Trinci had established a hermitage at Brugliano, and his Observant Franciscan followers soon claimed houses in the dozens across Italy.[2] In the same years the Augustinian Hermits had begun the reform of their order—most famously in Florence, where a return to discipline intertwined with a return to the ancients under Luigi Marsili and his disciples, among them Coluccio Salutati, Niccolò Niccoli and Roberto de' Rossi.[3] By 1400 Giovanni Dominici had established with his followers a network of Dominican Observant houses across northeastern and central Italy. From that foundation he sternly opposed the humanists' return to the ancients with a call to return to sound moral formation based on sound doctrine. "It is more useful for Christians to plow the earth," so Dominici put it, "than to waste time with pagan books."[4] Benedictines in Italy also renewed their observance, most successfully in small but eager congregations centered on the ancient communities of Subiaco, Farfa and Padua. In these communities, too, there emerged a fruitful interaction between religious and humanist returns to antiquity.[5]

---

[1] For an overview see the literature cited above, 4, nn. 13 and 14.
[2] Duncan Nimmo, "The Franciscan Regular Observance," in *Reformbemühungen und Observanzbestrebungen*, ed. Elm (Berlin, 1989), 189–205 as well as *Reform and Division in the Medieval Franciscan Order, from Saint Francis to the Foundation of the Capuchins* (Rome, 1987). See also Paul Nyhus, "The Franciscans in South Germany 1400–1530: Reform and Revolution," *Transactions of the American Philosophical Society* 65 (1975): 1–47 and "The Franciscan Observant Reform in Germany," in *Reformbemühungen und Observanzbestrebungen*, ed. Elm, 207–17.
[3] Kaspar Elm, "Mendikanten und Humanisten im Florenz des Tre- und Quattrocento. Zum Problem der Legitimierung humanistischer Studien in den Bettelorden," in *Die Humanisten in ihrer politischen und sozialen Umwelt*, ed. R. Stupperich and O. Herding (Bonn, 1976), 51–85, especially 64–67.
[4] Ibid., 55. Cf. Edmund Hunt, ed., *Iohannis Dominici Lucula Noctis*, (Notre Dame, IN, 1940), 252–56.
[5] Elm, "Verfall und Erneuerung," 222–23 and n. 81, with further literature.

To the north, reform took hold along a similar chronological arc. In Bohemia, regular canons at Raudnitz had begun to cultivate patterns of devotion that would nurture the new piety in central Europe.[6] Benedictine reform took hold at Kastl after 1380 and at St. Matthias in Trier after 1420.[7] At Windesheim by 1415, Thomas of Kempen and other regular canons had begun to fashion their own new devotion in dialogue with the Brothers and Sisters of the Common Life.[8] More slowly on the scene, but with lasting success, Dominicans under Raymond of Capua had also begun to lead their order back to pristine observance.[9] The Council of Constance then provided a catalyst for many of these fledgling reforms, especially in the Empire. Among the council's many measures, as Phillip Stump has shown, was a series of decrees focused on religious life.[10] The Council also heard disputes among the Franciscan Observants over whether to establish an independent reforming hierarchy within the order.[11] The council also provided a forum for the orders themselves to advance their own reforms independently. In 1417, a Benedictine chapter gathered at nearby Petershausen set out foundational guidelines for a return to strict observance.[12]

At the heart of these reforms, in ways particular to each of the orders' traditions, was a return to strict observance of religious community. Many of the particulars of that process have eluded sustained analysis, not least because so many details remain buried in the manuscripts. Some scholars have now begun to work toward more complex accounts

---

[6] Zibermayr, "Zur Geschichte der Raudnitzer Reform" (above, 8 n. 23).

[7] Petrus Becker, *Das monastische Reformprogramm des Abtes Johannes Rode von St. Matthias in Trier. Ein darstellender Kommentar zu seinen Consuetudines* (Münster, 1970). See also Becker's essays, "Erstrebte und Erreichte Ziele Benediktinischer Reformen im Spätmittelalter," in *Reformbemühungen und Observanzbestrebungen* ed. Elm, 23–34; and idem, "Benediktinische Reformbewegungen im Spätmittelalter. Ansätze, Entwicklungen, Auswirkungen," in *Untersuchungen zu Kloster und Stift*, ed. J. Fleckenstein (Göttingen, 1980), 167–87. For Kastl, see P. Maier, "Ursprung und Ausbreitung der Kastler Reformbewegung," *Studien und Mitteilungen zur Geschichte der Benediktinerordens* 102 (1991): 75–204.

[8] Van Engen, *Sisters and Brothers* (above, n. 11).

[9] Eugen Hillenbrand, "Die Observantenbewegung in der deutschen Ordensprovinz der Dominikaner," in *Reformbemühungen und Observanzbestrebungen*, ed. Elm, 219–271.

[10] See the discussion of the *Decretales reformationis* in Stump, *Reforms*, 158–67. Stump also briefly notes the place of Vener's *compendium* in this context on 158 and n. 40.

[11] Cf. Nimmo, "Franciscan Regular Observance," in *Reformbemühungen und Observanzbestrebungen*, 199–200 and Nyhus, "Franciscan Observant Reform" in idem, 212–13.

[12] Joseph Zeller, "Das Provinzialkapitel im Stift Petershausen im Jahr 1417. Ein Beitrag zur Geschichte der Reformen im Benediktinerorden zur Zeit des Konstanzer Konzils," *Studien und Mitteilungen zur Geschichte der Benediktinerordens* 41, NF 10 (1921/22): 1–73.

of reform ideologies of community, however, by devoting attention to its specific settings.[13] Building on the material surveyed in chapter two, this chapter offers its own account of the formation of another distinct Observant discourse of reformed community. It explains how reformers in the orders, working both within and beyond the Council of Constance, authored tracts of various lengths that attacked propertied religious of every order, prelates and subjects, men and women alike. In these treatises reforming religious adopted the same divisive tone, the same uncompromising stance, and in some cases the very language of the attacks that had emerged from beyond their ranks with figures such as Job Vener. And in doing so, as many treatises make clear, reformers inspired determined resistance. For decades after Constance, reformers still had to argue their case for the common life at length, even among their own brothers and sisters.

"To vituperate the perverse proprietors"
Reform's Publicist Foundations

At the Council of Constance an anonymous Cistercian attacked propertied religious of every order with remarkably incendiary rhetoric. Whether men or women, prelates or subjects, he argued, they could never be saved. What else but the mortal sin of the "vice of property" fueled the indignation of patrons, princes and parishioners, who now held back their support? What else gave rise to so much fornication and flattery, rebellion and ambition, gluttony and drunkenness?[14] The

---

[13] So, for example, the debates over poverty among Dominican Observants: Bernhard Neidiger, "Der Armutsbegriff der Dominikanerobservanten. Zur Diskussion in den Konventen der Provinz Teutonia (1389–1513)," *Zeitschrift für Geschichte des Oberrheins* 145 (1997): 117–58. See also Michael D. Bailey, "Religious Poverty, Mendicancy, and Reform in the Late Middle Ages," *Church History* 72 (2003): 457–83 and Sabine Von Heusinger, *Der observante Dominikaner Johannes Mulberg († 1414) und der Basler Beginenstreit* (Berlin, 1999).

[14] Heinrich Finke published a working edition of the treatise in his work on the acts of the Council of Constance (incipit: "Reverendissimo"): ACC 4, 671–76. The edition was based on Wolfenbüttel, Cod. Helmst. 1251, from the later fifteenth century. There are two recensions of the treatise. One of these, the recension upon which Finke's edition was based, survives in six manuscripts. More popular was a recension (apparently unknown to Finke) which circulated in subsequent years under the incipit "Manifestum videtur esse." The "Manifestum" recension survives in at least eleven manuscripts. I cite that recension here, from MS Vienna, Schottenkloster, Cod. 320, fols. 194–203. For other manuscripts see the Appendix, nos. 10 and 29. See also Dieter Mertens,

scandal owed much to the leaders of the orders themselves. Many abbots ruled not for the sake of their pastoral charges, but for their own comfort, honor and wealth. Some even welcomed a sorry state of affairs among their monks because it made their prelacy seem all the more holy. Some wanted to preserve pious outward appearances, but they refused to correct the intransigent because they were afraid of being denounced themselves. Weighed down by "a certain inertia and deadly sloth," they simply preferred to keep the peace rather than engage in the hard work of reform.[15] With "pharisaical falsehood," prelates male and female worked to excuse, to "gloss over" and "pervert" the writings and the intentions of the holy fathers. They were outwardly holy but inwardly rotten, and their way of life ensured the damnation of their flock.[16]

By the fifteenth century, calls for reform like these were both increasingly public and shaped by distinct regional landscapes. In England rebels and Wyclifites circulated letters and "bills" (*schedule*) in which they defended their ideas and actions.[17] In Bohemia, Hussites advanced their calls to reform through preaching, vernacular songs, painted images and broadsheets.[18] In a less visible but analogous way, the Council of Constance provided a public forum for reformist discourse in the Empire. Constance is best known for its confrontation with the Great Schism and all the related issues of ecclesiology and reform. But most who attended it experienced the council as an international public gathering

---

"Reformkonzilien und Ordensreform im 15. Jahrhundert," in *Reformbemühungen und Observanzbestrebungen*, ed. Elm, 437–8 and n. 29.

[15] MS Vienna, Schottenkloster, Cod. 320, fol. 195r–v: "Alii dimittunt ex propria perversitate, scilicet qui regimine praelationis non propter subditorum salutem susceperunt aut gerunt, sed propter suum commodum proprium, scilicet propter honores, voluptates et divitias. Alii, ut ipsi minus mali reputentur in sua mala vita in hoc gloriantur et gaudent, quod etiam subditi sui male vivunt...Alii vero.... quadam inertia et mortifera accidia commodum proprium querentes et quietem, neminem super iniquitatibus suis corripere praesumunt."

[16] Ibid., fol. 195r–v: "Hii omnes praclati et praelate...variis deceptionibus et pharisayica fictione divinas scripturas [et] sanctorum patrum intentiones nituntur verbis excusatoriis glosare et pervertere...."

[17] Cf. Kathryn Kerby-Fulton, *Books under Suspicion. Censorship and Tolerance of Revelatory Writing in Late Medieval England* (Notre Dame, IN, 2006), 174–87, here 176.

[18] See František Šmahel, *Die Hussitische Revolution* ed. Alexander Patschovsky, trans. Thomas Krzenck (Hannover, 2002) 1: 509 ff., discussing Hussite reform "propaganda," which included preaching, vernacular songs, wall-paintings and images painted on portable boards. There is also mention (p. 520) of what may have been a broadsheet used by one supporter of Hus. I am grateful to Dr. David Mengel of Xavier University for these references.

of unprecedented breadth and energy, one whose affairs ranged far beyond the familiar issues of reform in head and members. In some forty-seven official sessions, in scores of solemn sermons, countless open disputations and private conversations, the council's leaders, many of them public intellectuals in the mold of Gerson, Vener and others, debated with their many audiences not only the grand issues of conciliar and papal authority, but also a range of more mundane matters. And they did so in a way that was as intensely textual as it was public. As they took up their various positions, council participants energetically wrote, recorded, read and copied all of the arguments with care.[19] They also arranged for the most useful works to be read aloud slowly in open sessions so that others could copy them carefully—a process often termed a *reportatio* or *pronuntiatio*.[20] The same pattern of exchange repeated itself later at Basel. Along with discussion that produced tracts like the *Reformatio Sigismundi*, the council fostered the circulation and publication of the works of D'Ailly, Gerson, Nicholas of Cusa and others; of humanist works; and of popular twelfth-century texts such as Bernard's *De consideratione*. And alongside these more famous works, those who worked at Basel composed, copied and circulated countless other tracts, and even drafts of tracts, on issues great and small.[21]

This wider context helped reformers across the orders fashion a forceful call for a return to the common life. From 1415, drawing from both the work of outsiders and those within their own ranks, Observant religious composed, copied and circulated a flood of treatises attacking the "proprietors" (*proprietarii*). The insult was in one sense, as we have seen, at least as old as Peraldus. But at Constance and beyond, amid wider debates over papal taxation and provisions, simony and clerical morality, the old attack on the *proprietarii* took on new life. Consider the work of the anonymous Cistercian noted above, a sharp and sweeping condemnation of propertied religious, prelates and subjects, men and

---

[19] Helmrath, "Kommunikation auf den spätmittelalterlichen Konzilien" and Miethke, "Die Konzilien as Forum der öffentlichen Meinung," (above, 16 and n. 42). Older, but still useful, is Paul Lehmann, "Konstanz und Basel als Büchermärkte," in *Erforschung des Mittelalters*, ed. idem. (Stuttgart, 1959), 253–80.

[20] Cf. Hobbins, "The Schoolman as Public Intellectual: Jean Gerson and the Late Medieval Tract," esp. n. 117, with further literature. See especially A. I. Doyle, "Publication by Members of the Religious Orders," in *Book Production and Publishing in Britain, 1375–1475*, ed. Jeremy Griffiths and Derek Pearsall (Cambridge, 1989), 109–23.

[21] Miethke, "Die Konzilien as Forum der öffentlichen Meinung," 756–58, notes that at Basel, Nicholas of Cusa's *De concordantia catholica* was published in a draft which John of Ragusa then used as the basis for his own treatise *De ecclesia*.

women alike, across the orders. The manuscripts make clear that his screed was to be "published" (*publicare*) at the council, "in the hopes that it should come to the notice of many."[22] In England Wyclifites attacked "posessioner monks" and "private" religions, while in Bohemia Hussites denounced their priests as "concubinaries." At Constance, in an analogous fashion, reformers within the orders crafted their own slogan, clumsy but effective, to denounce the "proprietors" in their ranks.

The same catch phrase took on new life far beyond the council as well, as other reformers in search of a wider public began craft their own attacks on the *proprietarii*. Just as the anonymous Cistercian unleashed his invective at Constance, in Nuremberg the Augustinian Hermit Conrad Zenn composed the *De vita monastica*, a lengthy manifesto that called for a general reform of the religious orders.[23] The long and cumbersome work ultimately enjoyed only a limited circulation, largely within Zenn's own order. Yet as he composed it around 1415, Zenn hoped his call for reform would reach the broadest possible monastic audience. He addressed it explicitly to "all religious in Christ Jesus," and later readers described the book as having been "published" (*editus*) soon after its composition.[24] Zenn called for the orders to wake from their slumber, to turn sharply away from the world and sharply inward, and to return to the obligations of their estate.[25] He framed the call as a return to the "three essentials" of poverty, chastity and obedience—the model first articulated by Aquinas in quarrels with secular clergy that

---

[22] Cf. Finke, ACC 4: 671, note "d": "In Christo Jesu Domino nostro amen. Compendium de statu religiosorum moderni temporis 1415 in concilio Constanciensi...curavimus sequentem tractatum publicare, optantes, ut perveniat ad notitiam plurimorum."

[23] For a brief overview of Zenn's life and work see BBKL 14 (1998): 410–12. For a brief introduction to the *De vita monastica* see Adolar Zumkeller, "Der *Liber de vita monastica* des Conradus de Zenn O.E.S.A. (†1460) und die Spiritualität der spätmittelalterlichen 'Observantia regularis'," *Rivista Augustiniana* (1992): 921–38. See also idem, "Die Beteiligung der Mendikanten an der Arbeit der Reformkonzilien von Konstanz und Basel," in *Reformbemühungen und Observanzbestrebungen*, ed. Elm, 159–67. For general context, see Adalbero Kunzelmann, *Geschichte der deutschen Augustiner-Eremiten* (Würzburg, 1969) and, more recently, Francis Xavier Martin, "The Augustinian Observant Movement," in *Reformbemühungen und Observanzbestrebungen*, ed. Elm, 325–45. For detailed consideration of Zenn's work see Helmut Zschoch, *Reform und Monastische Spiritualität. Conrad von Zenn (†1460) und Sein Liber de Vita Monastica* (Tübingen, 1988). The *De vita monastica* is unedited. I cite it here from MS Vienna, ÖNB, Cod. 4934 (from 1459), described in Zschoch, *Reform und Monastische Spiritualität*, 51.

[24] Ibid., 55–56.

[25] See Zschoch, *Reform und Monastische Spiritualität*, especially ch. 3.

became standard for many fifteenth-century discussions of religious life. But Zenn's treatise also reflected the more immediate anxieties of his reforming peers at Constance. The purpose of his treatise was, as Zenn put it, to "vituperate the perverse *proprietarii*." He soon made good on that claim. A chain of some fifty chapters denounced the *proprietarii* as thieves, liars, murderers, traitors, flatterers and more, each chapter dedicated to different aspects of their many mortal sins. The commitment impressed Zenn's later readers. One copyist of the *De vita monastica* described its author as "the true enemy of all *proprietarii*, in word and script and deed."[26]

Within a decade another Cistercian known only as the "Poor Monk" sought to reach the same monastic public with the same divisive attacks. This author, too, had published his treatise in Vienna around 1422.[27] He pleaded with anyone considering entry into religious life that they not profess to a superior unworthy of the office, or to any who was not committed to ministering to them and sharing in common all the necessities of daily life.[28] The Cistercian then unleashed an invective against the *proprietarii* that rivaled even the sharpest of his day. In one vivid passage he denounced ingrate monks who thought themselves princes, and who stuffed their belongings into cases and chests, each bound tightly with iron and locks so that no monk stole from another.[29] These miserable *proprietarii*, who blindly defended their ways, were "more unfaithful than any infidel."[30]

Internal textual evidence from these treatises suggests concretely how the textual markets of the Constance era provided reformers the raw materials they needed for crafting their message. The reforming Cistercian treatises noted here, for example (the anonymous Cistercian

---

[26] Ibid., 5 n. 1: "Hunc librum edidit venerandus sacrae theologiae lector Conradus de czenn, pater conventus in Nuremberga...qui omnium proprietariorum verus inimicus semper fuit et hoc vita et moribus ac scriptis suis manifestissime ostendit."

[27] The unedited treatise survives in at least fourteen manuscripts. I take my readings from Vienna, ÖNB Cod. 3700 (see above, 67 and n. 1), fols. 147r–171r, here 149v–150r.

[28] Ibid.: "Ideo hortamur et supplicamus omnes fideles quicumque ordines intraverint ut non audeant profiteri abbatibus sive prioribus sive quibuscumque nisi sint tam [150a] digni et ydonei qui possint et velint omnino neccesaria ministrare et animas earum salvare verbis et exemplis per doctrinam Christi."

[29] Ibid., fol.167v: "Quare ergo nunc monachi per universa fere monasteria tronas et cistulas fero fortissime circumligatas et optimis feris iniunctas possident?"

[30] Ibid.: "Quia dicunt ideo archam et thecam habeo ut mihi concessa et data ibi ab infidelibus fratribus et extraneis furibus contuear et custodiam. Sed audi tu qui talia dicis proprietarie. Audi et considera quod infidelior es omnibus infidelibus."

treatise aired at Constance and the treatise of the Poor Monk published in Vienna in 1422) are only two of several tracts against the *proprietarii* that shared extensive common textual ground with the address Job Vener delivered at Constance. Both Vener's treatise and the anonymous Cistercian treatise, for example, discuss the problem of the abbot's license in a very similar way, and at one point with precisely the same words.[31] Other passages from one recension of the treatise (omitted in the printed edition of the Constance sources but available through another manuscript) reveal further parallels—again both treatises lament the excesses of license, and they also expose the fallacies of their opponents' arguments in almost identical language.[32] Extensive comparison reveals that these texts are by no means copies of one another. They have completely different structures and lines of argument. But they also share long passages in which the texts are nearly identical. It is possible the parallels had their origins in a common *pronuntiatio* of Vener's work at Constance, the various copies of which then found their way independently into each recension of the anonymous Cistercian treatise. Conversely, because the anonymous Cistercian treatise appears to have been "published" at the council in order to reach a broad audience, it is also possible that Vener borrowed from that treatise to shape his own arguments. Only the evidence of full, critical editions of these treatises could definitively resolve the uncertainty. For current purposes, it is sufficient to note their common textual ground as evidence of the

---

[31] To note only one of several examples (parallel passages are capitalized): "Manifestum", ed. Finke, ACC, 6:674: "Dicunt aliqui monachi: 'Res, quas habeo speciales, abbas meus dedit vel permisit michi, ergo non pecco,' false et perverse intelligentes et allegantes auctoritatem regule: 'Nichil licet habere monacho, quod abbas non dederit aut permisit.' Quibus videtur, quod abbas nulli monacho permittere peculii nisi racione amministracionis cuilibet, prout unicuique opus est. ERGO FALLUNT, QUI DICUNT, QUOD ABBAS POTERIT PERMITTERE, QUIBUS VOLUERIT, ET QUIBUS NOLUERIT. ITEM FALLUNT, QUI DICUNT, QUOD QUIDQUID ABBAS PERMISERIT, HOC NON SIT PROPRIUM, QUIA, NISI INCAUTE ET MALE PERMITTERE POSSET PROPRIUM DE FACTO, QUAMVIS NON DE IURE, UTIQUE PAPA ET ECCLESIA NON PROHIBERET." Cf. Vener, ed. Heimpel, 3:1269: "Habemus enim Extra *De statu monachorum primo* in hec verba in capitulo, quod sic incipit *Monachi*...[X 3, 35, 2]. Hic apparet, quod abbas nulli monacho poterit aliquid permittere peculii nisi officiali ratione officii sui dispensandi. QUO FALLUNT, QUI DICUNT, QUOD ABBAS POTERIT PERMITTERE QUIBUS VOLUERIT. ITEM FALLUNT, QUI DICUNT, QUOD QUIDQUID ABBAS PERMISERIT, HOC NON SIT PROPRIUM, QUIA, NISI INCAUTE ET MALE PERMITTERE POSSIT PROPRIUM, DE FACTO QUAMVIS NON DE IURE PAPA NON PROHIBERET. Et si dicunt, quod hoc loquitur contra peculium."

[32] Cf. MS Vienna, Schottenkloster, Cod. 320, fol. 196r with Vener, ed. Heimpel, 3:1277.

way in which the Constance environment helped shaped the reformers' attack on the "vice of property."

Other textual raw material for many of these tracts was to be found in William Peraldus' foundational treatments of the "vice of property."[33] Fifteenth-century Europe was awash in treatises of all kinds on virtues and vices, many of them compiled from excerpts of the works of Peraldus and others.[34] In keeping with that general trend, Observant publicists adapted Peraldus' teachings to their particular circumstance. To convince his audience that the *proprietarii* were the "worst kind of sinners," for example, the anonymous Cistercian at Constance appropriated nearly all of the rubrics Peraldus had provided in his *Summa*, in virtually the same order: The *proprietarii* were idolaters and thieves, lovers of sacrilege, perjurers and so on. Moreover, in each case the Cistercian cited most of the authorities available to him from Peraldus' text.[35] Soon after Constance, the anonymous Cistercian's brother in Vienna appropriated the same texts: the Poor Monk devoted a series of his chapters to all of the evils of the *proprietarii* as Peraldus had presented them, for example, in the Dominican's original sequence, but the Poor Monk elaborated on each more fully than had his predecessors. Conrad Zenn appropriated Peraldus as well, often using the Dominican preacher's standard epithets—thief, blasphemer, liar and so on—but also creating new rubrics that seem to have been of his own design.[36]

Zenn and his contemporaries did more, however, than merely recycle the older texts. They sharpened the tone of their material in ways that were almost without precedent. For Zenn the *proprietarii* were sacrilegious drunks "who shamefully wasted Christ's patrimony in taverns with whores."[37] Like a malformed sculpture that could be broken but not remade, propertied monks might be killed, but they could not be redeemed. No good deed, not even baptism itself, could save them.[38] Zenn's reforming zeal here led him onto dangerous theological ground,

---

[33] See above, 26.

[34] Richard Newhauser, *The Treatise on Vices and Virtues in Latin and in the Vernacular*, Typologie des Sources du Moyen Âge Occidental 68 (Turnhout, 1993), esp. 135–52.

[35] MS Vienna, Schottenkloster, Cod. 320, fols. 199v–200r.

[36] MS Vienna, ÖNB, Cod. 4934, fol. 61ra, c. 55.

[37] Ibid., fol. 52r: "partimonium crucifixi in tabernis cum meretricibus turpiter expendunt."

[38] Ibid., fol. 59v: "Proprietarii infideles sunt, quia fidem deo promissa franguunt.... Qui enim fidem perdit nihil plus perdere potest, et quamdiu cum proprio vivit neque baptismus [60r] neque elemosina quantacumlibet copiosa neque mors pro nomine Christi assumpta...nihil poterit proficere ad salutem."

and contemporaries noticed it. As one of its manuscripts relates, the *De vita monastica* had inspired a "new sect" of slanderers and pompous schoolmen who denounced Zenn's reform as foolishness that flirted with heresy.[39]

Reformers also deployed their material in ways that reflected their own era's communalist anxieties over "modern" domestic arrangements. By 1400 many had come to denounce lords, secular and ecclesiastical, who had retreated into the refined, secluded comfort of their private rooms.[40] Anonymous monks in the Constance era advanced similar critiques against the *proprietarii* who had appropriated community space. Recounting what he called a series of "modern miracles," the Cistercian "Poor Monk" told a story he had heard about a Benedictine monastery in the Rhineland.[41] In that community the more powerful and "better" brothers had contended with one another over separate living and sleeping quarters that were more "delightful" and "charming" than the rest (*delectabilior et venustior*). As a result of the discord the abbot had condemned that particular place, and had forbidden any brother to stay there. Nevertheless, the bursar, who saw himself as superior to the others, confidently appropriated it for himself. Soon after, in the dead of night, horrid noises began to echo through the abbey, startling the brothers from their sleep. They lit their lamps and looked all through the dormitory for the source. Finally they came to the bursar's appropriated cell. They heard the horrible cries of beasts within, and they dared not enter. Instead they gathered for prayer until the noises died away. After a long silence they entered, finding the bursar's miserably mutilated body drawn out on the stone floor. The monks later buried the corpse of their damned brother far from consecrated ground.

Inseparable from these attempts to demonize the *proprietarii* was the attempt to bind their excess back to the letter of the laws that governed the religious estate. Consider the anonymous Cistercian treatises noted above, which juxtaposed reforming appeals to the spirit with echoes of the jurist Job Vener. Both treatises appropriated Vener's citations from the *Decretals* and its commentaries, for example, especially Innocent

---

[39] Zschoch, *Reform und Monastische Spiritualität*, 67–68 and nn. 88, 89 and 93. The texts are from a later "supplement" to the *De vita monastica*, identified by Zschoch but unavailable to me.

[40] Dyer, *Standards of Living*, 106.

[41] The exemplum appears in chapter twenty three of his treatise (MS Vienna, ÖNB, Cod. 3700, fols. 154v–156r).

III's famous letter to Subiaco (X 3, 35, 6) and the Lateran decree condemning property (X 3, 35, 2).[42] In these works, and in most others like them, passages from the *Decretals* provided an arsenal of pithy "proof texts" for reformers to deploy in all of their engagements with their propertied antagonists. More rarely, compilers also grounded their arguments in laws particular to their own orders. The Cistercian "Poor Monk," for example, cited or paraphrased relevant passages from Pope Benedict XII's Cistercian legislation. He also cited relevant measures from "provincial statutes," including the stipulation that those who resisted reform openly could be thrown into prison.[43]

The marriage of reform and law is perhaps nowhere more visible, however, than in Conrad Zenn's *De vita monastica*. Zenn lamented those religious who resisted reform as "transgressors of the law of God," and denounced those who embraced the "crime of property."[44] To prove his case Zenn turned to the same texts Vener had used at Constance: the stern prohibitions of Innocent III, enshrined in the *Decretals*, and all of John Andreae's glosses. Zenn's devout legalism was even more forceful in his attacks on incompetent, negligent prelates. In a series of lengthy and challenging passages grounded in church law he equated the propertied prelates of the orders with the evil leaders of Christian history. They were like the Amalekites, whom God had commanded Saul to slay from the greatest to the least. They were like the evil men who tried to seduce and defame the pious Susanna, wife of Joachim. They were like Gehazi, who secretly took money from a soldier his master Elisha had healed of leprosy. They were like Ananias and Saphira, who paid with their lives for concealing property from the apostles.[45]

Conrad then unleashed his fiercest condemnations on the indulgence preachers of his day. He grounded the attack in several major precedents—decrees of Innocent III, Clement IV and Clement V.[46] From these texts Zenn drew up an exhaustive list of general points. Indulgence preachers were not to work in a given diocese without authorization from the papacy itself, and they were not to offer indulgences beyond what had been granted in official letters. As preachers they were to

---

[42] Cf. MS Vienna, ÖNB, Cod. 3700, fol. 152v, for example, with Heimpel, *Vener von Gmünd und Strassburg*, 3: 1271.
[43] Ibid., fol. 156a.
[44] Vienna, ÖNB, Cod. 4934, fol. 50va.
[45] Ibid., fols. 89r–v.
[46] For the precedents see: X 5, 38, 14 (CIC II: 888); VI 5, 2, 11 (CIC II: 1074); V 5, 9, 2 (CIC II: 1190).

be modest and discrete men. They were not to spend time in taverns and other suspect places; they were not to be wasteful or excessive in their expenses; they were not to preach while seeking their "charitable subsidies"; they were to advertise their indulgences only as they were licensed; and they were not to issue indulgences of their own accord or absolve anyone from perjury, murder or other sins. Nor were the preachers to remit sins according to the amount of money they had received.[47] Zenn then concluded his attack with a remarkable discussion of those he termed the "arch-proprietors"—prelates and other "sly officials," as well as "clever limitors" who licensed abusive indulgence campaigns. Zenn's discussion had wandered far from the "vice of property" as Peraldus and the others had traditionally framed it. There was no discussion here of the cash prebends, private rooms and so on that had inspired most discussions of the theme. Yet somehow in Zenn's mind these prelates were nevertheless the worst of the worst proprietors. In every religious order, these prelates and their followers "secretly planted their poison seeds of property" in the hearts of the professed. "Alas, alas!" Conrad cried, "it pains me to say it, how many of these sly beggars, obstinate proprietors, heed neither the church law nor the monastic law."[48] He then cited in detail all of the canons from the *Decretals* that condemned their excesses and abuses.

Zenn and his fellow reformers had begun to reduce the complexity of modern customs of property to sharp denunciations of "proprietors." They had begun to use that slogan effectively to accuse propertied religious in every order of mortal sin, and to bind their estate back to the letter of the law.[49] In doing so they had crafted a call to reform that was clearly something more complex than a benign recovery, within each order, of religious rules and monastic spirituality. To enrich that complexity further still, the analysis now turns to those who defended the old ways amid all of the attacks.

---

[47] MS Vienna, ÖNB, Cod. 4934, fol. 89v.

[48] Ibid., fol. 90v: "Hew, hew dolenter loquor plurimi versuti quaestioniarii, proprietarii obstinati, nec ecclesiasticam nec monasticam legem advertunt...."

[49] Vienna, ÖNB, Cod. 4934, fol. 92v: "Parcite, obsecro, omnes dominum timentes, ire mee, eo quod ad hoc me cogerunt adversarii regularis vite in hunc finem, ut hii peniterent et salvarentur."

"For such a long time that there is no memory of things being otherwise"
Property and Community between Custom and Vice

Around 1405, the Dominican Observant Giovanni Dominici wrote a tract attacking his order's culture of personal property. A veteran reformer of Dominican life in Venice and across northern Italy, Dominici had heard all of the arguments arrayed against him, and he began by rehearsing them in detail. One of the first and most forceful appealed to the ideal of good custom. The Dominicans justly enjoyed not only the licensed use of goods, so the argument ran, but even outright ownership (*dominium civile*), both corporate and individual. Indeed, for a hundred years and more, Dominici's antagonists boldly claimed, the universally approved custom (*consuetudo*) of their order had been one of vigorous commerce. The preachers bought and sold books among themselves and provided for their needs from the profits; they earned wages as singers, administrators and cooks; they argued in the courts, contending with their own prelates to win what they were owed; they even went to any length to get the quality clothing their status demanded.[50]

Dominici was shocked by these arguments, and they do seem strikingly at odds with most notions of an ideal religious community. But read carefully, Dominici's representation of his opponents' position

---

[50] For basic orientation to Dominici's career and works see Thomas Kaeppeli, ed., *Scriptores ordinis praedicatorum medii aevi*, 4 vols. (Rome, 1970–1993), 2: 406–13. Dominici's treatise, *De proprio*, is summarized in Gabrielle Maria Löhr, "Die Mendikantenarmut im Dominikanerorden im 14. Jahrhundert. Nach den Schriften von Johannes Dambach, O.P. und Johannes Dominici, O.P.," *Divus Thomas. Jahrbuch für Philosophie* (1940): 385–427. There is no edition of the *De proprio*. For manuscripts see Kaeppeli, *Scriptores*, #2283. I have consulted MS Bamberg, Staatsbibliothek, Theol. 117, fols. 201r–251r, here fols. 203ra–b: "Caritas enim, de qua scriptum est quod non querit que sua sunt, sic intelligitur quia communia propriis non propria communibus anteponit.... Ex tollerata consuetudine ordinis antedicti vendunt fratres et emunt a centum annis et citra, sicut patet per acta capitulorum generalium, libros sibi mutuo et etiam personis extraneis, et pretium cum lucro in res alias prout eis videtur communantur. Quinymmo repetunt alter ab altero debita sibi, ita quod etiam in capitulis tam generalibus quam provincialibus publici iudices ponuntur ad tales causas audiendas et per diffinitivam sententiam reddendum unicuique quod suum est, non tamen inter subditum et subditum sed inter subditos et suos prelatos, tamquam prelati non habeant potestatem super rebus temporalibus subditorum suorum aliam quam habeant priores et consules civitatum super rebus civium suorum quibus legitime praesunt. Hic petit sibi debitum quia fuit cantor vel officialis honoratus. Ille quia infirmatus de propria beneficia sibi subvenit, alter quoniam libros ligavit vel reparavit domum seu coquus fuit per annum, alius quoniam ambulavit in servitium conventus. Nonnulli petunt solitas vestes usque ad campanas pro pinguiore usurpantes." Löhr briefly noted this passage, but offered no sustained analysis of its significance.

provides a glimpse of the competing visions of community with which reformers had to contend. By 1400 a long Aristotelian tradition had upheld ownership as natural to the human condition, cash as a medium and measure of justice, and commerce as a marker of charity and community.[51] And a long-standing Dominican tradition had stressed the importance of inner virtue and higher ends with respect to material goods. In keeping with those principles, it seems, Dominici's opponents "bought and sold books among themselves and with other persons, and converted the price, with a profit, for other things." Dominici's opponents also seem to have deployed civic analogies to explain their circumstance, arguing their propertied brothers were "citizens" of a community whose priors were good "magistrates." In general and provincial chapters, the Dominicans argued, public judges had been brought in to hear property disputes among the brothers, "as if the prelates had no other power over the temporal goods of their subjects than do priors and consuls of cities over their subjects." Within the confines of the corporation, each pursued his own: "Here one seeks what is owed him because he was a singer or an honored official; this one because he was ill and supported himself from his own funds." All of it, Dominici's opponents presumed, was an expression of the common life of the apostles, who as they saw it had disposed of both personal property and cash "in abundance."[52] This was clear from the fourth chapter of the book of *Acts*, which told how "None who possessed anything presumed to say that it was their own, but all things were common to them." The propertied Dominicans took this to mean that the early apostles had possessed their goods individually, and that each had guarded their own "portions" in the spirit of the common good (*et quilibet suam portionem custodiebat, licet pro utilitate communi*).[53] In the same way, modern Dominicans enjoyed cash in notable amounts in order to meet the frequent and considerable expenses incumbent upon them as pastors, preachers and teachers. They had to send letters, buy books and make payments to other convents; they had to give pittances and *munuscula* (the same courtesy gifts that Henry of Langenstein had said

---

[51] Cf. Kaye, *Economy and Nature* (above, 76 and n. 36), 45 ff. and 168–69.

[52] MS Bamberg, Staatsbibliothek, Theol. 117, fol. 204vb: "Primo quod licet eis multas habere pecunias. Apostoli affluebant denariis, ergo et isti debent similiter. Consequentiam nota, quia, ut sepius dictum, et hii sunt imitatores eorum."

[53] Ibid.: "Hic habes quod nullus erat egens inter eos et quilibet suam portionem custodiebat, licet pro utilitate communi."

were so beloved of the canons at Klosterneuburg); they had often to provide for their own food and always for their own clothing, because only the most economically secure convents were able to provide both; and they had to lay out considerable expenses for advancement within the church, since without promotion to higher ranks, their preaching and counsel met only with disdain.[54]

Dominici rehearsed his opponents' arguments in a way that distorted and weakened each. But even his hostile representations are consistent with the arguments of another Dominican, Raymond Cabasse of Montpellier, who around 1400 rose in defense of his order's way of life. The occasion for the treatise is not known, but in one key passage Cabasse argued vigorously for the legitimacy of his fellow Dominicans' personal enjoyment of cash stipends. The cornerstone of the defense, again, was the legal force of long-held custom. So powerful was good custom's authority for this Dominican that, as Aquinas himself had taught, it interpreted and even abolished written law.[55] And for Cabasse, as for so many before him, custom's authority was perhaps nowhere more visible than in Christendom's routines of prayer and provision. From time out of mind, the faithful had brought endowments to churches of every kind to support all aspects of the divine cult. The Dominicans, as Cabasse saw it, therefore fully and legitimately participated in that same universal custom, one long ago approved by Innocent III and enshrined in the *Decretals*, in ways that brought them the personal enjoyment of cash incomes and other goods. "For such a long time that there is no memory of things being otherwise," Cabasse wrote,

---

[54] Ibid., fol. 205rb: "...sine pecunia non parva ad sui status perfectionem pervenire non possunt. Nam oportet eos insequi litteras toto orbe fugientes; libros ubique emere et maxime peregrinos, cum non ubique vigeat idem studium; conventibus extraneis contributiones solvere; pictantias repertis constudentibus facere; non parva munuscula donare; sibi de victu aliqualiter et de vestitu integraliter providere cum id non valeant conventus donec fuerunt largis possessionibus farciati. Ad ultimum cogitur non modicum eas exponere pro gradibus assequendis sine quibus verbum dei praedicatum et consilia data videntur hodie cum nausea vilependi. Sic ergo videtur quod sine magnis pecuniis fratres non valeant predicando et consulendo saluti animarum intendere, quod est praecipuus finis eroum."

[55] The treatise *Utrum sit licitum fratribus praedicatoribus tenere possessiones et redditus perpetuos*, Cabasse's only surviving work, is noted briefly in Löhr, "Die Mendikantenarmut," (above, n. 50), 415 n. 1. There is no edition. For its three surviving manuscripts see Kaeppeli, *Scriptores* 3: 280 (# 3390). I have consulted MS Florence, Bib. Naz. J.10.51, fols. 218r–225r, here fol. 219r–v: "Et dicit sanctus Thomas *prima secundae q. 97 articulo tertio* in corpore articuli: Consuetudo habet vim legis, et legem abolet, et est legum interpretatrix."

the preachers had disposed of land, tithes and other corporate wealth. They had also individually disposed of pensions, mass stipends and other pious donations, all brought to them by popes, kings, princes and common folk alike. The Dominicans had enjoyed these things without controversy for generations, "and no procurator of the pope or other lord of whatsoever rank" had prohibited them.[56] Indeed, if some now refused to pay what they owed the order, the papacy compelled them to do so.[57]

It is possible to dismiss all of this as feeble rationalization, but to do so robs Cabasse's argument of its original force. Cabasse must have encountered the wider culture of property outlined in previous chapters, along with all of its excesses. But he refused either to focus on the excesses alone, or to declare propertied life morally bankrupt. On the contrary, he grounded a dynamic, forward-looking reconciliation of personal incomes and religious community in an appeal to one of Christendom's most venerable legal principles. Whatever their origins, Cabasse vigorously defended his order's patterns of ownership as the mature expression of a wise and prudent adaptation to circumstance.

And that adaptation, because it had been sanctioned over so long a time, had now taken on legally binding force. Even if it were true (though Cabasse would not concede the point) that the founders of his order had not intended the Dominicans to own land, rents and personal incomes, times had changed. His brothers were now allowed these things so they could advance Dominic's ultimate ideal, a thriving order of students, teachers and preachers.[58] Indeed, Cabasse here noted, the

---

[56] MS Florence, Bib. Naz. J.10.51, fol. 219v: "Hec vero consuetudo omni iure est praescripta, quia a tanto tempore citra quod de opposito non est memoria habuerunt, tenuerunt et tenent possessiones et pensiones perpetuas et anniversaria et census in pluribus conventibus, et communiter in quolibet conventu pensiones annuales pro missis celebrandis, quas concesserunt reges et principes in suis terris...et alii fideles quam plures dimiserunt legata pia perpetua pro ornamentis et fabrica ecclesie conservanda, et pro fratrum necessitatibus in victualibus sublevandis."

[57] Ibid.: "Et fratres tenuerunt et tenent pacifice absque conditione...et nullus procurator pape vel alteri domini cuiuscumqe status eos impedivit; quinymmo si feodarii solvere recusarent, per officiales dominii nostri fratribus praedicatoribus ministrabatur iusititia et cogebantur feodarii ad solvendum. Ex quo apparet quod hoc consuetudo est legitime praescripta et per consequens est servanda."

[58] Ibid., fol. 224v: "...stante tempore ut est...id quod rationabiliter et iuste tunc per magistrum ordinis fuit ordinatum nunc rationabiliter per fratres mutatum est in melius, scilicet ut ordo in suo essentia servetur et fratres plenius possint predicationi verbi dei intendere et ita inrupta perfectione servetur beati Dominici fundatoris ordinis finalis intentio."

Church itself taught that obedience to outmoded laws was especially to be abandoned if blind adherence to them ultimately brought about the opposite intention of the legislators.[59] The best authority here was Aquinas himself, who argued in the *Summa* that it was licit to act against the letter of the law in cases where this was the only way to preserve the intent of the lawmaker, or where keeping the law ran counter to that intent.[60] Moreover, because the alms the Dominicans received had fallen so much that the brothers could hardly live from them, it was necessary that the preachers insist on something "secure and owned" to ensure sufficient support for their preaching and study.[61]

Cabasse's reasoning here suggests one Dominican's perception of the struggles of many religious corporations in the wake of the Black Death. His remarks also suggest something of the agency and creativity with which religious engaged that struggle. For Cabasse, the Dominican order was not in crisis. It was heir to an evolving way of life whose customs had become legally sanctioned by the passage of time. Even if there were somehow a dispute about the validity of the customs in question, Cabasse pointed out, the *Decretals* were clear that the status quo was to be preserved until the issue could be resolved by authority (*pendente probatione*). All the more ought the Dominicans' customs be preserved, Cabasse argued, because they had occasioned no dispute at all. Pontiffs and princes had not only approved but had themselves endowed the pensions and rents in question from time out of mind.[62] As Cabasse noted, citing a popular aphorism from the *Decretals*,

---

[59] Ibid.: "Hoc enim fiendum per ordinum rectores suo exemplo ecclesia docet. Nam quod ecclesia uno tempore sancte et iuste ordinavit alio tempore, cum subesset causa, aliud ordinat et disponit."

[60] Ibid.: "Et confirmatur *dicto sancti Thome prima secunde q. 96 articulo sexto*, ubi querit utrum liceat subditis legi agere contra legem. Et respondet quod in casu in quo oporteat aut infringere legem ut servetur perfecte legislatoris intentio aut legem servando ex legis observatione contrarium evenire illius quod legislator intendit, tunc licitum est subditis facere contra verba legis."

[61] Ibid.: "Et quia elemosine cottidiane sunt adeo parve quod decima pars fratrum non viverent ex eis congruenter, ideo ut fratres possint intendere praedicationi (quae est finis praecipuus propter quod beatus Dominicus instituit ordinem), oportet quod fratres habeant aliquid certum et proprietarium pro necessariis vitae subportandis; quia aliter non possunt nec possent studio vacare et predicationi intendere, et ideo nisi haberent possessiones perpetuas, neccessario ordo deficeret et praedicatio periret."

[62] Ibid., fol. 220r: "…probatione pendente non debent privari a sua possessione, ergo si pendente probatione praescriptionis debent teneri in sua possesione, a fortiori praescriptione probata consuetudinis tenebitur possessio. Iure ergo consuetudinis rationabilis et praescripte fratres praedicatores possunt tenere possessiones et pensiones

"He who remains silent appears to consent."[63] The remark highlights the importance of properly reading the long silences between the periodic condemnations of scandalous, propertied excess.

The scandals remained a part of everyday life, to be sure, and there were frequent condemnations of excess: Around the time Cabasse wrote, the Dominican general chapter gathered at Nuremberg complained of the brothers' drinking and gambling; their clamorous late-night songs and music; their games of chess and dice; their singing and other dissolute behavior in public; the lewd images of women in the brothers' private rooms. The chapter also denounced brothers who wore habits with slashed sleeves, belts, silver knives and other "costly and curious" ornaments.[64] Defenders of custom were fully aware of that kind of excess, however, and they worked to keep it distinct, in principle, from the modest, virtuous, professional enjoyment of cash incomes and worldly goods. Cabasse himself was very careful to point out that custom was no excuse for sin. He denounced his brothers who lived contrary to their rules and constitutions, enjoying a delicate life amid gold and silver treasures and abundant clothing, slothfully scorning the study and preaching that was the end of their profession.[65] But whatever the excesses, in their absence a tacit approval had long justified the virtuous disposition of cash incomes and goods.

Cabasse's arguments were consistent with wider understandings of good custom, not as something backward-looking or static, but as the mature expression of a long-established, evolving tradition. Romanists would soon defend communion in one kind against the Utraquists, for example, in analogous terms. Communion in one kind, so one defender of the practice argued, was the inheritance of a "modern" church whose long-held observance had been in place since the days of Pope

---

perpetuas. Et non solum permiserunt sed etiam fundaverunt dictis fratribus papa sive plures summi pontifices et reges et principes pensiones et annuos proventus."

[63] Ibid., fol. 220v: "Et confirmatur *De regulis iuris libri sexto*, 'Qui tacet consentire videtur.' Patet ergo quod posito tamen non concesso quod de iure non conveniret fratribus praedicatoribus habere perpetuos redditus et census annuos, quod hoc est eis licitum, cum de iure possunt eas tenere ratione consuetudinis rationalis et praescripte, ut patet ex dictis."

[64] Frühwirth 3: 121–22.

[65] Ibid., fol. 225r: "Voluit insuper tollere a fratribus possessiones et redditus superfluos, ne plene satiati intumescentes recalcitrarent et nollent praedicationi insistere, prout nonnulli fratres qui contra regulam et constitutiones aurum et argentum, iocalia et vestes habunde, decliciose viventes, studium contempnunt nec praedicationi intendere volunt."

Sylvester, or at least "for a couple of hundred years." Across that time, communion in one kind had become a "laudable and approved custom," one "introduced by the church," and one observed "for a very long time." It had therefore taken on the force of law. Communion in both kinds was the product of a primitive church, in a time when everything had been done "in a simpler and grosser way"—baptism had been performed with ordinary water, liturgies had been simpler, and so on.[66] In contrast, defenders of the custom of communion in one kind shared what Howard Kaminsky called a "confident acceptance of the existing order of civilization."[67] Like Cabasse and the Dominicans who defended their order's propertied ways, Romanists invoked good custom not in the name of blind obedience to the past, but in the name of progress and common sense. That same vision, moreover, was not inconsistent with inherited assumptions about status and its sensibilities. Consider how the Franciscan William Woodford had responded to John Wyclif's attacks on clerical dominion.[68] If what Wyclif said were true, what of the bishop's feasts and his magnificent horses? What of the sumptuous palaces and churchly splendor of bishops and religious prelates alike, their crowds of servants, their great halls and chambers and treasures, all of which secular lords also enjoyed? Surely to renounce all of that was not only too harsh, but repugnant to natural reason. For Woodford it was simply part of the natural order that priests and prelates, just as much as their noble peers beyond the clerical ranks, should represent themselves with the outward magnificence that marked their place in society. The same imperative had led Pope Benedict XIII to grant a Franciscan, the son of the count of Foix, an annual revenue of one thousand francs. It was essential that the friar be maintained in a manner appropriate to his family's *status*.[69]

Defenders of the established order continued to advance their arguments even amid the invectives of the Constance era. Soon after his anonymous brother wrote the pamphlet against the vice of property noted above, another Cistercian responded in defense of the principles of license.[70] Professed religious who enjoyed money for the purchase of

---

[66] Howard Kaminsky, *A History of the Hussite Revolution* (Berkeley, 1967), 117.
[67] Ibid. See also the arguments reproduced on 118–19, n. 71.
[68] Eric Doyle, "William Woodford's *De dominio civili clericorum* against John Wyclif" *Archivum Franciscanum Historicum* (1973): 49–109, here 106–7.
[69] Kaminsky, "Estate" (above, 33 n. 24), 690.
[70] The treatise is printed Mansi 28: 395–400. Cf. Mertens, "Reformkonzilien und Ordensreform," (above, 99 n. 14) 437 and n. 29. The section of the treatise in Mansi

clothing, wine, meat, fish and the like, or who enjoyed a private cell, he argued, did so fully in accord with church law and monastic tradition. He cited a canon of Gratian's *Causa* 28, Question 2, for example, a text that insisted "no monk...should presume through impulse of ambition or vanity to construct a cell without the permission of the bishop or the will of the abbot."[71] The implication was clear: abbots had the power to allow their subjects, through tacit or explicit consent, or simply out of kindness, to have private cells. By the same power abbots granted permission for the enjoyment of cash, food, clothing and other needs. Crucially, this Cistercian attacked excessive liberality as vigorously as he defended the ideal of virtuous use. It was nonsense for the professed to have unlimited use of material things, even if held at the pleasure of their superiors and in the name of their community. That was no different than living in the world.[72] But excess and abuse, which were of course to be corrected, were beside the point.[73] Superiors retained the right to grant license for proper personal use of incomes and goods. Indeed, when licensed and used properly, personal goods preserved peace and concord among the professed, and prevented the outbreak of scandal, as Gratian himself had taught.[74] There followed a citation of Aquinas, who had argued that true poverty was in any case interior and spiritual. The abdication of ownership was meant first, and most importantly, as a "preparation of the soul," an instrument for inner perfection, not as an end in itself.[75]

Others defended the established order in less principled ways—and in ways that perhaps reflected the knee-jerk reactions of an all-too-ordinary rank and file. Some argued that they had never been made aware of such a strict stance on the vow to live in community. They

---

seems to be a defense of inherited custom, one perhaps excerpted from a reforming tract written by the Carthusian Henry of Cosfeld († 1410).

[71] C. 18 q. 2 c. 14 (CIC I: 833): "Nullus monachus, congregatione monasterii derelicta, ambitionis et vanitatis inpulsu cellulam construere sine episcopi permissione vel abbatis sui voluntate presumat."

[72] Mansi 28. 395: "Etiam non videtur differentia quoad hoc inter personam monasticam, quae diceret prelato suo: 'Illa sunt vestra seu monasterii, et post mortem meam cedant monasterio,' et tamen ad usum fructum reservaret, et inter personam secularem, quae dominium omnium bonorum suorum resignasset, et tamen usum fructum sibi reservasset. Quod nullus credo sane mentis diceret."

[73] Ibid.: "Si vero sunt aliqui abutentes, corrigantur et praemoneatur. Si vero non volunt corrigi et emendari, sic poterit abbas propter abusum tollere usum."

[74] Ibid., 400.

[75] Ibid., 397.

had professed to the "modern" way of life, not to some hopelessly impractical dream of living like the ancient fathers.[76] Others scoffed at the impossibly harsh condemnation of ancient and venerable way of life, in its entirety, as the embodiment of mortal sin. How could a brother's precious soul, purchased through Christ's death and resurrection, be so easily damned over the slightest temporal thing? What of those who drew from their personal incomes to give to the poor? What of those who had served their orders so honorably for so many years? What of their singing in the choir, their work in erecting altars or restoring churches? Did their sacrifice merit damnation? Still others who resisted reform did so with an even more unrepentant indifference. These "lost and desperate" souls, as the reformers saw them, seemed not even to care whether some outsider thought them good or bad. Yes, they lived comfortably, they admitted. But God would be merciful to this generation of sinners, just as he had been to so many generations before. Others argued along similar lines: custom allowed monks and mendicants alike to enjoy all that had been granted to them through the license of their superiors—wages earned through writing, preaching and begging, and all of the treasures and other goods they had gathered. This was so, the argument ran, because surely the learned and pious prelates of their orders would not have allowed so many to live in mortal sin.[77] The men and women who articulated these sentiments may not have been opposed to calls for change, but in the end most remained too busy and too tangled in their own circumstance to respond to the occasional reforming barbs hurled at their conscience.

The force and longevity of these kinds of passive resistance should not be discounted. In the 1430s a colleague asked the renowned Dominican Observant John Nider to compose a general treatise for the reform of the "coenobitic estate." The son of a cobbler from the small Swabian community of Isny, Nider had risen from obscurity through the ranks of the Dominican Observants to become a leading reformer of his age, and a prominent figure at the Council of Basel.[78] Busied with the

---

[76] MS Vienna, Schottenkloster, Cod. 320, fol. 199r.

[77] For a sample of the arguments see ibid., 202r.

[78] No comprehensive study of Nider's life and work has appeared since K. Schieler, *Magister Johannes Nider aus dem Orden der Prediger-Brüder: Ein Beitrag zur Kirchengeschichte des fünfzehnten Jahrhunderts*, Mainz 1885. But see now Michael Bailey, *Battling Demons* (above, 7 n. 21), with further literature, along with standard dictionary articles: VL 6: 971–77 and BBKL 3: 502–5.

council's work, Nider paused to respond to his colleague's request. He soon completed a work most often titled *De reformatione religiosorum* or *De reformatione status cenobitici*. It was one of the most widely read treatments of its kind in all of the fifteenth century, and Nider began it, revealingly, by rehearsing some fifteen common counterarguments raised against reform.[79] Opponents argued that custom had long approved their way of life; that local superiors had the power to license the enjoyment of personal property through discretion and dispensation; that their "weak complexion" made modern Christians unsuited to the austerities of strict observance; and that strict reform was beneath the dignity of religious of noble blood. Throughout the rest of his work, Nider continued to vent his frustration at the opposition to reform. The halfhearted work of general and provincial priors, abbots and visitators did more harm than good. As soon as the talking was over, their call to reform was quickly forgotten.[80] On the ground, scheming religious appealed to friends, relatives and allies to stir up resistance.[81] Worse still, many of the utterly "lapsed" resisted reform, even though they themselves were not scandalous sinners. On the contrary, they were "adorned by a certain kind of tepid religion," a manner of life that effortlessly clothed outward piety with a certain social flair. So comfortable were these figures "eating and drinking with men of the world" that they could easily convince simple religious and ignorant laymen to resist reform.[82] To Nider they were heirs to the demons that had confounded reform from antiquity down to the days of Francis and Dominic, "false Christians" who abusively dispensed with essential

---

[79] There is no modern edition of the *De reformatione* (hereafter DRR). For my citations I have consulted MS Basel, Universitätsbibliothek, B. III. 15, fols. 186v–248v. See also Bailey, *Battling Demons*, Chapter Four, and as a complement my own essay: "The Setting and Resonance of John Nider's *De reformatione religiosorum*," in *Kirchenbild und Spiritualität. Dominikanische Beiträge zur Ekklesiologie und zum Kirchlichen Leben im Mittelalter. Festscrhift für Ulrich Horst OP zum 75. Geburtstag*, ed. Thomas Prügl and Marianne Schlosser (Paderborn, 2006), 319–38.

[80] DRR II. 11, fol. 218v.

[81] DRR II. 12, fol. 219v: "...ut etiam potestas procuretur et vigor secularis brachii, quia hoc expedit et sepe necessarium est propter rebelles aut propter astutos religiosos reformationi resistentes."

[82] DRR II. 4, fol. 211v: "Nec putandum quod in reformatione solum resistant religiosi de publicis aut gravibus facinoribus notati, sed nonnunquam nocent amplius hii qui talibus viciis carent, specie quadam tepide religionis decori. Talibus enim citius per simplices creditur qui speciem sanctitatis habent forinsecus. Conversari sciunt favorabiliter in esculentis et potibus cum huius mundi hominibus, et tanto amplius nocent reformationi quanto eis ab inexpertis secularibus citius creditur quidquid contra reformationem dixerint eo quod non videntur manifesta procurare scandala."

obligations like common property. Blinded by evil customs they defended as law, they were like the dead Lazarus stinking in his tomb. Yet these "perverse and astute men" managed to deceive others through their "most clever objections."[83] Nider bitterly recalled meeting one such figure in a gathering of great leaders, a doctor of divine law who was professed to a strict religious order—strict, if only its way of life had been properly observed. Nider knew this man would never openly admit how far his order had fallen, and how much it was in need of reform—even though quite the opposite was so clearly visible to all.[84]

The evidence presented thus far recaptures the way in which many must have first encountered the attacks on property in the Constance years, and for long after—the incisive polemic of the reformers and their pamphlets, the counter polemic of their opponents, the excuses and passive resistance of the ordinary rank and file caught in the middle, all reflecting a spectrum of competing interests and attitudes. Yet for all of their energy, these discussions were most often too heated or too partisan to allow a deeper consideration of the conceptual issues that calls to reform had raised. The analysis now turns to at least one reformer who wrestled with those issues, at more length and in more detail than most, in the years after Constance.

"The truth of justice"
Property and Community in the Commentaries of John Wischler

Born in 1383, John Wischler studied philosophy, theology and canon law at Heidelberg after 1400. After several years as a parish priest he entered the newly reformed community at Melk in Austria. There he became a prolific author and leader of Benedictine reform in the region.[85] More will be said in the following chapter about the reforms Wischler helped establish in practice. Here the focus turns to two of the many works he composed while advancing his community's cause: a pair of commentaries on the thirty-third chapter of Benedict's *Rule*, written

---

[83] DRR II. 5, fols. 211v–12v.
[84] DRR II. 9, fol. 217r: "...nequaquam admittere voluit verbis quod religio de qua assumptus erat lapsa esset ac reformatione indigeret, quamquam luce foret clarius toti mundo contrarium esse verum. Vix enim credi potest quanta cecitate premuntur et cordis duricia qui malis imbuuntur habitibus."
[85] There is no study of Wischler's life or work. See VL 4: 757–59.

most likely sometime in the 1430s.[86] Wischler's texts, still unedited and seldom noticed, are a baroque tour de force of subtle distinction, argument and counterargument, and no brief treatment can do them justice. But a careful reading of these texts, even in outline, repays the patience and effort required. They reveal how challenging the arguments for reformed community could be, even for learned leaders committed to establishing them on firm conceptual ground.

The opening chapters of Wischler's first commentary, entitled "On Property" provide a sense of the issue as he perceived and framed it. His aim was to determine "precisely that *proprium* by which a religious person is called a proprietor."[87] Wischler began with a set of distinctions. One concerned *proprium* as distinct from another person, another *proprium* as distinct from a community. Wischler then applied these distinctions to yet another, between true and "usurped" ownership. The purpose of the distinctions was to clarify a central point of confusion concerning the slogan "proprietor," so loosely thrown about in so many recent treatises. Some religious had argued that they were not technically "proprietors" because those professed to religious poverty could legally own nothing as individuals. Wischler now used his distinctions to point out that the passages of the *Rule* of Benedict that prohibited *proprium* (and similar texts from canon law) were not intended pointlessly to prohibit religious from the true ownership they could, by definition, not enjoy. Rather, the *Rule* condemned what Wischler called "similitudinous ownership" (*proprium similitudinarium*).[88] He used that phrase to denote "a substance that a religious person has usurped for himself alone with respect to its dominion, possession and use...having likeness to, but not the essence of true ownership."[89] Religious, in other words, could be guilty of the

---

[86] Cited here from MS Salzburg, St. Peter, a. III. 15, fols. 97r–147v. Another copy survives in MS Melk, CM 911, fols. 32r–60v.

[87] MS Salzburg, St. Peter, a. III. 15, fol. 103v: "ut inveniamus illud proprium praecise a quo persona religiosa proprietaria vocatur."

[88] Ibid., fol. 101r: "Non enim monachum vel aliam personam religiosam ideo proprietariam vocamus quia ipsa habeat verum alicuius rei dominium [sed] analogicum, id est similitudinarium…" Ibid., fol. 102r: "Patet iterum quod hoc nomen proprietarius equivoce dicitur de homine seculari et de homine religioso…. Patet tertio quod cum in hoc capitulo regule xxxiii dicitur 'nullus praesumat aliquid proprium habere' hoc 'proprium' non debet ibi accipi pro proprio vero quia illud frustra prohibetur monacho cum veraciter non possit aliquid tale proprium habere ut praedictum est, sed pro proprio similitudinario."

[89] Ibid., fol. 106r: "Proprium similitudinarium est substantia quam persona religiosa sibi soli usurpavit quoad eius dominium, possessionem et usum…cum vero proprio correspondente similitudinem habens, sed non veritatem."

mortal sin of *proprium/proprietas* not because they truly owned the things they had, which they could never do, but because they had usurped the "appearances" of lordship, possession and use. Just as a portrait of a person was not a true person, but only a likeness, so a lordly monk was only the likeness of a lord-proprietor, one who had merely "similitudinous" lordship over his worldly goods.[90] Like thieves, usurers and plunderers—the force of the similes should not be missed—monks who held property only seemed to own the things they enjoyed.

Wischler then had to counter the objection that the concept of *proprium similitudinarium* was ill-conceived. However things "looked," the argument ran, a "similitudinous *proprium*" was not true *proprium*, just as a painted likeness was not a real person.[91] Wischler sought to close the technical loophole by making a distinction between what he called the "truth of essence" and the "truth of justice." His concern, regardless of any of the conceptual technicalities, was with the justice of one's dominion, possession or use of a thing, as distinct from who technically owned it or physically controlled it.[92] There was no justice, Wischler argued, in monks who lorded it over others with property that was not rightfully theirs, who usurped dominion, possession or use and took everything in their own power (*potestas*) as if they were lords.[93] To develop his case Wischler had to confront the definitions of license and *proprium* as most knew them from the standard glosses on the relevant decretals. John Andreae had defined *proprietas* as "whatever was concealed from the abbot," for example, and anything that was held "without the license of the superior." But Andreae's definitions were too vague and imprecise, Wischler said, in that they did not sufficiently restrict the *modus habendi* of the individual monk. Andreae's definition also failed to account for those who granted "bad license" (*mala licentia*) or granted license too broadly (*large*).[94] Wischler thus shifted the emphasis of license away from the unquestioned authority of the superior toward

---

[90] Ibid.: "...cuius dominium a persona religiosa usurpatum non est verum dominium sicut homo pictus non est verus homo, sed est homo pictus et similitudinarius."

[91] Ibid.: "Sed proprium similitudinarium possessionis et proprim similitudinarum usus cum suis veris propriis habent non solum similitudinem, sed etiam veritatem."

[92] Ibid.: "Cum dicimus verum proprium dominii vel verum proprium possessionis, significamus veritatem iustitie et non veritatem essentie."

[93] Ibid., fol. 107r: "Ecce quod in omnibus his tribus veris propriis, hoc verum dicitur veritatem iustitie et non veritatem essentie."

[94] Ibid., fol. 108v: "Sed illud [quidquid concelatur] potest a monacho pluribus modis haberi quam uno, igitur etc. Preterea sicut elicitur ex presenti capitulo regule xxxiiio, quidquid monachus habet in propria potestate, hoc est sic proprium. Sed monachus

the *potestas* of the individual and individual disposition: the moment an individual monk desired to have a thing in a way contrary to the will of the superior, even in something as simple as a dish of food at the common table, there was the danger of mortal sin.

In one sense Wischler's theme and arguments recall a long tradition of debates over ownership and use reaching back to Francis and Olivi. Here again was a concern to uphold individual poverty, the concern for conceptual and legal precision regarding ownership, possession and use, a concern over the proportions of use, the dangers of prelates too liberal with their license and so on. There were even points at which Wischler framed his discussions in ways that recalled older debates over the use of "consumables."[95] Wischler's discussion of "usurped" dominion also in some ways recalled Wyclif's attacks on mortally sinful clerical dominion. In the end, however, Wischler and his work are better read on their own terms, as a product of their own immediate setting and horizons. Wischler was a recent convert to Observant monasticism. Yet he was also a former secular cleric, a veteran schoolman and pastor, and he remained something of a public scholar in the mold of Henry of Langenstein, Dietrich Kerkering, Job Vener and so many others. Indeed Wischler crafted certain key passages in his commentaries, it should be noted, as a full participant in the wider textual markets of the southern Empire after Constance. At one point in his discussion, for example, Wischler took issue with the treatment of *proprietas* that had been offered at Constance by Job Vener. He also cited other authors known to have authored texts on the "vice of property" within the orbit of the council as well, including Dietrich Kerkering's treatise to the nuns of Münster.[96] Drawing from these contemporary discussions Wischler sought not to engage in the

---

potest aliquam rem in propria potestate non solum ut dominus sed etiam ut possessor et non dominus, vel ut usurarius et non possessor et non dominus, etc."

[95] So, for example, one discussion that concerned a monk who offered food to another at table "as a lord," another that concerned how monks were to understand the use of candles. Cf. c. 18 (fols. 118r–120v).

[96] Wischler built one of his chapters, for example, around Kerkering's treatment of the various cases in which the enjoyment of individual cash incomes might justifiably be allowed. The citations themselves may have been drawn from the Melk manuscript that contained copies of Kerkering's text as well as several copies of Wischler's own works: MS Melk, Stiftsbibliothek, CM 900, fols. 56r–62r. Wischler also cited the Vienna jurist and reforming visitor Caspar Maiselstein (see below, 139 and n. 16, as well as the Appendix, no. 19), who had himself borrowed from a treatise by the Carthusian Henry of Cosvelt.

old academic debates, but to confront the particulars of property and community as lived and experienced in his day.

The result was a treatise that was legally and conceptually precise, yet also advanced with a keen eye for the human dimensions of daily life, and with what can be called a strong commitment to social justice. Consider the illustrations Wischler provided of his many scholastic distinctions between possession, ownership and use:[97] A monk who was dutifully assigned an office, and who then violently seized for himself the revenues he was to administer, was a proprietor "with respect to possession" (*quantum ad possessionem*). When the monk turned the property to his own use he became a proprietor "with respect to use" (*quantum ad usum*) as well. Monks who gave away property as if it were their own or who received treasure as surety on a loan were also proprietors "with respect to possession," even though they did not own the things given to them. Even if the debtor were a fellow monk, Wischler noted, the monk still possessed the surety "civilly as well as naturally, and so truly," and was guilty of *proprium*. Other revealing examples concerned monks who refused to be removed from a cell or a house at the will of the superior, or who refused to yield a book from the library; these monks were proprietors "with respect to use." Still more revealing are Wischler's complaints about "modern abbots" who dispensed prebends of bread, wine, meat and money as if they were lords, not only to their own monks but also to "outsiders" (*monachis extraneis*). The monks in turn hoarded these things as their own and gave them out to parents, relatives and friends, and did so without license or account.[98] Other abbots took in wandering monks or recruited monks from other monasteries because their numbers were too low to fulfill their obligations toward the anniversary masses in their communities. All received standard mass stipends and lived essentially as secular priests.[99] Still other abbots

---

[97] For these see MS Salzburg, St. Peter, a. III. 15, fols. 103v–107v.

[98] Ibid., fol. 120r: "Suis namque monachis quidam abbates dant portiones praebendales in pane, vino…carnibus ac pecuniis. Et quicumque eorum moneta residuat, hoc sibi retinet et moneta sibi thesaurizat, vel dat illud partentibus, cognatis et ceteris extraneis personis sine licentia sui abbatis et ad placitum suum."

[99] Ibid.: "Quidam etiam abbates habens defectum monachorum in suis monasteriis suscipiunt monachos extraneos et proprietarios undecumque ad se venientes, vel rogant aliorum monasteriorum abbates ut eis aliquos ex suis monachis concedat, qui eis legant missas in eorum monasteriis fundatas et statutas quas omnes per suorum monasteriorum monachos complere non possunt, et eosdem extraneos monachos ad legendum sibi huiusmodi missas conducunt pro annuo pecuniarum stipendio quasi illis

borrowed cash from their monks to restore dilapidated buildings, then paid them cash stipends in return.[100]

Wischler's portraits can be read from multiple perspectives. In one sense he had cast longstanding customs of prayer and provision, commerce and administration as mortal sin. Read against the grain, his laments thus provide another distorted glimpse of the human face of propertied religious life, of men and women who did what they could to keep their communities together and to fulfill the financial, social and spiritual obligations of their estate. Yet for all of that, whatever there might have been of the virtuous and sensible disposition of money and goods, there remained the unrepentant pomp and negligence of so many lordly abbots. Wischler provided some of the most captivating portraits of these figures in another of his commentaries on the thirty-third chapter of Benedict's rule.[101] There Wischler launched into a lengthy denunciation of the "foolishness or temerity of certain perverse abbots of our time," men who felt that the goods of the monastery were their own. Their very words were a witness to their error, for these lords called everything theirs—"my village, my carriage, my vassal, my slave, my men, my house, my horse, my money."[102] These pompous abbots usurped the better part of the community's goods for their own use and comfort, living "gloriously, or more truly I should say shamefully" with their great households and retinues in grand style. And because abbots drained their communities of resources, ordinary monks went without decent food and clothing, and they were forced to seek provision in cash and in kind from parents, relatives and friends. While monks suffered in indigence, abbots lived in luxury, dining with princes at tables resplendent with gold and silver vessels.[103] Wischler could

---

monachis liceret locare operas suas sicut presbyteris secularibus. Et huiusmodi stipendia dicti monachi sibi retinent quasi eorum vera propria."

[100] Ibid., fol. 122r.

[101] MS Melk, CM 911, fols. 3r–32r. In the manuscript are also copies of the commentary under study here, as well as one of the many manuscripts of John Nider's *De reformatione religiosorum*.

[102] MS Melk, CM 911, fols. 3r–32r, here fol. 7r: "Quorum errorem dampnabilem etiam verba eorum aperte testantur, quibus impudenter et intrepide solent dicere mea villa, meus currus, meus vasallus, meus colonus, mei homines, mea domus, meus equus, mea pecunia, et ita fere omnia bona monasteriorum suorum vocant sua."

[103] Ibid.: "Monachis autem monasteriorum suorum modica relinquunt, unde nec victum nec vestitum sufficientem habere possunt. Hinc coguntur a parentibus, cognatis et amicis suis petere et accipere necessaria quae eis deficiat aut aliis irregularibus modis et viis illa sibi acquirere."

barely contain his anger. Abbots provided prebends of food and drink at best, but nothing more, and they refused to provide for the needs of the sick. As a result, again, humble monks were compelled to work for a wage, to beg for assistance from their parents, kin and friends, or to suffer indigence and misery.[104] Wischler himself had known a monk who had fallen ill and who, though he lived in a wealthy community, had been left to fend for himself. When none of the monk's own brothers would come to his aid, he had been forced to flee his community and live among the laity. It was this kind of piteous neglect, aggravated by the prelates' crass carnality and spiritual weakness, that had made a mockery of the ideal of community.

To Wischler, such abuses of an abbot's unquestioned authority must have captured a range of wider frustrations about abuses of power in the church generally. At one point in his discussion, Wischler revealingly adopted language that recalled discussions of papal power. What of those abbots who resigned their offices, and who customarily (*consueverunt*) enjoyed an endowed pension in retirement? How were these to be called voluntarily poor? They enjoyed as their own all of the revenues assigned to them, and did with them as they pleased. Wischler then clothed the abbot's unassailability, cleverly, in a stock phrase canonists had long used in connection with discussions of papal absolutism: "And no one says to them 'why do you do this?'" The allusion could not have been lost on Wischler's readers, so many of whom were engaged in wider debates over reform "in head and members" and who would have been familiar with the citation. Wischler then concluded the invective with another clever allusion that was surely not to be lost on his audience: these retired pensioner abbots were accountable to none—"not the abbots of their monasteries (to whom they refuse to submit), not the bishops of their dioceses, not the pope, indeed not a soul"—*nullus omnino*, a caustic play on Benedict's *nihil omnino* in the thirty-third chapter of the *Rule*.[105]

---

[104] Ibid.: "Quapropter coguntur hec necessaria vel suis laboribus acquirere vel postulare et accipere ab eorum parentibus, cognatis et amicis vel, si ea habere non posssunt, magnas penurias pati, quod ego ipse expertus sum contigisse in quodam monasterio opulento...."

[105] MS Salzburg, St. Peter, a. III. 15, fol. 111r: "Dicti autem abbates omnia quae ex redditibus sibi assignatis percipiunt habent et tenent in propria potestate et faciunt cum eis sicut ipsis placet. Nec aliquis dicit eis 'cur sic facis,' non abbates monasteriorum suorum (quibus illi nolunt subesse), non episcopi de quorum diocesibus sunt, non papa, ymmo nullus omnino...." Cf. Pennington, *Prince and the Law*, 53–54. See also

In a second tract on the thirty-third chapter of the *Rule* of Benedict, Wischler turned to consider the precise nature of corporate ownership in a monastic community. He began with one of the most fundamental and contested issues of the era: Who owns the goods of the Church? Wischler recognized the difficulty of the task, and readily admitted that he was uncertain of the answer. But he noted what he called "two famous opinions" on the matter. The first was consistent with inherited papal theory: the hierarchical Church, with the pope as its head, held the *dominium* and *proprietas* of the goods donated by the faithful.[106] According to the second opinion, the Church held the right of possession and use alone. It thus had the right to dispose of its wealth, under leadership of the pope. But *proprietas* and *dominium*, the true ownership of those goods, rested with God alone.[107] Wischler then noted a third "very common" opinion: that the goods of the Church remained with those individual locales to which they were donated—presumably the opinion that accorded with the will of founding families, patrons and local custom. According to this model, religious houses and other corporations retained communal ownership of their goods, but allowed the particular members of the corporations to enjoy the goods individually.[108]

In the discussion that followed, Wischler defended the second of these opinions and used the others as foils to advance his case. The core issue turned on what can be called a theory of "shared" dominion for individual monks. Wischler's opponents held that though monks

---

Pennington's *Pope and Bishops. The Papal Monarchy in the Twelfth and Thirteenth Centuries* (Philadelphia, 1984), 16–30, here 17–18.

[106] MS Salzburg, St. Peter, a. III. 15, fol. 124r–v: "...unus qui dicit quod illorum bonorum proprietas sit apud universalem ecclesiam, per ecclesiam intelligendo totam congregationem fidelium, cuius auctoritate papa inter homines singulares supremam hebat potestatem eadem bona dispensandi.... Et sic videntur illa dedisse ecclesie et non deo...et per consequens earum proprietatem et dominium transtulerunt in ecclesiam; ergo proprietas est vel fuit apud ecclesiam. Ergo idem sentiendum est de donationibus quas postea fideles fecerunt et adhuc faciunt monasteriis et aliis ecclesiis."

[107] Ibid., fol. 125r: "Alia est opinio quae dicit quod proprictas bonorum ccclcsiasticorum...sit apud deum tantum, cui illa bona a fidelibus donata sit, et non ecclesie vel alicui alteri. Concedunt tamen illi cum priore opinione papa super talibus bonis auctoritate dei...plenam et supremam inter homines habet potestatem ea dispensandi...."

[108] Ibid., fol. 126r–v: "...tertia opinio valde communis quae dicit quod proprietas ecclesiasticorum bonorum sit aput singulas ecclesias ad quas donate sunt. Et illa opinio quantum ad monasteria et statum religionis attinet distinguit de duplici proprio, unum quod habetur in singulari, aliud quod habetur in communi, secundum quod duplex est rei dominium.... Et dicit quod monachus potest habere proprium in commune sed non proprium in singulari."

abdicated lordship as individuals upon profession, they did not do so as a community. Ownership was thus shared collectively by individuals.[109] As a single shareholder in a corporation, no individual monk could claim to be a sole owner. Wischler opposed the creative argument by pointing out that in the case of the death or departure of all but one member of the community, corporate ownership would devolve to the single monk. Wischler sought to clarify the issue through a rapid exchange with an imaginary adversary. Wischler asked whether a lone monk retained any dominion at all over the monastery's goods. If he did not, how could one say that there had been any ownership at all? Yet if some ownership did remain with that lone monk, Wischler asked whether it was held in common or individually. If one said that it was held in common, then in common with whom? If it were held individually, then the lone monk was a proprietor.[110] The opponent responded that though the monk might have a private dominion of sorts, it was only a share in the goods of the monastery. The monk could not be said to be lord of it all. The exchange continued, and at one point Wischler provided a teacher's clever example to illustrate his line of reasoning once again. He supposed that Socrates and Plato were monks, and that Plato left the monastery. Where, he asked, did Socrates' half of the dominion remain? If not with him, then with whom? If it departed with Plato in death, where did it go? If it departed with Plato to another monastery, how was it taken up into the common dominion of the second community? And what if Socrates should then receive another monk, Cicero, into his hapless little community? Whence did Cicero receive Plato's half of the dominion? The entire notion of shared dominion, if reduced to a single monk, resulted in a dominion that was neither common (because the monk was alone) nor *proprium* nor *alienum* (because it was shared)—"which seems," Wischler concluded, "to be absurd."[111]

---

[109] Ibid., fol. 129r: "Et ideo concedo quod omnium bonorum cuilibet monasterii dominium partim est aput singulos suos monachos. Nec hoc est inconsequens, quia omnis monachus cenobita bene potest habere rerum proprietatem sive dominium cum aliis, sed non potest hoc habere solus."

[110] Ibid., fol. 129v: "Si autem dixerit adversarius quod apud illum unicum monachum adhuc maneat aliquid dominium, quaero an illud sit commune vel privatum. Si dixerit commune, quaero cui sit commune. Nam tantum unus mansit per casum, et uni soli nihil poetst esse communi. Si dixerit privatum, tunc habeo intentum, scilicet proprietas omium bonorum monsterii illius devoluta sit ad illum unicum monachum et quod ipse factus sit dominus illorum."

[111] Ibid.

The arguments and counterarguments continued over six more conclusions. Their spiraling details need not detain the analysis here, but considered as a whole the exchanges make clear how difficult it remained for all sides to locate ownership in the monastic setting. Wischler's opponents continued to assert that the ownership of things donated to a religious community was retained by the household as a corporation. Wischler continued to counter that the true ownership was God's alone. As Wischler saw it, those offering goods to a monastery "abandoned" their dominion. The donor's ownership somehow disappeared, at least until it was taken up anew by those who received property from administrators and abbots (who for their part only controlled that property according to their right of use and possession, but not true *dominium*).[112] Another objection then seized on the conceptual problem of such "dominionless" property: If monks shared the "common use" of goods that God alone held as *dominium*, might they not be justified in seizing those goods according to their needs, just as one might make use of a city's common woodland?[113] The objection led into a concluding series of chapters that culminated in the discussion of a key issue: whether and under what circumstances monks might demand of their superiors the things they needed, yet not be found guilty of the vice of *proprietas*. It was a challenging question, one that again reflected Wischler's sensitivity to matters of "social justice" within the community. On one hand, monks had no right to demand things of their superiors as if "owed" to them, and superiors were not bound to provide for monks as if under contract. On the other hand, as experience proved almost daily, manifest necessity and indigence, the neglect of lordly prelates and so on could easily erode the foundations of community. In desperate circumstances, then, it seemed that monks did have the right to ask for and even demand things for their personal use. Again Wischler resorted to intricate distinctions that reveal his sophisticated training in Roman and canon law.[114] But more accessible and revealing are the

---

[112] Ibid., fol. 138v–139r: "Diecendum est enim quod homo aliquam rem suam donat seu offert deo ipse non transfert dominium in deum, sed omnem dominium quod sibi in illa re conpetit deserit propter deum, et ipsam rem reddit vel resignat deo, et sic in illa re...cessat omne dominium humanum et manet in ea dominium divinum...." Ibid., fol. 139v: "De novo acquiritur illi cui illa pecunia datur."

[113] Ibid., 141v.

[114] He began with the distinction between *ius ad rem* and *ius in re*. The former denoted the "just and proper power of asking for and requiring something as owed" (*potestas iusta et propinqua petendi et exiguendi aliquam rem tamquam sibi debitam*). The latter denoted

ways in which he illustrated his points with compelling examples from real life: Wischler noted the nature of a common granary of a city, or of a common fishery, whose administrators had the "right of use" (*ius utendi in re*) to provide for the community in the name of all. As another example he noted the community of the parish church, to which all parishioners had the right of use *in re* for their divine services. Should a rapacious lord somehow seize a granary or turn a parish church into a fortress, citizens and parishioners then had the right of use *ad rem*: the right to demand the thing unjustly taken from them.

The overall focus of Wischler's arguments here, and the social force of his examples, suggest something of the wider moment in which he wrote. By Wischler's day, ordinary townsfolk had embraced "communal" ideals in a variety of ways, not least by holding churchmen accountable both as pastors and as efficient administrators of the local church. The more radical expressions of the communal impulse have drawn much scholarly attention, whether in fifteenth century Bohemia or in the revolts of the early Reformation.[115] In Wischler's early Observant circles, less visibly and in more muted tones, was something of the same sensibility. Wischler articulated no vision of utopia or apocalypse, and he was no advocate of revolt or revolution. But he had a powerful sense of community, social justice and stewardship, and he sought to think through how these should shape daily life in a reformed religious community.

* * *

The discourse that has emerged in the last two chapters resists categorization within most familiar narratives of poverty, property and reform. It is a discourse that seems to have owed little to inherited arguments between seculars and mendicants, little to arguments over Franciscan poverty, or to concerns over prophecy or apocalypse. Rather, it was a call to community that reflected the commitments of the "new piety"

---

the "just and proper power of taking up a thing unto one's own disposition or use" (*potestas iusta et propinqua assumendi aliquam ad rem in sui facultatem vel usum*). Each of these rights, *ius ad rem* and *ius in re*, could in turn be applied to dominion, possession and use. Wischler first focused on each as they related to use alone (the *ius utendi ad rem* and *ius iutendi in re*). He then focused on each as they related to common and individual use—the *ius iutendi usu communi* and *ius iutendi privato vel proprio*.

[115] Cf. Ferdinand Seibt, "Hussitischer Kommunalismus," in *Häresie und Vorzeitige Reformation im Spätmittelalter*, ed. František Šmahel and Elisabeth Muller Luckner (Munich, 1998), 197–212. See also Peter Blickle, *From the Communal Reformation to the Revolution of the Common Man*, trans. Beat Kümin (Leiden, 1998).

of the region, commitments shared by university-trained lawyers and theologians as well as converts to religious life. It was also a divisive campaign of treatises and slogans, one that took the schoolman's arguments and counterarguments from the classroom out into the world, and applied them to daily life in the cloister. The formation of these Observant ideas is an important story in its own right, deserving of a place alongside more famous precedents among the Franciscans, or alongside fifteenth-century analogues among the Lollards, the New Devout and the Hussites. Just as important is the story of how reformers rendered all of these potential energies into actual ones, how they translated into reforming practice the pent-up frustration so often vented in their treatises. The final two chapters begin to outline that process, first as reform's energies broke in to unreformed communities from without, as a matter of law and order, and finally how reform worked to shape life from within, as a matter of the heart and spirit.

PART II

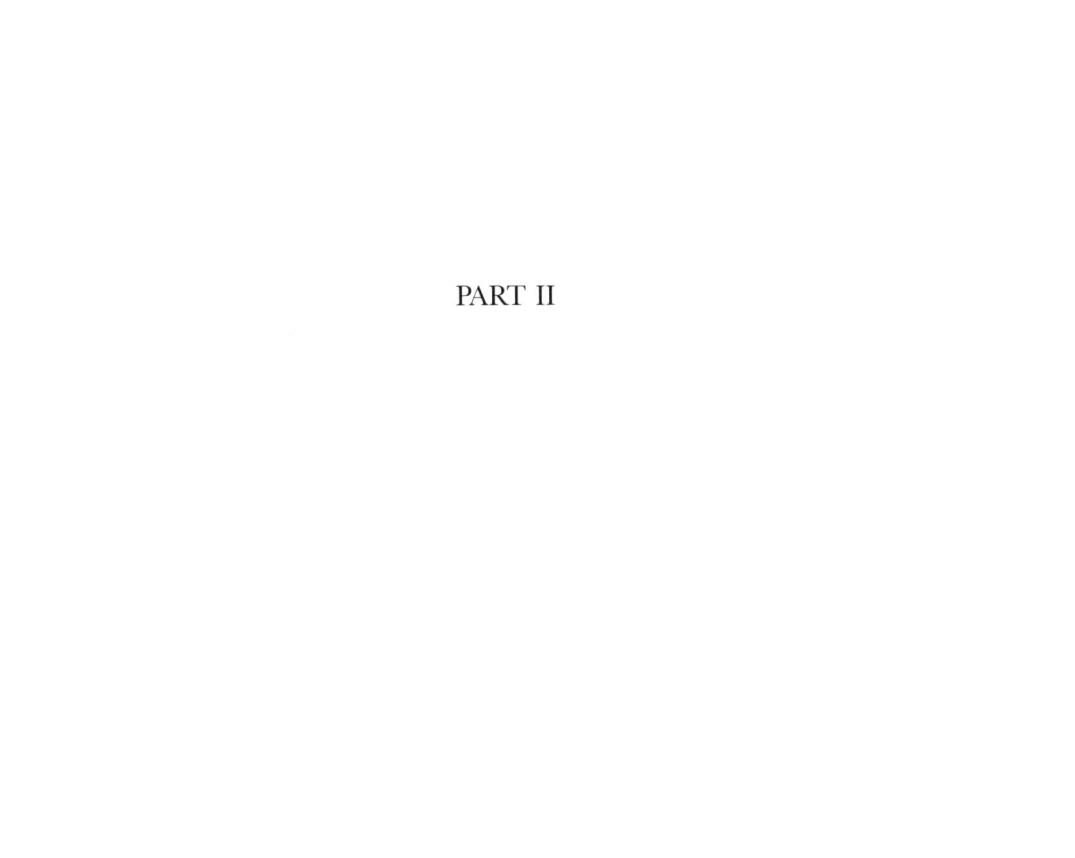

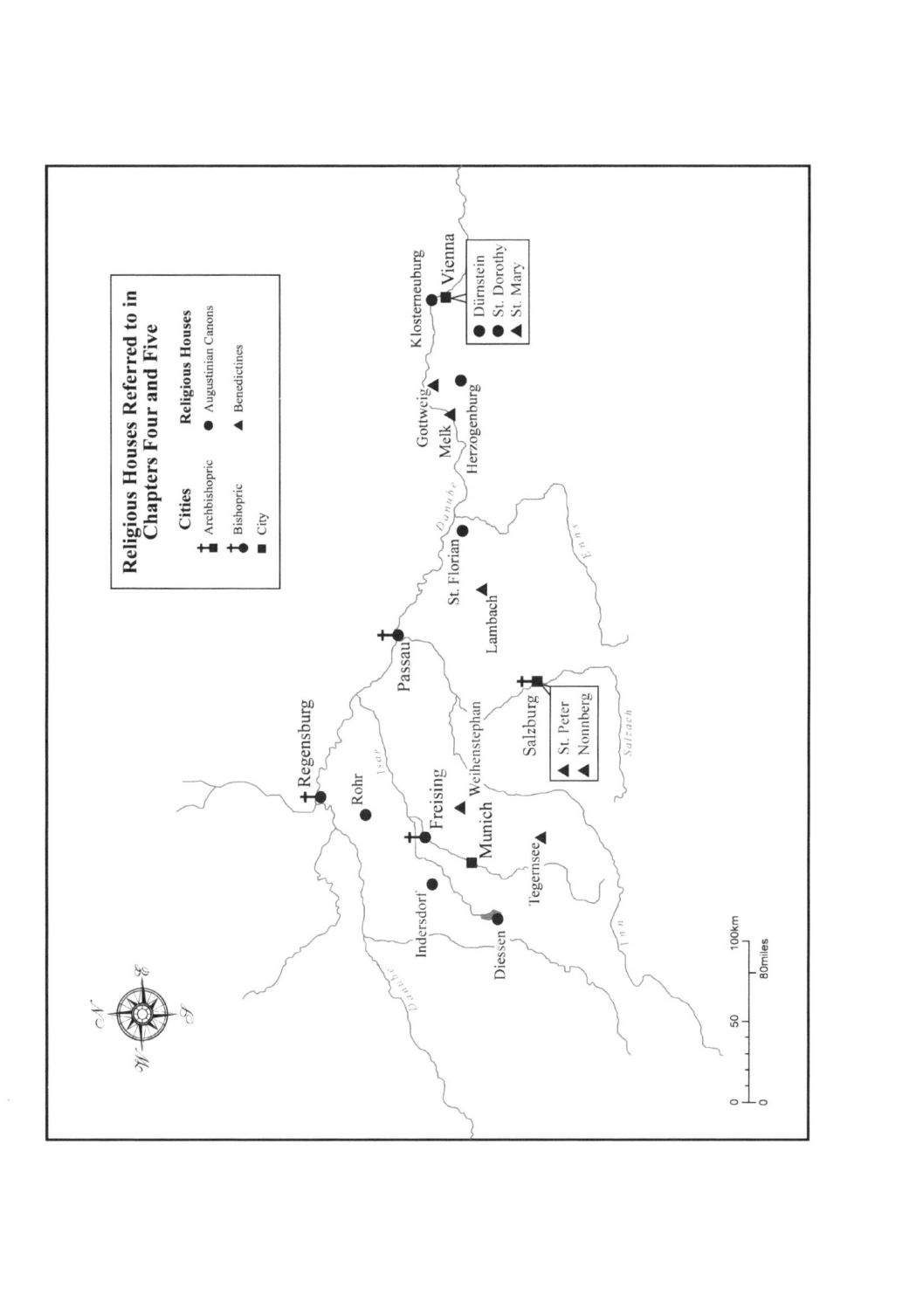

CHAPTER FOUR

PROPERTY AND COMMUNITY BETWEEN PRINCIPLE
AND PRACTICE

Writing around 1475, the Augustinian prior John Busch turned from recounting the reforms of the congregation of Windesheim to recall a colleague's stories of Benedictine reform in Austria.[1] In one household, as Busch told the story, the abbot and a minority of brothers hoped for reform, but a larger faction of *proprietarii* stood against them and swore to resist with all their might. The abbot approached Duke Albert of Austria, who agreed to come to the community personally. There the duke asked the abbot and members of the community, one by one, if they wished to embrace strict observance and the common life. Many, including the abbot, said that they did, and they were left in peace. Then the duke revealed how he dealt with the monks who had refused reform. He led the abbot to a chamber, where "rebellious and impudent" brothers were enduring what Busch called, strikingly, the *reformatio per suspensionem*: the monks were hanging by the neck from beams, some dead, some struggling to breathe their last. Busch also told of a Benedictine house reformed "through fire": frustrated with his dissolute and recalcitrant community, an abbot locked them all within the walls and burned them alive. Still another remembrance was of a community reformed "through chains and blows." Several "pestiferous and rebellious" brothers who refused to embrace reform were chained by the hands and feet to the pillars of the dormitory. There they were expected to sing the divine office at the appropriate time along with the rest of the community. When the defiant brothers refused, they were struck with the rod until they changed their minds. This, the chronicler noted, was a "more soft" method of reform than the other two, but it was quite successful.

These were dramatized remembrances of distant events, but they captured the forceful ways in which reformers often advanced their agenda. Numerous other passages in Busch's chronicle, and in others

---

[1] Johannes Busch, *De reformatione monasteriorum*, ed. K. Grube (Farnborough, 1968), 735–38.

like it, tell less fanciful but equally stern stories. Busch himself told again and again of how the Windesheim reformers and their secular allies deposed hostile superiors, or forced them to resign; how they rounded up the recalcitrant and sent them away in carts and carriages; how they brought in new members, converts to reformed life, to train others in the new discipline; how they often fought, legally and even physically, against the determined resistance of local communities and their patrons. The Dominican John Meyer recounted similar tales. The Dominicans, too, deposed superiors who stood against their agenda; forced communities to make sharp choices for or against reform; and worked closely with city councils and other secular allies to enforce change.[2] And in almost every instance, as these reforming chronicles repeatedly made clear, a central concern was to uproot the "vice of property." Busch often listed in detail all the worldly goods he and his colleagues had confiscated upon the reform of a community—rents in cash, silver rings and other dress accessories, spoons, plates and frying pans, goblets and chalices.[3] Meyer and other historians of mendicant reform recounted how brothers and sisters who refused to renounce their property were driven from their communities and forced to resign their incomes to city councils.[4]

Scholars have studied the strategies through which Observants and their allies advanced reform in practice, especially in studies of the expanding power of territorial princes.[5] Many have also recognized at least in passing how ideals of community shaped reform in practice,

---

[2] For an overview, see Eugen Hillenbrand, "Die Observantenbewegung in der deutschen Ordensprovinz der Dominikaner," in *Reformbemühungen und Observanzbestrebungen*, ed. Elm, 219–71. See also Bailey, *Battling Demons*, chapter four and von Heusinger, *Johannes Mulberg* (above, 99 and n. 13), 1–38.

[3] Busch, *De reformatione monasteriorum*, ed. Grube, 99.

[4] Hillenbrand, "Observantenbewegung," 237, following Meyer, *Buch der Reformacio Predigerordens*, ed. Reichert (Leipzig, 1907/8). See also Johannes Kist, *Das Klarissenkloster in Nürnberg bis zum Beginn des 16 Jahrhunderts* (Nüremberg, 1929), 23–25 (noting the legal resignation of property and incomes) and Paul Nyhus, "The Franciscan Observant Reform in Germany," in *Reformbemühungen und Observanzbestrebungen*, ed. Elm, 212–13 (noting the reform of finances related to anniversary masses).

[5] Manfred Schulze, *Fürsten und Reformation. Geistliche Reformpolitik weltlicher Fürsten vor der Reformation* (Tübingen, 1991), especially chapters 1 and 3, and Dieter Stievermann, *Landesherrschaft und Klosterwesen im spätmittelalterlichen Württemberg* (Sigmaringen, 1989). For the reforms under study here see Gerda Koller, *Princeps in Ecclesia. Untersuchungen zur Kirchenpolitik Herzog Albrechts V. von Österreich* (Vienna, 1964), and Helmut Rankl, *Das vorreformatorische landesherrliche Kirchenregiment in Bayern (1378–1526)* (Munich, 1971).

usually in the context of broader studies of reform.⁶ This chapter offers another study of the move from principle to practice. It traces how the reform ideology of property and community traced above came to be applied in the years after the Council of Constance. The analysis is limited to the reform of Benedictines and Augustinian canons because the textual trail of treatises, codices and authors has most often lead to their well-documented circles. From these sources emerges a sense of how contemporaries preached, argued over, applied and resisted their era's new reforming ideology of property and community.

Reformationis Methodus
The Foundational Visitations

John Busch's stories of Austrian reform were a distant reflection of one of the earliest and most lasting reforms of religious life in the Empire. The effort began at the Council of Constance, in the circle of advisers surrounding the young Duke Albert V of Austria. One of the leaders of that that circle was Nicholas of Dinkelsbühl, who at Constance rivaled his colleague "Lord Job" Vener in prestige and influence.⁷ As a student of Henry of Langenstein at Vienna, Nicholas developed a reputation as both an uncompromising moralist and a thrifty administrator, and he had served as Dean of the theology faculty by 1409. He also became a renowned preacher, and one of the most prolific and widely read of Vienna's many pastoral theologians. Albert V then chose Nicholas as his official representative to Constance, and at the council Nicholas worked tirelessly with delegates from the University of Vienna to advance the duke's interests.

Amid all of that work Nicholas paused to draw up the *Reformationis Methodus*, a brief treatise that offered concrete measures to bring about the reform of the Benedictine monasteries in Albert's domain.⁸ Above all, Nicholas noted, the duke needed "devout men" who from the beginning of their profession had lived a strictly observant religious

---

⁶ See especially the relevant treatments of Petrus Becker, *Das monastische Reformprogramm des Abtes Johannes Rode* (above, 98 n. 7) and Meta Niederkorn-Bruck, *Die Melker Reform im Spiegel der Visitationen* (above, 9 n. 23).

⁷ Alois Madre, *Nikolaus von Dinkelsbühl. Leben und Schriften. Ein Beitrag zur theologischen Literaturgeschichte* (Münster, 1965), 10 ff. and the works cited in VL 4: 1131.

⁸ For the *Reformationis Methodus* see Madre, *Nikolaus von Dinkelsbühl*, 269–71 and Niederkorn-Bruck, *Die Melker Reform*, 23.

life, and who could continue to do so "to the exclusion of all others" who would not willingly conform to reform's demands.[9] Another key step was to establish a reforming abbot in an appropriate community. Nicholas proposed several ways to make way for a suitable candidate. First, a current abbot might freely renounce his office, for example, or at least his right to administration of all temporal and spiritual affairs. In return, the abbot would receive comfortable provision. These more "soft and amicable" options, the least likely to raise serious opposition, were to be pursued first. Subsequent proposals were more aggressive and manipulative. Upon the death of the abbot of a suitable community, Nicholas suggested, Duke Albert and his allies might intervene to delay the election or confirmation of all candidates but their own. More aggressively still, they might lie in wait for an abbot whose administrative failure or notorious character opened the way for him to be deposed or suspended.[10] Upon their candidate's successful installation, Nicholas argued, reformers could then present a choice to any monks who did not wish to take on the rigors of Observant life: they could transfer to another monastery or they could accept pastoral or administrative positions elsewhere.[11] Nicholas knew that not every abbot would resign peacefully, and not every monk would agree either to strict observance or transfer. Anticipating the resistance, Nicholas therefore proposed that reformers obtain from the papacy and the bishops, for both exempt and nonexempt cloisters, the authority to transfer any who refused to submit to rigorous observance, and to expel any who refused to transfer.[12]

Nicholas' program came to life in January 1418, when newly elected Pope Martin V extended to Albert V a remarkable ten-year license to visit and reform every Benedictine and Augustinian house in the duke's domain.[13] The pope gave Albert's visitors the power to reform, censure and, where appropriate, depose abbots, abbesses, priors, prioresses and any other prelates, male or female, and to arrange for the election of suitable replacements. All who resisted the visitors' efforts,

---

[9] MS Melk, Stiftsbibliothek, CM 1094, fols. 271r–275v, here fol. 271r: "...ut advocentur viri devoti, qui sub regulari disciplina et iugo regulae praedicti ordinis a suae professionis exordio rigorosius enutriti sunt et sancte ac religiose vixerunt." Koller, *Princeps in Ecclesia*, 83.
[10] MS Melk, Stiftsbibliothek, CM 1094, fol. 272v.
[11] Ibid., fols. 271r–v.
[12] Ibid., fols. 273r–v
[13] Koller, *Princeps in Ecclesia*, 89–90 and fn. 47 (citing cod. Vat Reg suppl n. 108, fols. 245r–v).

moreover, were to be subject to temporal punishment. A commission was formed to carry the privilege into action. Its members represented an alliance of reforming interests and networks that bound together cloister, council, court and university. Two religious superiors, Angelus of Rein and Leonard of Gaming, were its nominal leaders. Pilgrim IV of Puchheim, one of Albert's advisers, represented Albert V. Two schoolmen represented the University of Vienna.[14] One was the theologian Peter of Pulka, who had succeeded Nicholas of Dinkelsbühl as dean of the arts faculty in the 1390s and had become a doctor of theology by 1410. Thereafter, both Peter and Nicholas had worked to police doctrine and preaching in Vienna.[15] Joining Peter was the jurist Caspar Maiselstein. Caspar had served as rector of the University of Vienna and dean of the faculty of law, and had become a doctor of law by 1405.[16] In September 1414, Caspar and Peter had then been chosen as Vienna's representatives to Constance. There they had worked closely with Nicholas of Dinkelsbühl to serve the interests of their duke and their university.

Albert's commission began its work at the ancient Babenberger foundation of Melk, where the Hapsburgs had long exercised their influence.[17] On June 30, 1418, just as Nicholas of Dinkelsbühl had outlined in the *Reformationis Methodus*, the commission accepted the resignation of Abbot John II, to whom they granted a lifelong pension. Abbot John's successor was Nicholas Seyringer.[18] A former canon of Olomouc in Moravia, Seyringer had studied under Henry of Langenstein and looked forward to a promising academic career at Vienna.[19] But in 1403 he turned away from academic ambitions to profess as a Benedictine at Subiaco in Italy. Several of Seyringer's closest colleagues

---

[14] Ibid., 66.

[15] Each, for example, had served on the tribunal that charged Jerome of Prague with heresy. For an overview of Peter of Pulka's career see VL 7: 443–48 and BBKL 7: 376, each with further literature. See also Dieter Girgensohn, *Peter von Pulkau und die Wiedereinführung des Laienkelches, Leben und Wirken eines Wiener Theologen in der Zeit des großen Schismas* (Göttingen, 1964).

[16] For Maiselstein see VL 5: 1183–91 and BBKL 5: 585–87.

[17] For the Melk reforms see Niederkorn-Bruck, *Die Melker Reform*, passim, as well as the chronologies, documents and further literature provided in the book's extensive appendices. For a brief overview see also Joachim Angerer, "Reform von Melk," in *Die Reformverbände und Kongregationen der Benediktiner im deutschen Sprachraum*, ed. Ulrich Faust and Franz Quarthal (St. Ottilien, 1999), 271–313.

[18] Koller, *Princeps in Ecclesia*, 83; Niederkorn-Bruck, *Die Melker Reform*, 23–25.

[19] BBKL 4: 928.

at Vienna followed him, most notably Peter of Rosenheim and Nicholas Respitz, who were to be central figures in the first generation of Melk reform. Seyringer was prior at Subiaco by 1410, and abbot by 1412. But he and his followers were soon driven out, and they retreated to Santa Anna in Rocca di Mondragone near Capua, where Peter of Rosenheim served as prior. By 1416 Seyringer, Peter of Rosenheim, Nicholas Respitz and others had returned north to Constance, where Nicholas of Dinkelsbühl convinced them to begin monastic reform in Austria.[20] The experiment they began at Melk proved too difficult for some. Six monks decided they could not bear the changes, and they departed for other houses. Those who remained, however, embraced a reformed observance whose customs would soon become dominant across the region.

Albert V's visitation commission continued its work at Göttweig, where the monks met the arriving visitors with ringing bells and a solemn, chanting procession.[21] The next morning, the abbot convened the gathering in the chapter room and Nicholas of Dinkelsbühl delivered a sermon so challenging that it offended the monk who recorded the proceedings. Nicholas "confounded our errors and negligence," the monk wrote, "and what was worse, said that we were Sarabites, the worst kind of monks."[22] In August Albert's commission then engaged in a difficult fight over the reform of the Irish Benedictines of St. Mary's in Vienna.[23] Established across the region by missionaries from Ireland, Irish Benedictine cloisters were deeply entrenched in their own customs, and fiercely independent. Indeed the abbot of St. Mary's, Thomas, told the visitors that his monks were neither willing nor able to live with any but their own kind. In fact they would sooner kill outsiders, or be killed by them, than live with them.[24] But in the end Thomas was persuaded to resign, and for his cooperation he too received an annual pension. The prior and five monks were then given safe conduct and provision

---

[20] Koller, *Princeps in Ecclesia*, 90; Niederkorn-Bruck, *Die Melker Reform*, 26–27 and 206.

[21] A detailed account of the visitation appears in FRA II/55, no. 2235. See also Niederkorn-Bruck, *Die Melker Reform*, 191.

[22] FRA II/55, no. 2235; Koller, *Princeps in Ecclesia*, 94; Niederkorn-Bruck, *Die Melker Reform*, 191.

[23] Cf. Koller, *Princeps in Ecclesia*, 95–96 and Niederkorn-Bruck, *Die Melker Reform*, 206–7.

[24] FRA II/18, no. 456: "...nos non possumus nec volumus commorari monachis aliarum quam nostrarum nacionum...quia nos interficeremus eos vel interficeremur ab eis."

to return to their homeland.[25] In the spring of 1419, Albert's commission visited the Augustinian communities of Herzogenburg, St. Florian and Klosterneuburg. In each community, the visitation commission established as the new norm for observance the statutes Bishop John of Draschitz had issued for the community of Raudnitz in Bohemia in the 1330s.[26] The Raudnitz statutes had also been established in two key communities that Albert V's immediate circle had founded in the previous decade: Dürnstein, established in February 1410 by Steven of Haalsach, and St. Dorothy, established by Albert's chancellor Andreas Plank in December 1414.[27]

A range of factors helped ensure the lasting success of these early reforms. The commitment of individual converts, figures such as Nicholas Seyringer and others who had turned away from their scholastic careers, was crucial. Just as important were the networks that bound converts to their old university colleagues and to other secular allies, figures such as Nicholas of Dinkelsbühl and Andreas Plank, whose pastoral and political interests were resonant with the rigorous piety of the Observants. Crucial as well was the backing of Albert V, who asserted his rights of advocacy and the reform for a variety of ends: to restore dignity to ancient dynastic foundations; to create alliances in ways that weakened competition from rival families; to assert an overall legal and moral order; and to promote economic efficiencies that increased his own revenues.[28]

A similar alliance of converts, schoolmen and princes soon established reformed religious life in Bavaria. By 1420 the territory had been fragmented into three smaller duchies. The dukes Ernest and William ruled the duchy of Bavaria-Munich, their rival cousins the duchies of Bavaria-Ingolstadt and Bavaria-Landshut.[29] The three lines had fought among themselves almost ceaselessly for years, and Bavaria's churches and cloisters were often targets for plunder in the region's frequent

---

[25] Koller, *Princeps in Ecclesia*, 95.
[26] See the literature cited above, 9 and n. 23, especially Zibermayr, "Zur Geschichte der Raudnitzer Reform."
[27] Koller, *Princeps in Ecclesia*, 98–99.
[28] Cf. the general remarks in Elm, "Verfall und Erneuerung," 227–30, with further literature.
[29] See the relevant material in Max Spindler, ed., *Handbuch der Bayerischen Geschichte 2: Das Alte Bayern. Der Territorialstaat vom Ausgang des 12. Jahrhunderts bis zum Ausgang des 18. Jahrhunderts* (Munich, 1969).

feuds. But each prince took seriously the role as patron and protector of his family's religious foundations.

The dukes of Bavaria-Munich, in particular, used their position as patrons to sponsor lasting Observant reform. In 1412, Ernest and William expressed their strong displeasure at what they perceived as the moral and temporal collapse of life at the community of Indersdorf. Nestled in a modest town on the Glann River northwest of Munich, the canonry had been one of the most important dynastic foundations of the Wittelsbach dukes of Bavaria for almost three hundred years.[30] To renew its reputation the dukes backed the election of the stern Eberhard Brunner as the new prior. Eberhard in turn convinced his half brother John Rothuet to join him in his effort to reform the community.[31] By October 1407 John had passed his baccalaureate exam in the arts at Vienna, and he returned to Indersdorf to serve as the schoolmaster of the canonry.[32] Eberhard convinced John to profess as a canon, and then sent him away to spend his novitiate among the Augustinian canons of Neunkirchen near Nuremberg. There John was trained in reformed observance according to the Raudnitz statutes. After his profession at Freising in 1413, John returned to Indersdorf to serve as deacon.

Already by 1417, months before even the first visitations in Austria, the canons of Indersdorf were wrestling with all of the challenges that faced any nascent reform: restoring the household's economy and administrative apparatus, copying all of the treatises and statutes that provided guidelines for reform, and establishing a renewed devotional

---

[30] The house was founded in 1120 in the diocese of Freising by Otto of Wittelsbach. See Romuald Bauerreiss, *Kirchengeschichte Bayerns 2: Von den Ungarneinfällen bis zur Beilegung des Investiturstreites* (St. Ottilien, 1950), 34 and Norbert Backmund, *Die Chorherrenorden und ihre Stifte in Bayern* (above, 9 n. 23), 93–97, with an overview of sources and a modest literature, e.g. Hundt, *Die Urkunden des Klosters Indersdorf* (Munich, 1863–64).

[31] John's mother had first married a Peter Brunner of Indersdorf, with whom she had Eberhard. She then married again and had John. For an overview of John of Indersdorf's career and works, see VL 4: 648–50 and the introduction to Bernhard Haage, "Der Traktat 'Von dreierlei Wesen der Menschen'" (PhD diss., Heidelberg, 1968). See also Ernst Haberkern, *Funken aus alter Glut. Johannes von Indersdorf: Von dreierlei Wesen der Menschen. Die theologischen, philosophischen und weltanschaulichen Grundlagen eines mystischen Traktats des 15. Jahrhunderts* (Frankfurt am Main, 1997).

[32] Andrea Klein, "Johannes von Indersdorf studierte in Wien," *Zeitschrift für deutsche Philologie* 115 (1996): 439–42.

life.[33] In the short term, division and disorder across the region prevented reform from taking root.[34] But by the 1420s new efforts were underway. The first came in 1424, when John Grünwalder—vicar-general of the diocese of Freising and half brother to the dukes of Bavaria-Munich—secured papal and episcopal privilege to establish a reforming visitation.[35] Dukes Ernest and William also officially backed their half brother's initiative with an open letter addressed to the prelates of all Benedictine monasteries and Augustinian canonries in their domain, exempt and nonexempt alike. The dukes reminded their subjects of Grünwalder's papal and episcopal privileges, and demanded all superiors submit obediently to the commission's will as their own.[36] Leading that commission were some of the region's most zealous of the recent converts to reformed life. John of Indersdorf, now with ten years' experience leading reform as a deacon, represented the Augustinian canons. Two veterans of Melk, Peter of Rosenheim and John of Ochsenhausen, joined John as representatives of Benedictine reform.[37] In Bavaria, as in Austria before, a vanguard of "devout men" were poised, with the backing of a bishop and a territorial prince, to press for reform.

---

[33] So, for example, the massive collection of charters and other documents concerning the household economy collected in Munich, BHStAM, KLI 146. For devotional texts and compilations, see Chapter Five below.

[34] Henry the Rich of Bavaria-Landshut had attempted to murder Ludwig the Bearded at the Council of Constance in 1417, and the formation of a "Constance League" against Ludwig quickly led to a war that ravaged the region from 1420 to 1422. See Spindler, ed., *Handbuch* (above, n. 29), 234–41.

[35] Grünwalder been elected bishop in 1422, but he had been forced to yield to Nicodemus Della Scala, who through the efforts Duke Henry of Bavaria-Landshut had won the favor of Martin V. There is no modern study of Grünwalder's important career, but see BBKL 3: 380–82, with further literature.

[36] The best account of the role of the dukes of Bavaria-Munich in the visitations is found in Rankl, *Kirchenregiment*, here 173–84. See also Niederkorn-Bruck, *Die Melker Reform*, 28–9 and Bauerreiss, *Kirchengeshcichte Bayerns* 5: *Das Fünfzehnte Jahrhundert* (St. Ottilien, 1955), 42–78.

[37] Peter of Rosenehim had retreated to Italy with Nicholas Seyringer and then returned to Austria. Thereafter he had served on the ducal visitation commission of 1418 and had risen to the position of prior under Seyringer at Melk. See VL 7: 518–21, BBKL 7: 377–79 and Franz Xaver Thoma, "Petrus von Rosenheim, OSB. Ein Beitrag zur Melker Reformbewegung," *Studien und Mitteilungen zur Geschichte des Benediktinerordens und seiner Zweige* (1927): 94–222. John of Ochsenhausen was successor to Nicholas of Respitz as the abbot of the reformed Irish Benedictines in Vienna.

Grünwalder's commission began its work at the ancient Benedictine cloister of Tegernsee. There, in keeping with the earlier program of the *Reformationis Methodus* and efforts at Melk and elsewhere, the visitors deposed the abbot, Hildebrand Kastner, and allowed him to retire with a pension. In Kastner's place the commission installed one of their own, the Munich patrician Kaspar Aindorfer, who was all of twenty-five years old.[38] By December 1426 the commission had visited the Augustinian canonry of Dietramszell, where the prior agreed to submit to the reformers' measures and issued a series of his own statutes; the Augustinian community of Rottenbuch; and the Benedictines of Tegernsee and Weihenstephan.[39] The record of the visitation's activities thereafter is incomplete, though fragmentary evidence suggests that their work continued at several other communities, among them Scheyern, Biburg, Altomünster, Rohr, Fürstenfeld and Beyharting, and the nunneries of Geisenfeld and Hohenwart.[40]

By the 1420s these visitations had established enclaves of reformed observance that soon became leadership academies, so to speak, for Observants of the coming generation.[41] For decades monks trained at Melk became leaders of reforming visitations, and leaders of allied communities. The first reformed abbot of the Irish Benedictines, Nicholas Respitz, was a veteran of Subiaco who had come to Melk with Seyringer. Similarly, Peter of Rosenheim, who had also retreated to Subiaco with Seyringer, helped establish reform both at Melk and at St. Peter in Salzburg, where he served as prior from 1431. Peter was also a prolific author and a leading voice for monastic reform at Basel.[42] At Tegernsee, the first reforming abbot, Kaspar Aindorfer, nurtured a generation of reformers in his community. Bernard of Waging, prior of Tegernsee, was a prominent figure in contemporary debates over mysticism. His fellow Benedictine John Keck, professed at Tegernsee in

---

[38] The details of the circumstances surrounding the deposition remain unclear. See Rankl, *Kirchenregiment*, 179–80 and n. 2. See also Thoma, "Petrus von Rosenheim," 135–37.

[39] Cf. Niederkorn-Bruck, *Die Melker Reform*, 211.

[40] Rankl, *Kirchenregiment*, 182. Thoma, "Petrus von Rosenheim," 129–30, suggests the commission may also have visited Schledorf, Diessen, Polling, Schliersee and Beuerberg,

[41] For an analogous dynamic among the Windesheim canons see Thomas Kock, "'Per totum Almanicum orbem.' Reformbeziehungen und Ausbreitung der niederländischen 'Devotio Moderna'," in *Die Neue Frömmigkeit in Europa im Spätmittelalter*, ed. Marek Derwich and Martial Staub (Göttingen, 2004), 31–56, especially 49–50.

[42] See the literature cited above, n. 37.

1442 after a long career at Vienna, became confessor to Albert III "the Pious" of Bavaria-Munich and a prolific author of treatises related to reform.[43] And at the canonry of Indersdorf, Deacon John established himself as a leader over a remarkably long career: He worked as a reformer for almost sixty years. He, too, served as confessor to Albert III of Bavaria-Munich, as a leader of several visitations until 1442, and thereafter as prior until his death in 1470. Moreover, as later chroniclers remembered it, canons trained under John's leadership at Indersdorf brought many more of the region's canonries to strict observance under the Raudnitz statutes.[44]

To midcentury and beyond, these enclaves and networks, with the support of the region's princes and bishops, continued to reform Benedictine life in accordance with the customs of Melk, and Augustinian life in accordance with the statutes of Raudnitz.[45] One of the most important later waves of reform came in 1441, when Albert III of Bavaria-Munich received a papal privilege authorizing another visitation. The commission was led once again by John Grünwalder (now bishop of Freising), Deacon John of Indersdorf, and Abbot Kaspar Aindorfer of Tegernsee. In keeping with established patterns, the visitors were authorized to reform all exempt and nonexempt cloisters and canonries, even mendicant communities. They were also authorized to depose abbots, administrators and other officers, and to replace them with anyone they deemed fit.[46] In a private letter to his confessor John, Albert III made clear to the visitors how he hoped the privilege would be used: Whether they were prelates or subjects, the duke wrote, if they were not obedient to the reformers, they were to be thrown into

---

[43] For Aindorfer see BBKL 1: 312, with further literature, especially Joachim Angerer, *Die Bräuche der Abtei Tegernsee unter Abt Kaspar Aindorffer (1426–1461), verbunden mit einer kritischen Edition der Consuetudines Tegernseensis* (Augsburg, 1968). For Waging see VL 1: 203 ff. and BBKL 1: 537, with further literature, e.g. Martin Grabmann, "Bernhard von Waging, Prior von Tegernsee. Ein bayerischer Benediktinermystiker des 15. Jahrhunderts," *Studien und Mitteilungen zur Geschichte des Benediktinerordens* 60 (1946), 82–98. For Keck, see VL 6: 1090–1104 and BBKL 3: 435–36. Also, for general context, see Virgil Redlich, *Tegernsee und die deutsche Geistesgeschichte im XV. Jahrhundert* (Munich, 1931). See also Martin, *Fifteenth-Century Carthusian Reform* (above, 21 n. 51), 209–11.

[44] Cf. Romuald Bauerreiss, *Kirchengeshichte Bayerns* 5: *Das Fünfzehnte Jahrhundert* (St. Ottilien, 1955), 46–47.

[45] Niederkorn-Bruck, *Die Melker Reform*, 29–32; Koller, *Princeps in Ecclesia*, 102–11; Rankl, *Kirchenregiment*, 189–90.

[46] Rankl, *Kirchenregiment*, 189–90.: "...a dignitatibus etiam abbatialibus necnon administrationibus et officiis penitus removendi et destituendi ac illorum loco alios ad hoc utiles et ydoneos...surrogandi et perficiendi...."

prison.[47] Another major round of visitations then made their way across the region in the early 1450s, when Nicholas of Cusa established two commissions for the archdiocese of Salzburg. Between June 1451 and September 1452, a Benedictine commission visited forty-four male and seventeen female monasteries according to the customs and statutes of Melk. Between September 1451 and December 1452, an Augustinian commission visited thirty-seven canonries and called for reforms in accordance with the statutes of Raudnitz.[48]

To conclude this overview of reforming visitation, a few general points about the visitation process, and about the cultural position of the visitors, deserve emphasis. By midcentury the Benedictines of Melk, taught by the long experience of the events outlined here, began to circulate detailed procedural guidelines for a typical reforming visitation.[49] After an arrival and a solemn reception, a sermon proclaimed the need for reform. Extending guarantees of both confidentiality and the right of all to defend themselves against accusation, visitors then interrogated each of the community's members about their way of life. The inquiry began with questions on the observance of the divine office; it then moved to questions about the observance of poverty, chastity and obedience. Several questions also focused intently on the abbot and his officials—their competence, reputation and so on. At the conclusion of all the questioning, the visitors weighed the evidence carefully, drew up the results in a visitation charter and passed judgment, as necessary, based on their findings. As a basis for future assessment and accountability, visitors then drew up a detailed reform charter and copies of other relevant documents. They also typically left behind a small group of zealots ("well-trained" in proper observance, as the charters sometimes put it), who would instruct the others in the new way of life.

---

[47] Ibid.: "Ob das waer ettlich prelat oder untertan solichem reformirn nicht gehorsam sein wolten, nach Inhald der vorgeschriben bull das sy dan dieselben in vangknuss nemen di so lanng darinn hallten und straffen muegen biss daz sy zu solicher gehorsam und geformierten leben bracht weren."

[48] The Cusanus commission's reform of the Augustinian canons is not as well documented as its efforts among the Benedictines, nor has it been as well researched. For a general overview, see Zibermayr, "Raudnitzer Reform" and the relevant passages in Bauerreiss, *Kirchengeshcichte Bayerns* (above, n. 44). For the Cusanus visitations generally, see Zibermayr, "Die Legation des Kardinals Nikolaus Cusanus und die Ordensreform in der Kirchenporvinz Salzburg," *Reformationsgeschichtliche Studien und Texte* 29 (1914): 1–128, and for the Augustinian canons especially 57–62.

[49] For an overview of the process see Niederkorn-Bruck, *Die Melker Reform*, 37–40.

Detailed procedural outlines like those the Benedictine sources provide are hard to come by in most other settings. Raudnitz canons did not document their activities as meticulously as the monks. Nor did male visitors, whether monks or canons, document the early visitations of women's communities as often or as fully as we would like. Read carefully, however, the available evidence suggests that what was coming into view by midcentury in Melk circles must have been a long-established and more widely applicable process. From the beginning, reformers active on the visitations outlined above—who most often knew one another personally and who often served together on the same commissions—worked with the same basic pattern of procedures and strategies, whether for houses of monks, canons or nuns.

In all of their work, moreover, visitors shared a common commitment to uprooting the "vice of property." In stinging sermons that denounced criminal *proprietarii*; in sworn interrogations that sought to ferret out those who concealed money and goods; in strategies that sought to depose the lordly superiors who resisted them; in charters that regulated the materiality of the cloister in ostentatious detail—in all these ways visitors, as authors, compilers and readers of their era's most widely circulated tracts on the "vice of property," translated ideology into practice. And as they did so they faced continual resistance. Consider two stories from the later fifteenth century, each authored decades after the earliest reform efforts. Sometime before 1464, the aging Benedictine Martin of Leibitz recalled in his memoirs (*Senatorium*) the reluctance to embrace the common life he had so often encountered during his years as a reformer in the archdiocese of Salzburg.[50] Martin proudly noted the rare successes: At St. Paul in Lavanttal the monks willingly embraced reform in both word and deed, confessing their sins and resigning their incomes—"one of thirty florins, another a bit more, another a bit less."[51] But most adopted strategies of resistance that ranged from passivity and dissimulation to overt violence. In most places, Martin noted, reform was largely superficial. The nuns of Göss, for example, resigned their rings and rosaries, the symbols of

---

[50] For Martin of Leibitz see VL 6: 154–57.
[51] Martin of Leibitz, *Senatorium*, cited here from MS Melk, Stiftsbibliothek, CM 193, fol. 195r: "Inter omnia monasteria non reformata in hoc laudo fratres illius monasterii, quod non solum verbo sed effectu assumpserunt reformationem, devotas fecerunt confessiones et in detestationem vite preterite coram nobis resignaverunt propria, alter 30 florenos, alter plus, alter minus." The treatise is also printed in Pez, *Rerum Austriacarum Scriptores* (Leipzig, 1725) 2: 626 ff.

their marriage to Christ and their piety. But they denied that they had any personal incomes, even though Martin suspected otherwise.[52] In another community (here likely a reference to an intractable *Damenstift*) elite women had no conception that they were under any obligation to a religious rule, and they marshaled the aid of their families and allies to resist visitation fiercely, even violently.[53] The power of local lords and the reverence for good custom were so great, Martin remembered, that only the privileges of the dukes of Austria and Bavaria-Munich allowed the visitation commission even to enter the communities, to say nothing of bringing about any reform.

Martin's story highlights how reforming visitors, for all of their commitment and for all of the backing of their secular allies, remained in a precarious cultural position. In each locale they found themselves confronted with a new circumstance, working through a complex reforming calculus whose equations demanded quick resolution from partial evidence. Visitors had to assert their own vision of reform against deeply entrenched local interests and long-held customs, dissimulation and passive resistance. Visitors had to discern the presence of any conspiracies in the community, whether against the superior or against the reformers. They had to discern the overall competence and reputation of an abbot or abbess, and his or her willingness to cooperate in reform. They had to evaluate the overall temporal and spiritual circumstances of the household. The visitors then had to pass judgment in a way that balanced respect for due process against the pressures to expedite reform. In all these ways, devout monks and canons on visitation found themselves outsiders within their own ranks, meddlesome intruders who worked from the margins to advance the divisive agenda of a new reforming regime.

To meet all of these challenges, visitors deployed the full force of a long-standing clerical culture of interrogation, evidence, argument and proof. Dyan Elliott has argued that the work of that culture—confession and penance, inquisition and canonization, along with all of their reading and writing, texts and methods—by the fifteenth century came to discredit many forms of female religious expression. In an analogous way, the same regime worked to discredit established customs of religious life, and to advance reform. Reforming visitors, most of

---

[52] Ibid. See also Niederkorn-Bruck, *Die Melker Reform*, 191.
[53] Zibermayr, "Legation des Kardinals Nikolaus Cusanus," (above, n. 48), 55.

them university-trained theologians and lawyers, in fact often described their overall visitation process as an *inquisitio*, a detailed "inquest." In doing so they framed reform within a legal tradition that, though most often associated with heresy trials, had long advanced investigations of many kinds of crimes within the ranks of the clergy.[54] The parallel should not be pressed too far. The aims, purposes and procedures of reforming visitors differed in important ways from those of inquisitors. But visitors availed themselves of the same cultural tools—confession and penance, interrogation, evidence and argument, and all of the schoolman's treatises and tracts, disputed questions, sermons and so on—to prosecute broken vows and other violations of religious rule and statute, the "vice of property" chief among them.

Ad regularem vitam reducta
Contesting Community Through Inquest

In 1418, as Albert V's commission began its work at Melk, University of Vienna theologian Peter of Pulka delivered the opening sermon. Peter chose for his sermon a passage that would become a favorite during many visitations to come, the same passage that Henry of Langenstein had chosen for Klosterneuburg years before: "Behold, we have left all and followed you."[55] Noting that it was for the monks of Melk to "live beyond the common measure of Christian law," and to work toward perfection "through certain spiritual and bodily training," Peter began by outlining the "three essentials" of poverty, chastity and obedience. But he then quickly focused his remarks only on the observance of the vow of poverty, or rather on its opposite, the vice of property. As Henry of Langenstein had before him, Peter cast an outsider's unsympathetic eye on all the old problems of custom and license, proportion and sensibility. As Peter saw it, a propertied malaise had strangled religious life in every order. In some houses, Peter noted, it was customary for prelates simply to provide equal sums of money to all in the community, whether annually or weekly, and to leave everyone to provide for their

---

[54] Henry Ansgar Kelly, "Inquisition and the Prosecution of Heresy: Misconceptions and Abuses," *Church History* 58 (1989): 439–51.

[55] MS Munich, BSB, Clm 16196, fol. 118v: "Hanc collationem fecit egregius Magister Petrus de Pulka in reformatione ordinis sancti Benedicti in Mellico et alibi, cuius anima requiescat in sancta pace." For other visitation sermons built around the same passage cf. Niederkorn-Bruck, *Die Melker Reform*, 37 and n. 125.

own needs, with no obligation to render any account of expenses. In other houses, though brothers ate at a common table, each was given license to enjoy personal incomes from any source available, whether from incomes in kind, annual or weekly cash stipends, alms or even from their own labors, again with no obligation to render an account of expenses.[56] All of it was a way of life "most foreign" to the intentions of its founders.

As Henry of Langenstein had before him, Peter also rehearsed the same counterarguments: surely prelates had the authority to license the enjoyment of cash incomes and other goods; surely cash prebends and other comforts were not only necessary and useful given modern circumstances, but also in accord with long-held customs. And as Henry had, Peter responded from a stance consistent with the theological and devotional commitments in Vienna. He focused intensely on the grotesque proportions of the monks' enjoyment of personal property, and all of the consequences, spiritual and social, of their excesses. In communities where each fended for himself from his own reserves, Peter noted, the strong, the healthy and the well-connected might flourish, but they and their superiors allowed others to live in indigence, lacking even basic necessities.[57] The rhetoric that had served the Constance era so well then followed: Their customary enjoyment of cash prebends inflamed the monks' passions and ensnared them in all manner of vice, from dice games to drunkenness to simony. Monks emboldened by their cash reserves simply refused to submit to any superior's authority.[58] Under the rule of a proper abbot, they might

---

[56] MS Munich, BSB, Clm 16196, fol. 118v: "Nam in nonnulla monasteria etiam diversorum ordinum practicatus est iste modus, quod praelatus singulis fratribus distribuit...pecuniales portiones, quolibet eorum relicto sue cure de procurandis sibi pro libito victu, vestitu et aliis necesariis...nulla de expositis reddita ratione. In quibusdam vero monasteriis, etsi fratres in communi edunt de una olla, habent tamen quilibet de licentia praelati pecunias aut alias res utiles, sive de bladiis, ut nominant, sive de annuis redditibus receptas, sive de elemonsina, aut etiam de laboribus aut undecumque alius provenientes, et quoad hoc derelictus est sue cure de procurandis sibi necessariis....."

[57] Ibid.: "Nonne apertum signum huius appropriationis rerum quo ad voluntatem et intentionem est id quod in monasteriis tam virorum quam mulierum sepissime fieri certum est, viz. quod una persona professa fortis et sana sibi habundat in omnibus etiam lucrosis et res sibi a priore utiles distributas aut a parentibus receptas vel undecumque eis provenientes...aliam personam in eodem monasterio professam...scienter permittit deficere [et] penuriam pati in necesariis."

[58] Ibid.: "...eis ministrat materiam unde remunerare possunt et ad se allicere personas quasdam in periculum castitatis. Et eis illo modo dantur instrumenta faciendi convivia inter et extra monasteria, et nonnumquam incurritur ebreitas, solivitur ieiuniam, fran-

be able to live "quietly" and to spend all of their energy in reading and study and daily spiritual exercise. But as it stood, with experience itself as the witness, the monks were forced to buy and sell and trade for their needs, weighed down by worldly cares, all of which drained them of devotion and distracted them from their duties as professed religious.[59] In contrast Peter held up his vision of the common life of Christian antiquity, the narrow way of the "holy primitive fathers." Each brother should receive their food from the common kitchen, their clothing from the vestiary, without excess and according to the "proper measure of religious life." Peter did not need to recite all the passages to prove his point; he noted that he was speaking to those who knew them. He only reminded his audience how well the common life had recently begun to take root among Benedictines, Cistercians, Carthusians and others who had been led back, "reduced" to the regular life of their primitive roots (*ad regularem vitam reducta*).[60]

Peter's sermon echoed Henry of Langenstein's at Klosterneuburg, and its view of Christian antiquity recalled the closing passages of Dietrich Kerkering's treatise. The sharpness of its stance was also consistent with the broadsides recently circulated at Constance. But Peter now applied the challenge to renounce the "vice of property" from a more forward, threatening position. Peter's was a sermon delivered "on point," so to speak, at the tip of the reforming spear. In the earliest moments of the first visitation after Constance, it brought to bear in practice all of the ideological energy that the Council had generated against the "vice of property." Among his visitation colleagues were monks who had personally returned *ad fontes*, to the origins of Benedictine community at Subiaco, and who intended to bind life at Melk back to those same origins. Consider also how Peter's sermon intersected with the interests of the patron of his visitation, Albert V of Austria. Albert was heir to a tradition of dynastic sanctity that cast the territorial lord as *paterfamilias* of his subjects, clergy and laity alike. One of Albert's

---

gitur silentium et tota dissolvitur claustralis disciplinam. Inde oriuntur ludi taxillorum, contentiones, blasphemii, percussiones, periuria, furta et cetera huiusmodi."

[59] Ibid., fol. 119v: "...se implicant curis et sollicitudinibus seculi in diminutionem devotionis, in negligentiam divine laudis, ymmo et in religiose vite exterminium, ut satis claret in nonnullis monasteriis, reipsa loquente, quod tamen non sine dolore ferendum est et referendum."

[60] Ibid., fol. 121r: "...et etiam monsteria aliorum ordinum ad regularem vitam reducta concorditer vivunt de communi sine proprio et secundum modum superius descriptum."

predecessors, Rudolph IV, had boldly claimed to be "pope, bishop, arch-dean and dean" in his domain. Henry of Langenstein had then energetically promoted Albert III as a "most Christian prince" and "most Christian archduke." Albert V now took his place as "prince in the church," one who used his sacred authority to properly order the spiritual, temporal and moral affairs of his realm, and of its church.[61] Peter's call for one of Austria's most venerable monasteries to renounce wasteful, scandalous claims to personal property must have seemed perfectly suited to that end.

By the 1420s, the most vocal leaders of reform and its visitations were no longer secular clergy and schoolmen like Peter of Pulka, but the first generation of devout converts to Observant reform. They too, however, enjoyed the backing of their prelates and princes. They too availed themselves of the same call to renounce the vice of property, and they advanced the call from the same forward positions. In 1426, Peter of Rosenheim, veteran of Melk and now leader of John Grünwalder's visitation in the diocese of Freising, delivered the visitation sermon for the Benedictine community of Weihenstephan.[62] Peter chose as his scriptural passage Romans 13:11: "It is now the hour for us to rise from sleep." Here was another favorite passage for reforming visitation sermons, and Peter used it to call the monks to turn from the vice of property.[63] Like the sleeping man who could neither see nor sense anything around him, these monks, bound by deeply rooted, inveterate custom, could no longer sense anything evil in the way they lived. Quite the contrary, Peter noted, they defended their customs as law, often so strongly that it caused scandal among princes and commoners alike.[64] Utterly forgetful of their vows, they had gathered money and goods from alms and gifts and other "irregular contributions," all of which they not only refused to resign, but actively defended. The *proprietarii* conspired openly against their superiors and countered any

---

[61] For the following see Koller, *Princeps in Ecclesia*, 40–44 and Elisabeth Kovács, "Die Heiligen und heilige Könige der frühen Habsburger (1273–1519)," in *Laienfrömmigkeit im späten Mittelalter. Formen, Funktionen, politisch-soziale Zusammenhänge*, ed. Klaus Schreiner (1992), 93–105.

[62] For the visitation see Niederkorn-Bruck, *Die Melker Reform*, 211.

[63] MS Munich, BSB, Clm 19638 fols. 14r–18v. Cf. Niederkorn-Bruck, *Die Melker Reform*, 37 and n. 125.

[64] Ibid., fol. 14r–v: "...ita sunt mala consuetudine firmata ut a plerisque quasi pro lege et tamquam pro iure ordinis sic serventur...."

perceived injustice with appeals to their secular allies, responding to demands for obedience with threats to destroy the very communities that had nurtured them.[65] Peter then offered a revealing insight into the social tensions reform had already caused: Those who sought to persuade their brothers to live a more strictly observant life, or who simply pursued strict observance alone for themselves, bore open insult and injury.[66] Derided as holier-than-thou hypocrites (*simulatores*) the pious either succumbed to the persecution and fell back into their old ways, or they were driven from the community. Even the visitors themselves, Peter lamented, had been subject to derision and persecution at Weihenstephan. The monks had even turned the visitors' own strategy against them, accusing Peter and others of greedily consuming the community's resources and unjustly seizing its goods.[67] The somnolent majority, for their part, continued to observe religious life only outwardly. Holy in habit and gesture alone, they feigned contempt for a world they knew and loved.[68] And though they fulfilled their carnal desires through their voluptuous care of the flesh, Peter reminded them how soon their bodies would be putrid food for worms, while their avaricious souls endured eternal torment.[69]

Early visitors preached these same divisive messages to women's communities. Here Dietrich Kerkering's address to the nuns of St. Giles in Münster surely proved useful. A Latin version of his treatise had made its way to Melk (most likely via Kerkering's trip to Constance as a representative of the University of Cologne) and there it shared a codex with the works of John Wischler and others.[70] Reformers likely adapted the text whenever their duties required them to visit women's houses. Nicholas of Dinkelsbühl, for example, who was active at both Constance and in the visitations in Austria, had a German translation of Kerkering's treatise among his many collections of sermons. One scholar has also suggested that Nicholas, who may have been confessor

---

[65] Ibid., fols. 14v–15r: "Et quod perversissimum est, subditi votorum suorum penitus immemores....propria resignare contempnunt atque peculia que tam diu per oblaias...aut alios irregulares obventiones tenuerunt, prelatis quibus subesse voverunt subesse renuunt ac contra eos conspirant."

[66] Ibid., fol. 15v.

[67] Ibid., fol. 17r: "Hinc virtuose et iuste viventes quasi scelerorum et malitie sue testes isti odiunt et simulatores nominant...."

[68] Ibid., fol. 16r.

[69] Ibid., fols. 16v–17r.

[70] MS Melk, Stiftsbibliothek, CM 900, fols. 56r–62r.

to the nuns of St. James in Vienna, delivered the sermon to women's communities in the city.[71] Further investigation of the manuscripts will establish more precisely the relationships among these texts, but it seems likely that Nicholas could have first encountered Kerkering's work in the vigorous textual exchanges of Constance, and thereafter appropriated it for his own purposes.

Following the sermon that announced their intentions, visitors worked to discern the overall temporal and spiritual state of the community before them. To that end their "culture of work" produced a range of texts of practice—anthologies of legal and moral treatises, visitation protocols, charters and so on, all of which collectively provided guidelines and strategies for the task at hand. The reforming handbooks of later Melk visitors provide the most visible evidence of the fruits of these efforts. One of the handbooks survives in the library of the Irish Benedictines in Vienna. Codex 152 is a massive compilation of texts related to the practice of reform. It includes a treatise on property by Caspar Maiselstein written in 1420, shortly after the jurist had served on Albert V's visitation; treatises on the eating of meat; a host of legal texts on excommunication; visitation charters and sermons; and miscellaneous correspondence concerning reform.[72] The codex is similar to other handbooks that the Melk reformer John Schlitpacher compiled for the Cusanus visitations in 1451 and 1452, and it is possible that codex 152 may have been used by the community's abbot, Martin of Leibitz, who served with Schlitpacher in that effort.[73] In any case, buried deep in the compilation are two interrogatories that outlined procedures very similar to those found in Schlitpacher's handbooks. The Irish Benedictine interrogatory instructed visitors to question household members one by one, under oath, beginning with the eldest.[74] It also framed its initial questions according to the principles of the *tria substantialia*: poverty, chastity and obedience. Under the rubric of poverty, the questions focused on the cloister's culture of property: how monks of a given community were provided with food and clothing and other necessities, for example, by whom, and from what revenues; how much

---

[71] Hermann Menhardt, "Nikolaus von Dinkelbühls deutsche Predigt vom Eigentum im Kloster," *Zeitschrift für deutsche Philologie* 74 (1955): 268–90 and 73 (1954): 1–39.

[72] MS Vienna, Schottenkloster, 152 (227) is noted in the appendix, no. 19.

[73] Cf. VL 4: 757–59 and Niederkorn-Bruck, *Die Melker Reform*, 30–32.

[74] For the following series of questions see fols. 185v–86v. See also the second *interrogatorium* at fol. 195r.

bread and wine was given to each, and whether that provision was given according to need or according to status. Visitors also asked the monks about money: Did they have an almonry that awarded cash sums for spiritual services? For what did the monks spend money they received? Did any monks pay mendicants or others to perform masses to which they themselves were obliged? Were any of the monks earning money as "merchants" or otherwise involved in secular ventures? Other questions concerned material comforts. The visitors asked, for example, if monks enjoyed individual cells, chests (*cistas*) or individual dwellings (*domos singulares*) and why; what they did there; what sort of furnishings and bedding they possessed; and whether the cells were at any point visited and searched for illicit personal goods. The visitors were also concerned about the fluid boundary between cloister and world: they asked if monks received courtesy gifts (*munuscula*); if they corresponded with friends or relatives; and if they played dice and other games for money, and if so where, when, with whom or in whose company they did so.

Reformers subjected women's communities to the same range of interrogations. In the Irish Benedictine formulary, for example, a separate section titled "On nuns" listed a series of questions that turned on matters of personal property:[75] if any of the women worked, and what habit they wore while they did so; what was the form of their provision; whether or not all had food and clothing in sufficient and equal measure; how they spent or gave away the money they earned from work; and if they owned annual rents, lands, vineyards or similar goods. Another question concerned possession of treasures or other valuables, and their purposes. The Vienna interrogatory also inquired into the cost of the women's veils and rings, and asked if the nuns played games of dice. Reformers asked similar questions of canonesses. Appended to a collection of statutes for the Augustinian communities of St. James, St. Lawrence and Mary Magdalen in Vienna, another procedural text outlined how each canoness should swear an oath on the gospel to discuss "all the things that I know or believe to be in need of reform in the cloister."[76] The questions that followed soon turned to personal property, or to the social tensions of material culture: Did

---

[75] MS Vienna, Schottenkloster 152, fol. 198r.
[76] See the "Modus visitandi brevis et planus" following the statutes for the canonesses of St. James, St. Lawrence and Maria Magdalena in Vienna in MS Klosterneuburg, Stiftsbibliothek, Cod. 1155, fol. 28r.

any of the women give or receive letters or courtesy gifts (*munuscula*) without permission? Did any of them have treasure or clothing that was either superfluous or excessively fine? Similarly, the procedural guide instructed reformers to beware of women who marked their status through veils, such that one woman might "seem like a lady," another "like a handmaid." Visitors were also to ask whether the provision of veils was delayed (*tarde ministrantur*) and whether any of the women "appropriated" veils or other things as if they were owed them "by right." The women were also to be asked whether they wanted to please others by virtue of what they wore.[77]

Here all of the concerns over the proportions and sensibilities of the cloister's culture of property, all of the concerns over status and excess that the treatises and sermons had raised, were now brought to bear on the local level. And as the visitors' own protocols suggest, the unprecedentedly focused and intrusive questions of reforming inquest inspired a variety of strategies of resistance. Notably, for example, Benedictine formularies suggested that visitors ask "whether there were any conspiracies among the monks, or between the monks and their superiors."[78] The key to controlling open conspiracy, the text noted, was to expel all servants, scholars and other extraneous members of the household at the beginning of a visitation, and to have all the gates and doors of the community secured.[79] Other passages suggest more subtle strategies: the monks were asked, for example, if because of the visitation, they might have hidden one another's goods within the monastery or elsewhere.[80] The time-honored strategy of dissimulation was also key. Peter of Rosenheim noted how, especially in the beginning, many feigned good will and commitment, only to turn on the reformers later. "Be cautious," Peter warned, "lest you trust them and yield to them too much through praise, consent or by confiding in them."[81]

Lists of questions and other procedural texts provide powerful suggestions of the tensions created by reforming visitation. But one text offers a more direct and vivid account of how those tensions actually played out in one community. In the early 1430s, Abbot John of Maulbronn

---

[77] Klosterneuburg, Cod. 1155, fol. 30r: "An pepla et alia tarde ministrantur.... An aliqua sibi appropriet peplum...."
[78] Ibid., fol. 185v.
[79] Ibid., fol. 193r.
[80] Ibid., fol. 186v.
[81] MS Melk, Stiftsbibliothek, CM 1094, fol. 276r.

attempted to reform the women's community of Rechentshofen in Swabia. A relatively detailed record of the proceedings survives.[82] To Abbot John and his team of lawyers, it was clear to "all whose reason is not depraved" that the women had to be returned to strict observance of the laws that governed their estate. The starting point for that program, notably, was not the *tria substantialia* so familiar in other interrogations, but rather the issue of enclosure enshrined in the famous decree *Periculoso*.[83] Yet the issue of enclosure was hard to distinguish from the issue of property and a superior's authority. It was precisely because they so often needed to provide for themselves and others, the reformers complained, that the women had wandered about beyond the cloister. The result, as Abbot John and his reformers saw it, was that the nuns became an endless bother to their family and friends. The women were impatient and even cursed others when they did not promptly receive the food and clothing and other things they needed. More seriously, the women's broken vows, publicly flaunted, were an open scandal to the wider world.[84] The women were "useless" to themselves, John argued, because their broken vows ensured their damnation. They were also "useless" to others, since their scandalous, mortally sinful intercession counted for nothing. Indeed, John noted, it would be easier for whores, thieves and murderers to make their way to heaven, since those sinners at least recognized and confessed their sins—here, in one local, judicial setting, a strong echo of Peraldus and the treatises of Job Vener and others. Bound and blinded by its inveterate, sinful custom, the nuns' community was nothing but a "devil's net" that trapped the souls of its noble women and carried them off to hell.

The same uncertainty that had haunted the reformers' rhetoric found its way into these proceedings. The women and their family members who were present at the confrontation responded indignantly with all of the corrosive counterarguments: that long-held and approved custom sanctioned their way of life; that to enclose the women, to deprive them

---

[82] Bruno Griesser, "Die Reform des Klosters Rechentshofen in der alten Speyerer Diözese durch Abt Johann von Maulbronn, 1431–33," *Archiv für Mittelrheinische Kirchengeschichte* (1956): 270–83. The text is cited here from MS Munich, BSB Clm 16196, fols. 121rb–124ra.

[83] Katherine Gill, "Scandala: Controversies Concerning Clausura and Women's Religious Communities in Late-Medieval Italy," in *Christendom and its Discontents: Exclusion, Persecution, and Rebellion, 1000–1500* ed. Peter D. Diehl and Scott L. Waugh (New York, 1996), 177–203.

[84] MS Munich, BSB Clm 16196, fols. 122rb and 122vb.

of their incomes and restrict their freedom would be an insult to their honor and a shame to their families. Did the women not confess their sins regularly and submit to the authority of their abbess? How then was it not an insult to call them no better than thieves and whores? It was a pitiless God indeed, they protested, who would not save the souls of such noble women, however sinful. Otherwise, why should they not uproot their monasteries like so many communities of heretics?

Caught in the middle of all the charges and countercharges were women such as Sister Margareta.[85] She protested to Abbot John that she had entered the community as a little girl, and she knew nothing other than her obligation to live as all the other "honest and noble" women—who had never been strictly enclosed, and who had never resigned their incomes and other goods. Had she known what would be required of her, Margareta certainly would have stayed in the world. Here in microcosm reformers like John confronted anew a longstanding tension. On the one hand, religious life was to be a voluntary embrace of ideals of poverty. On the other, all of the social pressures and obligations of custom ensured that practices such as child oblation remained necessary and intelligible. At Rechentshofen John tried to elide the tensions, reducing a complex matter to a simple equation of strict observance. Ignorance, he asserted, was no excuse. Just as laymen who were baptized had to learn the tenets of their faith, those professed to religious life were to be fully instructed in the rigors of true observance. Yet John repeatedly confronted concrete circumstances that demanded more discretion. He was lenient with the older women at Rechentshofen, for example, since they were not likely to be able to sustain the rigors of reformed life. He asked only that they remain enclosed and that they observe common property and other essential points of their vows. He would allow them to eat meat, and would allow them to participate in the divine office and other observances as they felt able. Taxing John's discretion far more, perhaps, was the case of Sister Katharina.[86] This woman asserted her willingness to submit fully to the way of life the reformers proposed. Indeed, Katharina testified that she had tried to be transferred to a reformed community. She had been refused, however, because the impoverished reformed household did not have the resources to sustain another member in the common

---

[85] Ibid., fol. 121 va–b.
[86] Ibid., fol. 122ra.

life. Katharina had even tried to resign her incomes to her abbess, asking in return that she be provided only the necessities of food and drink. The abbess promptly refused, and sharply accused Katharina of *singularitas*—of presuming that she was somehow more holy than her sisters. Was it not licit, then, for her to remain at Rechentshofen, and to maintain her customary way of life without mortal sin?

Across Bavaria and Austria, reformers quickly circulated the Rechentshofen court record, presumably because the text's rehearsal of the issues proved useful in preparations for similar confrontations elsewhere.[87] And as they did so, exporting the local issues from particular to universal, others confronted the same tensions independently, and framed them in remarkably similar ways. Nicholas of Dinkelsbühl, leading theologian at Vienna and Constance and author of the *Reformationis Methodus*, had confronted some of the issues at stake at Rechentshofen in an earlier treatise on women and reform. Recognizing that not every woman willing to embrace the common life would be in a position to do so, Nicholas had outlined a series of conditions and strategies that would allow those unable to live reformed life to preserve their conscience intact. First, it was imperative that the proportied way of life be genuinely displeasing to the woman, and that she truly desire to live the common life. Second, every woman who remained trapped within a house of unreformed observance was to be prepared, should the occasion ever arise, to resign her goods to the community. Third, she was to try eagerly to convince (*insinuare*) her abbess and other superiors of the benefits of the reformed common life, and she was to admonish others to embrace it whenever the opportunity arose. Fourth, if others would not hear of it, and if the abbess would not provide the proper necessities, then the trapped woman could, with the license of her superior, retain her goods. She was never to hide anything, and she was never to waste the money and goods she held by license on superfluous things. Indeed, she was to share her goods freely with others in the household who were less fortunate or who were otherwise in need. Notably, at Rechentshofen abbot John advised Katharina along these lines: she was to continue to approach her abbess "humbly and devoutly," asking her to accept the resignation of her incomes and to provide for her necessities only.

---

[87] At St. Nicholas in Passau, for example, immediately following Peter of Pulka's sermon to Melk (in Munich, BSB Clm 16196, as noted above, 149 n. 55) and at Klosterneuburg, Cod. 1155, fols. 38–55.

Should her repeated appeals fail, Katharina could seek his assistance for a transfer. Should even that strategy fail, she could live with her incomes in good conscience, as long as she was inwardly contemptuous of them and always willing to share them in common. Abbot John discretely kept all of these possibilities for compromise from the others; his conversation with Katharina was apparently held in private.

These passages add still more human dimensions to an already complex account of the fifteenth-century religious landscape, and of the range of women's religious experiences. Some, like the older Margareta, chose to remain set in their ways, embracing the relative comfort and security of status and estate in their more traditional, social and earthly forms. Others, like Katharina, chose to embrace more strongly the spiritual imperatives of the *status perfectionis* in the interstices, so to speak, of their earthly institutions. All of the choices, in any case, reflected women's agency within their circumstance. And to recover both the force and unpredictability of that agency helps make sense of the curious blend of intransigence and discretion with which reform's leaders confronted local circumstance.

"All of your work will be in vain"
Confronting the Religious Superior

Amid all of the interrogation and intrigue of a reforming inquest, the authority of the local superior was crucially at stake.[88] Perhaps more than any other figures, abbots and abbesses, priors and prioresses committed to reform could ensure success. Those committed to opposing reform, on the other hand, could bring every effort to ruin. That reality doubtless inspired John Wischler's tirade noted in the previous chapter, one that seemed to release a generation's frustration over excess and negligence among the heads of religious households.[89] It also inspired

---

[88] For general context, see Franz J. Felten, "Herrschaft des Abtes," in *Herrschaft und Kirche. Beiträge zur Entstehung und Wirkungsweise episkopaler und monastischer Organisationsformen*, ed. Friedrich Prinz (Stuttgart, 1988), 147–296 and Giles Constable, "The Authority of Superiors in Religious Communities," in *La notion d'autorité au Moyen Âge: Islam, Byzance, Occident. Colloques internationaux de la Napoule, session des 23–26 octobre 1978*, ed. George Makdisi, Dominique Sourdel, and Janine Sourdel-Thomine (Paris, 1982), 189–210. See also Klaus Schreiner, "Religiöse, historische und rechtliche Legitimation spätmittelalterlicher Adelsherrschaft," (above, 50 n. 89).

[89] See above, 123–25.

the more sober reflections of Peter of Rosenheim of Melk, veteran reformer and visitor. Peter's advice to a colleague on an upcoming visitation was to be cautious in dealing with the abbot, since without his willingness to cooperate "you'll accomplish nothing, and all of your work will be in vain."[90] Peter's remark reflected years of experience and touched on what was perhaps a visitor's most difficult challenge: how best to discern, quickly and efficiently, if a local superior was in fact willing and competent enough to sustain the reformers' vision of community.

The response to that challenge was the barrage of questions visible in so many visitation records, questions that reflected the Observants' sensibilities of diligent pastoral ministry: Did the abbot provide sufficiently in food and clothing? Were all monks served equally, or did some have more or less than others? And what were the other causes of inequality? Did the abbot, for example, allow his monks to dispose of money by granting a general license given once, or a special license for particular expenses? Just as important was the spiritual life of the prelate: to whom, if anyone, did the abbot and prior confess concerning waste, fraud or illicit use of the community's resources?[91]

Another Melk text suggests in even more detail how reformers confronted lordly superiors whose regimes could so easily thwart their efforts. CM 1094, a handbook similar to the Irish Benedictine codex in Vienna noted above, is a hefty compilation of procedural texts, treatises, sermons, charters and other material related to the practice of reform. Buried in the book is a text authored by John Wischler around 1429, when the archbishop of Salzburg directed him to visit the abbey of Lambach.[92] Here Wischler confronted in practice, in the figure of a powerful abbot, all of the matters of provision, ministry and communal sensibility his intricate commentary on the *Rule* of Benedict had raised. His first question asked whether the abbot wished in fact to subject himself to the regular observance the reformers were about to introduce, "in food and clothing" and "in all other things." Wischler then made several particular demands of the abbot personally. He was

---

[90] MS Melk, Stiftsbibliothek, CM 1094, fol. 276r: "Item si abbas non est voluntarius ad reformationem nihil facietis et perditis omnem laborem."

[91] MS Vienna, Schottenkloster, 152, fol. 186r.

[92] CM 1094, fols. 276v–79v. The text is found immediately following a copy of Nicholas of Dinkelsbühl's *Reformationis Methodus*. For Wischler's visitation to Lambach see Niederkorn-Bruck, *Die Melker Reform*, 29 and 194. For the manuscript, see 42.

not to use linen shirts or a feather cap, whether inside the monastery or without. In fact his habit was to be in no way significantly different from the habits of others. The abbot's bedding was also to be appropriately simple. He was to enjoy no meat unless he was ill, even in the company of "eminent" guests. He was to abstain from hunting and from having hunting dogs in his household. He was to keep all regular fasts with his community except when notably ill, or "out of charity" in the presence of certain company. Lastly, he was to be frequently in choir and refectory and chapter, especially on great feast days.

The second question of Wischler's interrogatory turned to the wider community and its culture of personal property. Wischler insisted the abbot of Lambach demand "immediately and above all" that his monks surrender to him all of their money, individual dwellings (*domos*), clothes and books. The abbot in turn was to gather all in common and dispose of it according to need, ensuring that the household thereafter had but one cellarer and one vestiary to feed and clothe the entire community. The question then ended with a revealing aside regarding monks who might be assigned to live elsewhere as parish priests. Since it would be difficult for them to return to live in the abbey without outsiders constantly calling on them, it seemed expedient that all parish duties be handed over to secular clerics.

Wischler's third question, the longest in the document, asked whether the abbot was truly committed to providing for his monks sufficiently in food and clothing and all other necessary things from the common goods of the monastery. A meticulously detailed description of that provision followed. For bedding the monks were to have a simple straw mattress, simple pillows and pillowcases, and other basic necessities. For clothing, they were to receive both short and long tunics; one ankle-length cloak; two cowls, one with sleeves, one without; two scapulars, one for day and one for night; and appropriate boots, shoes and the like for both summer and winter. Other details followed concerning caps, gloves, tunics and other items.[93] All of the clothing, Wischler insisted, was to be "decent," suitable for use by those professed to religious life, and when worn out, old garments were to be returned for replacement. There were hints here of how divergent assumptions and sensibilities may have shaped different attitudes about precisely what "decent" cloth-

---

[93] MS Melk, Stiftsbibliothek, CM 1094, fols. 278r–v.

ing and food were supposed to look like: Wischler noted in particular that the shape of the cowls at Lambach was "indecent." They were excessively (fashionably?) pleated and wide (*minis rugate et ample*), and Wischler insisted that they be reshaped by a tailor.[94] He then turned from clothing to the common table. The abbot was to see to it that the meals were alternated from day to day so as to avoid monotony, and again the abbot himself was to offer a good example. He was not to eat grand meals in front of his monks, nor was he to have a crowd of secular servants about him. At best he might allow a single brother from the community to serve him, and with that the lord abbot was to be content. Moreover, it was not fitting that the abbot should enjoy more refined food than did the rest. He was to be a good example to the others, especially in the refectory, by eating in common with the brothers and sharing the same food.[95]

That Wischler drew up such a long list of demands is no proof that the abbot of Lambach complied, and it is easy to imagine the abbot did not. But the demands themselves, read carefully, capture how the wider tensions over lordship and church property took root in reforming practice. John Wischler had complained at length about the human costs of tolerating negligent and incompetent abbots who lorded it over their monks, figures he may have encountered in his efforts as a visitor. He had also argued at length and with great sophistication, against the grain of legal and social reality, that not even abbots were lords or owners of the goods of their communities. Wischler's vision—a community whose abbot served as a minister to his flock with humility and compassion—was as ancient as monasticism itself. But here it was applied anew, in a particular setting and in a particular way. Wischler's contemporaries at the councils were concerned over the excesses of authority and wealth in the church, and sought to bind head and members back to an earlier simplicity. His contemporaries at princely courts, lawyers and other schoolmen at their side, sought to bind recalcitrant excess, especially in the church, back to the letter of the law. Others, especially Wischler's contemporaries in Bohemia, embraced a more radical utopian communalism that sought to overthrow established authority altogether, and communalist impulses remained strong in cities, towns and villages

[94] Ibid.
[95] Ibid.

across the region until their explosion during the Reformation. In a way, Wischler's circumstance captured another inflection of these many impulses. His pointed questions and bothersome demands sought to bind head and members, both a prelate's majesty and authority and the lives of his flock, back to an original simplicity. And though Wischler was no radical or revolutionary, his was still an upstart's insistence on a kind of utopian communalism—modest clothing shared from a common closet; modest provision of humble food from a common table; strict regulation of the enjoyment of cash and the appropriation of space, all asserted and applied locally, face-to-face.

What then were visitors to do with local superiors deemed incapable, uncooperative or unsuited to lead a reformed community? The authority of local superiors, whatever their shortcomings, remained in many ways unquestioned, and no superior could be simply thrown out of office. Yet only they were the best local guarantors of the observance of community. Reformers recognized the difficulty from the beginning, and they preferred negotiation over strife. In 1416, as noted above, Nicholas of Dinkelsbühl suggested that reformers begin by persuading an abbot to renounce his office, or at least to resign his right to administration of all temporal and spiritual affairs. And, as noted above, the strategy worked at Melk in June 1418: Abbot John was persuaded to resign in return for a comfortable pension, and Nicholas Seyringer quietly replaced him. Other sources reflect the same preference for compromise: visitation handbooks and charters provide evidence of superiors who were publicly "chastened" for their faults and excesses, for example, but who ultimately remained in office.[96] If an abbot were found to be so scandalous, wasteful or negligent that there was clearly no hope for reform, or if he were simply judged too old to be able to lead a reformed household, he could be invited to renounce his office, and offered the incentive of lifelong provision as a consolation.[97] If the abbot agreed to resign, one handbook suggested, he was to be handled gently—no one would presume to recite any of his particular misdeeds or faults openly, for example, and he was to be told of the favor he

---

[96] Note the visitation charter for the community of Göttweig (1418), for example, which records how the abbot there, though "chastened" by the visitors, retained his office (FRA II/55, no. 2235). Note also the protocols for "chastening" a superior in the reforming handbook of the Irish Benedictines in Vienna (MS Vienna, Schottenkloster, 152, fol. 202v).

[97] MS Vienna, Schottenkloster, 152, fol. 199v.

would find not only with God, but with the prince and the bishop. A formula for renunciation followed, stressing the abbot's free consent and the absence of even a hint of simony in the negotiations.[98]

Where persuasion and negotiation failed, reformers schemed to engineer a deposition. Nicholas of Dinkelsbühl offered one early model. He suggested that reformers might lie in wait for an abbot whose incompetence or notorious character opened the way for him to be deposed.[99] The handbook of the Irish Benedictines in Vienna suggested a similar strategy.[100] Visitors might freely entertain all manner of public accusations against a recalcitrant superior—from laity, servants, neighbors or "whoever else" they might find.[101] The text then suggested that the visitors throw in the abbot's face (*obiciatur*) not only his own negligence, but the sins of all in his household.[102] Here was a shrewd manipulation of the moral politics of visitation and inquest, where few were without fault and where, in principle, the abbot was responsible for all the failings of his flock. But to create such a volatile circumstance, the reformers recognized, could be dangerous. The handbooks advised visitors to guard the monastery carefully, to anticipate violence and rebellion, and to be prepared to have the deposed abbot seized and thrown into prison. A formula for deposition then followed, emphasizing how the abbot's manifest vice and negligence merited the sentence.[103]

Testimony alone, however, was insufficient for a solid conviction. Crucial to their success, the reformers knew, was that they somehow fit all of the information their inquest produced into established precedents that sanctioned deposition. To that end one reformer, most likely John Schlitpacher, compiled a brief and practical synthesis of those precedents, organized under the rubrics of specific cases.[104] The text merits careful attention here for several reasons. First, this particular

---

[98] Ibid., fols. 199v–200r.
[99] MS Melk, Stiftsbibliothek, CM 1094, fol. 272v.
[100] MS Vienna, Schottenkloster, 152, fol. 201v.
[101] Ibid.: "...domini visitores possunt audire adhuc plures contra ipsum deponentes, videlicet laicos, vicinos, famulos etc. quoscumque."
[102] Ibid., fol. 202r: "Deinde monasterium caute custoditur et fiat recitatio et obiciatur sibi negligentia sua et omnium fratrum, quia ipse debuit vitia corrigere et esse diligens ne fieret in monasterio suo talia."
[103] Ibid.
[104] The text is found in Melk, Stiftsbibliothek, CM 959, fols. 189r–v, immediately preceding the *Modus procedendi in reformatione monasteriorum* edited by Niederkorn-Bruck, *Die Melker Reform*, 214–22. See pp. 42–43 for the dating of the codex to 1456–57, and the attribution of its contents to Schlitpacher.

collection of categories and precedents could be found in no one place in all the laws of the church. It was a legal *florilegium*, artfully arranged, that revealed one reformer hard at work crafting the textual and legal tools he needed to depose a superior. Second, though compiled in Benedictine circles, these precedents were much more widely applicable. As the compilation itself noted explicitly, they applied to Augustinian canons as well. Finally, trace evidence suggests that these precedents may actually have applied from the early days of the region's visitations. The same evidence also suggests that the mortal sin of the "vice of property" remained a central moral and legal concern.

The first case that justified deposition was the most fully developed. It concerned an abbot found to be a "waster" (*dilapidator*). The precedents were many, including a decretal of Honorius III that had empowered visitors to denounce all nonexempt abbots deemed to be "wasters" to the bishops, who were to depose them.[105] The Melk compilation also cited canon eight of the Fourth Lateran Council, the famous *Qualiter et quando*. In that text, Innocent III summarized and clarified from his own precedents how best to investigate and prosecute suspect clerics.[106] Taken up into Gregory IX's *Decretals*, the canon became foundational for a range of procedures that came to be used in church and civil courts in a variety of ways. It was here that the link between a visitation inquest and the investigation of crime was most explicit: administrative waste was one of the many "grave excesses" that Innocent III said justified clerical inquisition, and reformers seized on the precedent to prosecute abbots. Another precedent, from a text from Gratian, suggested that even an abbot who was only suspected of wasteful administration might be removed from office.[107] A second case in the compilation concerned abbots who were unchaste. The main precedent was another of Gratian's canons, included in a larger question about a bishop's rights over abbots. The text was most likely relevant to visitors of the mid-fifteenth century because it provided a long list of moral qualities that, when absent, justified an abbot's deposition.[108] Precedents from Lateran IV and other decretals governing the election of prelates and the renuncia-

---

[105] X 3,35,8 (CIC II: 601–2).
[106] X 5,1,24 (CIC II: 745–47). For context see Kelly, "Inquisition and the Prosecution of Heresy" (above, n. 54) 439–451.
[107] C 3 q. 2 c. 9 (CIC I: 509).
[108] C 18 q. 2 c. 15 (CIC I: 833).

tion of offices underscored a third cause for deposition, one that must have resonated strongly with the stance shaped by Vienna's theologians: manifest ignorance and incompetence, especially in matters of pastoral care.[109] Fourth, any abbot could be deposed who was grossly negligent either in providing a good overall moral example for his community, or in correcting his monks. A brief survey of extreme cases—heresy, simony and homicide—then concluded the series of rubrics.

The superiors against whom these texts were arrayed might have scoffed at outsiders who presumed to challenge their authority through centuries-old laws. As the embodiment of good custom, superiors were entitled to used their discretion and authority to confront all the challenges of maintaining both their household's reputation and its fiscal solvency. But they now faced devout, disciplined and university-trained scholars armed with powerful tools and bent on holding them accountable with renewed intensity.

The compiler of these precedents then brought his textual creature to life through a very aggressive reading of the last lines of *Qualiter et quando*, Innocent's decree that had established inquisitions for the crimes of clerics. At the end of that decree the pope had noted, with rather uncharacteristic brevity and imprecision, that the rules for due process he had outlined need not apply to regular clergy. The Melk compiler now exploited that generality. Prosecutions against religious prelates suspected of any of these crimes, they argued, could advance without due process (*absque strepitu iuris*).[110] "Since many prelates are guilty of these things," fifteenth-century reformers revealingly concluded, visitations that vigorously applied precedent were vital, and Innocent's decree gave them justification for doing so more expeditiously.[111]

The text examined here survives from a handbook of the 1450s. Its categories, however, and presumably all of its precedents, seem to have been deployed a generation before. By early October 1427, the visitation commission sponsored by the bishop of Freising and Duke William of Bavaria-Munich had begun its work at the Benedictine community of

---

[109] E.g. X 1, 9,10 (CIC II: 108).
[110] MS CM 959, fol. 189v: "Et sciendum quod quando de crimen simonie, periurii, dilapidationis, incontientie et similibus agitur contra prelatum regularem absque strepitu iuris potest deponi, quia ex facili causa potest a sua administratione removeri, ut patet in c. *Qualiter et quando*." Cf. X 5,1,24 (CIC II: 747).
[111] Ibid.

Ebersberg.[112] In the presence of Duke William, the vicar-general John Grünwalder, several nobles and some forty soldiers as well as several reforming monks and other churchmen, the commission interrogated Ebersberg's ten members. The proceedings quickly turned to focus on the reputation of the abbot, Simon Kastner. Simon had allied his fortunes with William's cousin and rival, Duke Henry the Rich of Bavaria-Landshut. Simon was also subject to a series of accusations from his own monks. In the presence of Duke William and the vicar-general, the monks charged that their abbot had not only paid Duke Henry two hundred gulden to back his election, but a further two hundred gulden for protection against the visitors. The visitors took down all of the accusations, found Abbot Simon guilty of a long list of crimes, deposed him and cast him into prison.

The list of Abbot Simon's crimes is of particular interest because it is consistent with the categories and precedents visible in the later Melk compilation. Abbot Kastner was declared a "waster" (*dilapidator*) and a perjurer. He was also found guilty of simony and concubinage, declared incompetent in administration and denounced as a "proprietor."[113] The list suggests the possibility that well-known precedents and slogans centered on notorious crimes, such as the "vice of property," had shaped the outcome of the trial. A host of pressures—the presence of the duke who sponsored the visitation not least among them—may well have encouraged the visitors to fit all of the testimony into categories they knew could make an solid case for deposition of an abbot who was supported by a rival duke. There was perhaps too much pressure; Abbot Simon was soon set free, and he quickly accused the reformers of unjust deposition and seizure of his incomes. He then launched a vigorous countersuit that occupied all parties in multiple appeals for years. Decades later, after the death of Martin V in 1431, Simon won back his position, ruling again at Ebersberg until his death in 1442.

---

[112] Thoma, "Petrus von Rosenheim," 135–37 (recounted from Munich, archdiocesan archive, Cod. F. 64, fols. 432–33).

[113] Ibid. "Invenimus gravibus culpis obnoxium, intrusum videlicet symoniacum, periurum, concubinarium publicum, dilapidatorem, subtractorem sigilii conventus, proprietarium, sacrilegium, nescientem facere rationem."

"First and Above All"
Property, Community and the Visitation Charter

In the wake of their inquests, visitors left behind detailed charters in which they outlined the rigors of reformed observance. The charters addressed a wide range of reforming concerns, but central to most were a series of stipulations concerning the dangers of the "vice of property." The focus typically turned, more concretely, to the indiscriminate, unregulated enjoyment of cash incomes. The lengthy charter that Albert V's visitation issued for the Benedictine community of Seitenstetten in 1419 captures some of the best representative language.[114] "With experience as a witness," the visitors lamented, many monasteries in the region had "collapsed," both temporally and spiritually, not least because of so much illicit appropriation.[115] The charter then prohibited the distribution of money to individual monks from an almonry or by virtue of any other offering. Here the reformers dismissed a long-held custom in religious houses across the region as something that seemed "not very far" from the vice of property.[116] Still stronger language followed. The charter condemned the enjoyment of cash incomes as an "abusive corruption, one that endures in this monastery despite all rules and statutes to the contrary." Almost identical language can be found in the early visitation charters for the monks and Augustinian canons of Bavaria. At the canonries of Dietramszell and Beuerberg in 1426, the Grünwalder visitation commission demanded that the prior was "first and above all" to uproot the vice of property in his community by providing both wine and "regular food" for his brothers. The prior was also to prohibit any within the community from receiving personal cash stipends. Those who were discovered to have concealed cash were to be condemned as *proprietarii*. The visitation commission also demanded that only officers be allowed to retain even moderate cash sums, but only with license and only if circumstance required it, and then only to the appropriate extent. Notably, in many instances the language of

---

[114] MS Vienna, Schottenkloster, 152, fols. 164r–68r.
[115] Ibid., fol. 165v: "...districte...precepimus et mandamus quod nulla persona regularis huius monasterii proprium aut peculium habeat sive occulte retineat nec quovis quesito colore ad sibi appropriandum acquirat, sed omnia et singula ad dominum abbatis arbitrium distribuenda integraliter assignentur."
[116] Ibid.: "Et specialiter quod nulla fiat deinceps de oblaya seu quibuscumque aliis obventionibus inter monachos distributio pecuniarum, cum ipsa non videatur fori a proprietatis vitio aliena."

the Augustinian charters was nearly identical to the provisions of the Benedictine reform charters of Tegernsee and Weihenstephan. Later adaptations of Raudnitz statutes recorded at the canonry of Diessen articulated even more strongly the need to uproot the customary provision of cash for masses. All of the community's spiritual revenues were to be "faithfully presented" to the prior, who was then to allow his officers to purchase only what necessity demanded. All cash expenditures, moreover, were to be counted out (*nummeratam pecuniam*) and recorded carefully and frequently (*diligenter conscribendo*).[117]

In the place of appropriated incomes, reforming visitors sought to establish a culture of diligent, charitable ministry of the necessities of food, drink and clothing. Again the charter of Seitenstetten provides a useful example of the typical language. It instructed the abbot and household officers to work to provide "sufficiently and honestly" for the community's food, clothing and other needs, and to do so equally for all. Detailed stipulations about provision then followed. The refectory was to provide eggs, cheese, fish and other basic staples in proper measure. The reformers were also concerned that superiors provide good wine for good monks—not in excess, but in proper, modest proportion, and in a way that discouraged strife. In the same spirit, the monks were to eat together daily, never excusing themselves from the common meal without good reason, and never hoarding any excess for themselves or for others. Only officers were to dispose of any excess and to provide for the poor. At Tegernsee, bread, wine, eggs and fish were to replace the cash of the mass stipend and other cash distributions from the almonry.[118] At Weihenstephan, the foundational reform charter of 1426 made similar demands: that the abbot and cellarer provide for the monks "not in money or rents, but in the provision itself" (*in ipsis victualibus*), that they provide only what the monks' needs required, and that they do so "in all charity." Only officers were to dispose of cash, and even they were to do so only in moderate proportions suited to circumstance. Austrian charters articulated similar measures for women's communities. In Vienna, superiors were to provide Augustinian canonesses with, among other things, two tunics (one for daily wear and

---

[117] Eusebius Amort, *Vetus Disciplina Canonicorum Regularium et Secularium* (Farnborough, 1971), 5: 767 [773].
[118] MS Munich, BSB Clm 1008, fol. 23v.

one for festivals); two or three veils; and shoes and socks according to season and need.[119]

Reformers also recorded in their visitation charters detailed measures regulating the cloister's appropriated spaces. Visitation sermons and charters hardly ever reveal the contours of those spaces as reformers encountered them from locale to locale. But in the 1430s, John Nider offered one revealing glimpse of the proportions intimate comfort could reach in his *De reformatione religiosorum*. Nider lamented the number of glorious private cells he had seen in many religious houses in the region, their finely appointed spaces adorned with images of sirens, monkeys and jousters, and even sculptures of women "so well executed as to not only distract from devotion, but to threaten the vow of chastity!"[120] Not every monk, nun or canon lived in such comfortable domesticity. But whatever the arrangements they encountered, early visitors uniformly railed against the excesses of appropriated space. In its place they articulated their communalist vision. At Seitenstetten in 1419 the monks were to share a common dormitory, "as has been customary in well-ordered monasteries" (*sicut hactenus in monasteriis ordinatis fieri est consuetum*). The generality of the phrase obscures precisely what the reformers had in mind, but some passages allow for sound conjecture. In one way reform seems to have presumed the quiet, long-term transformation that had made individual rooms integral to daily life generally—monks are described as having individual cells in the dormitory suitable for both study and sleep. But those spaces were now fully subject to the reformed regime: monks were to sleep in clothing properly bound with a belt or cord. No monks were to enjoy beds made comfortable with feather pillows or linen bed coverings. All were to use simple pallets or straw mattresses diligently provided for them by the abbot or other officers. Moreover, superiors were to "scrutinize" the dormitory's cells regularly, not least to ensure that monks did not hide or otherwise retain money or other goods there.[121] These lines suggest how reformers appropriated for themselves a new domestic mood. It was one of stern and well-ordered frugality, modesty and discipline,

---

[119] MS Klosterneuburg, Cod. 1155, fols. 9r–10r.
[120] For Nider see above, 117 and n. 78. Here, DRR I.17, fol. 206v: "Sed iste sepe in privatis reperiuntur habtaculis non sub typo divinorum ymaginum, sed sub syrenarum et symearum scemate, sub hastilusorum et feminarum pene nudata ymagine, ita ut ex hiis non modo perdatur religionis devotio, sed etiam castitatis minetur naufragium."
[121] MS Vienna, Schottenkloster, 152, fol. 167r.

encountered across the Empire after 1400 in so many urban hospitals and apartments, in the neighborhood houses of the New Devout in the Low Countries and so on. Something of the same "bourgeois" sensibility, often rugged, but not uncomfortable, helped reformers give expression to their renunciation of propertied life, and their retreat to the imagined simplicity of early monasticism.

Sleeping arrangements in women's communities were subject to similar regulation and scrutiny. Statutes for Augustinian canonesses in Vienna allowed each woman to have her own cell, for example, yet also demanded that each sleep alone, clothed, in her own bed.[122] The statutes also demanded that the younger girls of the community clean the dormitory regularly, and that each cell be open at all times to inspection. The superior was to ensure that each woman had appropriate bedding, here described in detail: a simple mattress (though the superior might exceptionally allow the young or the infirm to enjoy a feather bed); two simple feather pillows; and bed coverings and other necessities according to the community's means, without exception for status. The women's reform charters also suggested that they should be allowed needle, thread, scissors "and other such small things"—all of the tools essential for the needlework so important to women's religious life throughout the Middle Ages. Just as revealingly, the statutes prohibited the women from having "sculpted or carved images made from silver" in their individual cells. The women were permitted to have painted images, presumably for devotional purposes, but even these were to be allowed only with the license of the superior.[123]

Religious houses and orders had long recorded guidelines of observance in their customaries, and they had long issued statutes aimed at governing excess. After 1400, however, reform of the orders strengthened and concentrated the old links between written statute and observance in a distinct way. The charters and other sources studied here provided a more consistent textual basis for accountability and regulation, and their guidelines in principle trumped many local customs. It is important not to overestimate the impact of the new regime; deep into the fifteenth century, as reformers themselves complained, local communities ignored or lost the documents, or otherwise allowed the reformers' whole agenda to slide into oblivion soon after the visi-

---

[122] MS Klosterneuburg, Cod. 1155, fols. 9r–10r.
[123] Ibid.

tors had left. But the ground had begun to shift in a notable way. By midcentury the reformers' "culture of work" had brought all of the textual and cultural energy of their era to bear on regulating the lives of monks, nuns and canons, regionally and locally, in unprecedented length and detail. By 1450, religious communities were coming to be governed, like so much else, by diligent writing and record-keeping, by standard statutes and other written documents, and by repeated scrutiny and accountability.

The movements for reform surveyed thus far have been focused and directed in different ways, outwardly and most often negatively—secular theologians and jurists who denounced propertied religious from beyond the cloister; religious who revolted from within; visitors who sought to break in from the outside to carve out enclaves for renewed religious life. But as reformers themselves recognized from the beginning, perhaps the most difficult and lasting struggles were inward and spiritual. No rhetorical attack, no mere citation of the laws, no visitation and inquest could by itself establish a lasting renunciation of the "vice of property." Any lasting transformation required that reform's energies work from within, in ways that helped individuals embrace the reforming vision of community as their own. A final chapter turns now to explore that important process.

CHAPTER FIVE

PROPERTY AND COMMUNITY BETWEEN
PENANCE AND PERFECTION

Around 1460, Martin of Leibitz, prior of the reformed Irish Benedictines in Vienna and a veteran of years of visitation across Bavaria and Austria, recounted in his *Senatorium* (c. 1460) why he had chosen to profess Benedictine religious life. Martin remembered that as a young schoolman he had been impressed by how many of the "holy doctors" he studied—Augustine, Gregory, Aquinas, Bonaventure and so many more—had themselves been professed to religious life.[1] Martin considered conversion himself, but wavered for a time, choosing instead to take a pilgrimage to Rome and to purchase indulgences to pay for his sins. While in Italy he was deeply impressed by reformed Benedictine observance at Subiaco, however, and realized that religious life's "second baptism" could give him the safeguard against sin he had long sought. Martin had difficulty adjusting to the rigors of Subiaco's regime, but he soon made his way to Austria, where he began his long career in the service of the reformed Irish Benedictines at Vienna.

Martin's reflections capture something of the broader religious mood of his day—the embrace of penitential devotion, pilgrimage, indulgences and other acts of piety; an overall desire for holiness and for the assurance of salvation; and the related sense of the need to return churches and communities to order and accountability. Observant religious shared that common ground with their contemporaries beyond the cloister, and cultivated it in a variety of ways: through sermons, pastoral treatises, and an attentiveness to law and a rightly ordered daily life. At the same time, Observants remained particularly conscious of their own sin and moral weakness, and they embraced the obligations of *religio* with a distinct energy and seriousness of purpose. For leaders of reform like Martin of Leibitz, John Wischler, John of Indersdorf

---

[1] MS Melk, CM 193, fol. 190v–191r: "Adverti quod sancti doctores quasi omnes fuerunt claustrales—sanctus Hieronimus, Augustinus, Gregoius, Bernardus, Thomas de Aquino et alii nobiles: Scotus, Alexander de Halles, Bonaventura." For Martin's career and a discussion of his memoir, the *Senatorium*, see VL 6: 154–57.

and others—many of them former schoolmen and mature converts to religious life—the strictures of Observant life provided safety and security in the battle against sin, and the best environment for progress in the virtues.

These broader commitments drove Observant reformers to reshape and redeploy their attack on the "vice of property" from yet another cultural position, in a way different from those surveyed thus far. Looking in one direction, reformers saw themselves surrounded by the unrepentant comfort of those in their own ranks who did not share their zeal. Among themselves, reformers held the belief that a measured charity of life in community remained one of the best guarantees of moral discipline and spiritual progress. Looking beyond the cloister, reformers knew princes, pious women and other laity who shared their spiritual goals and admired their ordered, communal sensibilities, but who themselves were not under formal religious vows. The "vice of property" became meaningful in this field of relationships, not primarily as a publicist's slogan or as a rubric for reforming visitation, but as a far-reaching penitential theme, and as a pastoral and administrative concern. Within their reformed enclaves, Observants placed renunciation of their modern world of cash and comfort at the foundation of a program of penance and spiritual progress. In a way consistent with their pastoral commitment, they also extended that penitential call through translation to wider circles of lay brothers, nuns and the laity. At the same time, as professed religious, they remained keenly conscious of their vows, and they continually returned to their own commitment to conversion and community through strict observance of written statute.

"Against the Proprietors, On Penance"
Texts, Contexts and Resonance

In 1441 a visitation commission sponsored by Duke Albert III of Bavaria-Munich reformed the Augustinian canonry of Diessen.[2] In 1447, the canons there copied out two codices for their newly reformed

---

[2] See above, 145. For the reform of Diessen see Bauerreiss, *Kirchengeschichte Bayerns*, 5, 47. Also see Backmund, *Die Chorherrenorden und ihre Stifte in Bayern* (above, 9 n. 23), 72, with further literature.

community.[3] In each book the canons included several widely read treatises on the instruction of novices. Arnulf of Boheries' *Speculum monachorum*—addressed to any who would be a "diligent examiner" of thought, word and deed—provided readers with instruction on how to raise up a flagging spirit of devotion.[4] One of the most effective strategies was a diligent meditation on death.[5] Arnulf's readers were to meditate on bodies being prepared for burial, on how the head and limbs "fall around" as the body is turned; how it is carried away for burial and then consumed by worms and putrefaction. Diessen canons also copied out David of Augsburg's *De exterioris et interioris compositione*, an remarkably popular work that instructed novices to cultivate "purity of heart" and outward discipline, above all by focusing on the life and the suffering of Christ.[6] In each of the Diessen codices, Adam Scotus' *Soliloquium anime* also offered reforming readers a dialogue on the nature of religious life and its obligations, including careful considerations of the many temptations and challenges novices might face—thoughts of beautiful girls, the burdens of a superior's many demands, the rigors of proper chanting, and so on.[7] Other treatises in the two Diessen codices focused on more widely popular devotional themes. One anonymous fourteenth-century treatise offered a series of brief but vivid meditations on Christ's passion, organized around the seven traditional hours of prayer.[8] Two other works—a *Speculum peccatoris* attributed to Augustine and a *Speculum amatorum mundi*, attributed to Denis the Carthusian—recovered all of the sharp imagery and compelling rhetoric

---

[3] MSS Munich, BSB Clm 5690 and 5607.

[4] Cf. BSB Clm 5690, fols. 1r–6r. The treatise is printed in PL 184: 1175–78. Cf. Morton Bloomfield, *Incipits of Latin Works on the Virtues and Vices: 1100–1500* (Cambridge, MA, 1979), no. 5582, p. 480.

[5] PL 184: 1178.

[6] MSS Munich, BSB Clm 5607, fols. 139v–51r and 5690, fols. 20r–41r, printed in PL 184: 1167–69. The work, composed around 1240, was actually a trilogy whose three parts, whether copied and circulated together as a independent works, were explosively popular in the later Middle Ages. There are nearly 400 Latin manuscripts, along with numerous vernacular adaptations. Cf. Bloomfield, no. 3897, pp. 328–9 and Bert Roest, *Franciscan Literature of Religious Instruction Before the Council of Trent* (Leiden, 2004), 211 and n. 16.

[7] The treatise is printed in Pez, *Thesaurus* 1: 335–72 and PL 198: 843–72. Cf. Bloomfield, *Incipits*, no. 5366. It appears in Clm 5607, fols. 48ra–51rb and 5690, fols. 42r–57r.

[8] MSS Munich, BSB Clm 5607, fols. 159r–61r and 5690, fols. 99v–106v. The treatise, which survives in over 100 manuscripts, is printed in PL 94: 561–68. See Thomas H. Bestul, *Texts of the Passion. Latin Devotional Literature and Medieval Society* (Philadelphia, 1996), 54–56 and 190.

of a traditional monastic contempt of the world.[9] "And what is more vile in this world than man," asked the author of the *Speculum peccatoris*, "whose body, without a soul, cannot remain three days before it begins to stink; then it is thrown out like vile dung, hidden in the depths of the earth, handed over to rotting, given up as food for worms, made into a corpse?"[10]

By midcentury, diligent reforming scribes in communities across the Empire had produced a flood of books like these.[11] Each was a witness to a wider cultural flowering of reading, writing and devotion that emerged across Europe after 1400.[12] Its earliest manifestations are visible in the circles of the New Devout and the canons of Windesheim.[13] With a bookish diligence they gathered together an extensive *Patrologia devota*—Gregory, Ambrose and Jerome; Bernard, William of St. Thierry, Arnulf of Boheries, Hugh and Richard of St. Victor; Aquinas, Bonaventure, even Petrarch. These works and others they read carefully, closely and repeatedly, copying out personal collections (*rapiaria*, "grab bags")

---

[9] For the *Speculum peccatoris* (Incipit: " Quoniam fratres karissimi) see MSS Munich, BSB Clm 5607, fols. 221r–23r and 5690, fols.115r–24r. For the *Speculum amatorum mundi* (Incipit: "Videte quomodo caute ambuletis") see MSS Clm 5607, fols. 162v–64r and 5690, fols 125r–34r. The treatise is also found in PL 184: 487–89. For broader context, see Kent Emery, Jr., "Lovers of the World and Lovers of God and Neighbor: Spiritual Commonplaces and the Problem of Authorship in the Fifteenth Century," in *Historia et Spiritualitas Cartusiensis Colloquii Quarti Internationalis Acta* (Destelbergen, 1983), 177–219.

[10] PL 40: 988: "Et quid huic mundo tantum vilescit, sicut homo, cuius corpus cum sit exanime, non permittitur esse intra domum triduo prae fetore, sed ut vile stercus foras proiicitur, in profundo terrae absconditur, putredini traditur, vermibus in escam datur, cadaver efficitur?" Cf. Bloomfield, *Incipits*, no. 4918, pp. 414–15.

[11] To note only a very few representative examples: MS Munich, BSB Clm 18551, containing a copy of a popular collection of "pious meditations" attributed to Bernard (Incipit: "Multi multa sciunt," found in PL 184: 485–87) as well as most of the other treatises noted here. The Benedictine codices Clm 18558 and 18600 (Tegernsee); Clm 9726 (Oberalteich); and Clm 7531 (Indersdorf) also contain many of the same works.

[12] For general context see Uwe Neddermeyer, *Von der Handschrift zum gedruckten Buch: Schriftlichkeit und Leseinteresse im Mittelalter und in der frühen Neuzeit. Quantitative und Qualitative Aspekte* (Wiesbaden, 1998) and for a specialized study Matthew Wranovix, "Parish Priests and their Books in the Fifteenth-Century Diocese of Eichstätt" (PhD diss., Yale University, 2007).

[13] See the works of Nikolaus Staubach, especially "Von der persönlichen Erfahrung zur Gemeinschaftsliteratur. Entstehungs- und Rezeptionsbedingungen geistlicher Reform-texte im Spätmittelalter," *Ons geestelijk erf* 68 (1994): 200–28; and idem, "'Memores priscae perfectionis.' The Importance of the Church Fathers for Devotio moderna," in *The Reception of the Church Fathers in the West: From the Carolingians to the Maurists*, ed. Irena Backus and Antoinina Bevan (Leiden, 1997), 1: 405–74; John Van Engen, *Devotio Moderna. Basic Writings* (New York, 1988), especially the introduction, and his *Sisters and Brothers of the Common Life* (above, 3 n. 11).

of excerpts they found stirring, meaningful or useful. They did so not as an end in itself, or as a way to advance their own knowledge or careers, but rather as a means to spiritual advancement—to persevere in their conversion to the apostolic life; to uproot vices and to progress in the virtues; to cultivate genuine charity and purity of heart.

The New Devout and the Windesheim canons are justly celebrated as pioneers of this culture of reading and devotion. Consider the phenomenal popularity of the *Imitation of Christ*, a work that survives in some 750 manuscripts and thousands of printed editions, and that remains among the most widely-read in Western history. But analogous patterns took hold elsewhere in the Empire, and the reforming enclaves of Bavaria and Austria were among the most energetic and successful.[14] Their monks, canons and nuns embraced reading, writing and copying anew as well, and soon their libraries and *scriptoria* had become a cultural force in the region. At Melk, to note only one well-researched setting, the monks considered writing, copying and bookbinding to be essential to their labors, more important than traditional manual labor in the garden or other menial tasks.[15] In time their discipline bore fruit—they copied some six hundred manuscripts in the fifteenth century, and John Schlitpacher, one of their most visible leaders, copied some fifty books alone. Other reformed communities self-consciously ennobled the *exercitium scribendi* in similar ways, and in all reformed houses the diligent work of texts and books served the same devotional ends. Reformers stuffed their *libri devoti*, books like those at Diessen noted above, with texts and excerpts they deemed "devout" or "useful" (as they so often

---

[14] Uwe Neddermeyer, "'Radix Studii et Speculum Vitae.' Verbreitung und Rezeption der 'Imitatio Christi' in Handschriften und Drucken bis zur Reformation" in *Studien zum 15. Jahrhundert: Festschrift für Erich Meuthen*, ed. Johannes Helmrath et al. (Munich, 1994), 1: 457–81.

[15] Felix Heinzer, "Labor Scribendi—Überlegungen zur Frage einer Korrelation zwischen geistlicher Reform und Schriftlichkeit im Mittelalter," in *Die Präsenz des Mittelalters in seinen Handschriften. Ergebnisse der Berliner Tagung in der Staatsbibliothek zu Berlin—Preußischer Kulturbesitz, 6.–8. April 2000*, ed. Hans-Jochen Schiewer and Karl Stackmann (Tübingen, 2002), 107–27; Freimut Löser, "Im Dialog mit Handschriften. 'Handschriftenphilologie' am Beispiel der Laienbrüderbibliothek in Melk," in *Die Präsenz des Mittelalters in seinen Handschriften*, 177–208; S. H. Steinberg, "Instructions in Writing by Members of the Congregation of Melk," *Speculum* 16 (1941): 210–15 notes a *De modo recte scribendi* that survives from the library of Tegernsee (Clm 18799, fol. 117r ff.). For general context see Klaus Schreiner, "Verschriftlichung als Faktor monastischer Reform. Funktion von Schriftlichkeit im Ordenswesen des hohen und späten Mittelalters," in *Pragmatische Schriftlichkeit im Mittelalter. Erscheinungsformen und Entwicklungsstufen*, ed. Hagen Keller et al. (Munich, 1992), 37–75.

put in their titles, colophons and marginalia) because they helped establish and sustain a disciplined *forma vivendi*. Here Observants drew their inspiration from all of the "classics" of the monastic tradition, and especially engaged all of the twelfth-century themes that Giles Constable and others have shown to be so central to fifteenth-century spirituality: an affective piety based on the individual will; reflection on penance and death leading to introspection, self-knowledge and spiritual progress; reflection on the humanity of Christ, his life and sufferings; and reflection on the tensions between contemplation and action.[16]

The long-term victory of reforming religious culture has made these devotional themes commonplace. But it is important to return the themes to their original setting, to ground them and hold them in tension with competing sensibilities of custom and status. Consider the monks of Tegernsee, who over the course of the fifteenth century compiled a massive library of the devout texts so popular in the reformed circles of their day. During the Council of Basel, the monks also recorded a series of "advisements" (*avisamenta*) regarding the excesses that still cried out for reform. Too many abbots, the Tegernsee monks complained, ignored the laws of the church by usurping the regalia of bishops and their rights to bless and to consecrate. Too many surrounded themselves with grand feast tables (*credentias*) "like secular lords" and allowed all manner of "curious and irreligious gestures" amid the festivities. They enjoyed games with laymen and allowed minstrels and actors into their households.[17] Others insisted on being addressed by pompous titles such as "Glorious Lord," "Your Gloriousness," "Your Grace" and the

---

[16] See espeially Giles Constable, "The Popularity of Twelfth-Century Spiritual Writers in the Late Middle Ages," in *Renaissance Studies in Honor of Hans Baron*, ed. Anthony Molho and John A. Tedeschi (Florence and DeKalb, 1971), 5–28 and "Twelfth Century Spirituality and the Late Middle Ages," in *Medieval and Renaissance Studies 5*, ed. O.B. Hardison, Jr. (Chapel Hill, 1971), 27–60; Ulrich Köpf, "Monastische Theologie im 15. Jahrhundert," *Rottenburger Jahrbuch für Kirchengeschichte* 11 (1992): 117–35 and idem, "Die Passion Christi in der lateinischen religiösen und theologischen Literatur des Spätmittelalters," in *Die Passion Christi*, ed. Walter Haug and Burghart Wachinger (Tübingen, 1993), 21–41; Jean Leclercq, "Monastic and Scholastic Theology in the Reformers of the Fourteenth to the Sixteenth Century," in *From Cloister to Classroom: Monastic and Scholastic Approaches to Truth*, ed. E. Rozanne Elder (Kalamazoo, 1986), 178–201; and Dennis Martin, *Fifteenth-Century Carthusian Reform*, especially Chapter Two and 63 and n. 102.

[17] MS BSB, Clm 19697, fol. 158r: "Item aliqui ludos varios et indecentes solent exercere cum laycis...in suis domibus ioculationes et truffas hystrionicas admittere, comessationibus et potationibus dissolutis hominibus inibi frequenter indulgere, ut iam non domus abbatis, sed potius taberna vel theatrum habeatur."

like. Still others went about with great retinues, their horses adorned with splendidly decorated saddles, reins and precious cloth—and so, as one devout monk scribbled in the lower margin, "made knights out of monks."[18] Ordinary monks, for their part, carried on their belts individual "purses" or "bags" to hold the many things they had appropriated for themselves. They also jealously guarded their personal chalices, cups or vases used for drinking.[19] Monks also sang masses for money, but their priors actually kept the proceeds for themselves, often to buy spices for special occasions or to flavor meals.[20] The condemnations continued: fashionable hats and other clothing worn pompously and in public; monks who could be found naked in the public baths, scandalously indistinguishable from the rest of the worldly throng; abbots who had women in their households and at their tables, even with monks present. Some even treated the women to a stroll around the gardens within the precincts of the cloister. "O, Danger!" wrote the sensitive monk recording the custom.[21] Still other monks enjoyed bloodletting sessions in rooms decked with sumptuous tapestries, wearing pearl-studded ligatures and gold and jeweled rings "on almost every finger."[22] Bloodletting involved the monks in drinking in the presence of worldly laymen and "base people" who sang "ridiculous songs" and who made everyone laugh with their gestures and jokes.[23]

[18] Ibid.: "Item quidam in familia et in equitatura contra decentiam status sui sunt nimis sumptuosi et omnino superflui, non advertentes vel potius contemptui habentes quorundam summorum pontificum instituta hoc ipsum prohibentia etc. [i. m. infra]: Equos faleratos cum frenis et sellis splendide decoratis, sellasque vestitas de pannis pretiosis equitantes, ex monachis milites facientes."

[19] Ibid.: "...monachi singuli bursas seu sacculos quottidie portant in cingulis et in eisdem deferunt que non decent.... Insuper cantros et piccaria seu vasa pro potu in mensa sibi ad voluntatem eligunt et eadem consignant...."

[20] Ibid.: "Item in nonnuliis monasteriis servatur consuetudo detestanda quod fratres legunt missas pro pecunia, quam pecuniam priores apud se retinent, et suo tempore pro certa summa emunt species aromaticas, quas inter se distribuunt ac semper secum ferunt in pixidibus et in bursis, ut...cum eis condiant fercula sua quae alias male condiuntur."

[21] Ibid.: "Item, quidam infra domos suos abbatiales admittunt feminas, easque ad suas mensas, etiam monachis presentibus.... Similter admittunt easdem infra clausuram monasteriorum ad viridaria et pomeria et cetera. O, pericula!"

[22] Ibid.: "...annulis aureis et gemmatis quasi omnes digitos muniunt, sed et ligaturas venarum margaritas intextas habentes...et loca ubi habitant tapetibus pretiosis...ac ceteris similibus paramentis, ut si quis illuc introerit paradisum terrestrem sibi videatur introisse."

[23] Ibid.: "Insuper vocant et admittunt laycos scientes cantare cantilenas ridiculosas aut alias seculares, sed et viles persone aliquando admittuntur, gestibus et instrumentis suis scientes provocare risu et ioca facere dissoluta."

It is important neither to make excuses for nor to domesticate the force of the excesses so vividly denounced in these lines. But it is also important to discern how the reformers' laments offered another photographic negative, as it were, of longstanding practices that most often appeared in more muted tones. Abbots still marked their social and spiritual status through material splendor and lordly titles. Monks still had to make a living from the spiritual marketplace and its intercessory masses. Some might enjoy the conviviality of the baths, of feasts and festivals, or the refined company of ladies on a stroll through the garden. Still others might enjoy an intimate, refined gathering for bloodletting—complete with the pearls and other jewels whose properties were believed to help balance the humors.[24] While these pastimes might involve excess, they could also be followed in more moderate and measured ways.

Reformers committed to the common life thus had to continually remind their peers of the scandal of so much propertied excess, and to establish a lasting commitment to a life of penance and community. To that end, the minority of "well trained" and "devout" zealots who led reform had to establish a solid "basic training" in the tenets of an observant life in community, to anchor renewed observance in steady indoctrination. Reform's leaders had to explain the precise nature of the "vice of property" and the evils of the *proprietarii*, and why meticulous attention to universal precepts or once-distant laws should trump long-standing local arrangements or the force of custom. Yet in all of their twelfth- and thirteenth-century texts, reformers found almost nothing that quite fit their fifteenth-century circumstance. Adam Scotus' *Soliloquium*, for example, had offered some relevant reflections, but only in passing. When *Anima* asked if it is a serious sin to have property (*proprium*), *Ratio* responded sternly: "How is it not a serious sin to have something of your own when blessed Benedict prohibits you even to name something as your own? Is theft a serious sin, or lying, or sacrilege, or apostasy?"[25] But the discussion then quickly moved on to other matters. The brief treatment must have seemed wholly inadequate to fifteenth-century reformers surrounded by so many unrepentant proprietors. Most of the older discussions of poverty, mysticism and prophecy

---

[24] Cf. the discussion of bloodletting in Nancy Siraisi, *Medieval and Early Renaissance Medicine. An Introduction to Knowledge and Practice* (Chicago, 1990), 141.
[25] PL 198: 843–72, here 863–64.

were similarly too distant or specialized to be of much immediate use. Even Peraldus' treatment of the vice of property, though focused in a way that spoke to reformers' moral concerns, had been articulated only in a general way, and had to be adapted to fifteenth-century experience. Reformers thus had to forge new textual tools that helped them grapple with the propertied figures before their eyes—the canon who smugly refused to renounce an annual cash stipend, the monk who went around in fashionable clothing, the abbot or prior who licensed it all in the name of authority, status or custom.

To that end reformers compiled in their books all of the most popular treatises on property that circulated across the region. They did so most commonly by collecting the texts within the gatherings of larger collections. In the two Diessen codices noted above, for example, alongside the works of the older monastic reforming tradition, the canons copied Henry of Langenstein's sermon and Job Vener's *compendium*, along with several other miscellaneous citations from canon law regarding the vice of property.[26] A Tegernsee codex containing autographs of the mystical works of Bernard of Waging also reveals how property treatises traveled together within a larger codex. The eighth of that book's thirteen gatherings contained three treatments on property: the anonymous Cistercian treatise aired at Constance; a disputed question on property by an anonymous "Doctor of Erfurt" and another question disputed at Vienna concerning "whether a monk should have property."[27] Many other codices exhibited the same pattern.[28] As late as 1491, the Benedictine Georg Phrayter of Oberalteich, a community reformed from Tegernsee in 1483, copied the entire contents of the Tegernsee codex Clm 18558, a book compiled by the industrious Tegernsee monk Oswald Nott, who was a former canon of Indersdorf. The Oberalteich copy, now Munich's Clm 9810,

---

[26] MS Munich, BSB, Clm 5690, fols. 58r–98r contains Henry's sermon, followed by excerpts from Vener and other texts on the vice of property. Henry's sermon and Vener's compendium are also found in Clm 5690 at fols. 26ra–32rb and 33va–36rb, respectively.

[27] MS Munich, BSB, Clm 18600 contains treatises number 3, 10 and 19 in the appendix below. See VL 1: 779–89 for Bernhard von Waging's life and works and for examples of the various texts in Clm 18600, (e.g. 781–82 nos. 8 and 9, the *Defensorium laudatorii doctae ignorantiae* and the *De cognoscendo deum*). See also, for general context, Bernard McGinn, *The Harvest of Mysticism in Medieval Germany (1300–1500)* (New York, 2005), ch. 10.

[28] E.g. MS Munich, BSB, Clm 18551 (Tegnernsee), fols. 301vb–2vb (Master of Paris) and fols. 303ra–6ra ("Non Dicatis").

included Job Vener's treatise and two anonymous tracts.[29] By century's end these collective efforts had produced dozens of treatises surviving in scores of manuscripts. Job Vener's Constance treatise alone survives in at least sixty-five copies. Henry of Langenstein's sermon in at least thirty-nine.[30] Typical for most of these codices was some inflection of the general pattern noted above: treatises on property combined with both a variety of works of basic instruction in religious life, and with all of the monastic tradition's most popular treatises on penance and spiritual progress.

More rarely, but revealingly, reformers gathered together anthologies devoted exclusively (or almost exclusively) to the most popular treatises on property. One of the best and earliest examples comes from the canonry of Indersdorf around 1417, when the parish priest John copied much of the codex that now survives in the Bavarian State Library as Clm 7720. As noted in the previous chapter, soon after 1417 Indersdorf's deacon John would lead the visitation effort that established key reforming enclaves across the region by midcentury. It is thus tempting to speculate, though it is difficult to prove, that in Clm 7720 we are able to look over the shoulder of John of Indersdorf himself, a recent reforming convert, scribbling out the texts foundational to his movement's new ideology. In any case, the overall contents of the book are revealing. In it John and other copyists wrote out the *Rule* of St. Augustine, texts on the canonical hours and the annunciation, miscellaneous "devout" sayings of the fathers, hymns and so on. A majority of the book's folios, however, were devoted to newly popular tracts against the vice of property. Someone other than the parish priest John copied out Henry of Langenstein's sermon to Klosterneuburg and Job Vener's widely read *compendium* from Constance. John himself appears to have copied out a third treatise, the "Exhortation to regular canons on the vice of property," a miscellany of citations of patristic and canon law and arguments against *proprietas*, much of it culled from other popular works.[31] Though these property treatises were not the only texts in this book, the Indersdorf canons notably considered it essentially a handbook on the issue. A contemporary parchment label on the front cover lists the contents of the book as *Regula sancti Augustini;*

---

[29] See the colophons on fols. 64r, 182v and 193v.
[30] See the manuscripts listed in the Appendix below.
[31] Munich, BSB, Clm 7720 fols. 30r–33r.

Epistola magistri Heinrici de Hassia contra vitium proprietatis; Item alia exhortatio contra proprietatem, et plura alia puncta ibidem. A Mondsee codex copied in the third quarter of the fifteenth century provides another example of an anthology devoted almost entirely to the vice of property.[32] The book begins with a brief text in praise of Catherine of Siena by Pius II, followed by Raymond of Capua's *Vita* of the saint. The remainder of its folios contain three of the most popular works on *proprietas*: the treatise of the "Poor Monk"; the brief, anonymous treatise written by the "Master of Paris"; and Henry of Langenstein's sermon to Klosterneuburg.

Physical evidence also suggests the frequent use of these texts. The copy of Henry of Langenstein's sermon gathered into the Indersdorf handbook noted above, for example, is faded, worn and heavily creased from frequent folding—suggestive evidence that it may have been passed around and frequently copied before coming to rest in the binding of a book at Indersdorf. Other evidence of frequent usage survives in Munich's Clm 18644, a Tegernsee codex from the mid-fifteenth century. The second and third gatherings of that book contain a pattern of circulation familiar from other books—the *Contra vitium proprietatis* of the anonymous Cistercian "Poor Monk" published in Vienna; Henry of Langenstein's sermon on property; and Job Vener's *Compendium*. On many of the folios in these gatherings, moreover, underlining and marginalia highlight fervent language or the meticulous citations of canon law characteristic of so many reforming texts. One user also took the trouble to place a leather tab—the only one in the book—on the first folio of the "Poor Monk's" treatise. The tab thereby seems to have marked something like a "property gathering" for easier reference amid so much other material. Similar tabs and marginal notations suggestive of frequent consultation can be found in many other books; one used by the nuns of Nonnberg in Salzburg provides another excellent example.[33]

These texts and anthologies likely proved most useful for training novices and others in the rigors of reformed life—hence their circulation in many books with the works of David of Augsburg and others

---

[32] MS Vienna, ÖNB, Cod. 3700, from which Henry's sermon was cited above. See 67 and n. 1.

[33] MS BSB Clm 18644 (Tegernsee), fols. 140r–81v. The leather tab is on fol. 140. For the nuns of Salzburg, cf. MS Salzburg St. Peter, Stiftsbibliothek, a. III. 13 and a. IV. 23.

on the novitiate, and their association with the work of deacons and priors, who were in charge of cloister discipline.[34] But it is important also to recall how a keen awareness of temptation and sin and a strong commitment to penance remained the foundation of reformed life, even for its veterans. For novices and veterans of reformed life alike, the era's property treatises provided precisely the textual tools they needed to establish that foundation: passionate calls to conversion; penetrating rehearsals of the psychological landscape of temptations centered around cash and status; a host of penitential epithets from Peraldus; and strings of legal "proof texts." Here a generation of denunciations of the vice of property, most of them directed outwardly and socially, now came to bear on the inner life. They helped devout religious of all stripes discern and confront the temptations of property and status, wherever they might be encountered from day to day.

These considerations help restore contemporary resonance to the ways in which fifteenth-century reformers returned to an earlier monastic spirituality. Consider the monks of Melk, for example, who copied Hugh of Fouilloy's twelfth-century moral treatise *De rota verae religionis*, probably from a thirteenth-century exemplar from nearby Heiligenkreuz.[35] In both texts, two illustrations contrast life in a well-ordered, disciplined cloister with life in a dissolute one. Among the disciplined monks, an abbot ministers to his flock as a pastor who holds his office "in dignity, but humbly and with charity," reluctantly acting as lord over the others. The abbot's prior ascends in his career reluctantly; his counterpart resigns his office out of true humility and a distaste for power, while the humble cloistered monk sits quietly below, diligently reading a book and embracing his life of poverty and obedience. In the dissolute cloister, an abbot reigns in pride and "curiosity" while a prior aspires to his seat through simony. A former abbot laments his fall from grace through negligence, and a lazy cloistered monk sits idly and shamefully in his poverty. Their entire course of life turns on the "axis of the brothers' perversity," its spokes each representing a different vice.

---

[34] Cf. Clm 7720, for example, possibly associated with deacon John of Indersdorf; Clm 18600, containing the works of the prior Bernard von Waging; and Melk, CM 900 and 911, containing numerous works of John Wischler of Melk.

[35] Cf. Constable, *Reformation of the Twelfth Century*, Plates 4 and 5 (MS Heiligenkreuz, Stiftsbibliothek, 226, fols. 146r and 149r). The Melk images are from CM 737, fols. 96v and 100r.

The reformers' recovery of Hugh's treatise and its images seems, at first glance, unremarkable. There are a few subtle but revealing differences in the thirteenth-century images and their fifteenth-century Melk counterparts, however, that merit careful attention. (See Plates I and II on pp. 188 and 189.) The prideful Melk abbot who rules over his undisciplined cloister, unlike his predecessor at Heiligenkreuz, is soaked in fifteenth-century perceptions of lordly sensibility and its material excess. The image is a kind of visual sumptuary law: the abbot, enthroned at the top, wears a red habit, a red tunic adorned with buttons at the wrists, and a red beret. He wears red boots adorned with golden spurs and a luxuriously adorned dagger on a golden belt. He holds a falcon in his left hand, and nearby are a backgammon board and a lyre. To the left of the image, the prior wears a red tunic adorned with buttons and fashionable long-toed boots. He also clutches a blue bag, presumably filled with the cash he is said to use for funding his ascent. To the right, the deposed abbot is pulled down by a demon who clutches his habit, and the cloistered monk sleeps below with a pair of dice nearby. There is no explicit mention in either text or image of the "vice of property." But the contextual evidence provided here suggests that the monks would have read these images precisely through that cultural lens. The library at Melk held numerous treatises denouncing the *proprietarii* in the bitter language of Peraldus and Vener. Melk's prior John Wischler had reflected on the vice extensively in theory and worked against it in practice through visitation. And the Tegernsee *avisamenta*, noted above, complained of the social experience of precisely this kind of excess—pompously attired abbots, monks with sacks and purses, and quarrels between subjects and superiors.

As Thomas Lentes has noted, moral theorists in the later Middle Ages often stressed the importance of the "inner eye" of the soul, which had to be kept clean from sin in order to ensure moral progress.[36] Like dust in the outer eye, so one treatise attributed to Bonaventure taught, sin in the inner eye prevented a clear vision of perfection. Only constant vigilance against sinful images in the imagination would ensure a properly "composed," properly ordered inner sense. In a way consistent with that model, the Melk text seems to have juxtaposed images of a

---

[36] Thomas Lentes, "Inneres Auge, Äusserer Blick und Heilige Schau. Ein Diskussionsbeitrag zur visuellen Praxis in Frömmigkeit und Moraldidaxe des späten Mittelalters," in *Frömmigkeit im Mittelalter. Politisch-soziale Kontexte, visuelle Praxis, körperliche Ausdrucksformen*, ed. Klaus Schreiner (Munich, 2002), 179–220.

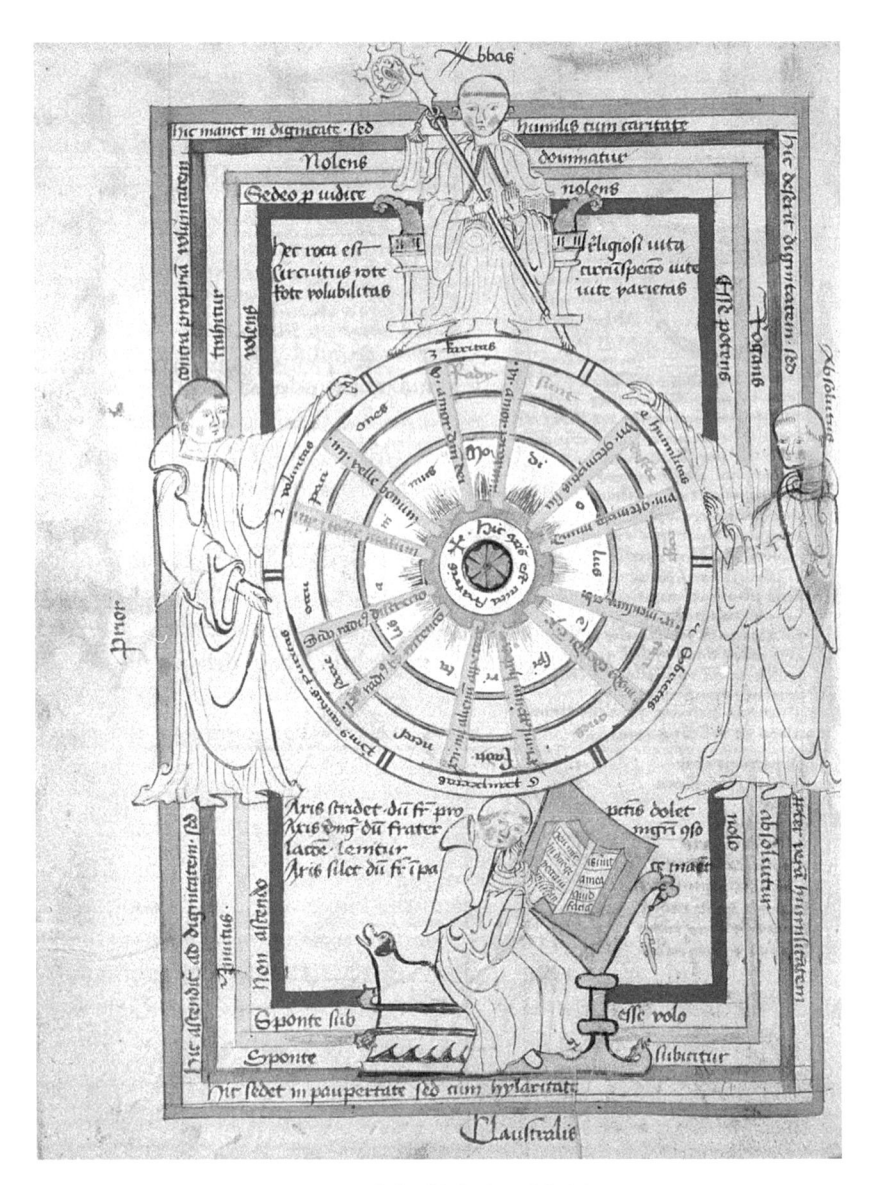

Plate I. Melk CM 737, fol. 96v.

Plate II. Melk CM 737, fol. 100r.

propertied abbot and his followers, adorned in worldly excess, with contrasting images of poverty and discipline. Both text and image highlighted sharp choices between sin and repentance, and reinforced commitments to discipline and devotion. In a similar way, in their books reformers seem to have juxtaposed texts that demonized the carnality of the world with those that upheld the purifying carnality of Christ's suffering—so the circulation of excerpts of Ludolph of Saxony with texts like the *Speculum amatorum mundi*, the *Speculum monachorum*, the compilation *On the Seven Canonical Hours*, and so on, all of which were read alongside more recent demonizations of propertied mortal sin like Henry of Langenstein's, with its calls to conversion and its colorful, vivid satire of lordly excess.[37]

In one sense, these examples reflect all of the old commonplaces about contempt of the world, but in another sense these devotional compilations had a distinct fifteenth-century cultural edge. Thomas Bestul has argued that the carnality of Passion narratives served variously as a polemic against the Jews, as a narrative struggle over the representation of woman and the body, and as a narrative reinforcement of the revival of judicial torture, all in ways consistent with the rise of a "persecuting society" in the later Middle Ages.[38] In an analogous way, reformers can be seen as agents of their own kind of narrative "persecution," one directed both outwardly and socially against the carnality of the *proprietarii*, yet also inwardly, against the "vice of property." One brief devotional tract "Against the proprietors, on penance" in fact frames the issue in precisely these terms.[39] The *proprietarii*, its author lamented, not only defended their inveterate customs as law, but also denounced reformers explicitly as "persecutors" who introduced schism and division.[40] The same treatise also turned the aggressive impulse inward, walking its reader systematically through a six-step scrutiny of conscience. First, the reader was to consider the eternal obligations of the religious estate; second, the obligation, under vows, to tend to perfection; third, the detestable state of this life and the horror of sin among those who lived against rule and constitutions; fourth, the futility of life among those who lived obstinately (*pertinaciter*) against the rule—dead in the mortal sin of property, their prayer, psalms, fasting

---

[37] See above, 69 ff.
[38] Bestul, *Texts of the Passion*, chs. 3–5, and 157.
[39] The text is found in MS Melk, Stiftsbibliothek, CM 1801, fols. 106r–110v.
[40] Ibid., fol. 106r.

and the rest were worthless before God; fifth, the certainty of death, and the uncertainty of its day and hour; sixth, and lastly, the fragility and vileness of the human body, a flower that though beautiful today would tomorrow be trampled underfoot. All of our love and desire and care for the flesh, the reader was reminded, would soon be dissolved into putrid food for worms and vile dust.

Here again was in one sense a return to ancient monastic commonplaces—in fact much of this treatise appears to have been compiled from excerpts of Bernard, Arnulf of Boheries and others. Yet the "harvest" was something other than a simple recovery of an earlier tradition. The fifteenth-century, as Thomas Lentes has shown, expressed an almost unprecedented enthusiasm for counting and calculation in matters of devotion.[41] It was directed outwardly in increasingly elaborate and refined schemes to calculate prayers, masses, indulgences and so on. It was also expressed inwardly in the ordering of lists of virtues and vices for catechesis, for example, or in programs whose numbered points anchored methodical meditation and spiritual exercises centered on the Passion. And an important catalyst for the overall trend, Lentes notes, was the diffusion of the learning of the schools, where numbered conclusions, divisions, lists of propositions and so on had so long shaped moral thought. The text noted here suggests how reforming monks—many of them former schoolmen converted to reformed religious life—embraced and fostered the same trend. In a way that blended "scholastic" and "monastic" habits of mind, reformers crafted new texts that helped direct reform both outwardly "against the proprietors," and inwardly as a call to penance.

As it began to take root across the orders, all of the textual energy surveyed thus far also found expression in the vernacular.[42] Building

---

[41] Thomas Lentes, "Counting Piety in the Late Middle Ages," in *Ordering Medieval Society: Perspectives on Intellectual and Practical Modes of Shaping Social Relations*, ed. Bernhard Jussen and Pamela E. Selwyn (Philadelphia, 2001), 55–91.

[42] Werner Williams-Krapp, "Ordensreform und Literatur im 15. Jahrhundert," *Jahrbuch der Oswald von Wolkenstein Gesellschaft* 4 (1986): 41–51, citing the estimates of Kurt Ruh, notes that some 70–80% of the overall production of vernacular writing was devoted to religious texts. See also Williams-Krapp's other important essays: "Frauenmystik und Ordensreform im 15. Jahrhundert," in *Literarische Interessenbildung im Mittelalter. Mauracher Symposion 1991*, ed. J. Heinzle (Stuttgart, 1993), 301–13; "Observanzbewegungen, monastische spiritualität und geistliche Literatur im 15. Jahrhundert," *Internationales Archiv für Sozialgeschichte der deutschen Literatur* 20 (1995): 1–15; idem, "'Praxis Pietatis.' Heilsverkündung und Frömmigkeit der illiterati im 15. Jahrhundert," in *Die Literatur im Übergang vom Mittelalter zur Neuzeit*, ed. Werner Röcke and Marina Münkler

on a tradition reaching back to the works of Suso, Observant monks and canons celebrated everyday language of the "simple" and the "devout," the language best suited to bringing the pastoral theology of the learned to wider circles of pious readers. In that spirit, reformed religious houses became crucial centers for the translation of the most popular and useful devotional texts. Of 260 known fifteenth-century manuscripts (including excerpts) of Suso's *Büchlein der ewigen Weisheit*, for example, nearly half belonged to cloisters, and of the hundred or so that can be located precisely, nearly every one belonged to a reformed community—including several that were copied in the houses of the Melk Benedictines and the Raudnitz circles of Augustinian canons. At Melk, while busied with all of the other work of visitation and reform, John Wischler himself translated and copied treatises into books for the lay brothers' use, such as Gregory the Great's *Dialogues* and the *Rule of Benedict*.[43] Religious women, too, in ways that need much more research in the region studied here, copied and compiled works of their own—some of the most industrious seem to have been the women of Nonnberg in Salzburg.

In keeping with these trends, the reforming impulse to repent from the "vice of property" soon found expression in a variety of German translations and compositions.[44] A translation of Dietrich Kerkering's treatise, attributed to Nicholas of Dinkelsbühl, survives in eight manuscripts.[45] Translations of Job Vener's and the Master of Paris' treatises survive in at least four manuscripts each.[46] The remaining works were independent compositions or miscellanies of translated authorities and *exempla*. By far the most popular among these was a two-part compilation that circulated with the works of John of Indersdorf, and that

---

(Munich/Vienna, 2004), 139–65. For the significance and context of vernacular literature and piety generally see also Klaus Schreiner, "Laienfrömmigkeit—Frömmigkeit von Eliten oder Frömmigkeit des Volkes?," in *Laienfrömmigkeit im späten Mittelalter. Formen, Funktionen, politisch-soziale Zusammenhänge*, ed. Klaus Schreiner (Munich, 1992), 1–78.

[43] Freimut Löser, "Anselm, Eckhart, Lienhart Peuger. Zu einer deutschen Übersetzung der 'Orationes et Meditationes' Anselms von Canterbury der Melker Laienbruder," in *Latein und Volkssprache im deutschen Mittelalter*, ed. Nikolaus Henkel and Nigel F. Palmer (Tübingen, 1992), 233–55.

[44] Texts and manuscripts are listed in Bernard Haage's entry, "Privatbesitz im Ordensleben," in VL 7: 845–50.

[45] VL 7: 847 (no. IV, incipit: *Ewer sitt, ewr gewonhait oder owr leben*).

[46] For the translation of Vener's treatise, VL 7: 846 (no. II, incipit: *Zu heil denen*). Haage followed the older literature in erroneously attributing this treatise to Henry of Langenstein. For the various translations of the treatise by the "Master of Paris" see VL 7: 846–47 (no. III).

may have been authored by the deacon himself.[47] It seems to have been remarkably popular among the reformed Benedictines of St. Peter in Salzburg. They alone had seven of its twenty-three manuscripts, some shared among the women of Nonnberg and the lay brothers. These vernacular treatises are a crucial witness to the shared penitential culture of the "devout" and "simple" that took root in reforming households. In these works lay brothers and women read along with monks and canons all of the now familiar citations from canon law—the texts of Innocent III, Gratian, John Andreae and others—that condemned property and upheld the common life. They also read in their everyday language the fervent passages that had been appropriated from so many widely circulated Latin treatises. So one treatise admonished that though a monk be equal to Gregory the Great, more devout than St. Martin, St. Bernard or St. Dominic, though he be adorned with the stigmata like St. Francis, should he die guilty of the mortal sin of property, his soul would be eternally damned.[48]

In all of these works, Latin and vernacular, fervent and accessible devotional language helped meet Observant demands for renewed conversion, penance and spiritual progress. Across the reforming ranks, for monks, canons, nuns and lay brothers alike, they helped promote penance and progress in the virtues. At the same time, in a way consistent with the broader aims of the new piety, reformers also sought to share the fruits of that culture with those beyond their ranks. As Observant reform took hold, reformers themselves remained in close contact with an increasingly diverse and pastorally demanding audience beyond the cloister, one that sought access to the tradition of moral progress long cultivated within.

Raising Lazarus
Penance and Spiritual Progress Within and Beyond the Cloister

By the fifteenth century, princes and court officials, pious laywomen, jurists, merchants and others beyond the ranks of the clergy constituted an increasingly literate and learned community. These "subtle" laymen, some of whom could appear more educated than their clerical peers, were often full participants in the broadening textual and intellectual

---

[47] VL 7: 848 (no. VI, incpit: *Sand Benedict redt in seiner regel*).
[48] MS Salzburg St. Peter, Stiftsbibliothek, b. III. 11, fols. 147r–v.

markets of their day. And much of that participation was driven by a growing demand for the pastoral theology of the schools.[49] Across the southern Empire, the authors and treatises of Vienna's new piety were especially popular: works like Henry of Langenstein's *Erchantnuss der sund*, for example, the *Büchlein von der Liebhabung Gottes* of Thomas Peuntner, or the pastoral works and sermons of Nicholas of Dinkelsbühl. Reforming religious, both men and women, remained the most immediate audience for these works. Eighteen of the seventy surviving manuscripts of Peuntner's treatise, for example, were copied in houses of reformed Benedictines, including Melk; St. Peter and Nonnberg in Salzburg; the Irish Benedictines in Vienna; Tegernsee; St. Ulrich in Augsburg; and Andechs. And of all the copies of the work that survive among the Augustinian canons, each was to be found in a house associated with the Raudnitz reform.[50] But in most cases reforming translators, women as well as men, worked in ways that made their texts available to ever-wider circles of laity and clergy, and the reformers' growing libraries provided a key point of cultural contact between university, reformed cloister and the wider public.[51]

In the same collaborative spirit, around 1441 John of Indersdorf composed a German devotional treatise called *Dreierlei Wesen der Menschen*.[52] John appeared above as the deacon and prior who introduced the Raudnitz reform to one of the leading canonries in Bavaria, and who helped lead the most important early visitations in the region.[53] But John was also a pastor and author in the best tradition of Vienna's pastoral theology and the new piety. He served as confessor and coun-

---

[49] Essential is Schreiner, "Laienfrömmigkeit—Frömmigkeit von Eliten oder Frömmigkeit des Volkes?" (above, n. 42), esp. 27–29.

[50] Williams-Krapp, "Ordensreform und Literatur im 15. Jahrhundert," esp. 48.

[51] Karl-Heinz Steinmetz, "Schule der heiligen Katharina. Trianguläre Wissenstransfer in der *Katharinenpredigt* und der *Vierzehnten Harfe* des Johannes Nider O.P.," in *Kirchenbild und Spiritualität. Dominikanische Beiträge zur Ekklesiologie und zum kirchlichen Leben in Mittelalter. Festschrift für Ulrich Horst O.P. zum 75. Geburtstag*, ed. Thomas Prügl and Marianne Schlosser (Paderborn, 2007), 339–55.

[52] The *Dreierlei Wesen der Menschen* (hereafter DWM) is edited by Bernhard Haage, "Der Traktat Von dreierlei Wesen der Menschen'" (PhD diss., Heidelberg, 1968). For the textual history of the work see especially the studies by Haage, "Ein neues Textzeugnis zum spätmittelalterlichen Traktat 'Von Dreierlei Wesen der Menschen'," *Zeitschrift für deutsches Altertum* 100 (1971), 227–30; idem, "Ein Vorausentwurf des mittelalterlichen Traktats 'Von Dreierlei Wesen der Menschen'," *Leuvense Bijdragen* 58 (1969), 138–68; and idem, "Zur Textgeschichte des Traktats 'Von Dreierlei Wesen der Menschen': Hs. Salzburg, St. Peter, Cod. b III 11," *Zeitschrift für deutsches Altertum* 105 (1976), 122–25.

[53] See above, 143.

selor to the dukes of Bavaria-Munich, and in that setting composed several pastoral and devotional treatises for both clergy and laity. These included a series of meditations on the passion; two prayer books for the noblewoman Elizabeth Ebran; a "mirror of princes" for Duke Albert III; and a collection of devotional "table readings" for Albert and his wife. The *Dreierlei Wesen*, also a work of spiritual instruction for Albert III and his wife, originated in this same context.[54]

John crafted the *Dreierlei Wesen* according to the ancient threefold way of purgation, illumination and perfection. John associated those stages of spiritual development with three allegories: purgation with the figure of Lazarus, whom Jesus raised from the dead; illumination with the figure of Martha, who was "busy about much serving" upon Jesus' visit to her home; and perfection with Mary of Bethany, who sat at Jesus' feet while Martha served.[55] As Giles Constable has noted, the tradition of commentary passages was so rich and ancient that there was very soon hardly any truly new interpretation to be drawn from the texts. At the same time, the long tradition had inspired "changes in tendency and emphasis" that revealed much about their various historical moments.[56] That insight is useful here. Though the program of moral progress outlined in the *Dreierlei Wesen* had deep roots in the monastic tradition, by John's day its franchise had been extended to an increasingly diverse and pastorally demanding audience. A Cistercian work called the *Pomegranate* is one of the best examples. Composed in reforming circles in Bohemia, the Latin work that was comparable in spirit to the *Imitation of Christ* and Suso's *Horologium*. It extended a threefold call to penance, progress and perfection to "devout" readers of every condition.[57] In a similar way, John of Indersdorf's German work

---

[54] For a brief overview of John's career and these works, see VL 4: 648–50 with further literature, e.g. Gerhard Eis, "Die Tobiaslehre des Johannes von Indersdorf," *Neophilologus* 47 (1963):198–203 and Brigitte Weiske, "Bilder und Gebete vom Leben und Leiden Christi. Zu einem Zyklus im Gebetbuch des Johannes von Indersdorf für Frau Elisabeth Ebran," in *Die Passion Christi in Literatur und Kunst des Spätmittelalters*, ed. Walter Haug and Burghart Wachinger (Tübingen, 1993), 113–68.

[55] Cf. Luke 10: 38–42 and John 12: 1–8.

[56] Giles Constable, *Three Studies in Medieval Religious and Social Thought* (Cambridge, 1995), 14.

[57] The work survives in some 150 manuscripts. See Manfred Gerwing, *Malogranatum, oder der dreifache Weg zur Vollkommenheit: Ein Beitrag zur Spiritualität des Spätmittelalters* (Munich, 1986). Also see now Gerwing's essay, "'...state in fide vera, viriliter agite, omnia vestra in caritate fiant.' Zum dreifachen Weg im 'Malogranatum'," in *Die Neue Frömmigkeit*, ed. Derwich and Staub, 85–110, esp. 97–98.

staked out common ground among reforming religious and a audience beyond the cloister. At least thirty-three complete copies of the work survive, along with numerous excerpts and abridgments. Most circulated in reformed monasteries and canonries across the region, but copies found their way into the households of lay nobility and burghers as well.[58] The *Dreierlei Wesen* made thus made accessible a rich legacy of penance and spiritual progress to all who copied or excerpted from it, or who read from it or heard it read. In certain ways it upheld ideals of the cloister, and many passages preserved the language of monastic spirituality. But the work also distilled and translated that same tradition in a new setting, rendering it more accessible to a growing number of ordinary people who sought moral progress.

At the core of the *Dreierlei Wesen* was an insistent call to genuine and eager conversion (*becherung*). Here the treatise recalled both ancient traditions of religious life, and contemporary calls to conversion in settings as diverse as the New Devout and the Lollards. It also intersected with a long German mystical tradition: For John the *anhebender mensch*, one who had eagerly embraced conversion and penance and fully embraced the diligent pursuit of perfection, became a true "Friend of God." Precedents for that turn of phrase reached back to David of Augsburg and Mechtild of Magdeburg, but it had come to be used more widely since the fourteenth century. At times it described in a general way the apostles, saints and other "prefect souls" who lived exemplary lives. With Suso and Tauler, the phrase began to mark particular Rhineland circles of religious and laity who shared the Dominican authors' spiritual aims and sensibilities. And perhaps most famously, the Strasbourg banker Rulman Merswin established his Green Isle community for "friends of God" of every estate.[59] In the *Dreierlei Wesen*, John of Indersdorf drew from this long tradition to extend an invitation to all "converted souls," whatever their condition or estate, to embrace spiritual progress. In doing so he turned away from or attenuated much that had characterized the mysticism of the fourteenth century. There is no language in the *Dreierlei Wesen* that recalled the earlier *Book of Spiritual Poverty*, no language of self-emptying and annihilation, no taking leave of the virtues and so on. Rather, John's treatise was anchored in all of the

---

[58] For a discussion of the manuscripts see the introduction to Haage, "Der Traktat 'Von dreierlei Wesen der Menschen'" (above, n. 52).
[59] For a useful overview see McGinn, *Harvest*, Ch. 9, especially 408–15.

themes that had become characteristic of the Modern Devotion and the "new piety." John's call to conversion and penance was meant to spur all who read it, or who heard it read, to pursue "purity of heart" and devotion (*andacht*). Its entire program of spiritual progress was grounded in a constant concern for both "utility" (*nucz*) and "diligence" (*fleys*) in spiritual exercises (*ubung*), especially those centered on the life and suffering of Christ.[60]

The call to repentance and conversion was most pronounced in the "Lazarus" tract, the longest portion of the work. John called his audience to rise up from spiritual death and to embrace the life of the *anhebender mensch*, the penitent soul. Here the work overflowed with all of the energy of the penitential tradition as it flowered in the fifteenth century. At times the admonitions were addressed to a general audience. John urged his readers to think of their last moments, of death, of the last judgment and of the "unspeakable pain of hell" that awaited the unrepentant. He called for them to wake from their slumber, to stop making excuses that put off repentance.[61] At other times the call to repent seemed directed more to the elite, especially those in circles that would have surrounded a duke like Albert III. John denounced what was encountered everywhere in the houses of the nobility: the singing and pompous talk; the lust and proud ambition; the time wasted playing cards and dancing; the eating and drinking early and late.[62] John then turned to noblewomen in his circle, and in particular to all of the ways they marked their status through clothing: What would the noblewomen say when they were called to judgment on the last day, wearing those peacock tails on their long dresses, those silk cloaks, those narrow shoes and golden rings, their necks bare and breasts pointed, "with all

---

[60] DWM, 309: "Das erczaigt sich an dem, das sy nit suchen daz ewig gut mit ernstlichem fleys. Besunder tag und nacht, frü und spat ist ir hercz und ir gemüt mit zeittlichen dingen bekumert und wenn sy in hocher andacht solten sein gen got, so ist ir hercz gestrött hin und her und bekümert und verzeren die zeit der gnaden unnüzlich ir sel."

[61] DWM, 294: "...die gedachtnüsz deiner leczten zeit, dy grösz unauszsprechenlich pen der hell, dy forchtsame zwkunft des strengen richters und dem jungsten tag..."; Ibid., 297: "O du liebhaber der welt, wie lang willdu warten? Dy zeit der gnaden gett da hin, der tod stett dir vor der tür. Es sey dir lieb oder layd, du must im auff thun, und darumb verzeuch dein becherung nit bis morgen, als Salomon spricht. Hab selber fleys und sorg deiner sel, und enpflich sy nyemant, so wirdest du nit versaumpt." Ibid., 298: "O lieber mensch, stee auff von dem schalff deiner torhait, gib urlaub dem posen feindt, seyt du pist ein vernünftige creatur."

[62] Ibid., 321–23.

of the pomp of your dead corpse, through which you have poisoned so many souls and brought them to evil thoughts and desires?"[63] All of the penitential commonplaces were in turn part of John's overall appeal to pious action. Again and again the Lazarus tract pleaded with its audience to "note with diligence" (*merck mit fleys*) its admonitions; to "be diligent" (*fleissig*) in uprooting sin through scrutiny of conscience and thorough confession; to be diligent and attentive in hearing mass, and so on.[64]

For readers in the orders, the Lazarus tract provided a rich textual ground for private study, meditation and affective identification with religious life's ideals. A generation after John of Indersdorf compiled the *Dreierlei Wesen der Menschen*, reforming monks in Salzburg still read it carefully, and one of them excerpted from the "Lazarus tract" to craft his own miscellany on the "vice of property," obedience and conversion.[65] The converted religious, as an *anhebender mensch*, was to turn from the vice of property, rise up from the death of sin and turn to "true penance." After that "good beginning"—unlike so many who turned back again so easily to their old customs—he was to persist in the pursuit of perfection. Saved from damnation, the grateful convert then became a true "friend of God" through diligent confession and constant vigilance against future sin. Such an appropriation suggests how all of the heated rhetoric over the "vice of property" could settle down into more quiet but durable programs of personal reading, writing and devotion among monks, canons, women, lay brothers and others who excerpted from the *Dreierlei Wesen* in similar ways.

The call to repent and return to order and discipline also appealed to the powerful lay patrons who sponsored reform. The *Dreierlei Wesen* was composed just as Albert III of Bavaria-Munich (whom John of Indersdorf served as confessor) received a papal privilege for another round of reforming visitations in his duchy, and the *Dreierlei Wesen* itself offers what may have been a veiled reference to the coming visitation: With

---

[63] Ibid., 323–24.

[64] Ibid., 331: "...deine gutte werck, die du on todsünd verpracht hast, werden getött und pringen kaynen nucz zu dem ewigen leben, als wenig als sy geschehen waren in tod sunden. Hebst du aber an zepussen dein sünd mit rew und layd deynes herczen, so wirt dein sel wider erkükt zu dem leben."

[65] See the works by Haage noted above, n. 52, "Ein neues Textzeugnis," and "Zur Textgeschichte des Traktats 'Von Dreierlei Wesen der Menschen." Cf. Salzburg St. Peter, Stiftsbibliothek, Cod. b. III. 11, fols. 145r–67r and the Mondsee manuscript now in Vienna, ÖNB Cod. 2968, fols. 176r–89v.

all available powers secular and spiritual, and "with great diligence," so the Lazarus tract urged, an upright and spiritual life according to the rule was to be enforced in religious houses. Only then would land and people be spared God's wrath.[66] A passage like this would have been continually relevant as visitations continued across the region to the 1450s and beyond, not only for reformers themselves, but for an audience of lay princes and nobility. And while more research into the patterns of reception of the *Dreierlei Wesen* would be needed in this regard, it seems reasonable that an even wider audience of "brothers and sisters" who fancied themselves "friends of God" could also have accessed the Lazarus tract and the *Dreierlei Wesen*, and so become participants in the culture of penance and progress that was so fashionable in their day.[67]

John continued to cultivate a broad devotional ground in the second part of the *Dreierlei Wesen*. Here he led his audience toward the life of the "rising soul," the *aufhebender mensch*, allegorized as the life of Martha. John first treated the outward manifestations of spiritual progress. Humble clothing, notably, was held up in contrast to the pomp of the nobility so vehemently attacked in the Lazarus tract. There followed admonitions to frequent hearing of mass and other good works. John then shifted his focus inward, demanding "diligent exercise" of the virtues. His program of spiritual progress moved to a series of spiritual exercises centered on the life of Christ, and culminated in meditations on the Passion.[68] And all the while, John framed his material in a way that rendered it intelligible to both lay and professed audiences. His starting point was Christ's admonition to the rich young man to "sell all and follow me." Only by entering the "school of Christ" would the *aufhebender mensch* move on to perfection.[69] Here readers professed to religious life would have recognized the traditional call to abandon the world to enter a religious order. John's next chapter further admonished readers to abandon their bodies and embrace obedience, a command that again would have been familiar to his professed readers. Yet there was no explicit discussion of religious life. Rather, John offered a general

---

[66] DWM, 311.
[67] Cf. DWM, 354: "Nun, ir lieben prüder und schwester in got, den dy obgeschriben matery zehanden kumpt sy zelesen oder zehoren...."
[68] Ibid., 339: "...so ist im fast notturftig, dise lere offt zebetrachten und uberlesen oder horen lesen und besunder sich zu regieren nach den zwain regimen, dy zu dem lesten geschriben stend."
[69] Ibid., 340.

invitation to turn from the world as a preparation for inward reflection on Christ's suffering at the crucifixion. "Lift up the inner eyes of your reason," John wrote, "and take hold of the powers of your soul, and gaze upon Jesus Christ."[70] There followed a series of invitations to visualize, detail by detail and "with diligence," Christ's suffering and death on the cross.[71] The devotional pattern focused its energy on breaking what John called, revealingly, the "custom of sin." Those fettered by custom could break their way into a "progressive spiritual state" only with diligent "work and exercise." John then offered a seven-step daily program to aid in that work. The reader was first to focus on recent sins—"twenty or thirty," John recommended—though the reflection should not last too long, and should not cause despair. Second, the reader was to think on all the good things God had provided, especially the redemptive sacrifice of Christ. Third, the reader was to think on the joys of the angels and the saints long enough to rouse genuine desire for spiritual progress. Fourth, the reader was to ask God for protection against sin. Fifth, the reader was to hold up before the inner eye a spiritual model (*ebenbild*)—a pious, virtuous person whose example would help order daily life. Sixth, the reader was to think continually on death and the eternal pains of hell. Seventh, the reader was to think daily and "with particular diligence" on the works and sufferings of Jesus. There followed a series of strongly emotional prayers and other exercises for the reader to undertake upon receiving the Eucharist.[72] John remained focused on how best to spur his audience to action, and he was humanely attentive to all of the inward obstacles and excuses that might get in the way. The good pastor knew how easily everyday laziness and self-doubt could smother good spiritual intentions: "You perhaps say to yourself," he wrote, "'I can't give myself over to all of these exercises and follow these teachings...I am neither cold nor warm.'" In response he encouraged his audience to "put on the armor of Christ," and to "fight like a knight."[73]

In the third part of the *Dreierlei Wesen* John turned to the life of the "perfect soul," allegorized as the life of Mary of Bethany. Again, his text made a long ascetic tradition accessible and intelligible for religious

---

[70] Ibid., 379.
[71] Ibid.: "...bis fleyssig indeiner betrachtung und sich in an in hocher andacht und wart genaden von im."
[72] DWM, 392–4.
[73] DWM, 395.

and others beyond their ranks. It began, revealingly, with a note of caution: Asked by an interlocutor what perfection in fact was, John responded that he himself did not presume to know. He could only try to summarize what others had said. Reaching back to the teachings of Aquinas, John notably began with the religious orders. He reminded his readers that only the cloistered, as Thomas had taught, rightfully belonged to the "estate of perfection." But John then quickly lamented how far religious life had fallen from its golden age. He then turned from the notion of perfection as an institutional rank to perfection as an inward state of "detachment" (*abgeschaidenheit*).[74] The concept had a long history in the vernacular mystical tradition, reaching back to Suso.[75] Here it appeared in a more general, attenuated way, a way accessible to all who sought progress in the virtues. Although John encouraged his audience to reach more lofty spiritual heights, he cautioned that they should not aim "too high." The best meditations were to remain careful, fearful and "devout."[76] Even in these closing discussion of the "perfect soul," John recommended readers "faithfully exercise" (*trewlich üben*) meditation on of the pains of hell and the strict judgment of God. At the summit of their progress, his "friends of God" were to "sink in to the wounds of Christ," and to continually purge their sin through contemplation of the passion.[77]

These considerations further illustrate the ways in which core reforming concerns over the cloister's culture of personal property resonated more widely, and in ways that rendered them something other than an intramural recovery of an earlier monastic spirituality. For one scribe who copied the *Dreierlei Wesen* in 1447, the treatise offered guidance for a well-ordered spiritual life not only to professed religious, but to everyone who embraced its program, whatever their particular estate or condition.[78] Yet for all of the common cultural ground that a penitential turn from the world provided, reformed religious remained keenly conscious that they alone had embraced the call to conversion through

---

[74] DWM, 411–12.
[75] For general context see the many discussions in McGinn, *Harvest*, e.g. 164–68.
[76] John Nider, for example, deployed many concepts and turns of phrase found in the work of Eckhart, Tauler and Suso, but in most instances he emptied their language of its original mystical content. See Gundolf Gieraths, "Johannes Nider O.P. und die 'deutsche Mystik' des 14. Jahrhunderts," *Divus Thomas* 30 (1952): 321–46, esp. 327–30.
[77] DWM, 450–51.
[78] DWM, 454: "...dar inn ein yeglich mensch nach seinem standt underweisung vinden mag, wie er sein leben hye inder zeyt ordnen sol seiner sel zu heyl..."

solemn vows. That consciousness issued in a distinct scrupulosity and an attention to rule and statute that remained a hallmark of Observant piety for all of the fifteenth century.

Scrupulosity and Statute
The Letter and the Spirit of the Law

Around 1417, as noted above, Augustinian canons as Indersdorf in Bavaria compiled a book that was essentially an anthology of the latest pamphlets on the "vice of property."[79] In the back of the codex, one of the canons (most likely the parish priest John, who had copied out several of the other texts in the book) wrote out a series of questions concerning property and community. Written in the hurried, practical manner of so many fifteenth-century miscellanies, these unselfconscious scribblings suggest that reformers thought hard about the practical implications of the treatises they gathered together.

One question, for example, addressed whether religious might receive and use money donated to them by their parents. In keeping with the reformers' fundamental rejection of that widespread custom, the answer insisted that all donations be presented to the community, never to a canon personally.[80] Another question asked whether a canon might administer a plot of land outside the community. The "brief answer" was no, since the *Rule* of Augustine prohibited anyone from calling anything his own.[81] Other questions further confirm the practical pastoral nature of the concerns at stake in the Indersdorf codex. One asked whether religious might have "spiritual treasures" (presumably liturgical items) with license of the superior. The brief response was in line with a long tradition: the canons could have such things if there were some special need, but they were not to be held or possessed "as if legally their own." More revealing was the next admonition: the licensed liturgical items were not to be "splendid"—of precious metals and so on. The magnificence deemed appropriate to the divine cult

---

[79] See above, 184.
[80] MS BSB Clm 7720, fol 66v: "Item religiosus habens pecuniam sibi ordinatam a parentibus vel alias a patrimonio, utrum liceat eum uti talibus pecuniis an non? Respondetur quod talis debet presentare communitati et personaliter obtinere non debet, quia esset proprietarius."
[81] Ibid.

and the clerical estate in so many settings was thrust aside in the name of a more humble and stern sensibility.[82]

Further questions rehearsed even more delicate dilemmas of practice. One asked whether reformed canons should celebrate divine services on behalf of the *proprietarii*.[83] Job Vener had argued at Constance only a few years before, in the very treatise copied into this book, that propertied monks polluted the church and heaped damnation on themselves every time they celebrated mass and other divine services.[84] The response in the Indersdorf codex was similarly stern, though it offered a slight concession to the exigencies of circumstance. Celebrating mass for *proprietarii* (whose mortal sin excommunicated them) was "very dangerous." Since strict adherence to this rule might cause scandal among the laity, however, this "lesser evil" might be tolerated. The reformers seem to have been worried about patrons who might be deeply offended should otherwise pious and upstanding religious men and women be denied intercession. A further question wrestled with the practical implications of Gregory the Great's command that the monk Justus be buried in a dung heap. What was to be done with a brother who was discovered after his death to have hidden away something of his own? The answer again reveals a seriousness of principle tempered with a certain common sense: The brother was not to be thrown on a dung heap, but he was to be denied burial in the community, and he was not to benefit from their intercessory prayers. Moreover, the body was not even to be buried in consecrated ground, "if this can be done conveniently," since to do so might unduly cause scandal among the laity.[85] Here again, perhaps, was a certain sensitivity to pressures to be felt from outside

---

[82] Ibid., fol. 67v: "Utrum religiosus posset habere sibi spiritualia clenodia cum licentia superioris. Respondetur quod bene potest habere quoad usum de quibus habet speciale indigentiam. Sed non debet habere nec possidere tamquam proprium legale, nec splendida debet possidere, videlicet argenta vel consimilia."

[83] Ibid.: "Item. Utrum liceat aliqui celebrare divina erga proprietarios. Respondetur quod valde periculosum est, quia omnes tales sunt excommunicate, ut manifeste patet per omnes doctores. Sed...minus malum potest sustineri ne layci per tales scandalizantur."

[84] Heimpel, *Vener von Gmünd und Strassburg*, 3: 1271–2.

[85] MS BSB Clm 7720, fol 67v: "Item religiosus qui inventus est habuisse proprium in hoc mundo et tunc discedit, quod est de eo faciendum? Respondetur quod non debeat sepeliri in sepulturam fratrum, nec est particeps bonorum. Et debet cadaver poni extra cymiteriam, si commode fieri potest, ne scandilizentur laycii per hac. *Extra De statu monachorum*."

the cloister, this time from outsiders who refused to share sacred space with those they deemed to be in mortal sin.

Some five years later, the same reformed scrupulosity remained strong at Indersdorf. In 1422, remembered as "the fourth year of our reformation," another Indersdorf canon again copied out the *Rule* of Augustine, the "Exhortation" on property found in Clm 7720 and the statutes of Raudnitz.[86] In the same bundle of texts was another revealing set of disputed questions, most of which turned on the psychological and moral dilemmas of strict observance—whether all points in the rule were to be observed under threat of mortal sin, for example, and whether a monastery could be thought a safe haven when so many temptations arose there, even among the reformed.[87] One of these questions is of particular interest. It concerned the tensions between the contemplative and active lives: Should reformed canons take on pastoral duties? Those outside the monastery, responded the anonymous author, were unable to live "spiritually according to the requirements of religion and the vow." This was especially true of younger canons. Moreover, the author pointed to the "collapse" of religion where formerly strict communities had taken on such responsibilities.[88] "Dismissing many arguments on both sides," the author outlined a nuanced middle way. Canons, even in ancient times, had been assigned pastoral duties, "at least by dispensation, according to the quality of the person and the place." The author omitted the many standard legal authorities for this, though he said he was prepared to show them to anyone who wished to see them. He decided in the end that only able and mature persons were suitable for such positions.[89] Raymond Cabasse and others had long defended money and goods as essential to an active life of preaching, teaching and pastoral care. The Indersdorf Observants rejected

---

[86] BHStAM, KLI 145, fol. 30r: "Expliciunt statuta canonicorum regularium scripta et collecta in monasterio Undersdorf finita in vigilia purificationis sanctissime virginis marie anno Christi 1422, anno vero reformationis dicti monasterii 4to." Ibid., fol. 36 and 39r, each with explicits dating their texts to 1422.

[87] Ibid., fol. 43v.

[88] Ibid., fol. 40r: "Utrum canonici regulares debeant praefici cure ecclesiarum parochialium non obstante observantia religionis deo devota. Quod non arguitur, quia extra monasterium spiritualiter vivere secundum religionis et voti exigentiam non valeant, presertim iuvenes.... Quoniam experientia docente multis in locis ubi monastica a primordio viguit et Deo devota fuit vita, plures heu contra sui votum et etiam precepta legis divine cum applicati erant talismodi ecclesiarum cure...collapsi fuerunt...."

[89] BHStAM, KLI 145, fol. 40v.

that proposition soundly. They worried at length about the dangers of money and worldly goods, dangers they could read about in the property treatise adjoining these questions. The financial convenience of pastoral incomes, they reasoned, did not justify the risk to the souls of those professed who dared venture out in the world. It was better to have secular clergy tend to such matters if at all possible.[90] What indeed, the author asked, had been the major cause of the great and broad collapse of the religious life, which the Council of Constance had recently worked so hard to reform, if not cash prebends and personal property?

A remarkable citation followed: The authority for all of the arguments against the active life was Henry of Langenstein's sermon to the canons of Klosterneuburg. The unexpected, offhand remark bears independent witness to the contemporary popularity of one of this project's most important unedited texts.[91] The citation also provides further evidence of the bond between the reformers' scrupulous stance on the "vice of property" and the wider religious mood. For the reformed canon who cited Henry's sermon, an active life of pastoral care and service sustained by personal incomes, so long presumed and accepted, was now a source of overwhelming temptation. His reforming readers at Indersdorf seem to have shared the worry—hence their rehearsal of questions and cases related to concrete circumstance, and their embrace of Henry's text and so many others like it as a guide to the answers. And though Henry's treatise was cited here among Augustinian canons, the work's broader popularity suggests how much these same concerns informed Observant sensibilities elsewhere.

The cultural complement to the searching scrupulosity revealed in these questions was a meticulous attention to rule and statute. The Observants embraced their prescriptive texts with a legalism that that is seldom fully thematized in the scholarship on reform, and that can seem quite at odds with modern notions of religion and spirituality. But their attention to the letter of the law was an essential guard against

---

[90] Ibid., "...ratio prohibitionis est periculum distractionis et casus a devocione.... Nec puto tantum lucrum facere monasteria regimen ecclesiarum per fratres super id quod possetis habere si per seculares regeretis ipsas ecclesias...."

[91] Ibid.: "Cum enim ceperant implicari temporalibus...collabi ceperant a devotione Deo devoti, de quo colligere poteritis plura...ex tractatu Magistri Hainrici de Hassia, qui incipit 'Ecce nos reliquimus omnia et secuti sumus te'."

the ravages of sin.[92] The result was a remarkable flowering of prescriptive texts that guided reformed life. Especially in leading Benedictine communities such as Melk and Tegernsee, massive new customaries regulated daily routines anew, often in unprecedented detail.[93] And while reformed Augustinian circles have not yet benefited from the commitment to text editing and research that has revealed so much about Benedictine reform, the evidence suggests that Augustinian canons shared with the Benedictines an enthusiasm for detailed regulation. In a mere four decades, roughly from the first visitations in the 1420s to those of the 1460s, Augustinian circles in the Bavarian region alone produced enough legislation to fill some 150 pages of small print in their early-modern editions. There can be no comprehensive effort here to evaluate this material thoroughly, but a few soundings suggest how the scrupulous inner life of penitential renunciation surveyed thus far inspired an outwardly disciplined, highly-regulated life in community.

One starting point is provided by the customary of Tegernsee and a collection of statutes issued in 1422 by the papal legate Cardinal Branda for the Augustinian canonries of Rebdorf, Walsee, Neunkirchen and Langenzenn.[94] The reformers' general scrupulosity about sin and their desire to promote inward humility is visible in many different passages of these texts. The customs of Tegernsee, for example, detailed the many cases in which the monks were expected to demonstrate their humility through prostration: whenever they were before their superiors; whenever they were late to choir or to the refectory; whenever they made an error in singing or reading; whenever they spilled food or drink. Further detailed guidelines followed concerning how to conduct the traditional monastic chapter of faults: its opening, which included readings centered on martyrdom; formulas for expressing fault; instructions on how to administer the discipline (the abbot or prior was to strike "once or twice" with the rod during each verse of Psalm 51,

---

[92] Cf. Denis Martin, *Fifteenth-Century Carthusian Reform*, 133 and n. 72, with further literature.

[93] Joachim Angerer, *Die Bräuche der Abtei Tegernsee unter Abt Kaspar Aindorffer* (above, 145 n. 44); Eusebius Amort, *Vetus Disciplina Canonicorum Regularium et Secularium* 5 (Farnborough, 1971), 609–30.

[94] Amort, *Vetus Disciplina* 5: 613: "...ut certum modum vivendi, et uniformitatem in moribus teneretis, circa hoc misericorditer providere dignaremur, et quadam statuta per vos de antiquioribus statutis, et monasteriorum vestrorum consuetudinibus, quae professioni et statui vestro conveniunt, simul in unum collecta, et nobis oblata, examinata et correcta pro pleniori reformatione vobis ad observandum traderemus...."

though during intense cold the customary allowed for the shorter Psalm 130). Other guidelines followed concerning daily confession, and how best to treat brothers who were cast into prison for major offenses.[95] The Augustinian canons' texts offered similar guidelines. Their chapter of faults began with a recital from Psalm 115, "Precious in the sight of the Lord is the blood of his saints."[96] After receiving the blessing of their superior, each canon was to "diligently examine his conscience" regarding his own sins. As appropriate, each was to come before the assembly and prostrate himself before the prelate until bidden to rise. If he were also accused of faults by others, he was to ask forgiveness, and in no way defend himself. Any who presumed to do so were to remain silent for as many days as the prelate required. The prelate, for his part, was to be on guard against false or excessive accusations, and was to punish anyone he found to have accused another falsely. Instructions for giving and receiving disciplinary blows followed, along with guidelines for confession.

Within this broader regime, one that disciplined and humbled both body and conscience, matters of property and community were regulated in great detail. In 1426, as noted above, the first reform charter at Tegernsee had already legislated against the distribution of cash and demanded the provision of food and drink in kind.[97] It also prohibited the enjoyment of cash stipends from anniversary masses, individual incomes and so on. Presuming those earlier measures, the later Tegernsee customary articulated the same forceful commitment more fully: To give or to receive anything without license was a scandalous sin, on par with rebellion, and the abbot reserved the judgment of all such cases for himself. To be caught giving or receiving without license merited either discipline with the rod or imprisonment.[98] Monks whom necessity required to serve as parish priests were to render strict accounting of their alms and other receipts to the abbot, and other officers within the community were to do the same.[99] The cellarer was to be "solicitous" in his provision of food and other items to the brothers, and was to render "a distinct and faithful account" of his activities as often as

---

[95] Angerer, *Bräuche der Abtei Tegernsee*, 148–9.
[96] Amort, *Vetus Disciplina* 5: 621–2.
[97] See above, 170.
[98] Angerer, *Bräuche der Abtei Tegernsee*, 154–55.
[99] Ibid.

the abbot required.[100] The kitchen-master was to petition the abbot or the cellarer for all of his needs, to "write down diligently" all of the things he received, and to render an account of his activities as often as was requested. The *vestiarius* was to keep a detailed inventory of the community's clothing, all of which was to be held under his care. He was also granted the right to search the brothers' cells to ensure that their habits and bedding were kept clean, and he was to denounce to the prior those who were negligent.[101]

Augustinian canons confronted the dangers of cash and personal property with equal vigor. Cardinal Branda's statutes from 1422 equated concealment of property with apostasy and theft, and the punishment was imprisonment.[102] In a similar spirit, a later *Liber officiorum* detailed how each officer was to preserve community and guard against vice. It fell to the prelate to guard against this crime "above all." In language that echoed the *Rule* of Benedict, the canons' statutes demanded the prior uproot the vice of property "in head and members." A long clause then detailed all that the prior and the brothers were not to "appropriate" for themselves—movable or immovable goods, whether inherited, given as gifts, purchased or otherwise acquired—and insisted that the prelate was to minister to the needs of all from common resources.[103] From the *Decretals*, the Augustinian texts cited Innocent III's warning that no prelate could dispense with *proprium*, and then, remarkably for a text of this kind, fell into the rehearsal of disputed questions regarding particular cases—canons who were sent to school, performed official business and so on.[104] Finally, the statutes stipulated that all of the community's cash was to be stored in a common safe, its three keys held by the prior, the procurator and the sacristan. The prior was also to have counted out precisely any money he gave to the procurator (*numeratam pecuniam*).[105]

---

[100] Ibid., 229–30.
[101] Ibid., 233.
[102] Amort, *Vetus Disciplina* 5: 623.
[103] Ibid., 699: "...aut sibi appropriet bona quaecumque mobilia aut immobilia, ad ipsum hereditatis iure devoluta aut devolvenda, data, propinata, legata, empta sive quoqunque titulo ad ipsum vel monasterium perventa, cuiuscunque nominis, utilitatis aut necessitatis existant, sed omnia talia bona aut iura...monasterio et communitati conventus cedant, et iam habita prelato et fratribus sint communia, et de his unicuique, prout opus fuerit, provideatur."
[104] Ibid., 700.
[105] Ibid.

Apart from matters of appropriation, cash and the like, reforming statutes also bound Raudnitz canons back to disciplined, communal sensibilities of space, food and clothing. Cardinal Branda's statutes presumed individual cells, for example: each was to have an aperture to allow those within to be seen. Each brother was to be provided basic bedding and to sleep decently clothed. The prelate himself was to read and sleep in his own cell in the common dormitory. He was also to "scrutinize" every cell regularly, above all to ensure that no brothers concealed chests or boxes within.[106]

Meticulously orchestrated meals were also a marker of reformed sensibility.[107] Unreformed abbots and priors feasted amid the entertainments of jugglers and actors, leaving their communities to provide for themselves from cash prebends. Reformed canons, in contrast, gathered in disciplined silence, washed their hands, then entered the refectory, two by two, in procession. The prelate and the brothers exchanged a series of blessings; the meal was blessed with the sign of the cross as the brothers bowed their heads. The lector received a blessing from the prior, and each brother was to sit in his place, silently and without complaint, in an orderly fashion, "religiously and honestly, not curiously, looking around at the others." No canon was to give or receive anything on his own. If the prelate sent something to him, the canon was to nod slightly in appreciation. Even if he did not want the food or could eat no more, he was to make an attempt to eat it to show his gratitude before having the food passed on to others. The statutes took special care to stress that the meal was to be a reflection of the precept of the *Rule* of Augustine that "all was to be common to all."

The canons' reformed regime also devoted considerable attention to outward appearance. Canonries like Klosterneuburg had once paid their members cash prebends to supplement the purchase of clothing. Reformed canonries in Bavaria now subjected themselves to the regime of the *vestiarius*, who governed a disciplined ministry of provision in kind. He was to collect and redistribute the canons' clothes according to season, and to care for tablecloths, bedding, shoes and so on. He was to keep all things "decent and clean," and to repair or replace items as needed, according to his discretion and conscience. To these ends he was to maintain a separate workshop whose affairs he was to manage

---

[106] Ibid., 700 and 701.
[107] Ibid., 617–18.

carefully. In all of his affairs the *vestiarius* was to show neither favor nor ill will, and he was to be conscious of even the unspoken needs of all. There followed detailed regulations that sought to capture the "devout" sensibility of the reformed habit.[108] The canons' white tunics were to be of modest quality and of "moderate" length and width, with plain sleeves—of a hand's width or so, with no slits, buttons or fur linings. The canons' cloaks were to be of cloth that was "sufficient for honesty" and "not too subtle," of modest width and length, and without pleats or other adornments. The furs of the canons' habits were to be of "simple" cut and quality. Even the prelate's headwear was to be lined only with squirrel fur. "Accessories," too, were to be simple and plain—the belts three fingers in width, with only iron buckles and with no ornamentation, the knives and purses "without curiosity."

Here again was the old impulse to control through legislation the links between status and consumption, but it was localized and internalized in distinct ways. In the wake of all of the treatises and visitations, devout reformers worked from within their own enclaves to establish a lasting commitment to the common life and to reformed simplicity. Two final soundings from the statutes help illustrate this dynamic from different angles.

In January 1460, Pius II and Bishop John IV of Tülbeck confirmed a set of statutes for the canons of Indersdorf. The canons, so the prologue to the statutes noted, had "lived laudably under regular observance for forty years or so," and they intended to do so in the future.[109] The prologue also noted explicitly that the canons wanted to commit their way of life to writing because of what they called the "variety of priors" who might come along in the future.[110] The canons may well have seen their aging prior John nearing the end of his long life, and in these statutes sought to ensure that the program begun under their exceptionally zealous and able leader would remain in force. In any case, the impulse itself is revealing. After a generation of composing and imposing written statutes, both across the region and in their own community, the reformed Augustinian canons of Indersdorf drew up

---

[108] Ibid., 708–9.
[109] BHStAM, KLI 146, fol. 3: "Ipsi per quadraginta annos vel citra sub regulari observantia ordinationibus et statutis tam apostolica quam ordinaria auctoritate eis traditis laudabiliter vixerint et similiter vivere intendunt...."
[110] Ibid.: "Nihilominus propter varietatem praepositorum dicti monasterii dubitant contra huiusmodi ordinationes et statuta posse turbari tempore procedente."

still another list of rules and routines, this one longer than any of its predecessors. The regime of statutes, they hoped, would preserve the vigor and momentum of their reforming experiment.

Much of that regime followed the general language of the regional prescriptions that had so often been issued. But appended to the collection was a stunning catalog of specific regulations—there were no fewer than 130 for this one community alone—that touched on every aspect of daily life. Some of the most revealing focused on the tensions of lordship, material culture and community that had so often been at stake over the previous generation.[111] The prior himself, for example, was not to have his own place to bathe, no special place to sleep, no special kitchen, no special place to eat. He was to wear a simple choral miter of wool, "as do other reformed prelates." Nothing about his habit was to be particularly distinguished, and he was especially not to wear rings or belts, or gold or silver. He was to eat with his brothers in the refectory as often as possible, and never with "pompous ostentation." Not even his servants were to offer him his food and drink with pompous, servile gestures, and the prelate was never to surround himself with an excessive retinue of servants, followers, horses and so on. The prior was to stand before his community as a "true sign of humility," one whose dress, manner and bearing sent a pointed religious and cultural message about the seriousness of Observant reform. The stern John of Indersdorf himself had, by all accounts, sent that message his entire life. John's community now wanted to record his way of life, and to make binding upon his successors.

Only two years later, in 1462, the Benedictine lay brothers at Mondsee recorded the vernacular treatise on property and obedience, noted above, that had drawn from the "Lazarus Tract" of the *Dreierlei Wesen der Menschen*. Following that text, the lay brothers copied out statutes of their own that regulated their life in ways consistent with the devotional stance of the *Dreierlei Wesen*.[112] The statutes emphasized that the brothers were under the same spiritual obligations as professed priests, though they were expected to work with their hands and serve in capacities from which the priests were exempt. The statutes regulated the lay brothers' dress, their chapter of faults and other routines, even

---

[111] Ibid., fol. 29vb.
[112] MS Vienna, ÖNB, Cod. 2968, fols. 167v–73v.

the conditions under which they were allowed to speak. The statutes also stipulated that the cells of the lay brothers were to be subject to frequent searches by the prior or other officers. And here the anxieties over the vice of property emerged again, as they had in other similar collections of statutes: any brother found with money or goods held against the rule or against the will of the prelate was to be declared a proprietor (*aygenschafter*) and punished accordingly. If the value of the goods came to more than twenty-four pfennig, the statutes made clear, the brother was to be thrown into the community's prison. For lesser amounts the brother was to receive a suitable penance according to the superior's discretion.

Following these detailed statutes, remarkably, are what appear to be one brother's unselfconscious, seemingly private reflections on the spiritual life the rules were supposed to guide. These lines recorded a kind of intimate inner dialogue about the spirit that inspired the letter of the law.[113] "The first thing that you are to observe," wrote the brother, "is voluntary poverty. And have patience within it while you are here on earth." Three further reflections called for humility, for the renunciation of power (*gewalt*), of pride in work and deed, and of bodily comfort. The brother then turned to the inner life. In a fifth admonition, he instructed his reader to "have compassion in your heart at all times for your neighbor." The list continued: Sixth, the reader was to love God with all of his heart and strength; seventh, to think always of how God had saved him; eighth, "that you willingly and patiently suffer"; and ninth, that the brother give body and soul to God "with great devotion." A tenth admonition was for the brother to remember that he had come from God, and that he comport himself at all times as if he were about to come before God again. Eleventh, the brother was to think of the shortness of life, the certainty of death, and the uncertainty of the time. Twelfth, and finally, the brother was to "always have sorrow and devotion concerning your sin, and ask God to forgive you."

By midcentury the distinctly scrupulous, methodical piety captured in these texts had helped establish some of the most self-consciously regulated religious communities of the era. In those communities, the Observants had transformed the "vice of property" from a publicist's slogan and an instrument for reforming visitation into a devotional

---

[113] Ibid., fols. 174v–75r.

theme that nurtured both outward discipline and inward moral progress. To an extent, reformers had shared that penitential ground with the laity and clergy beyond their ranks. But they alone had bound themselves back to penance, progress and community through meticulous attention to a flood of local statutes of their own design.

* * *

In 1507, a canon of Indersdorf made his last entries into a new chronicle for his community. Much of the work was typical of its genre—a patchwork of stories of the Wittelsbach family, stories of the founding of his house, and brief descriptions of the achievements of its prelates over the generations. Toward its end, however, the work began to blend history and living memory. On the one hand, the author noted proudly that he had been the "most secret servant" of prior John of Indersdorf, whose "life, morals, customs and all of his spirituality" he had witnessed in abundance.[114] On the other hand, he wrote nearly a century after most of the events he described, and more than thirty years after the death of the old prior John. In that sense the stories reflected at best the distant memories of conversations with an aging reformer. In any event, as the chronicler came to recount the history of Indersdorf's recent reforms, the narrative came to life. He began with what he perceived as a time of decline that had set in around 1400. The cloister had been burned down, and the house was in such debt that it had pawned all of its liturgical treasures to the Jews in Augsburg. And as economic fortunes had waned, so the tale went, discipline had faltered. The community reached its nadir as it turned to the mortal sin of property (*im convent kam die aigenschafft herfur*). In those evil times one canon had even stabbed another after a dispute over money.[115] A dramatic tale of conversion followed. The convent and the dukes of Bavaria-Munich elected the "eloquent" Eberhard, rector of the convent's parish of Glannersdorf.[116] Prior Eberhard found his

---

[114] Ibid., fol. 19v: "Von seiner tugend, guter regierung und geystlichem leben wär vil zu schreiben, das ich umb kurz willen vermeid. Dann ich als sein gehaymister diener sein leben, siten, gewonhait und alle geystlichait uberflussig gesehen han."

[115] BHStAM, KLI 7, fol. 17r: "Im convent kam die aigenschafft herfur, und was ein erstats leben im convent. Ein Herr stach den andern...Das kloster kam in solich nachtail bey im [the former prior, Peter Fries] und in schuld, das die clainaten des gotzhauses, als kelch, munstranz, messgewant, silbergeschir, stund als den Iuden zu Augsburg. So warn die guter alle versetzt und vil ewiges gelts iarlich zegeben...."

[116] Ibid., fol. 18r: "Als man zelt tausend vierhundert und zwelff jar, ward werwelt von dem convent und von baiden fursten der wirdig herr der Erhart Rothuet, ein

community in a sorry state, "with great debt and a disordered way of life." He quickly "took to heart" the call of the Council of Constance to reform the cloisters, and resolved to return "spiritual discipline" (*geystlich zucht*) to his house. To that end, he approached his brother John, a "learned young man" who had been the schoolmaster at the canonry. John reluctantly agreed to take part in his brother's experiment[117] and after a brief novitiate in the reformed community of Neuenkirchen am Brand near Nuremberg he returned to Indersdorf "with three well-trained persons" to begin "a spiritual, godly life." John soon became deacon, and his first concern, the Indersdorf chronicler tellingly noted, was the eradication of the vice of property. John then enforced strict enclosure and took up learned, able recruits. They threw out the old ways "with great impatience," meeting daily with resistance from the "old ones and their helpers," resistance so fierce that they thought it easier to build a reformed community anew, "from the ground up," than to confront head-on all of the inveterate "bad customs" of their enemies.[118] Other remembrances from the later fifteenth century recalled how prior Eberhard had enjoined his brother John to make the canons dig up the ground near the refectory and pile it up in the same area. The point of the seemingly fruitless and tiresome exercise was clear from the name that tradition came to accord the resulting mound—the "hill of obedience," which the canons noted was still visible in their own day.[119]

Soon after our chronicler wrote, the Reformation transformed much of the world he knew. Yet his memories and stories captured in only

---

redlicher man, aus dem convent, die zeit verweser der ausseren pfarr glanerdorf mit iren kirchen, ein wol thunder man, weltlewffig in allen handeln."

[117] Ibid., fol. 18r: "Lieber herr und bruder, was solt ich in dem orden thun, so es ein solichs grobs und zerstrats, verlassens leben ist? Han hoffnung in der welt unserem herren vil nachner zukommen, dann also pin ich zu nichte verpunden. Wo aber recht geystlich ordnung da wär, wie es dann sein sol, ließ ich mich e bereden. Doch wil ich des ein bedenckhen nemen und pald ein antwort wissen lassen mit solicher red wo ich gewisz wär, das solichs beshcach."

[118] Ibid.: "Nach osteren kam er herwider, bracht mit im drey wol geubt person. Von den namen sy auff und huben an ein geystlichs gotlichs leben mit abnemen der aigenshcafft, mit beschließung des convents und anderen handeln, dar zu gehorend, namen auff in den convent wolgelert person. Da das die alten sachen, die luffen all auß mit grosser ungeduld...."

[119] BHStAM, KLI 4, fol. 12r: "....terram refectorio vicinam effodiendo minorans et eadem monticulum in orto faciens, ex re nomen eidem imposuerunt quod et usque hodie retinuit. Vocatus est autem non incongrue mons obedientie, quia operibus obedientie in unum collectus est."

a few lines something of the story that has unfolded in the foregoing chapters: narratives and memories of moral crisis and decline that justified reform; sharp conversions and an embrace of reform that took lasting root during the era of the Council of Constance; the leadership of zealous prelates and converts; a process of expulsion and exclusion, and a culture of discipline and devotion. And at the heart of the story, still strong in local memory, was a sharp, penitent rejection of the "vice of property," and a call to return to the common life of the apostles.

CONCLUSION

Some fifty years ago, the Benedictine historian David Knowles wrote that by the fourteenth century the "tide of monastic fervor, after flowing far up the shores, had receded towards the horizon." The golden age of monasticism had faded, Knowles wrote, and even the friars had "ceased to be a marvel." For Knowles, the "heavy weight of the social and economic fabric of the world was pinning the monks to the earth."[1] Knowles' eloquent metaphors reveal how deeply into our own day historians of religious life—many of them, like Knowles, professed to uphold its ideals—framed their accounts in ways that echoed reforming chroniclers of the fifteenth century. John Busch, John Meyer, and John of Indersdorf's anonymous confidant all told of a propertied moral malaise that had reached its nadir on the eve of reform. Only in the 1970s did scholars began in earnest to question the assumptions that had long informed such compelling narratives. Kaspar Elm took the lead, grounding older generalizations within more historically concrete settings of crisis and reform. Others, including a growing number of Anglophone scholars, have since begun to work toward new histories of late-medieval religious life. Old generalizations about crisis and reform are still with us, but they now giving way to new histories: studies of leading Observant figures; studies of key texts; studies of the social structures, economic networks and political powers that sustained reform; and studies of reform's influence on the lives of religious women.

This book has contributed to these reconsiderations of religious life and reform in several ways. One the one hand, it has taken seriously how many religious men and women found themselves in the difficult circumstances captured under the rubric of "crisis." This study has introduced men like Raymond Cabasse, who noted explicitly how tough it could be to make a living as his order's incomes fell. It has introduced women like the nuns of St. Giles, who in dialogue with Dietrich Kerkering wrestled with the challenges of communities reduced to indigence through poverty, fire or other calamity. It has also

---

[1] *The Religious Orders in England*, 3 vols. (Cambridge, 1948–1959), I: 319.

recovered the presence of men and women whose incomes and goods, fashionable habits, private cells and so on marked religious life's full participation in its era's wider culture of property. At the same time, without making excuses for excess, this study has also refused to read these patterns of life too strongly as a consequence of crisis. It has instead suggested the ways in which propertied religious life remained fully intelligible within the conceptual and cultural "common sense" of custom and status that had long sustained it. That common sense was rugged enough to endure the challenges of the fourteenth century, even as it made room for a culture that allowed religious to enjoy cash, personal property and domestic comfort in seemingly unprecedented proportions. Future scholarship will perhaps better measure the orders' perceptions of crisis against the social and economic particulars of so many different locales, and contextualize propertied life more fully in long-term patterns of continuity and change. But the beginnings offered here have hopefully begun to restore a humanity and agency to propertied life that centuries of change have eroded, and that models of crisis have never been able to recapture.

A better understanding of propertied life's cultural legitimacy has also helped this book offer its main contribution: from new source material, a close reading of fifteenth-century reforming ideas and practices of the common life. Scholars of religious life long tended to present Observant ideals of community as self-evident, drawn from transparent readings of religious rules and inspired by a return to an earlier spirituality. For fifteenth-century contemporaries, however, as recent scholarship has begun to show, the matter was more complex. This study has offered another account of that complexity, grounding reform ideals more firmly in their fifteenth-century sources and settings. From close readings of dozens of unpublished or little-known texts, it has explored the genesis, impact and legacy of a distinct reforming discourse of property and community. It has shown how a constellation of reforming authors—secular theologians and lawyers like Henry of Langenstein and Job Vener, as well as anonymous publicists from within the orders—drew from a long penitential, legal, and moral tradition to build a common front against the *proprietarii*. It has also traced how, against steady resistance, reformers advanced their agenda through the circulation of tracts, through visitation and inquest, statute and devotion. The call to reformed community has thus appeared here as something other than simply a reaction to crisis, something other than simply a return to rules or twelfth-century spirituality. As fifteenth-century cultural agents, reformers redeployed old ideas and texts to shape and even distort inherited circumstance, with often unpredictable results.

Our most familiar narratives of religious poverty, it should now be clear, can accommodate the evidence presented here only with some difficulty. Poverty is almost always associated with the story of Francis and his followers, with all of their famous debates over observance, or with the mendicants generally, and the life of the spirit that their movement inspired and cultivated. Without question, inherited discourses of poverty, property and the spirit remained vital. They continued to inspire ongoing debates among the Franciscans; debates between seculars and mendicants; debates over ecclesiology and political theory; anxiety over perceived heresies; suspicion of Beguines, Lollards and other radicals, even the New Devout.[2] The sources adduced here only suggest the importance of keeping future scholarship open to still other possibilities. These texts have revealed how a range of factors shaped other choices and other experiments, and allowed fifteenth-century reformers to redeploy inherited discourses in new settings and in new ways. The emergence of a "new piety" of penance and spiritual progress; the intellectual and textual energy of Constance and Basel; the marriage of reforming interests among Vienna's graduates and the region's territorial princes; something of a wider enthusiasm for the common life, and for more order, discipline and accountability in daily life generally—all of these forces inspired a new contest over religious community distinct from what had come before. It was a contest that drew in religious of many stripes, from monks to canons to mendicants, men and women alike. It was a contest that focused on the social contours of daily life, yet it also spoke to larger anxieties about clerical property and clerical morality, as well as the reformers' own inner anxieties about personal holiness. It was a contest over matters of the spirit, yet it was argued out and expressed in ways that bound matters of the spirit to the letter of the law.

Much more must be done to refine what has been begun here—more work to illuminate the social, political and intellectual networks that fostered or limited reform; more work on key texts and manuscripts; more work on so many other patterns of reception and application.

---

[2] Cf. Christopher Ocker, "Die Armut und die menschliche Natur: Konrad Waldhauser, Jan Milíč von Kroměříč und die Bettelmönche," in *Die Neue Frömmigkeit in Europa im Spätmittelalter*, ed. Marek Derwich and Martial Staub (Göttingen, 2004), 111–29 and Kathryn Kerby-Fulton, *Books under Suspicion* (above, 100 n. 17).

But already this study has helped provide a more precise account of the mechanics of the Observant Movement—or rather one of many possible mechanics. As scholars now rightly emphasize, "the" Observant Movement was in fact a strikingly diverse patchwork whose many inflections await further investigation. And as the evidence of the appendix below suggests, there were many other climates in which the ideas about reform of community surveyed here took shape and took root. Future work may turn to those climates, too, for more accounts of how general calls for reform crystallized into militant and focused movements for change.

These considerations, in turn, intersect with some of the larger interpretive challenges facing historians of medieval religion and church life. The study of medieval religion now encompasses a remarkable range of themes: spirituality and mysticism, heresy, magic and witchcraft; clerical power and persecution; and relationships between clergy and laity, men and women. The challenge, most now recognize, is how best to hold all of these themes, perspectives and possibilities in tension, and in full scholarly view.[3] This study's account of property, community and reform suggests how the history of institutional religious life and reform can engage that challenge. As most people experienced or encountered it, daily life in religious households captured a wide range of competing and contradictory impulses. It could be a life of dull routine and resigned mediocrity, a way for ordinary men and women to keep themselves fed and clothed and funded in ways fitting to their station. It was a life that intertwined the secular and the spiritual, the social and the sacred. It could also blend courtly refinement and lordly excess with "Renaissance" domesticity. Cloister life was dominated by imposing prelates, figures such as the abbot of Lambach and his peers. It was also lived out among a less visible rank and file—religious women such as Margareta and Katharina of Rechentshofen (contemporaries of Joan of Arc and Margery Kempe), who found themselves faced with hostile reforming visitors and sharp decisions about their way of life. Religious life's reform, too, also captured its own range of energies and experiences. Many of those energies were directed outwardly: the sharp resentment of the *proprietarii*; the often radical, public critiques that resentment inspired; the sharpness and shrewdness of reforming

---

[3] Cf. Van Engen, "Future of Medieval Church History," and "Multiple Options" (above, 12 n. 31).

prelates and visitors, who often advanced reform in ways that reflected a wider culture of clerical power and inquisition. Other energies were focused inward: how to balance the attraction of the pursuit of perfection against the dangers of spiritual pride and legalism; how to discern the boundaries of mortal sin in matters of conscience; how to bind the individual to practices of community in ways that promoted spiritual progress.

Historians of the Reformation era have often looked back on the fifteenth century from the sixteenth, explaining the events Luther inspired within the context its earlier precedents. Historians of medieval religion and church life, for their part, have looked forward to the fifteenth century from the twelfth, suggesting all of the ways that later spirituality and reform drew inspiration from the era of Bernard and Francis. These approaches continue to raise issues that remain unresolved: how best to balance continuity and change; where to locate the true turning points and caesuras; how to organize our narratives. And those unresolved tensions, it is clear, remain at stake in any account of religious life and reform. On the one hand, twelfth century spirituality was clearly decisive for fifteenth-century Observants, and Observant reforms are fully intelligible only within a longer history of religious movements in "Old Europe" that stretches the twelfth to the sixteenth century and beyond.[4] Well into the eighteenth century monasteries, nunneries and canonries like those studied here, their patterns of life inflected by the changes of the Baroque era, continued to dominate many local landscapes. Imposing prelates, their power and splendor captured in fashionable early-modern portraits, continued to play prominent social and sacred roles, and their communities continued to participate in patterns of religious life whose roots reached back centuries.[5] In the same years the bookish piety of the Modern Devotion, with all of its affinity to the "classics" of twelfth-century spirituality, continued to inspire the devotional lives of men and women both within and beyond the ranks of the orders. Yet for all of the long-term continuities, it is also impossible to deny the direct and lasting impact of the Reformation. Luther, once a young Observant monk, wore the spiritual obligations of his reformed religious life heavily, and ultimately cast off its burdens.

---

[4] See the concluding remarks to Kaminsky's "Problematics of 'Heresy' and 'The Reformation,'" (above, 12 n. 31), especially 21–22.
[5] Cf. *Krone und Schleier. Kunst aus Mittelalterlichen Frauenklöstern* (Munich, 2005), 496–7.

Luther's heirs then eventually dissolved and expelled religious life's presence in many locales across Europe.

Within the interstices of these larger questions of periodization, continuity and change, this study has explored the possibilities of a more focused account, one more fully attentive to fifteenth-century sources and circumstances on their own terms. It has recovered a reform that participated in long-standing debates about ownership and religious community, and that drew inspiration from a long tradition of reform spirituality. At the same time, this study has emphasized a distinct fifteenth-century genealogy of reform, one whose ideas took shape and took root in ways that were historically conditioned, contested and contingent within fifteenth-century horizons. In restoring life and energy to that story, this study has also suggested how many new sources have yet to be uncovered, and how many more histories of religious life and Observant reform have yet to be written.

APPENDIX

AN INVENTORY OF WORKS "ON PROPERTY" AND THEIR MANUSCRIPTS

The following is a preliminary inventory of works concerning the "vice of property" and their manuscripts. Given the current state of research, it can in no way pretend to be comprehensive or complete. It is offered here only to give an indication of the broad reception of the theme. To capture something of that breadth I have included a sampling of many genres—treatises, sermons, rule commentaries, disputed questions and so on. There are many other works in which the "vice of property" figures prominently—Conrad Zenn's *De vita monastica*, for example, and a variety of texts related to the enforcement of reform. As noted above, there are also a number of vernacular treatises on the theme. In the interest of brevity, however, these works have not been included here.

Treatises are listed alphabetically by incipit. Drawing from available catalogues and databases, and from the literature provided in the notes above, I have provided as much information as is currently available to me regarding each treatise and each manuscript. Where possible I have also provided reference numbers from the manuscript projects of the Hill Monastic Manuscript Library (HMML) and the *Institut de recherche et d'histoire des textes* (IRHT).

1.

Incipit: "Caveant praesumptuosi proprietarii"
Author: Anonymous/Unknown
Date: Unknown
References: N/A
Manuscripts:
　1. COLOGNE, Stadtarchiv, GB8° 152, fol. 50; IRHT 1019632

2.

Incipit: "Christus Jesus Dei Eterni Filius"
Author: "Magister Parisiensis" (Franciscus de Bar?)
Date: Unknown
References: *Thesaurus*, ed. Marténe-Durand, 1: 1738–42

Manuscripts:
1. DOUAI, Bibliothéque Municipale, 812, fol. 16; IRHT 57528
2. VIENNA, ÖNB, Cod. 3702, fols. 303v–305v
3. WÜRZBURG, Universitätsbibliothek, Cod. M. ch. q. 14, fol. 268v; IRHT 1030488
4. WÜRZBURG, Universitätsbibliothek, Cod. M. ch. q. 98, fols. 228–30; IRHT 57530
5. WÜRZBURG, Universitätsbibliothek, Cod. M. ch. q. 110, fols. 86–9v; IRHT 57529

3.

Incipit: "Cum status religionis cessatio quedam sit"
Author: "Doctor Erfordiensis"
Date: Unknown
References: N/A
Manuscripts:
1. MUNICH, BSB, Clm 18600, fols. 418r–419v
2. WÜRZBURG, Universitätsbibliothek, Cod. M. ch. q. 111, fols. 79–91; IRHT 82872

4.

Incipit: "Ecce nos reliquimus omnia"
Author: Henry of Langenstein
Date: c. 1386
References: Hohmann, 229; Kreuzer, 147 n. 680; Lang, 55
Manuscripts:
1. ADMONT, Cod. 156, fols. 1–14; HMML 9247
2. ADMONT, Cod. 319, fols. 162v–171r; HMML 9390
3. ADMONT, Cod. 430, fols. 105–135; HMML 9461
4. COLOGNE, Stadtarchiv, GB4° 124
5. COLOGNE, Stadtarchiv, W 236, fols. 210r–220r
6. ERFURT, Amplon, Q 150, fols. 225–235
7. KLOSTERNEUBURG, 384, fols. 180–87; HMML 5397
8. KLOSTERNEUBURG, 907, fols. 89–101; HMML 5911
9. MELK, Stiftsbibliothek, CM 361, fols. 291–309; HMML 1364
10. MUNICH, BSB, Clm 1892, fols. 67r–90v
11. MUNICH, BSB, Clm 3038, fols. 120r– 132v
12. MUNICH, BSB, Clm 5607, fols. 26r–32r
13. MUNICH, BSB, Clm 5690, fols. 58r–83v
14. MUNICH, BSB, Clm 7320, fols. 130 152
15. MUNICH, BSB, Clm 7321, fols. 227v–235r
16. MUNICH, BSB, Clm 7531, fols. 192r–199v
17. MUNICH, BSB, Clm 7720, fols. 14r–29r
18. MUNICH, BSB, Clm 7750, fols. 110r–120r
19. MUNICH, BSB, Clm 22404, fols. 177r–182r
20. MUNICH, BSB, Clm 26876, fols. 11r–18r (listed as "Pro salute eorum" by Hohmann)

21. MUNICH, BSB, Clm 28416, fols. 21r–27r (listed as "Pro salute eorum" by Hohmann)
22. MUNICH, BSB, Clm 11749, fols. 64r–75r
23. MUNICH, BSB, Clm 16464, fols. 263r–273r
24. MUNICH, BSB, Clm 18544b, fols. 217r–219v
25. MUNICH, BSB, Clm 18644, fols. 168v–181r
26. PRAGUE, Universitätsbibliothek, Cod. Lat. 2613, fols. 59r–79r
27. ST. FLORIAN, Stiftsbibliothek, 71, fols. 272–283; HMML 2321
28. ST. FLORIAN, Stiftsbibliothek, 96, fols. 218–226; HMML 2355
29. VIENNA, ÖNB, Cod. 3700, fols. 173–185; HMML 16919
30. VIENNA, ÖNB, Cod. 3702, fols. 305v–321r
31. VIENNA, ÖNB, Cod. 4119, fols. 113–123
32. VIENNA, ÖNB, Cod. 4159, fols. 113v–123v
33. VIENNA, ÖNB, Cod. 4173, fols. 187r–192v
34. VIENNA, ÖNB, Cod. 4242, fols. 37–57
35. VIENNA, ÖNB, Cod. 4444, fols. 274–282; HMML 14458
36. VIENNA, ÖNB, Cod. 4610, fols. 170–184
37. VIENNA, ÖNB, Cod. 4816, fols. 104r–112v; HMML 17997
38. VIENNA, ÖNB, Cod. 5352, fols. 194r–201v
39. WOLFENBÜTTEL, Herzog-August-Bibliothek, Cod. Guelf. 18 Aug. fols. 167v–179v

5.

Incipit: "Ecce nos reliquimus omnia"
Author: Peter of Pulkau (Also attributed to Nicholas of Dinkelsbühl and John Wischler)
Date: 1418
References: Madre, *Nikolaus von Dinkelsbühl*, 329
Manuscripts:
1. MELK, Stiftsbibliothek, CM 793, fols. 244r–247r; HMML 1634
2. MELK, Stiftsbibliothek, CM 911, fols. 208r–213v; HMML 1729
3. MELK, Stiftsbibliothek, CM 955, fols. 232r–238v; HMML 1765
4. MUNICH, BSB, Clm 16196, fols. 118–121
5. RIMINI, Bibl. Civica Gambalunga, Cod. 71, fols. 174r–178r
6. VIENNA, Schottenklolster, Cod. 21; IRHT 118810; HMML 3869
7. VIENNA, Schottenkloster, Cod. 152, fols. 154r–162r; IRHT 1065596; HMML 4071

6.

Incipit: "Igitur uniusquisque"
Author: "Pauper Monachus"
Date: c. 1422
References: N/A
Manuscripts:
1. KREMSMÜNSTER, Stiftsbibliothek, Cod. CXI, fols. 148r–194r
2. MELK, Stiftsbibliothek, CM 1241, fols. 165r–193v; HMML 1885
3. MELK, Stiftsbibliothek, CM 746, fol. 126r–159v; HMML 1595

4. MUNICH, BSB, Clm 3038, fols. 86 ff.
5. MUNICH, BSB, Clm 4396
6. MUNICH, BSB, Clm 5051
7. MUNICH, BSB, Clm 7008
8. MUNICH, BSB, Clm 18644, fols. 140r–168v
9. SALZBURG, St. Peter, a. IV. 23, fols. 90r–126r; HMML 10016
10. STAMS, Stiftsbibliothek, Cod. 55, fols. 212–250
11. VIENNA, ÖNB, Cod. 3549, fols. 67r–103r
12. VIENNA, ÖNB, Cod. 3551, fols. 1r–43r
13. VIENNA, ÖNB, Cod. 3700, fols. 147r–171r; HMML 16919
14. VIENNA, ÖNB, Cod. 3702, fols. 273r–303v

7.
Incipit: "In Domino dominorum continuam conscientie pacem"
Author: Geert Groote
Date: Unknown
References: N/A
Manuscripts:
   1. LEUVEN, Bibl. van der Fac. der Godgeleerdh., Mechlen 30, fol. 28; IRHT 180139
   2. PARIS, Bibliotheque de l'Arsenal 532 (581 Y. TL.) 13o, fol. 94; IRHT 180138

8.
Incipit: "Invectio in vitium proprietatis"
Author: Unknown
Date: Unknown
References: IRHT 1028947
Manuscripts:
   1. BERLIN, Staatsbibliothek Preußischer Kulturbesitz, Lat 400 (Th. Lat. Qu. 78), fols. 110r–116r

9.
Incipit: "Notandum quod diligenter debemus"
Author: Unknown
Date: Unknown
References: N/A
Manuscripts:
   1. NIJMEGEN, UB 98, fols. 13v–14v; IRHT 203448

10.
Incipit: "Manifestum videtur esse, quod personae religiosae" (a segment of Constance tract "Reverendissimo" (no. 29 below) that circulated independently.
Author: Anonymous
Date: c. 1415
References: See no. 29 below.

Manuscripts:
1. COLOGNE, Stadtarchiv, GB8° 152, fols. 27–40; IRHT 1119082
2. COLOGNE, Stadtarchiv, GB4° 196 (pastedown, fragment); IRHT 1001965
3. DARMSTADT, Hessische Landes- und Hochschulbibliothek, Cod. 792, fols. 100r–111v
4. DARMSTADT, Hessische Landes- und Hochschulbibliothek, Cod. 767, fols. 125v–130v
5. MUNICH, BSB, Clm 3025
6. MUNICH, BSB, Clm 6963
7. MUNICH, BSB, Clm 8180, fols. 249r–258r
8. MUNICH, BSB, Clm 14820, fols. 73r–93v
9. MUNICH, BSB, Clm 16196, fols. 124r–136r
10. MUNICH, BSB, Clm 18152
11. MUNICH, BSB, Clm 18600, fols. 408r–413v
12. VIENNA, Schottenkloster, Cod. 320, fols. 194–203; IRHT 1119083; HMML 4253

11.

Incipit: "Modus vivendi quem tenetis"
Author: Dietrich Kerkering of Münster
Date: 1412
References: VL 4: 1129–32
Manuscripts:
1. FRANKFURT, Stadt-und Universitätsbibliothek, MS Barth. 141, fols. 190r–197v
2. LAMBACH, Stiftsbibliothek, Cod. Ccl 254, fols. 100v–109r
3. MAINZ, Stadtbibliothek Cod. II 122, 234v–240r
4. MELK, Stiftsbibliothek, Cod. 900, fols. 56r–62r; HMML 1720
5. TRIER, Stadtbibliothek, Cod. 2316, 34r–48r

12.

Incipit: "Monachi proprietarii quomodo salvari possunt"
Author: Anonymous
Date: Unknown
References: N/A
Manuscripts:
1. FRENSWEGEN, Klosterbibl. 83, fol. 368va; IRHT 1426380
2. STRASSBOURG, BNU 107 (Latin 104), fol. 368v; IRHT 230217

13.

Incipit: "Nolite diligere mundum neque ea que in mundo sunt" [I. John 2:15].
Author: Henry of Cosfeld
Date: Unknown
References: N/A

Manuscripts:
  1. DEVENTER, Stads-en-Athenaeumbibl. 1.78, fols. 46–84; IRHT 241189

14.

Incipit: "Non dicatis"
Author: Anonymous
Date: Unknown
References: N/A
Manuscripts:
  1. MUNICH, BSB, Clm 7320, fols. 153v–160v
  2. MUNICH, BSB, Clm 7720, fols. 30r–35v
  3. MUNICH, BSB, Clm 16512, fols. 168r–174v
  4. MUNICH, BSB, Clm 18551, fols. 303ra–306ra

15.

Incipit: "Nota diligenter"
Author: Anonymous
Date: Unknown
References: N/A
Manuscripts:
  1. VIENNA, Schottenkloster, Cod. 258, fols. 412–413; HMML 4008
  2. VIENNA, Schottenkloster, Cod. 325, fols. 193a–193b; HMML 4255

16.

Incipit: "Notandum quod monachus proprietarius peccator pessimus"
Author: Anonymous
Date: Unknown
References: N/A
Manuscripts:
  1. COLOGNE, Historisches Archiv, W 140, fol. 275v; IRHT 1090193

17.

Incipit: "Noverint singuli et universi"
Author: "Magister Parisiensis"
Date: Unknown
References: N/A
Manuscripts:
  1. BERLIN, Staatsbibliothek Preußischer Kulturbesitz, Theol. Lat. Qu. 167, fols. 221r–222r
  2. KREMSMUNSTER, Stiftsbibliothek, Cod. CXI, fols. 194a–195a
  3. MUNICH, BSB, Clm 7320, fol. 153v
  4. MUNICH, BSB, Clm 18551, fols. 301v–306r
  5. MUNICH, BSB, Clm 18655, fols. 164–167
  6. SALZBURG, St. Peter, b.V. 18, fols. 1–2; HMML 10449
  7. VIENNA, ÖNB, Cod. 3700; HMML 16919

18.
Incipit: "Omnis religiosus existens in monasterio proprietarius est Dei inimicus"
Author: Anonymous
Date: Unknown
References: N/A
Manuscripts:
   1. Würzburg, UB Cod. M ch. q. 124, fols. 281–301; IRHT 263893

19.
Incipit: "Personam aliquam habere proprietatem"
Author: Caspar Maiselstein
Date: Unknown
References: VL 7: 443–448
Manuscripts:
   1. Vienna, Schottenkloster, Cod. 152, fols. 142b–145a; HMML 4071
   2. Munich, BSB, Clm 18600, fols. 416v–417v

20.
Incipit: "Praecipue hoc vitium"
Author: John Wischler
Date: Unknown
References: VL 4: 757–9
Manuscripts:
   1. Melk, Stiftsbibliothek, CM 911, fols. 32r–60v; HMML 1729
   2. Salzburg, St. Peter a. II. 22, fols. 261–265v; HMML 9919
   3. Salzburg, St. Peter a. III.15, fols. 97r–122v; HMML 9954

21.
Incipit: "Pro salute eorum, qui vitia fugere cupiunt"
Author: Job Vener (Often attributed to Henry of Langenstein)
Date: 1415
References: ed. Heimpel, *Vener*, 3: 1269–97; Kreuzer, *Heinrich von Langenstein*, 148
   1. Admont, Stiftsbibliothek, Cod. 209, fols. 131v–137r; IRHT 297990; HMML 9294
   2. Augsburg, Staats- und Stadtbibliothek, Cod. 4° 13 fol. 27r–32r
   3. Bamberg, Staatsbibliothek Cod. Theol. 172 (Q.V.14) fol. 90v–96r
   4. Darmstadt, Hessische Landes- und Hochschulbibliothek, Cod. 792, fols. 100r–111v
   5. Berlin, Staatsbibliothek Preußischer Kulturbesitz, Th. Lat. Qu. 710, fols. 287v–292r
   6. Berlin, Staatsbibliothek Preußischer Kulturbesitz, Th. Lat. Fol. 732, fols. 71v–76v
   7. Cambridge, Corpus Christi College, Ms. 156 II; IRHT 297985
   8. Cologne, Stadtarchiv, GB 8° 61, fol. 128; IRHT 1155020
   9. Dresden, Landesbiliothek P 157
   10. Frankfurt, Stadt- und UB Praed. 129, fol. 202; IRHT 1155022

11. GRAZ, UB 900, fols. 133r–139r; IRHT 1155024
12. GRAZ, UB 951, fol. 25; IRHT 1155025
13. GRENOBLE, BM 587 (639), fols. 75 and 83v; IRHT 297983
14. HARBURG, Oettingen Wallersteinische Bibliothek, Cod. II 1. 40 15
15. HARBURG, Oettingen Wallersteinische Bibliothek Cod. II.1 40 30 fols. 111r–117r
16. HERZOGENBURG, Stiftsbibliothek, Cod. 6, fol. 109; IRHT 1405803; HMML 3185
17. LILIENFELD, 113, fols. 193–223
18. MAINZ, II, 37
19. MELK, Stiftsbibliothek, CM 62, fols. 155–176
20. MELK, Stiftsbibliothek, CM 299, fols. 47–65; HMML 2140
21. MELK, Stiftsbibliothek, CM 280, fols. 497–519; HMML 1904
22. MUNICH, BSB, Clm 3038, fols. 123r–129v
23. MUNICH, BSB, Clm 5009, fols. 168r–179v
24. MUNICH, BSB, Clm 7720, fols. 45v–52v
25. MUNICH, BSB, Clm 8258, fols. 152r–160v
26. MUNICH, BSB, Clm 8445, fols. 245v–247v
27. MUNICH, BSB, Clm 9726, fols. 81r–84r
28. MUNICH, BSB, Clm 9804, fols. 280–297
29. MUNICH, BSB, Clm 14520, fols. 35r–41r
30. MUNICH, BSB, Clm 14820, fols. 145r–167r
31. MUNICH, BSB, Clm 15631, fols. 11r–21v
32. MUNICH, BSB, Clm 16196, fols. 114v–117v
33. MUNICH, BSB, Clm 16512, fols. 212r–224v
34. MUNICH, BSB, Clm 18526b, fols. 170r–176r
35. MUNICH, BSB, Clm 18551, fols. 106r–114r
36. MUNICH, BSB, Clm 18644, fols. 185r–196r
37. MUNICH, BSB, Clm 18655, fols. 156–64
38. MUNICH, BSB, Clm 22404, fols. 177r–182r
39. MUNICH, BSB, Clm 24816, fols. 21r–27r
40. MUNICH, BSB, Clm 26876, fols. 11r–18r
41. PRAGUE, Kar. Knih. 2382 (XIII.G.15), fols. 269r–275v; IRHT 1370186
42. NIJMEGEN, UB 95, fols. 1–9v; IRHT 297980
43. NIJMEGEN, UB 98, fols. 3–6v; IRHT 297981
44. SALZBURG, St. Peter, a. III. 15, fols. 148–149v; HMML 9959
45. SALZBURG, St. Peter, a. III.13, fols. 103–115; HMML 10483
46. SALZBURG, St. Peter, b.VI. 6, fols. 32–38; HMML 10583
47. SALZBURG, St. Peter, b. IX. 20
48. SCHLÄGL, Stiftsbibliothek, 122 (452 a.102), fols. 149–153; IRHT 1155018
49. ST. GALLEN, Stiftsbibliothek, Cod. 780, fols. 415–431
50. ST. GALLEN, Stiftsbibliothek, Cod. 937, fols. 505–514
51. STAMS, Stiftsbibliothek 62, fols. 14v–22v; IRHT 1155019
52. STRASSBOURG, BNU 83 (Latin 80) fol. 174; IRHT 297984

53. SUBIACO, Biblioteca della Abbazia, Cod. CCXCVII, fols. 57v–73v
54. TRIER, Stadtbibliothek, Cod. 879 (680), fols. 36v–43v
55. UTRECHT, Bibl. d. Rijksun. 236, fols. 28–34; IRHT 297982
56. VIENNA, ÖNB, Cod. 4059, fols. 160v–171v
57. VIENNA, ÖNB, Cod. 4065, fols. 213r–227r
58. VIENNA, ÖNB, Cod. 4409, fols. 164r–169r
59. VIENNA, ÖNB, Cod. 4732, fols. 42v–50v
60. VIENNA, ÖNB, Cod. 4760, fols. 85r–97v
61. VIENNA, ÖNB, Cod. 4948, fols. 49–56
62. VIENNA, Schottenkloster, 63, fols. 168–78; IRHT 297989; IRHT 1155021; HMML 3985
63. VIENNA, Schottenkloster, 305, fols. 116–127; IRHT 297988; IRHT 1155023; HMML 4250
64. WÜRZBURG, Universitätsbibliothek, Cod. M. ch. o. 35 fols. 55v–69r
65. WÜRZBURG, Universitätsbibliothek, Cod. M. ch. q. 111, fols. 85–95; IRHT 1155028

22.
Incipit: "Queritur sic: Numquid episcopus abbas prelatus seu superior dumtaxat propria"
Author: Rudolfus Spizlin
Date: Unknown
References: N/A
Manuscripts:
 1. STAMS, Stiftsbibliothek 55, fols. 253v–261; IRHT 1162826

23.
Incipit: "Queritur utrum religiosus usum alicuius rei"
Author: Unknown/Anonymous
Date: Unknown
References: N/A
Manuscripts:
 1. NIJMEGEN, UB 98, fols. 7r–13r; IRHT 316464

24.
Incipit: "Qui habet aures audiendi audiat"
Author: Unknown
Date: Unknown
References: N/A
Manuscripts:
 1. MUNICH, BSB, Clm 7748, fols. 84r–86v
 2. MUNICH, BSB, Clm 11749, fols. 184–188
 3. MUNICH, BSB, Clm 18558, fols. 65r–70r

25.

Incipit: "Quia vitium proprietatis"
Author: John Nider?
Date: Unknown
References: N/A
Manuscripts:
  1. Munich, BSB, Clm 21625, fols. 234–256
  2. Munich, BSB, Clm 18152, fols. 1–5

26.

Incipit: "Quod fratres non obstante sua mendicitate"
Author: John Nider?
Date: Unknown
References: N/A
Manuscripts:
  1. Besançon, BM 388, fol. 214v; IRHT 299082

27.

Incipit: "Quomodo fratres debeant se habere, ne sint proprietarii"
Author: Unknown
Date: Unknown
References: N/A
Manuscripts:
  1. Kórnik, Bibl. Publ. 119, fol. 157; IRHT 335358

28.

Incipit: "Regularium sive claustralium sacra religio"
Author: Henry of Langenstein?
Date: Unknown
References: Hohmann, *Initienregister*, 426
Manuscripts:
  1. Admont, Stiftsbibliohtek, Cod. 156; HMML 9247
  2. St. Florian, Stiftsbibliohtek, Cod. XI 82

29.

Incipit: "Reverendissimo in Christo patri ac dd.Cistercii…Pro eveidenti et necessaria salute animarum nostrarum"
Author: Anonymous
Date: Unknown
References: cd. Finke, ACC 4, 671–76; Mertens, "Reformkonzilien und Ordensreform," 437 n. 29
Manuscripts:
  1. Berlin, Staatsbibliothek Preußischer Kulturbesitz, Th. Lat. Qu. 28
  2. Berlin, Staatsbibliothek Preußischer Kulturbesitz, Th. Lat. Qu. 167
  3. Berlin, Staatsbibliothek Preußischer Kulturbesitz, Th. Lat. Qu. 844
  4. Copenhagen, Gl. Kgl. S. 72, fols. 73–78

5. Munich, BSB, Clm 7066, fols. 212–225
  6. Wolfenbüttel, Cod. Helmst. 1251, fols. 107–131

30.
Incipit: "Sanctis in Christi fratribus"
Author: Petrus Monachus
Date: Unknown
References: N/A
Manuscripts:
  1. Prague, Kar. Knih. 1805 (X.A.2) fols. 143–147; IRHT 1368822

31.
Incipit: "Utrum absque nota et vitio proprietatis liceat fratribus"
Author: Heinricus Stirer de Nuremberg
Date: Unknown
References: N/A
Manuscripts:
  1. Munich, BSB, Clm 8485, fols. 34r–41v

32.
Incipit: "Utrum monachus possit proprium habere"
Author: Anonymous
Date: Unknown
References: N/A
Manuscripts:
  1. Munich, BSB, Clm 18600, fols. 420r–423v

33.
Incipit: "Utrum religiosi habentes"
Author: John Wischler
Date: Unknown
References: VL 4: 757–9
Manuscripts:
  1. Melk, Stiftsbibliothek, Cod. 900, fols. 280–90; HMML 1720

BIBLIOGRAPHY

Archives and Manuscripts

Bamberg, Staatsbibliothek, Theol. 117
Basel, Universitätsbibliothek, B. III. 15
Florence, Biblioteca Nazionale, J.10.51
Frankfurt, Stadt-und Universitätsbibliothek, MS Barth. 141
Klosterneuburg, Stiftsbibliothek, Cod. 1155
Melk, Stiftsbibliothek, CM 193; 737; 746; 793; 900; 911; 959; 1094; 1801
Munich
– Bayerische Staatsbibliothek, Clm 1006; 7531; 5607; 5690; 7720; 9726; 16196; 18551; 18558; 18600, 18644; 19638; 19697
– Bayerisches Hauptstaatsarchiv, Klosterliteralien Indersdorf 4; 7; 145; 146
Salzburg, St. Peter, a. III. 15; a. IV. 23; a. VI. 6; b. II. 15; b. III. 11
Vienna
– Österreichische Nationalbibliothek, Cod. 2968; 3700; 4934
– Schottenkloster, Cod. 152; 320

Printed Sources

Conciliorum Oecumenicorum Decreta. Basel: Herder, 1962.
Monumenta Boica. Munich: Typis Academicis, 1763–.
Amort, Eusebius, ed. *Vetus Disciplina Canonicorum Regularium et Secularium*. 5 vols. Venice, 1747. Reprint Farnborough: Gregg, 1971.
Andreae, Johannes. *In sextum decretalium librum nouella commentaria*. Venice, 1581.
Angerer, Joachim, ed. *Caeremoniae regularis observantiae sanctissimi patris nostri Benedicti ex ipsius regula sumptae, secundum quod in sacris locis, scilicet Specu et monasterio Sublacensi practicantur.* Corpus consuetudinum monasticarum XI/1. Siegeburg: F. Schmitt, 1985.
———. *Die Bräuche der Abtei Tegernsee unter Abt Kaspar Aindorffer (1426–1461), verbunden mit einer kritischen Edition der Consuetudines Tegernseensis*. Augsburg: Winfried-Werk, 1968.
Bihl, M. "Statuta Generalia ordinis edita in capitulo generali an. 1354 Assisii celebrato communiter Farneriana appelata." *Archivum Franciscanum Historicum* 35 (1942): 35–112; 177–253.
Canivez, J.-M., ed. *Statuta capitulorum generalium ordinis Cisterciensis ab anno 1116 ad annum 1786*. 8 vols. Louvain: Bureaux de la Revue, 1933–41.
Finke, Heinrich, ed. *Acta Concilii Constanciensis*. 4 vols. Münster: Regensbergsche buchhandlung, 1896–1928.
Friedberg, Emil, ed. *Corpus Iuris Canonici*. 2 vols. 1879–81. Leipzig, 1879–81. Reprint Union, NJ: Lawbook Exchange, 2000.
Frühwirth, A., ed. *Acta capitulorum generalium Ordinis Praedicatorum*. 3 vols, *Monumenta Ordinis Praedicatorum Historica 3, 4, 8*. Rome, 1898–1900.
Fry, Timothy et al., ed. *RB 1980: The Rule of St. Benedict in Latin and English with Notes*. Collegeville: Liturgical Press, 1982.
Gregory the Great. *Dialogues*. 3vols. SC 251, 260, 265. Paris: Cerf, 1978.
Grube, Karl, ed. *Des Augustinerpropstes Iohannes Busch Chronicon Windeshemense und Liber de reformatione monasteriorum*. 1886. Reprint Farnborough: Gregg, 1968.
Hoffmans, J., ed. *Le Dixième Quodlibet de Godefroid de Fontaines (Texte Inédit)*. Louvain: Institut supérieur de philosophie, 1931.
Hostiensis. *Decretalium Commentaria*. Turin: Bottega d'Erasmo, 1965.

Hundt, Friedrich. *Die Urkunden des Klosters Indersdorf*. Munich: Wolf, 1863–64.
Koller, Heinrich, ed. *Reformation Kaiser Siegmunds*. MGH Staatschriften VI. Stuttgart: Anton Hiersemann, 1964.
Künzle, P. *Heinrich Seuse's Horologium Sapientiae. Erste kritische Ausgabe unter Benützung der Vorarbeiten von Dominikus Planzer O.P.* Freibourg, 1977.
Mansi, Giovan Domenico, ed. *Sacrorum conciliorum nova et amplissima collectio*. 31 vols. 1758–1798. Reprint Paris: H. Welter, 1901–21.
Marténe, Edmund, and Ursinus Durand. *Thesaurus Novus Anecdotorum*. 5 vols. Farnborough: Gregg, 1969.
Meyer, Johannes. *Buch der Reformacio Predigerordens*. Edited by B. M. Reichert. Leipzig, 1908/9.
Peraldus, William. *Summa aurea de virtutibus et vitiis*. Cologne, 1546.
Pez, Bernhard. *Bibliotheca ascetica antiquo-nova*. 12 vols. Farnborough: Gregg, 1967.
Salimbene de Adam Cronica. I A. 1168–1249. Edited by Giuseppe Scalia. CCCM 125. Turnhout: Brepols, 1998.
Suso, Henry. *Wisdom's Watch Upon the Hours*. Translated by Edmund Colledge. Washington: Catholic University of America, 1994.
Zeibig, Hartmann. *Urkundenbuch des Stiftes Klosterneuburg*. 2 vols. *Fontes Rerum Austriacum* 10/28. Vienna, 1857/65.

Secondary Works

Adelige Sachkultur des Spätmittelalters: Internationaler Kongress Krems an der Donau 22. bis 25. September 1980. Vienna: Austrian Academy of Sciences, 1982.
Klösterliche Sachkultur des Spätmittelalters. Internationaler Kongress Krems an der Donau 18. bis 21. September 1978. Vienna: Austrian Academy of Sciences, 1982.
Krone und Schleier. Kunst aus Mittelalterlichen Frauenklöstern. Munich: Hirmer, 2005.
Ames, Christine Caldwell. "Does Inquisition Belong to Religious History?" *American Historical Review* 110 (2005): 11–37.
Andenmatten, Bernard, and Agostino Paravicini Bagliani, eds. *Amédée VIII—Felix V, Premier duc de savoie et pape (1383–1451). Colloque international Ripaille-Lausanne, 23–26 octobre 1990*. Lausanne: Bibliothèque historique Vaudoise, 1992.
Angerer, Joachim. "Reform von Melk." In *Die Reformverbände und Kongregationen der Benediktiner im deutschen Sprachraum*, edited by Ulrich Faust and Franz Quarthal, 271–313. St. Ottilien: EOS, 1999.
———. "Zur Problematik der Begriffe: Regula—Consuetudo—Observanz und Orden." *Studien und Mitteilungen zur Geschichte des Benediktinerordens* 88 (1977): 312–23.
Armstrong, Megan. *The Politics of Piety: Franciscan Preachers during the Wars of Religion, 1560–1600*. New York: University of Rochester Press, 2004.
Austin, David. "Private and Public: An Archaeological Consideration of Things." In *Die Vielvalt der Dinge. Neue Wege zur Analyse mittelalterlicher Sachkultur. Internationaler Kongress Krems an der Donau 4. Bis 7. Oktober 1994*, 163–206. Vienna: Austrian Academy of Sciences, 1998.
Backmund, Norbert. *Die Chorherrenorden und ihre Stifte in Bayern*. Passau: Neue-Presse, 1966.
Baernstein, P. Renée. *A Convent Tale: A Century of Sisterhood in Spanish Milan*. New York: Routledge, 2002.
Bailey, Michael D. *Battling Demons. Witchcraft, Heresy and Reform in the Later Middle Ages*. University Park, PA: Penn State University Press, 2003.
———. "Religious Poverty, Mendicancy, and Reform in the Late Middle Ages." *Church History* 72 (2003): 457–83.
Banner, Lisa A. "Private Rooms in the Monastic Architecture of Habsburg Spain." In *Defining the Holy: Sacred Space in Medieval and Early Modern Europe*, edited by Sarah Hamilton and Andrew Spicer, 81–94. Aldershot: Ashgate, 2005.

Bast, Robert J. *Honor Your Fathers. Catechisms and the Emergence of a Patriarchal Ideology in Germany, 1400–1600*. Leiden: Brill, 1997.
Bauerreiss, Romuald. *Kirchengeshcichte Bayerns. Das Fünfzehnte Jahrhundert*. St. Ottilien: EOS, 1955.
Bean, J. M. W. *From Lord to Patron*. Philadelphia: University of Pennsylvania Press, 1989.
Becker, Petrus. "Benediktinische Reformbewegungen im Spätmittelalter. Ansätze, Entwicklungen, Auswirkungen." In *Untersuchungen zu Kloster und Stift*, edited by J. Fleckenstein, 167–87. Göttingen: Vandenhoeck and Ruprecht, 1980.
——. *Das monastische Reformprogramm des Abtes Johannes Rode von St. Matthias in Trier. Ein darstellender Kommentar zu seinen Consuetudines*. Münster: Aschendorf, 1970.
——. "Erstrebte und Erreichte Ziele Benediktinischer Reformen im Spätmittelalter." In *Reformbemühungen und Observanzbestrebungen im spätmittelalterlichen Ordenswesen*, edited by Kaspar Elm, 23–34. Berlin: Duncker and Humblot, 1989.
Bellomo, Manlio. *The Common Legal Past of Europe, 1000–1800*. Translated by Lydia G. Cochrane. 2nd ed. Washington: Catholic University of America Press, 1995.
Berlière, U. "Le nombre des moines dans les anciens monastères." *Revue Bénédictine* 41 (1929): 231–61; 42 (1930): 19–42.
——. "Les chapitres généraux de l'ordre de S. Benoît." *Revue Bénédictine* 18 (1901): 364–98; 19 (1902): 38–75; 22 (1905): 377–97.
Berman, Constance. *The Cistercian Evolution. The Invention of a Religious Order in Twelfth-Century Europe*. Philadelphia: University of Pennsylvania Press, 2000.
Bestul, Thomas H. *Texts of the Passion. Latin Devotional Literature and Medieval Society*. Philadelphia: University of Pennsylvania Press, 1996.
Biraben, Jean-Noël. *Les hommes et la peste en France et dans les pays européens et méditerranéens*. 2 vols. Paris: Mouton, 1975.
Bisson, Thomas. "Medieval Lordship." *Speculum* 70 (1995): 743–59.
——, ed. *Cultures of Power: Lordship, Status and Process in Twelfth-Century Europe*. Philadelphia: University of Pennsylvania Press, 1995.
Blickle, Peter. *Communal Reformation. The Quest for Salvation in Sixteenth-Century Germany*. Translated by Thomas Dunlap. New Jersey: Humanities Press, 1992.
——. "Communalism as an Organizational Principle Between Medieval and Modern Times." In *From the Communal Reformation to the Revolution of the Common Man*, 1–15. Leiden: Brill, 1998.
——. *From the Communal Reformation to the Revolution of the Common Man*. Translated by Beat Kümin. Leiden: Brill, 1998.
Bloomfield, Morton. *Incipits of Latin Works on the Virtues and Vices: 1100–1500*. Cambridge, MA: Medieval Academy of America, 1979.
Boner, Georg. "Das Predigerkloster in Basel von der Gründung bis zur Klosterreform 1233–1429." *Basler Zeitschrift für Geschichte und Altertumskunde* 33 (1934): 195–303.
Boockmann, Hartmut. "Zur Mentalität spätmittelalterlicher gelehrter Räte." *Historische Zeitschrift* 233 (1981): 295–316.
Brandmüller, Walter. *Das Konzil von Konstanz*. Paderbron: Schöningh, 1991.
Britnell, R. H. *The Commercialisation of English Society*. Cambridge: Cambridge University Press, 1993.
Brown, Peter. *The Rise of Western Christendom. Triumph and Diversity, A.D. 200–1000*. 2nd ed. Oxford: Blackwell, 2003.
Buchholz, Werner. "Anfänge der Sozialdisziplinerung im Mittelalter. Die Reichstadt Nürnberg als Beispiel." *Zeitschrift für Historische Forschung* 18 (1991): 129–47.
Buisson, Ludwig. *Potestas und Caritas: Die Päpstliche Gewalt im Mittelalter*. Colonge: Böhlau, 1959.
Bulst, Neithard. "Der Schwarze Tod. Demographische, wirtschafts- und kulturgeschichtliche Aspekte der Pestkatastrophe von 1347–1352." *Saeculum* 30 (1979): 45–67.
——. "Feste und Feiern unter Auflagen. Mittelalterliche Tauf-, Hochzeits- und Begräbnisordnungen in Deutschland und Frankreich." In *Feste und Feiern im Mittelalter*, edited

by Detlef Altenburg, Jörg Jarnut and Hans-Hugo Steinhoff, 39–51. Sigmaringen: Thorbecke, 1991.

———. "La législation somptuaire d'Amédée VIII." In *Amédée VIII—Félix V: Premier duc de Savoie et pape (1383–1451). Colloque international, Ripaille-Lausanne, 23–26 octobre 1990*, edited by Bernard Andenmatten and Augusto Paravicini Bagliani, 191–200. Lausanne: Bibliothèque historique Vaudoise, 1992.

———. "Les ordonnances somptuaires en Allemagne: expression de l'ordre social urbain (XIVe–XVIe siècle)." *Académie des inscriptions et belles-lettres. Comptes-rendus des séances* 3 (1993): 771–83.

———. "Zum problem städtischer und territorialer Kleider- Aufwands- und Luxusgesetzgebung in Deutschland (13.- Mitte 16. Jahrhundert)." In *Renaissance du puvoir législatif et genèse de l'état*, edited by André Gouron and Albert Rigaudiere, 29–57. Montpellier, 1988.

Bumke, Joachim. *Courtly Culture. Literature and Society in the High Middle Ages*. Translated by Thomas Dunlap. Berkeley: University of California Press, 1991.

Burr, David. *Olivi and Franciscan Poverty: The Origins of the usus pauper Controversy*. Philadelphia: University of Pennsylvania Press, 1989.

———. *The Spiritual Franciscans. From Protest to Persecution in the Century after Saint Francis*. University Park, PA: Pennsylvania State University Press, 2001.

Bynum, Caroline Walker. *Wonderful Blood. Theology and Practice in Late Medieval Northern Germany and Beyond*. Philadelphia: University of Pennsylvania Press, 2007.

Chiffoleau, Jaques. *La comptabilité de l'au-delà: les hommes, la mort et la religion dans la région d'Avignon à la fin du Moyen Âge (vers 1320–vers 1480)*. Rome: École française de Rome, 1980.

———. "Sur l'usage obsessionnel de la messe pour les morts à la fin du moyen-âge." In *Faire croire. Modalités de la diffusion et de la réception des messages religieux du XIIe au XVe siècle*, 236–56. Rome: École française de Rome, 1981.

Cipolla, C. M. "Une crise ignorée. Comment s'est perdue la propriété ecclésiastique dans l'Italie du nord entre le XIIe et le XVIe siècle." *Annales E. S. C.* 3 (1947): 248–80.

Clark, James G. "Reformation and reaction at St Albans Abbey, 1530–58." *English Historical Review* 115 (2000): 297–328.

———, ed. *Religious Orders in Pre-Reformation England*. New York: Boydell, 2002.

Clunas, Craig. "Modernity Global and Local: Consumption and the Rise of the West." *American Historical Review* 104 (1999): 1497–1511.

Samuel Cohn, Jr. *The Black Death Transformed: Disease and Culture in Early Renaissance Europe*. London: Arnold, 2002.

Coleman, Janet. "Property and Poverty." In *The Cambridge History of Medieval Political Thought c. 350–c. 1450*, edited by J. H. Burns, 607–52. Cambridge: Cambridge University Press, 1991.

Comba, Rinaldo. "Les *Decreta Sabaudiae* d' Amédée VIII: un projet de société." In *Amédée VIII—Félix V, Premier duc de Savoie et Pape (1383–1451). Colloque international, Ripaille-Lausanne, 23–26 octobre 1990*, edited by Bernard Andenmatten and Agostino Paravicini Bagliani, 179–90. Lausanne: Bibliothèque historique Vaudoise, 1992.

Congar, Yves. "Aspects ecclésiologiques de la querelle entre mendiants et séculiers dans la second moitié du XIIIe siècle et la début du XIVe." *Archives d'histoire doctrinale et littéraire du moyen âge* 28 (1961): 35–151.

Constable, Giles. "The Authority of Superiors in Religious Communities." In *La notion d'autorité au Moyen Age: Islam, Byzance, Occident. Colloques internationaux de la Napoule, session des 23–26 octobre 1978*, edited by George Makdisi, Dominique Sourdel and Janine Sourdel-Thomine, 189–210. Paris: Presses Universitaires de France,1982.

———. "The Ceremonies and Symbolism of Entering Religious Life and Taking the Monastic Habit, from the Fourth to the Twelfth Century." *Segni e riti nella chiesa altomedievale occidentale: Settimane di Studio del centro italiano di studi sull'alto medioevo* 33 (1987): 771–834.

———. "The Popularity of Twelfth-Century Spiritual Writers in the Late Middle Ages." In *Renaissance Studies in Honor of Hans Baron*, edited by Anthony Molho and John A. Tedeschi, 5–28. Florence and DeKalb: Northern Illinois Univeristy Press, 1971.
———. *The Reformation of the Twelfth Century*. Cambridge: Cambridge University Press, 1996.
———. *Three Studies in Medieval Religious and Social Thought*. Cambridge: Cambridge University Press, 1995.
———. "Twelfth Century Spirituality and the Late Middle Ages." In *Medieval and Renaissance Studies 5*, edited by O. B. Hardison, Jr., 27–60. Chapel Hill: University of North Carolina Press, 1971.
Courtenay, William J., Jürgen Miethke, and David B. Priest, eds. *Universities and Schooling in Medieval Society*. Leiden: Brill, 2000.
Davies, Wendy, and Paul Fouracre, eds. *Property and Power in the Early Middle Ages*. Cambridge: Cambridge University Press, 1995.
Davis, Adam J. *The Holy Bureaucrat. Eudes Rigaud and Religious Reform in Thirteenth-Century Normandy*. Ithaca: Cornell University Press, 2006.
De Wulf, Maurice. *Un Théologien-Philosophe du XIIIe Siècle. Étude sur la vie, les oevres et l'influence de Godefroid de Fontaines*. Brussels: Hayez, 1904.
Delaruelle, E., E.-R. Labande, and Paul Ourliac. *L'Église au temps du Grand Schisme et de la crise conciliaire (1378–1449)*. Paris: Bloud et Gay, 1964.
Derwich, Marek and Martial Staub, eds. *Die Neue Frömmigkeit in Europa im Spätmittelalter*. Göttingen: Vandenhoeck and Ruprecht, 2004.
Dirlmeier, Ulf. *Geschichte des Wohnens 2, 500–1800: Hausen, Wohnen, Residieren*. Stuttgart: Deutsche Verlags-Anstalt, 1998.
———. *Untersuchungen zu Einkommensverhältnissen und Lebenshaltungskosten in oberdeutschen Städten des Spätmittelalters (Mitte 14. bis Anfang 16. Jahrhundert)*. Heidelberg: Winter, 1978.
Dirlmeier, Ulf, Gerhard Fouquet, and Bernd Fuhrmann. *Europa im Spätmittelalter 1215–1378*. Munich: Oldenbourg, 2003.
Doyle, A. I. "Publication by Members of the Religious Orders." In *Book Production and Publishing in Britain, 1375–1475*, edited by Jeremy Griffiths and Derek Pearsall, 109–23. Cambridge: Cambridge University Press, 1989.
Doyle, Eric. "William Woodford's *De dominio civili clericorum* against John Wyclif." *Archivum Franciscanum Historicum* (1973): 49–109.
Drossbach, Gisela. "Die sogenannte Devotio moderna in Wien und ihre geistigen Träger zwischen Tradition und Innovation." In *Die Neue Frömmigkeit in Europa im Spätmittelalter*, edited by Marek Derwich and Martial Staub, 267–81. Göttingen: Vandenhoeck and Ruprecht, 2004.
Dubar, G. L. *Recherches sur les offices du monastère de Corbie jusqu'à la fin du XIIIe siècle*. Paris: Picard, 1951.
Dyer, Cristopher. *An Age of Transition? Economy and Society in England in the Later Middle Ages*. Oxford: Clarendon Press, 2005.
———. *Standards of Living in the Later Middle Ages. Social Change in England 1200–1500*. Cambridge: Cambridge University Press, 1989.
Eis, Gerhard. "Die Tobiaslehre des Johannes von Indersdorf." *Neophilologus* 47 (1963): 198–203.
Elliott, Dyan. *Proving Woman. Female Spirituality and Inquisitional Culture in the Later Middle Ages*. Princeton: Princeton University Press, 2004.
Elm, Kaspar. "Die 'Devotio moderna' und die neue Frömmigkeit zwischen Spätmittelalter und früher Neuzeit." In *Die Neue Frömmigkeit in Europa im Spätmittelalter*, edited by Marek Derwich and Martial Staub, 13–30. Göttingen: Vandenhoeck and Ruprecht, 2004.
———. "Mendikanten und Humanisten im Florenz des Tre- und Quattrocento. Zum Problem der Legitimierung humanistischer Studien in den Bettelorden." In *Die Humanisten in ihrer politischen und sozialen Umwelt*, edited by R. Stupperich and O. Herding, 51–85. Bonn, 1976.

——. "Reform- und Observanzbestrebungen im spätmittelalterlichen Ordenswesen. Ein Überblick." In *Reformbemühungen und Observanzbestrebungen im spätmittelalterlichen Ordenswesen*, edited by Kaspar Elm, 3–19. Berlin: Duncker and Humblot, 1989.

——, ed. *Reformbemühungen und Observanzbestrebungen im spätmittelalterlichen Ordenswesen*. Berlin: Duncker and Humblot, 1989.

——. "Termineien und Hospize der westfälischen Augustiner-Eremitenklöster Osnabrück, Lippstadt und Herford." *Jahrbuch für Westfälische Kirchengeschichte* 70 (1977): 11–40.

——. "Verfall und Erneuerung des Spätmittelalterlichen Ordenswesens: Forschungen und Forschungsaufgaben." In *Untersuchungen zu Kloster und Stift*, edited by J. Fleckenstein, 189–238. Göttingen: Vandenhoeck and Ruprecht, 1980.

Emery, Kent, Jr. "Lovers of the World and Lovers of God and Neighbor: Spiritual Commonplaces and the Problem of Authorship in the Fifteenth Century." In *Historia et Spiritualitas Cartusiensis Colloquii Quarti Internationalis Acta*, 177–219. Destelbergen: De Grauwe, 1983.

Erler, Adalbert, and Ekkehard Kaufmann, eds. *Handwörterbuch zur deutschen Rechtsgeschichte*. Berlin: Schmidt, 1971.

Faust, Ulrich, and Franz Quarthal, eds. *Die Reformverbände und Kongregationen der Benediktiner im deutschen Sprachraum*. St. Ottilien: EOS, 1999.

Faust, Ulrich, and Walter Krassnig, eds. *Die benediktinischen Mönchs- und Nonnenklöster in Österreich und Südtirol*. 2 vols. St. Ottilien: EOS, 2000–2001.

Felten, Franz J. "Die Ordensreformen Benedikts XII. unter institutionengeschichtlichem Aspekt." In *Institutionen und Geschichte*, edited by Gert Melville, 369–436. Cologne: Böhlau, 1992.

——. "Herrschaft des Abtes." In *Herrschaft und Kirche. Beiträge zur Entstehung und Wirkungsweise episkopaler und monastischer Organisationsformen*, edited by Friedrich Prinz, 147–296. Stuttgart, 1988.

Felten, Franz J., and Nikolas Jaspert, eds. *Vita Religiosa im Mittelalter. Festschrift für Kaspar Elm zum 70. Geburtstag*. Berlin: Duncker and Humblot, 1999.

Fichtenau, Heinrich. *Living in the Tenth Century*. Translated by Patrick Geary. Chicago: University of Chicago Press, 1991.

Fieback, Andreas. "*Necessitas non est legi subiecta, maxime positivae*. Über den Zusammenhang von Rechtswandel und Schriftgebrauch bei Humbert de Romanis O. P." In *De ordine vitae: zu Normvorstellungen, Organisationsformen und Schriftgebrauch im mittelalterlichen Ordenswesen*, edited by Gert Melville, 125–51. Münster: Lit, 1996.

Findlen, Paula. "Possessing the Past: the Material World of the Italian Renaissance." *American Historical Review* 103 (1998): 83–114.

Freed, John. *The Friars and German Society*. Cambridge, MA: Medieval Academy of America, 1977.

Ganz, David. "The Ideology of Sharing: Apostolic Community and Ecclesiastical Property in the Early Middle Ages." In *Property and Power in the Early Middle Ages*, edited by Wendy Davies and Paul Fouracre, 17–30. Cambridge: Cambridge University Press, 1995.

Garnsey, Peter. *Thinking about Property: From Antiquity to the Age of Revolution*. Cambridge: Cambridge University Press, 2007.

Geary, Patrick. *Medieval Germany in America*. Washington, D.C.: German Historical Institute, 1996.

Gerwing, Manfred. *Malogranatum, oder der dreifache Weg zur Vollkommenheit: Ein Beitrag zur Spiritualität des Spätmittelalters*. Munich: Oldenbourg 1986.

——. "'…state in fide vera, viriliter agite, omnia vestra in caritate fiant.' Zum dreifachen Weg im 'Malogranatum'." In *Die Neue Frömmigkeit in Europa im Spätmittelalter*, edited by Marek Derwich and Martial Staub, 85–110. Göttingen: Vandenhoeck and Ruprecht, 2004.

Gieraths, Gundolf. "Johannes Nider O.P. und die 'deutsche Mystik' des 14. Jahrhunderts." *Divus Thomas* 30 (1952): 321–46.

Gilchrist, Roberta. *Gender and Material Culture. The Archaeology of Religious Women*. London: Routledge, 1994.
Gilissen, John. *La Coutume*. Typologie des Sources du Moyen Âge Occidental 41. Turnhout: Brepols, 1982.
Gill, Katherine. "Scandala: Controversies Concerning Clausura and Women's Religious Communities in Late-Medieval Italy." In *Christendom and its Discontents: Exclusion, Persecution, and Rebellion, 1000–1500*. Edited by Peter D. Diehl and Scott L. Waugh, 177–203. New York: Cambridge University Press, 1996.
Glassner, Christine. "'Schreiben ist lesen und studiern, der sel speis und des herczen jubiliern': Zu den mittelalterlichen Handschriften des Benediktinerstiftes Melk." *Studien und Mitteilungen zur Geschichte des Benediktinerordens* 108 (1997): 283–320.
Goldsmith, James L. "The Crisis of the Late Middle Ages: The Case of France." *French History* 9 (1995): 417–50.
Goldthwaite, Richard. *Wealth and the Demand for Art in Italy 1300–1600*. Baltimore: Johns Hopkins University Press, 1993.
——. "The Empire of Things: Consumer Demand in Renaissance Italy." In *Patronage, Art and Society in Renaissance Italy*, edited by F. W. Kent, Patricia Simons and J. C. Eade, 153–75. Oxford, 1987.
Grabmann, Martin. "Bernhard von Waging, Prior von Tegernsee. Ein bayerischer Benediktinermystiker des 15. Jahrhunderts." *Studien und Mitteilungen zur Geschichte des Benediktinerordens* 60 (1946): 82–98.
Graus, František. "The Church and its Critics in Time of Crisis." In *Anticlericalism in Late-Medieval and Early Modern Europe*, edited by Peter A. Dykema and Heiko A. Obermann, 65–81. Leiden: Brill, 1993.
——. *Pest, Geißler, Judenmorde: Das 14. Jahrhundert als Krisenzeit*. Göttingen: Vandenhoeck and Ruprecht, 1987.
Gribbin, Joseph A. *The Premonstratensian Order in Late Medieval England*. Woodbridge: Boydell and Brewer, 2001.
Griesser, Bruno. "Die Reform des Klosters Rechentshofen in der alten Speyerer Diözese durch Abt Johann von Maulbronn, 1431–33." *Archiv für Mittelrheinische Kirchengeschichte* 8 (1956): 270–83.
Groiß, Albert. *Spätmittelalterliche Lebensformen der Benediktiner von der Melker Observanz vor dem Hintergrund ihrer Bräuche. Ein darstellender Kommentar zum Caeremoniale Mellicense des Jahres 1460*. Münster: Aschendorf, 1999.
Grundmann, Herbert. *Religiöse Bewegungen im Mittelalter. Untersuchungen über die geschichtlichen Zusammenhänge zwischen der Ketzerei, den Bettelorden und der religiösen Frauenbewegung im 12. und 13. Jahrhundert und über die geschichtlichen Grundlagen der deutschen Mystik*. 2nd ed. Hildesheim: Olms, 1970.
Haage, Bernhard. "Der Traktat 'Von dreierlei Wesen der Menschen'." PhD diss., Heidelberg, 1968.
Haage, Bernhard D. "Ein neues Textzeugnis zum spätmittelalterlichen Traktat 'Von Dreierlei Wesen der Menschen'." *Zeitschrift für deutsches Altertum* 100 (1971): 227–30.
——. "Ein Vorausentwurf des mittelalterlichen Traktats 'Von Dreierlei Wesen der Menschen'." *Leuvense Bijdragen* 58 (1969): 138–68.
——. "Zur Textgeschichte des Traktats 'Von Dreierlei Wesen der Menschen': Hs. Salzburg, St. Peter, Cod. b III 11." *Zeitschrift für deutsches Altertum* 105 (1976): 122–25.
Haas, Alois M. "Civitatis Ruinae. Heinrich Seuse's Kirchenkritik." In *Festschrift Walter Haug und Burghart Wachinger*, edited by Johannes Janota et al., 389–406. Tübingen: Niemeyer, 1992.
——. "Sinn und Tragweite von Heinrich Seuse's Passionsmystik." In *Die Passion Christi in Literatur und Kunst des Spätmittelalters*, edited by Walter Haug and Burghart Wachinger, 94–112. Tübingen: Niemeyer, 1993.
Haberkern, Ernst. *Funken aus alter Glut. Johannes von Indersdorf: Von dreierlei Wesen der Menschen. Die theologischen, philosophischen und weltanschaulichen Grundlagen eines mystischen Traktats des 15. Jahrhunderts*. Frankfurt am Main: Peter Lang, 1997.

Hallinger, Kassius. "Consuetudo. Begriff, Formen, Forschungsgeschichte, Inhalt." In *Untersuchungen zu Kloster und Stift*, edited by J. Fleckenstein, 140–66. Göttingen: Vandenhoeck and Ruprecht, 1980.

Hamburger, Jeffrey. *Nuns as Artists. The Visual Culture of a Medieval Convent*. Berkeley: University of California Press, 1997.

———. *The Visual and the Visionary. Art and Female Spirituality in Late-Medieval Germany*. New York: Zone Books, 1998.

Hamilton, Sarah, and Andrew Spicer, eds. *Defining the Holy: Sacred Space in Medieval and Early Modern Europe*. Aldershot: Ashgate, 2005.

Hamm, Berndt. "Das Gewicht von Religion, Glaube, Frömmikeit und Theologie innerhalb der Verdichtungsvorgänge des ausgehenden Mittelalters und der frühen Neuzeit." In *Krisenbewußtsein und Krisenbewältigung in der Frühen Neuzeit—Crisis in Early Modern Europe. Festschrift für Hans-Cristoph Rublack*, edited by Monika Hagenmaier and Sabine Holtz, 163–96. Frankfurt: Peter Lang, 1992.

———. "Frömmigkeit als Gegenstand theologiegeschichtlicher Forschung. Methodischhistorische Überlegungen am Beispiel von Spätmittelalter und Reformation." *Zeitschrift für Theologie und Kirche* 74 (1977): 464–97.

———. "Normative Centering in the Fifteenth and Sixteenth Centuries: Observations on Religiosity, Theology and Iconology." *Journal of Early Modern History* 3 (1999): 307–54.

———. "Von der spätmittelalterlichen reformatio zur Reformation: der Prozeß normativer Zentrierung von Religion und Gesellschaft in Deutschland." *Archiv für Reformationsgeschichte* 84 (1993): 7–82.

Harvey, Barbara F. *Living and Dying in England, 1100–1540: The Monastic Experience*. New York: Oxford University Press, 1993.

———. *Westminster Abbey and its Estates in the Middle Ages*. Oxford: Clarendon, 1977.

Hatcher, John. "England in the Aftermath of the Black Death." *Past and Present* 144 (1994): 3–35.

Haug, Walter, and Burghart Wachinger, eds. *Die Passion Christi in Literatur und Kunst des Spätmittelalters*. Tübingen: Niemeyer, 1993.

Heimpel, H. *Die Vener von Gmünd und Strassburg 1162–1447: Studien und Texte zur Geschichte einer Familie sowie des gelehrten Beamtentums in der Zeit der abendländischen Kirchenspaltung und der Konzilien von Pisa, Konstanz und Basel*. Göttingen: Vandenhoeck and Ruprecht, 1982.

Heinzer, Felix. "Labor Scribendi—Überlegungen zur Frage einer Korrelation zwischen geistlicher Reform und Schriftlichkeit im Mittelalter." In *Die Präsenz des Mittelalters in seinen Handschriften. Ergebnisse der Berliner Tagung in der Staatsbibliothek zu Berlin—Preußischer Kulturbesitz, 6.–8. April 2000*, edited by Hans-Jochen Schiewer and Karl Stackmann, 107–27. Tübingen: Niemeyer, 2002.

Heldewein, Johannes. *Die Klöster Bayerns am Ausgang des Mittelalters*. Munich, 1913.

Helmrath, Johannes. "Capitula. Provinzialkapitel und Bullen des Basler Konzils für die Reform des Benediktinerordens im Reich. Mit einer Konkordanz und ausgewählten Texten." In *Studien zum 15. Jahrhundert. Festschrift für Erich Meuthen*, edited by Johannes Helmrath and Heribert Müller, 87–121. Munich: Oldenbourg, 1994.

———. "Kommunikation auf den spätmittelalterlichen Konzilien." In *Die Bedeutung der Kommunikation für Wirtschaft und Gesellschaft*, edited by Hans Pöhl, 116–72. Stuttgart: Franz Steiner Verlag, 1989.

———. "Reform als Thema der Konzilien des Spätmittelalters." In *Christian Unity. The Council of Ferrara-Florence 1438/9–1989*, edited by Giuseppe Alberigo, 75–153. Louvain, 1991.

———. "Theorie und Praxis der Kirchenreform im Spätmittelalter." *Rottenburger Jahrbuch für Kirchengeschichte* 11 (1992): 41–70.

Hemmerle, Josef. *Die Benediktinerklöster in Bayern*. Augsburg: Winfried-Werk, 1970.

Henkel, Nikolaus, and Nigel F. Palmer, eds. *Latein und Volkssprache im deutschen Mittelalter*. Tübingen: Niemeyer, 1992.

Herzig, Tamar. *Savonarola's Women: Visions and Reform in Renaissance Italy*. Chicago: University of Chicago Press, 2007.
Hillenbrand, Eugen. "Die Observantenbewegung in der deutschen Ordensprovinz der Dominikaner." In *Reformbemühungen und Observanzbestrebungen im spätmittelalterlichen Ordenswesen*, edited by Kaspar Elm, 219–71. Berlin: Duncker and Humblot, 1989.
Hilton, Rodney. *Class Conflict and the Crisis of Feudalism: Essays in Medieval Social History*. London: Verso, 1990.
Hinnebusch, William A. *The History of the Dominican Order*. 2 vols. New York: Alba House, 1966; 1973.
Hlaváček, Ivan, and Alexander Patschovsky, eds. *Reform von Kirche und Reich: zur Zeit der Konzilien von Konstanz (1414–1418) und Basel (1431–1449): Konstanz-Prager historisches Kolloquium (11.–17. Oktober 1993)*. Constance: Universitätsverlag, 1996.
Hobbins, Daniel. *Authorship and Publicity before Print. Jean Gerson and the Transformation of Late Medieval Learning*. Philadelphia: University of Pennsylvania Press, 2009.
——. "The Schoolman as Public Intellectual: Jean Gerson and the Late Medieval Tract." *American Historical Review* 108 (2003): 1308–37.
Hodges, Laura F. *Chaucer and Clothing. Clerical and Academic Costume in the General Prologue to the Canterbury Tales*. Cambridge: D. S. Brewer, 2005.
Hohmann, Thomas. "Initienregister der Werke Heinrichs von Langenstein." *Traditio* 32 (1976): 399–426.
Horst, Ulrich. *Evangelische Armut und Kirche. Thomas von Aquin und die Armutskontroversen des 13. und beginnenden 14. Jahrhunderts*. Berlin: Akademie Verlag, 1992.
——. *Evangelische Armut und päpstliches Lehramt. Minoritentheologen im Konflikt mit Papst Johannes XXII. (1316—34)*. Stuttgart: Kohlhammer, 1996.
Hourlier, Jacques. *L'âge classique, 1140–1378: Les religieux. Histoire du droit et des institutions de l'Eglise en Occident 10*. Paris: Editiones Cujas, 1973.
Hudson, Anne. "Poor preachers, poor men: Views of Poverty in Wyclif and his Followers." In *Häresie und Vorzeitige Reformation im Spätmittelalter*, edited by František Šmahel and Elisabeth Muller Luckner, 41–53. Munich: Oldenbourg, 1998.
Isenmann, Eberhard. "Norms and Values in the European City, 1300–1800." In *Resistance, Representation, and Community*, edited by Peter Blickle, 185–215. Oxford: Clarendon, 1997.
Jannssen, W. "'...na gesetze unser lande...' Zur territorialen Gesetzgebung im späten Mittelalter." In *Gesetzgebung als Faktor der Staatsentwicklung*, edited by Dietmar Willoweit, 7–40. Berlin: Duncker and Humblot, 1984.
Jardine, Lisa. *Worldly Goods: A New History of the Renaissance*. New York: Norton, 1998.
Jaritz, Gerhard. "Kelidung und Prestige-Konkurrenz. Unterschiedliche Identitäten in der städtischen Gesellschaft unter Normierungszwängen." *Saeculum* 44 (1993): 9–31.
——, ed. *Norm und Praxis im Alltag des Mittelalters und der frühen Neuzeit. Internationales Round-Table-Gespräch Krems an der Donau. 7 October 1996*. Vienna: Austrian Academy of Sciences, 1997.
——, ed. *Terminologie und Typologie mittelalterlicher Sachgüter: Das Beispiel der Kleidung. Internationales Round-Table-Gespräch, Krems an der Donau, 6. Oktober 1986*. Vienna: Austrian Academy of Sciences, 1988.
——. "Zur Sachkultur österreichischer Klöster des Spätmittelalters." In *Klösterliche Sachkultur des Spätmittelalters*, 147–68. Vienna: Austrian Academy of Sciences, 1982.
Jaspert, Nikolas. *Stift und Stadt: Das Heiliggrabpriorat von Santa Anna und das Regularkanonikerstift Santa Eulàlia del Camp im mittelalterlichen Barcelona (1145–1423)*. Berlin: Duncker and Humblot, 1996.
Jordan, William C. *The Great Famine*. Princeton: Princeton University Press, 1996.
Justice, Steven. *Writing and Rebellion. England in 1381*. Berkeley: University of California Press, 1994.
Kaelber, Lutz. *Schools of Asceticism: Ideology and Organization in Medieval Religious Communities*. Universtiy Park, PA: Penn State University Press, 1998.

Kaeppeli, Thomas, ed. *Scriptores ordinis praedicatorum medii aevi*. 4 vols. Rome: Ad S. Sabinae, 1970–1993.
Kaminsky, Howard. "Estate, Nobility and the Exhibition of Estate in the Later Middle Ages." *Speculum* 68 (1993): 684–709.
———. "From Lateness to Waning to Crisis. The Burden of the Later Middle Ages." *Journal of Early Modern History* 4 (2000): 85–125.
———. *A History of the Hussite Revolution*. Berkeley: University of California Press, 1967.
———. "The Problematics of 'Heresy' and 'The Reformation'." In *Häresie und vorzeitige Reformation im Spätmittelalter*, edited by František Šmahel, 1–22. Munich: Oldenbourg, 1998.
Karras, Ruth Mazo, Joel Kaye, and E. Ann Matter, eds. *Law and the Illicit in Medieval Europe*. Philadelphia: University of Pennsylvania Press, 2008.
Kaye, Joel. *Economy and Nature in the Fourteenth Century: Money, Market Exchange, and the Emergence of Scientific Thought*. Cambridge: Cambridge University Press, 1998.
———. "Monetary and Market Consciousness in Thirteenth and Fourteenth Century Europe." In *Ancient and Medieval Economic Ideas and Concepts of Social Justice*, edited by Todd Lowry and Barry Gordon, 372–99. Leiden: Brill, 1998.
Kelly, Henry Ansgar. "Inquisition and the Prosecution of Heresy: Misconceptions and Abuses." *Church History* 58 (1989): 439–51.
Kempshall, M. S. *The Common Good in Late Medieval Political Thought: Moral Goodness and Political Benefit*. Oxford: Clarendon Press, 1999.
Kerby-Fulton, Kathryn. *Books under Suspicion: Censorship and Tolerance of Revelatory Writing in Late Medieval England*. Notre Dame, IN: University of Notre Dame Press, 2006.
Kieckhefer, Richard. "Major Currents in Late-Medieval Devotion." In *Christian Spirituality, High Middle Ages and Reformation*, edited by Jill Raitt, 75–108. New York: Crossroad, 1987.
Killerby, Catherine Kovesi. "Practical Problems in the Enforcement of Italian Sumptuary Law 1200–1500." In *Crime, Society and the Law in Renaissance Italy*, edited by Trevor Dean and K. J. P. Lowe, 99–120. Cambridge: Cambridge University Press, 1995.
———. *Sumptuary Law in Italy, 1200–1500*. Oxford: Oxford University Press, 2002.
Kist, Johannes. *Das Klarissenkloster in Nürnberg bis zum Beginn des 16. Jahrhunderts*. Nüremberg: Sebaldus-Verlag, 1929.
Klein, Andrea. "Johannes von Indersdorf studierte in Wien." *Zeitschrift für deutsche Philologie* 115 (1996): 439–42.
Knowles, David. *The Religious Orders in England*. 3 vols. Cambridge: Cambridge University Press, 1948–59.
Kock, Thomas. "'Per totum Almanicum orbem.' Reformbeziehungen und Ausbreitung der niederländischen 'Devotio Moderna'." In *Die Neue Frömmigkeit in Europa im Spätmittelalter*, edited by Marek Derwich and Martial Staub, 31–56. Göttingen: Vandenhoeck and Ruprecht, 2004.
Koller, Gerda. *Princeps in Ecclesia. Untersuchungen zur Kirchenpolitik Herzog Albrechts V. von Österreich*. Vienna: Austrian Academy of Sciences, 1964.
Koller, Heinrich. *Die Universitätsgründungen des 14. Jahrhunderts*. Salzburg: Pustet, 1966.
König, Eberhard. *Boccaccio, Decameron. Alle 100 Miniaturen der ersten Bilderhandschrift*. Stuttgart: Belser, 1989.
Köpf, Ulrich. "Die Passion Christi in der lateinischen religiösen und theologischen Literatur des Spätmittelalters." In *Die Passion Christi in Literatur und Kunst des Spätmittelalters*, edited by Walter Haug and Burghart Wachinger, 21–41. Tübingen: Niemeyer, 1993.
———. "Monastische Theologie im 15. Jahrhundert." *Rottenburger Jahrbuch für Kirchengeschichte* 11 (1992): 117–35.
Kovács, Elisabeth. "Die Heiligen und heiligen Könige der frühen Habsburger (1273–1519)." In *Laienfrömmigkeit im späten Mittelalter. Formen, Funktionen, politisch-soziale Zusammenhänge*, edited by Klaus Schreiner, 93–105. Munich: Oldenbourg, 1992.

Kreuzer, Georg. *Heinrich von Langenstein: Studien zur Biographie und zu den Schismatraktaten unter besonderer Berücksichtigung der Epistola pacis und der Epistola concilii pacis.* Paderborn: Ferdinand Schöningh, 1987.
Kühnel, Harry. "Beiträge der Orden zur materiellen Kultur des Mittelalters und weltliche Einflüsse auf die klösterliche Sachkultur." In *Klösterliche Sachkultur des Spätmittelalters*, 9–30. Vienna: Austrian Academy of Sciences, 1982.
Kunzelmann, Adalbero. *Geschichte der deutschen Augustiner-Eremiten.* Würzburg: Augustinus-Verlag, 1969.
Lahey, Stephen. *Philosophy and Politics in the Thought of John Wyclif.* Cambridge: Cambridge University Press, 2003.
Lambert, Malcom. "The Franciscan Crisis under John XXII." *Franciscan Studies* 32 (1972): 123–143.
———. *Franciscan Poverty: The Doctrine of the Absolute Poverty of Christ and the Apostles in the Franciscan Order, 1210–1323.* 2nd ed. New York: Franciscan Institute, 1998.
Lang, Paul Justin. *Die Christologie bei Heinrich von Langenstein.* Freiburg i. Br.: Herder, 1966.
Langholm, Odd. *Economics in the Medieval Schools: Wealth, Exchange, Value, Money, and Usury According to the Paris Theological Tradition, 1200–1350.* Leiden: Brill, 1992.
———. "The Medieval Schoolmen." In *Ancient and Medieval Economic Ideas and Concepts of Social Justice*, edited by Todd Lowry and Barry Gordon, 439–502. Leiden: Brill, 1998.
Lawless, George. *Augustine of Hippo and his Monastic Rule.* Oxford: Oxford University Press, 1987.
Lawrence, C. H. *The Friars: The Impact of the Early Mendicant Movement on Western Society.* London, New York: Longman, 1994.
———. *Medieval Monasticism. Forms of Religious Life in Western Europe in the Middle Ages.* 3rd ed. New York: Longman, 2001.
Leclercq, Jean. "Monastic and Scholastic Theology in the Reformers of the Fourteenth to the Sixteenth Century." In *From Cloister to Classroom: Monastic and Scholastic Approaches to Truth*, edited by E. Rozanne Elder, 178–201. Kalamazoo: Cistercian Publications, 1986.
———. *The Love of Learning and the Desire for God.* 2nd ed. New York, 1974.
LeGoff, Jacuqes. "Apostolat mendiant et fait urbain dans la France médiévale: L'implantation des ordres mendiants." *Annales E. S. C.* 23 (1968): 335–352.
Lehmann, Paul. "Konstanz und Basel als Büchermärkte." In *Erforschung des Mittelalters*, edited by idem, 253–80. 1921. Reprint Stuttgart: Hiersemann, 1959.
Lehner, Julia. *Die Mode im Alten Nürnberg: Modische Entwicklung und Sozialer Wandel in Nürnberg, Aufgezeigt an der Nürnberger Kleiderordnungen.* Nuremberg: Stadtarchiv Nuremberg, 1984.
Leiberich, H. "Die Anfänge der Polizeigesetzgebung des Herzogtums Baiern." In *Festschrift Max Spindler zum 75. Geburtstag*, edited by Dieter Albrecht, 307–78. Munich: Beck, 1969.
Lentes, Thomas. "Counting Piety in the Late Middle Ages." In *Ordering Medieval Society: Perspectives on Intellectual and Practical Modes of Shaping Social Relations*, edited by Bernhard Jussen and Pamela E. Selwyn, 55–91. Philadelphia: University of Pennsylvania Press, 2001.
———. "Inneres Auge, Äusserer Blick und Heilige Schau. Ein Diskussionsbeitrag zur visuellen Praxis in Frömmigkeit und Moraldidaxe des späten Mittelalters." In *Frömmigkeit im Mittelalter. Politisch-soziale Kontexte, visuelle Praxis, körperliche Ausdrucksformen*, edited by Klaus Schreiner, 179–220. Munich: Wilhelm Fink, 2002.
———. "*Vita perfecta* zwischen *Vita Communis* und *Vita Privata*. Eine Skizze zur klösterlichen Einzelzelle." In *Das Öffentliche und Private in der Vormoderne*, edited by Gert Melville and Peter von Moos, 125–64. Cologne: Böhlau, 1998.
Lentze, Hans. "Begräbnis und Jahrtag in mittelalterlichen Wien." *Zeitschrift für Rechtsgeschichte, Kanonische Abteilung* 67 (1950): 328–64.

———. "Das Seelgerät in mittelalterlichen Wien." *Zeitschrift für Rechtsgeschichte, Kanonische Abteilung* 75 (1958): 35–103.

———. "Die rechtsform der Altarpfründen im Mittelalterlichen Wien." *Zeitschrift für Rechtsgeschichte, Kanonische Abteilung* 68 (1951): 221–302.

———. "Pitanz und Pfründe im Mittelalterlichen Wilten." In *Veröffentlichungen aus dem Stadtarchiv Innsbruck*, edited by Karl Schadelbauer, 5–15. Innsbruck: Wagner, 1954.

LePointe, Gabriel. "Réflexions sur des textes concernant la propriété individuelle de religieuses cisterciennes dans la région Lilloise." *Revue d'histoire ecclésiastique* 49 (1954): 743–69.

Lesne, Emile. "Une source de la fortune monastique: les donations à charge de pension alimentaire du VIIIe au Xe siècle." *Mélanges de philologie et d'histoire, publiés à l'occasion du cinquantenaire de la Faculté des lettres de l'Université catholique de Lille. Mémoires et travaux publiés par des professeurs de Facultés Catholiques de Lille* 32 (1927): 33–45.

Leyser, Conrad. *Authority and Asceticism from Augustine to Gregory the Great*. Oxford: Oxford University Press, 2000.

Little, Lester K. *Religious Poverty and the Profit Economy in Medieval Europe*. Ithaca: Cornell University Press, 1978.

Löhr, Gabrielle Maria. *Beiträge zur Geschichte des Kölner Dominikanerklosters im Mittelalter*. 2 vols. Quellen und Forschungen zur Geschichte des Dominikanerordens in Deutschland 15 and 17. Leipzig, 1920–22.

———. "Die Mendikantenarmut im Dominikanerorden im 14. Jahrhundert. Nach den Schriften von Johannes Dambach, O. P. und Johannes Dominici, O. P." *Divus Thomas. Jahrbuch für Philosophie* (1940): 385–427.

Lopez, Roberto. "Hard Times and the Investment in Culture." In *Social and Economic Foundations of the Renaissance*, edited by Anthony Molho. New York: Wiley, 1969.

Löser, Freimut. "Anselm, Eckhart, Lienhart Peuger. Zu einer deutschen Übersetzung der 'Orationes et Meditationes' Anselms von Canterbury der Melker Laienbruder." In *Latein und Volkssprache im deutschen Mittelalter*, edited by Nikolaus Henkel and Nigel F. Palmer, 233–55. Tübingen: Niemeyer, 1992.

———. "Im Dialog mit Handschriften. "Handschriftenphilologie" am Beispiel der Laienbrüderbibliothek in Melk." In *Die Präsenz des Mittelalters in seinen Handschriften*, 177–208.

Lübeck, K. "Der Privatbesitz der Fuldaer Mönche im Mittelalter." *Archiv für Katholisches Kirchenrecht* 119 (1939): 52–99.

Lynch, Joseph H. *Simoniacal Entry Into the Religious Life from 1000 to 1260: A Social, Economic, and Legal Study*. Columbus: Ohio State University Press, 1976.

Madre, Alois. *Nikolaus von Dinkelsbühl. Leben und Schriften. Ein Beitrag zur theologischen Literaturgeschichte*. Münster: Aschendorf, 1965.

Maier, P. "Ursprung und Ausbreitung der Kastler Reformbewegung." *Studien und Mitteilungen zur Geschichte der Benediktinerordens* 102 (1991): 75–204.

Mäkinen, Virpi. *Property Rights in the Late Medieval Discussion on Franciscan Poverty*. Leuven: Peeters, 2001.

Mann, Jill. *Chaucer and Medieval Estates Satire. The Literature of Social Classes and the General Prologue to the Canterbury Tales*. Cambridge: Cambridge University Press, 1973.

Martin, Dennis. *Fifteenth-Century Carthusian Reform: The World of Nicholas Kempf*. Leiden: Brill, 1992.

Martin, Francis Xavier. "The Augustinian Observant Movement." In *Reformbemühungen und Observanzbestrebungen im spätmittelalterlichen Ordenswesen*, edited by Kaspar Elm, 325–345. Berlin: Duncker and Humblot, 1989.

———. *Friar, Reformer, and Renaissance Scholar: The Life and Work of Giles of Viterbo, 1469–1532*. Villanova: Augustinian Press, 1992.

McGinn, Bernard. *The Harvest of Mysticism in Medieval Germany (1300–1500)*. New York: Crossroad, 2005.

McGuire, Brian Patrick. *Jean Gerson and the Last Medieval Reformation*. University Park, PA: Penn State University Press, 2005.

McLaughlin, Megan. *Consorting with Saints: Prayer for the Dead in Early Medieval France*. Ithaca: Cornell University Press, 1994.

Mecham, June. "A Northern Jerusalem. Transforming the Spatial Geography of the Covent of Wienhausen." In *Defining the Holy: Sacred Space in Medieval and Early Modern Europe*, edited by Sarah Hamilton and Andrew Spicer, 139–60. Aldershot: Ashgate, 2005.

———. "Reading Between the Lines: Compilation, Variation, and the Recovery of an Authentic Female Voice in the Dornenkron Prayer Books from Wienhausen." *Journal of Medieval History* 29 (2003): 109–28.

Melville, Gert, ed. *De ordine vitae: Zu Normvorstellungen, Organisationsformen und Schriftgebrauch im mittelalterlichen Ordenswesen*. Münster: Lit, 1996.

———, ed. *Institutionen und Geschichte*. Cologne: Böhlau, 1992.

Melville, Gert, and Jörg Oberste, eds. *Die Bettelorden im Aufbau: Beiträge zu Institutionalisierungsprozessen im mittelalterlichen Religiosentum*. Münster: Lit, 1999.

Menhardt, Hermann. "Nikolaus von Dinkelbühls deutsche Predigt vom Eigentum im Kloster." *Zeitschrift für deutsche Philologie* 74 (1955): 268–90 and 73 (1954): 1–39.

Mertens, Dieter. "Monastische Reformbewegungen des 15. Jahrhunderts: Ideen—Ziele—Resultate." In *Reform von Kirche und Reich: Zur Zeit der Konzilien von Konstanz (1414–1418) und Basel (1431–1449). Konstanz-Prager historisches Kolloquium (11.–17. Oktober 1993)*, edited by Ivan Hlavácek and Alexander Patschovsky, 157–82. Constance: Universitätsverlag, 1996.

———. "Reformkonzilien und Ordensreform im 15. Jahrhundert." In *Reformbemühungen und Observanzbestrebungen im spätmittelalterlichen Ordenswesen*, edited by Kaspar Elm, 431–57. Berlin: Duncker and Humblot, 1989.

Meuthen, Erich. *Cusanus und die Orden: Aus der geistlichen Welt des späten Mittelalters*. Basel: Helbing and Lichtenhahn, 1996.

———. *Das 15. Jahrhundert*. 3rd ed. Munich: Oldenbourg, 1996.

Meyer, Ulrich. *Soziales Handeln im Zeichen des 'Hauses.' Zur Ökonomik in der Spätantike und im früheren Mittelalter*. Göttingen: Vandenhoeck and Ruprecht, 1998.

Miethke, Jürgen. "Die Konzilien as Forum der öffentlichen Meinung." *Deutsches Archiv* 37 (1981): 736–73.

———. "Kirchenreform auf den Konzilien des 15. Jahrhunderts. Motive—Methoden—Wirkungen." In *Studien zum 15. Jahrhundert. Festschrift für Erich Meuthen*, edited by Johannes Helmrath and Heribert Müller, 13–42. Munich: Oldenbourg, 1994.

———. "Paradiesischer Zustand—Apostolisches Zeitalter—Franziskanische Armut. Religiöses Selbstverständnis, Zeitkritik und Gesellschaftstheorie im 14. Jahrhundert." In *Vita Religiosa im Mittelalter. Festschrift für Kaspar Elm zum 70. Geburtstag*, edited by Franz J. Felten, 503–32. Berlin: Duncker and Humblot, 1999.

Milis, Ludo. "Reformatory Attempts within the Ordo Canonicus in the Late Middle Ages." In *Reformbemühungen und Observanzbestrebungen im spätmittelalterlichen Ordenswesen*, edited by Kaspar Elm, 3–19. Berlin: Duncker and Humblot, 1989.

Mixson, James D. "The Setting and Resonance of John Nider's De reformatione religiosorum." In *Kirchenbild und Spiritualität. Dominikanische Beiträge zur Ekklesiologie und zum Kirchlichen Leben im Mittelalter. Festschrift für Ulrich Horst OP zum 75. Geburtstag*, edited by Thomas Prügl and Marianne Schlosser, 319–38. Paderborn: Schöningh, 2006.

Moorman, John R. H. *A History of the Franciscan Order from its Origins to the Year 1517*. Oxford: Oxford University Press, 1968.

Moraw, Peter. *Von offener Verfassung zu gestalteter Verdichtung. Das Reich im späten Mittelalter, 1250 bis 1490*. Berlin: Propyläen, 1985.

Mormondo, Franco. *The Preacher's Demons. Bernardino of Siena and the Social Underworld of Early Renaissance Italy*. Chicago: University of Chicago Press, 1999.

Neddermeyer, Uwe. "'Radix Studii et Speculum Vitae.' Verbreitung und Rezeption der 'Imitatio Christii' in Handschriften und Drucken bis zur Reformation." In *Studien zum 15. Jahrhundert: Festschrift für Erich Meuthen*, edited by Johannes Helmrath et al., 1: 457–81. Munich: Oldenbourg 1994.

———. *Von der Handschrift zum gedruckten Buch: Schriftlichkeit und Leseinteresse im Mittelalter und in der frühen Neuzeit. Quantitative und Qualitative Aspekte*. Wiesbaden: Harrassowitz 1998.
Neidiger, Bernhard. "Der Armutsbegriff der Dominikanerobservanten. Zur Diskussion in den Konventen der Provinz Teutonia (1389–1513)." *Zeitschrift für Geschichte des Oberrheins* 145 (1997): 117–58.
———. "Die Observanzbewegungen der Bettelorden in Südwestdeutschland." *Rottenburger Jahrbuch für Kirchengeschichte* 11 (1992): 175–96.
———. *Mendikanten zwischen Ordensideal und städtischer Realität: Untersuchungen zum wirtschaftlichen Verhalten der Bettelorden in Basel*. Berlin: Duncker and Humblot, 1981.
———. "Selbstverständnis und Erfolgschancen der Dominikanerobservanten." *Rottenburger Jahrbuch für Kirchengeschichte* 17 (1998): 67–122.
Nelson, Janet. "Medieval Monasticism." In *The Medieval World* edited by Peter Linehan and Janet Nelson, 576–604. London, 2001.
Newhauser, Richard. *The Treatise on Vices and Virtues in Latin and in the Vernacular*. Typologie des Sources du Moyen Âge Occidental 68. Turnhout: Brepols, 1993.
———, ed. *In the Garden of Evil: The Vices and Culture in the Middle Ages*. Toronto: Pontifical Institute of Mediaeval Studies, 2005.
Newton, Stella Mary. *Fashion in the Age of the Black Prince. A Study of the Years 1340–1365*. Woodbridge: Boydell, 1980.
Nicholas, Barry. *An Introduction to Roman Law*. Oxford: Oxford University Press, 1962.
Niederkorn-Bruck, Meta. *Die Melker Reform im Spiegel der Visitationen*. Vienna: Oldenbourg, 1994.
Nimmo, Duncan. "The Franciscan Regular Observance." In *Reformbemühungen und Observanzbestrebungen im spätmittelalterlichen Ordenswesen*, edited by Kaspar Elm, 189–205. Berlin: Duncker and Humblot, 1989.
———. *Reform and Division in the Medieval Franciscan Order, from Saint Francis to the Foundation of the Capuchins*. Rome: Capuchin Historical Institute, 1987.
Nuechterlein, Jeanne. "The Domesticity of Sacred Space in the Fifteenth-Century Netherlands." In *Defining the Holy: Sacred Space in Medieval and Early Modern Europe*, edited by Sarah Hamilton and Andrew Spicer, 49–80. Aldershot: Ashgate, 2005.
Nyhus, Paul. "The Franciscan Observant Reform in Germany." In *Reformbemühungen und Observanzbestrebungen im spätmittelalterlichen Ordenswesen*, edited by Kaspar Elm, 207–17. Berlin: Duncker and Humblot, 1989.
———. "The Franciscans in South Germany 1400–1530: Reform and Revolution." *Transactions of the American Philosophical Society* 65, no. 8 (1975): 1–47.
Oakley, Francis. *The Western Church in the Later Middle Ages*. Ithaca: Cornell University Press, 1979.
Oberste, Jörg. *Visitation und Ordensorganisation: Formen sozialer Normierung, Kontrolle und Kommunikation bei Cisterziensern, Prämonstratensern und Cluniazensern, 12.–frühes 14. Jahrhundert*. Münster: Lit, 1996.
Ocker, Christopher. "Die Armut und die menschliche Natur: Konrad Waldhauser, Jan Milíč von Kroměříč und die Bettelmönche." In *Die Neue Frömmigkeit in Europa im Spätmittelalter*, edited by Marek Derwich and Martial Staub, 111–29. Göttingen: Vandenhoeck and Ruprecht, 2004.
Oexle, Otto Gerhard, ed. *Nobilitas. Funktion und Repräsentation des Adels in Alteuropa*. Göttingen: Vandenhoeck and Ruprecht, 1997.
Ogris, Werner. *Der mittelalterliche Leibrentenvertrag. Ein Beitrag zur Geschichte des deutschen Privatrechts*. Vienna: Herold, 1961.
———. "Die Konventualenpfründe im Mittelalterlichen Kloster." *Österreichisches Archiv für Kirchenrecht* 13 (1962): 104–42.
Oliva, Marilyn. *The Convent and the Community in Late Medieval England: Female Monasteries in the Diocese of Norwich, 1350–1540*. Rochester: Boydell, 1998.
Pacaut, Marcel. "La visite, institution fondamentale du régime cistercien." In *Vita Religiosa im Mittelalter. Festschrift für Kaspar Elm zum 70. Geburtstag*, edited by Franz J. Felten, 183–191. Berlin: Duncker and Humblot, 1999.

Pastoureau, Michel. *The Devil's Cloth. A History of Stripes and Striped Fabric*. Translated by Jody Gladding. New York: Columbia University Press, 2001.
Patschovsky, Alexander. "Der Reformbegriff zur Zeit der Konzilien von Konstanz und Basel." In *Reform von Kirche und Reich: zur Zeit der Konzilien von Konstanz (1414–1418) und Basel (1431–1449). Konstanz-Prager historisches Kolloquium (11.–17. Oktober 1993)*, edited by Alexander Patschovsky and Ivan Hlaváček, 7–28. Constance: Universitätsverlag, 1996.
Pennington, Kenneth. *Pope and Bishops. The Papal Monarchy in the Twelfth and Thirteenth Centuries*. Philadelphia: University of Pennsylvania Press, 1984.
———. *The Prince and the Law, 1200–1600: Sovereignty and Rights in the Western Legal Tradition*. Berkeley: University of California Press, 1993.
Peters, Edward. "More Trouble With Henry: The Historiography of Medieval Germany in the Angloliterate World." *Central European History* 28 (1995): 47–72.
Piponnier, Françoise and Perrine Mane. *Dress in the Middle Ages*. Translated by Caroline Beamish. New Haven: Yale University Press, 1997.
Raitt, Jill, ed. *Christian Spirituality, High Middle Ages and Reformation*. New York: Crossroad, 1987.
Rankl, Helmut. *Das vorreformatorische landesherrliche Kirchenregiment in Bayern (1378–1526)*. Munich: R. Wölfe, 1971.
Rapp, Francis. "Les abbayes, hospices de la noblesse: l'influence de l'aristocratie sur les couvents bénédictines dans l'Empire à la fin du Moyen Age." In *La noblesse au Moyen Age, XIe–XVe siècle. Essais à la mémoire de Robert Boutruche*, edited by Phillipe Contamine, 167–74. Paris: Presses Universitaries de France, 1976.
———. "Religious Belief and Practice." In *The New Cambridge Medieval History*, edited by Cristopher Allmand, 284–331. Cambridge: Cambridge University Press, 1998.
Redlich, Virgil. *Tegernsee und die deutsche Geistesgeschichte im XV. Jahrhundert*. 1931. Reprint Aalen: Scientia Verlag, 1974.
Reuter, Timothy. "Property Transactions and Social Relations Between Rulers, Bishops and Nobles in Early Eleventh-Century Saxony: the Evidence of the Vita Meinwerci." In *Property and Power in the Early Middle Ages*, edited by Wendy Davies and Paul Fouracre, 165–99. Cambridge: Cambridge University Press, 1995.
Roest, Bert. *Franciscan Literature of Religious Instruction before the Council of Trent*. Leiden: Brill, 2004.
Röhrig, Floridus. "Die materielle Kultur des Chorherrenstiftes Klosterneuburg unter besonderer Berücksichtigung der Aussage von Rechnungsbüchern." In *Klösterliche Sachkultur des Spätmittelalters*, 217–24. Vienna: Austrian Academy of Sciences, 1982.
———. *Klosterneuburg*. Vienna: Zsolnay, 1972.
Rosenwein, Barbara. "Views from Afar: American Perspectives on Medieval Monasticism." In *Dove va la storiografia monastica in Europa? Temi e metodi di ricerca per lo studia della vita monastica e regolare in età medievale alle soglie del terzo millennio. Atti del Convegno internazionale Brescia-Rodengo, 23–25 marzo 2000*, edited by Giancarlo Andenna, 67–84. Milan: Vita e Pensiero Università, 2001.
———. *To be the Neighbor of Saint Peter: The Social Meaning of Cluny's Property, 909–1049*. Ithaca: Cornell University Press, 1989.
Rubner, Heinrich. "Die Landwirtschaft der Münchener Ebene und ihre Notlage im 14. Jahrhundert." *Vierteljahrschrift für Sozial- und Wirtschaftsgeschichte* 51 (1964): 433–53.
Rüther, Andreas. *Bettelorden in Stadt und Land: Die Strassburger Mendikantenkonvente und das Elsaß im Spätmittelalter*. Berlin: Duncker and Humblot, 1997.
———. "Schreibbetrieb, Bücheraustausch und Briefwechsel: Der Konvent St. Katharina in St. Gallen während der Reform." In *Vita Religiosa im Mittelalter. Festschrift für Kaspar Elm zum 70. Geburtstag*, edited by Franz J. Felten, 653–77. Berlin: Duncker and Humblot, 1999.
Scase, Wendy. *Piers Plowman and the New Anticlericalism*. Cambridge: Cambridge University Press, 1989.

Schimmelpfennig, Bernhard. "Das Papstum und die Reform des Zisterzienserordens im späten Mittelalter." In *Reformbemühungen und Observanzbestrebungen im spätmittelalterlichen Ordenswesen*, edited by Kaspar Elm, 399–410. Berlin: Duncker and Humblot, 1989.

——. "Zisterzienserideal und Kirchenreform: Benedikt XII (1334–42) als Reformpapst." *Zisterzienser-Studien* 3: 11–43.

Schneider, Reinhard. "Lebensverhältnisse bei den Zisterziensern im Spätmittelalter." In *Klösterliche Sachkultur des Spätmittelalters*, 43–72. Vienna: Austrian Academy of Sciences, 1982.

Schreiner, Klaus. "Benediktinische Klosterreform als zeitgebundene Auslegung der Regel. Geistige, religiöse und soziale Erneuerung in spätmittelalterlichen Klöstern Südwestdeutschlands im Zeichen der Kaslter, Melker und Bursfelder Reform." *Blätter für württembergische Kirchengeschichte* 86 (1986): 105–95.

——. "Dauer, Niedergang und Erneuerung klösterlicher Observanz im hoch- und spätmittelalterlichen Mönchtum. Krisen, Reform- und Institutionalisierungsprobleme in der Sicht und Deutung betroffener Zeitgenossen." In *Institutionen und Geschichte. Theoretische Aspekte und mittelalterliche Befunde*, edited by Gert Melville, 295–341. Cologne: Böhlau, 1992.

——. "Laienfrömmigkeit—Frömmigkeit von Eliten oder Frömmigkeit des Volkes?" In *Laienfrömmigkeit im späten Mittelalter. Formen, Funktionen, politisch-soziale Zusammenhänge*, edited by Klaus Schreiner, 1–78. Munich: Oldenbourg, 1992.

——. "Legitimation, Repräsentation, Schriftlichkeit. Gedankliche Begründungen und symbolische Formen mittelalterlicher Abtsherrschaft." In *Political Thought and Realities of Power in the Middle Ages*, edited by Joseph Canning and Otto Gerhard Oexle, 67–111. Göttingen: Vandenhoeck and Ruprecht, 1998.

——. "Nobilitas Mariae. Die edelgeborene Gottesmutter und ihre adeligen verehrer. Soziale Prägungen und politische Funktionen mittelalterlicher Adelsfrömmigkeit." In *Maria in der Welt. Marienverehrung im Kontext der Sozialgeschichte 10.–18. Jarhundert*, edited by Claudia Opitz, 213–42. Zurich: Chronos Verlag, 1993.

——. *Mönchsein in der Adelsgesellschaft des hohen und späten Mittelalters. Klösterliche Gemeinschaftsbildung zwischen spiritueller Selbstbehauptung und sozialler Anpassung*. Munich: Cotta, 1989.

——. "Religiöse, historische und rechtliche Legitimation spätmittelalterlicher Adelsherrschaft." In *Nobilitas. Funktion und Repräsentation des Adels in Alteuropa*, edited by Otto Gerhard Oexle and Werner Paravicini, 376–430. Göttingen: Vandenhoeck and Ruprecht, 1997.

——. *Sozial und standesgeschichtliche Untersuchungen zu den Benediktinerkonventen im östlichen Schwarzwald*. Stuttgart: Kolhammer, 1964.

——. "Verschriftlichung als Faktor monastischer Reform. Funktion von Schriftlichkeit im Ordenswesen des hohen und späten Mittelalters." In *Pragmatische Schriftlichkeit im Mittelalter. Erscheinungsformen und Entwicklungsstufen*, edited by Hagen Keller et al., 37–75. Munich: Fink, 1992.

——. "Vom adeligen Hauskloster zum "Spital des Adels." Gesellschaftliche Verflechtungen oberschwäbischer Benediktinerkonvente im Mittelalter und in der frühen Neuzeit." *Rottenburger Jahrbuch für Kirchengeschichte* 9 (1990): 27–54.

Schuller, Helga. "*Dos—Praebenda—Peculium*." In *Festschrift Friedrich Hausmann*, edited by Herwig Ebner, 453–87. Graz: Akademische Druck- und Verlagsanstalt, 1977.

Schulze, Manfred. *Fürsten und Reformation. Geistliche Reformpolitik weltlicher Fürsten vor der Reformation*. Tübingen: Möhr, 1991.

Schuster, Peter. "Die Krise des Spätmittelalters. Zur Evidenz eines sozial- und wirtschaftsgeschichtlichen Paradigmas in der Geschichtsschreibung des 20. Jahrhunderts." *Historische Zeitschrift* 269 (1999): 19–55.

Seibt, Ferdinand. "Hussitischer Kommunalismus." In *Häresie und Vorzeitige Reformation im Spätmittelalter*, edited by František Šmahel and Elisabeth Muller Luckner, 197–212. Munich: Oldenbourg, 1998.

Seibt, Ferdinand, and Winfred Eberhard, eds. *Europa 1400: Die Krise des Spätmittelalters*. Stuttgart: Klett-Cotta, 1984.

Shank, Michael H. *Unless You Believe, You Shall Not Understand: Logic, University, and Society in Late Medieval Vienna*. Princeton: Princeton University Press, 1988.

Šmahel, František. *Die Hussitische Revolution*. Translated by Thomas Krzenck. Edited by Alexander Patschovsky. 3 vols. Hannover: Hahnsche Buchhandlung, 2002.

Šmahel, František, and Elisabeth Muller Luckner, eds. *Häresie und Vorzeitige Reformation im Spätmittelalter*. Munich: Oldenbourg, 1998.

Snape, R. H. *English Monastic Finances in the Later Middle Ages*. Cambridge: Cambridge University Press, 1926.

Spindler, Max, ed. *Handbuch der Bayerischen Geschichte. Das Alte Bayern. Der Territorialstaat vom Ausgang des 12. Jahrhunderts bis zum Ausgang des 18. Jahrhunderts*. Munich: Beck, 1969.

Staubach, Nickolaus. " 'Memores priscae perfectionis.' The Importance of the Church Fathers for Devotio moderna." In *The Reception of the Church Fathers in the West: From the Carolingians to the Maurists*, edited by Irena Backus and Antoinina Bevan, I: 405–74. Leiden: Brill, 1997.

———. "Von der persönlichen Erfahrung zur Gemeinschaftsliteratur. Entstehungs- und Rezeptionsbedingungen geistlicher Reformtexte im Spätmittelalter." *Ons geestelijk erf* 68 (1994): 200–28.

Steinberg, S. H. "Instructions in Writing by Members of the Congregation of Melk." *Speculum* 16 (1941): 210–15.

Steinmetz, Karl-Heinz. "Schule der heiligen Katharina. Trianguärer Wissenstransfer in der *Katharinenpredigt* und der *Vierzehnten Harfe* des Johannes Nider O.P." In *Kirchenbild und Spiritualität. Dominikanische Beiträge zur Ekklesiologie und zum kirchlichen Leben in Mittelalter. Festschrift für Ulrich Horst O.P. zum 75. Geburtstag*, edited by Thomas Prügl and Marianne Schlosser, 339–55. Paderborn: Ferdinand Schöningh, 2007.

Stievermann, Dieter. *Landesherrschaft und Klosterwesen im spätmittelalterlichen Württemberg*. Sigmaringen: Thorbecke, 1989.

Stuard, Susan Mosher. *Gilding the Market. Luxury and Fashion in Fourteenth-Century Italy*. Philadelphia: University of Pennsylvania Press, 2006.

Stump, Phillip H. *The Reforms of the Council of Constance*. Leiden: Brill, 1994.

Sydow, Jürgen. "Sichtbare Auswirkungen der Klosterreform des 15. Jahrhunderts. Beobachtungen an historischen Quellen südwestdeutscher Klöster." *Rottenburger Jahrbuch für Kirchengeschichte* 11 (1992): 209–22.

Szittya, Penn R. *The Antifraternal Tradition in Medieval Literature*. Princeton: Princeton University Press, 1986.

Thoma, Franz Xaver. "Petrus von Rosenheim, OSB. Ein Beitrag zur Melker Reformbewegung." *Studien und Mitteilungen zur Geschichte der Benediktinerordens und seiner Zweige* 45 (1927): 94–222.

Thornton, Dora. *The Scholar in his Study. Ownership and Experience in Renaissance Italy*. New Haven: Yale University Press, 1998.

Thornton, Peter. *The Italian Renaissance Interior, 1400–1600*. New York: Abrams, 1991.

Tisset, P. *L'abbaye de Gellone au diocèse de Lodève des origines au XIIIe siècle*. 1933. Reprint Troyes: Editions du Beffroi, 1992.

Toubert, P. "Les statuts communeaux et l'histoire des campagnes lombardes au XIVe siècle." *Mélanges d'archéologie et d'histoire de l' École française de Rome* 72 (1960): 397–508.

Uhrle, Susanne. *Das Dominikanerinnenkloster Weiler bei Esslingen (1230–1571/92)*. Stuttgart: Kohlhammer, 1968.

Valous, G. *Le monachisme clunisien des origines au XVe siècle: vie intérieure des monastères et organisation de l'ordre*. Ligugé (Vienne): Abbaye Saint-Martin, 1935.

Van Engen, John. "The Christian Middle Ages as an Historiographical Problem." *The American Historical Review* 91 (1986): 519–52.

———. "The Church in the Fifteenth Century." In *Handbook of European History 1400–1600*, edited by Thomas Brady, Heiko Oberman and James Tracy, 305–30. Leiden: Brill, 1994.

———. *Devotio Moderna. Basic Writings*. New York: Paulist, 1988.

———. "The Future of Medieval Church History." *Church History* 71 (2002): 492–522.

———. "Illicit Religion: The Case of Friar Matthew Grabow O.P." In *Law and the Illicit in Medieval Europe*, edited by Ruth Mazo Karras, Joel Kaye and E. Ann Matter, 103–16. Philadelphia: University of Pennsylvania Press, 2008.

———. "Multiple Options: The World of the Fifteenth-Century Church." *Church History* 77 (2008): 257–84.

———. "Sacred Sanctions For Lordship." In *Cultures of Power*, edited by Thomas Bisson, 203–30. Philadelphia: University of Pennsylvania Press, 1995.

———. *Sisters and Brothers of the Common Life: The Devotio Moderna and the World of the Later Middle Ages*. Philadelphia: University of Pennsylvania Press, 2008.

Vargas, Michael. "Administration in a Time of Change: The Dominican Province of Aragon, 1301–1378." PhD diss., Fordham, 2006.

Vauchez, André. "The Religious Orders." In *The New Cambridge Medieval History*, edited by Cristopher Allmand, 220–54. Cambridge: Cambridge University Press, 1998.

Verheijen, Luc. *La Règle de saint Augustin*. 2 vols. Paris: Études augustiniennes, 1967.

Von Heusinger, Sabine. *Der observante Dominikaner Johannes Mulberg († 1414) und der Basler Beginenstreit*. Berlin: Akademie Verlag, 1999.

Walsh, Katherine. *A Fourteenth-Century Scholar and Primate: Richard FitzRalph in Oxford, Avignon and Armagh*. Oxford: Oxford University Press, 1981.

Warren, Nancy Bradley. *Spiritual Economies. Female Monasticism in Later Medieval England*. Philadelphia: University of Pennsylvania Press, 2001.

Watzl, Hermann. "Über Pitanzen und Reichnisse für den Konvent des Klosters Heiligenkreuz." *Analecta Cisterciensia* 47 (1978): 40–147.

Waugh, Scott. "Tenure to Contract: Lordship and Clientage in Thirteenth-Century England." *English Historical Review* 101 (1986): 811–39.

Weiske, Brigitte. "Bilder und Gebete vom Leben und Leiden Christi. Zu einem Zyklus im Gebetbuch des Johannes von Indersdorf für Frau Elisabeth Ebran." In *Die Passion Christi in Literatur und Kunst des Spätmittelalters*, edited by Walter Haug and Burghart Wachinger, 113–68. Tübingen: Niemeyer, 1993.

White, Stephen D. *Custom, Kinship and Gifts to Saints. The Laudatio Parentum in Western France 1050–1150*. Chapel Hill, NC: The University of North Carolina Press, 1988.

Wickberg, Daniel. "What is the History of Sensibilities? On Cultural Histories, Old and New." *American Historical Review* 112 (2007): 661–84.

Williams-Krapp, Werner. "Frauenmystik und Ordensreform im 15. Jahrhundert." In *Literarische Interessenbildung im Mittelalter. Mauracher Symposion 1991*, edited by J. Heinzle, 301–13. Stuttgart, 1993.

———. "Observanzbewegungen, monastische spiritualität und geistliche Literatur im 15. Jahrhundert." *Internationales Archiv für Sozialgeschichte der deutschen Literatur* 20 (1995): 1–15.

———. "Ordensreform und Literatur im 15. Jahrhundert." *Jahrbuch der Oswald von Wolkenstein Gesellschaft* 4 (1986): 41–51.

———. "'Praxis Pietatis.' Heilsverkündung und Frömmigkeit der illiterati im 15. Jahrhundert." In *Die Literatur im Übergang vom Mittelalter zur Neuzeit*, edited by Werner Röcke and Marina Münkler, 139–65. Munich/Vienna: Carl Hanser Verlag, 2004.

Willoweit, Dietmar. "Dominium und Proprietas. Zur Entwicklung des Eigentumsbegriffs in der mittelalterlichen und neuzeitlichen Rechtswissenschaft." *Historisches Jahrbuch* 94 (1974): 131–56.

Winston-Allen, Anne. *Convent Chronicles. Women Writing About Women and Reform in the Late Middle Ages*. University Park, PA: Penn State University Press, 2004.

Wood, Diana. *Medieval Economic Thought*. Cambridge: Cambridge University Press, 2002.
Wranovix, Matthew. "Parish Priests and their Books in the Fifteenth-Century Diocese of Eichstätt." PhD diss., Yale, 2007.
Zaddach, Bernd. *Die Folgen des Schwarzen Todes (1347–51) für den Klerus Mitteleuropas*. Stuttgart: G. Fischer, 1971.
Zeller, Joseph. "Das Provinzialkapitel im Stift Petershausen im Jahr 1417. Ein Beitrag zur Geschichte der Reformen im Benediktinerorden zur Zeit des Konstanzer Konzils." *Studien und Mitteilungen zur Geschichte der Benediktinerordens* 41, NF 10 (1921/22): 1–73.
Zeschick, J. *Das Augustinerchorherrenstift Rohr und die Reformen in bairischen Stiften vom 15. bis 17. Jahrhundert*. Passau: Verlag des Vereins für Ostbairische Heimatforschung, 1969.
Zibermayr, Ignaz. "Die Legation des Kardinals Nikolaus Cusanus und die Ordensreform in der Kirchenprovinz Salzburg." *Reformationsgeschichtliche Studien und Texte* 29 (1914): 1–128.
——. "Zur Geschichte der Raudnitzer Reform." *Mitteilungen des Instituts für Österreichische Geschichtsforschung. 11. Ergänzungsband* (1929): 323–53.
Zimmermann, Gerd. *Ordensleben und Lebensstandard. Die Cura Corporis in den Ordensvorschriften des abendländischen Hochmittelalters*. Münster: Aschendorff, 1973.
Zschoch, Helmut. *Reform und Monastische Spiritualität. Conrad von Zenn († 1460) und Sein Liber de Vita Monastica*. Tübingen: Möhr, 1988.
Zumkeller, Adolar. "Der *Liber de vita monastica* des Conradus de Zenn O.E.S.A. (†1460) und die Spiritualität der spätmittelalterlichen 'Observantia regularis'." *Revista Augustiniana*, 33 (1992): 921–38.
——. "Die Beteiligung der Mendikanten an der Arbeit der Reformkonzilien von Konstanz und Basel." In *Reformbemühungen und Observanzbestrebungen im spätmittelalterlichen Ordenswesen*, edited by Kaspar Elm, 459–67. Berlin: Duncker and Humblot, 1989.

INDEX

abbots/abbesses, 25, 27, 29, 30, 31, 34–36, 42, 45–47, 81, 86–87, 95–96, 100, 103–4, 106, 115–16, 120–21, 123–25, 128, 135, 138–40, 160–69, 180–81, 186, 187
Admont (OSB), 38
Aindorfer, Kaspar, OSB, 144–45
Albert III, Duke of Austria, 71, 152
Albert III "the Pious," Duke of Bavaria-Munich, 145, 176, 195, 197, 198
Albert V, Duke of Austria, 16, 135, 138, 139–41, 149, 151–52
Altomünster (OSB), 144
Amadeus VIII, Duke of Savoy (antipope Felix V), 93
Ambrose, 178
Andechs, (OSB), 194
Andreae, John, 44, 75, 94, 107, 121, 193
Angelus of Rein, OSA, 139
antifraternal tradition, 3 and n. 9, 56
apostolic community, *see* common life
Aquinas, Thomas, 39, 102, 111, 113, 116, 175, 178, 201
Arnulf of Boheries, 177, 178, 191
Augustine of Hippo, 1, 175, 176
Augustinian canons, 1, 3, 4, 98, 135–36, 138, 141–45; and visitation, 152–73
Augustinian Hermits, 8, 40 n. 32, 97, 102
Avignon, 52

Babenbergers, 139
Basel, Dominicans of, 54; Dominican nuns of, 61
Bavaria, 38, 51, 141
Bavaria-Ingolstadt, Duchy of, 141
Bavaria-Landshut, Duchy of, 141, 168
Bavaria-Munich, Duchy of, 141–43, 145, 168, 176, 195, 213
Beguines, 219
Benedict of Nursia, 1, 25
Benedict XII, 47, 53, 61, 107
Benedict XIII, 115
Benedictines, 4, 97, 98, 119, 135, 137–39, 141–47; and visitation, 152–73

Bernard of Clairveaux, OCist, 101, 178, 191
Bernard of Waging, OSB, 144, 183
Bernardino of Siena, OFM, 6
Beuerberg (OSA), 169
Beyharting (OSB), 144
Biburg (OSB), 144
Black Death, 11, 72; and consequences for material culture, 55–56; and religious orders, 53–54, 56; and "vice of property," 54 and n. 109, 113
Boccaccio, 3, 56, 63
Bonaventure, 175, 178, 187
Book of Spiritual Poverty, 196
Bridget of Sweden, 4
Brothers and Sisters of the Common Life, 3, 81, 98
Brunner, Eberhard, OSA, 142, 213–14
Burr, David, 2 n. 8, 13
Busch, John, OSA, 135, 217

Cabasse, Raymond, OP, 111–15, 203, 217
Capua, 140
Carmelites, 56
cash, 29, 30, 34–40, 42–48, 80, 81–82, 85–86, 112–14, 116, 124, 149; and critiques of excess, 78–79, 82–85, 108, 150–53, 187; and theories of money, 110 and n. 51; and reform visitation, 155, 169–70
Catherine of Siena, 6, 185, 207
Chaucer, 3, 56, 57
chess, 114
Cistercians, 1; defense of propertied life, 115; and Observant reform, 99, 101–7; religious habit of, 32, 38; statutory legislation of, 46–47, 57–58, 62, 107
Clement IV, 44, 107
Clement V, 107
Cluny (OSB), and Black Death, 55; prebends and pittances of 30, 31; religious habit of, 32; and *status*, 49–50, 114, 124, 162; and sumptuary law, 51, 55; and worldly clothing, 31, 32

Cologne, Dominicans of, 54, 153; New Devout of, 88; University of, 71, 81, 89
comfort (*commodità, commodum*), 60, 85
common life, 1, 3, 7–8, 68, 77, 84, 88–89, 93, 103, 110, 126–30, 135–36, 151, 217, 219; and reforming legislation, 207–13; and reforming memory, 213–15; and reforming visitation, 158–59, 162, 169–72
Constable, Giles, 2 and n. 5; 21 and n. 50, 180, 195
conversion, 19, 68, 70–71, 102, 139–40, 197–98, 196
Council of Basel, 8, 16, 101, 117, 144, 180
Council of Constance, 8, 16, 17, 89–91, 93, 98, 99, 121, 137, 139, 140, 151, 153, 205, 214, 215; as public forum, 100–103, 154
Council of Vienne, 52, 53
courtesy gifts (*munuscula*), 75, 110, 155, 156
crisis, historiography of, 9–10 and n. 24; rhetorical uses of, 80, 84–85, 88
curialitas, 49, 52, 56, 58–59
custom (*consuetudo*), 14, 18, 28–29, 31, 95, 214; and cash prebends, 41, 68 and n. 3, 80; as justification for appropriated space, 62; as justification for eating meat, 58; as justification for propertied life in general, 109–15, 117, 118
customaries, 29, 206

D'Ailly, Peter, 101
David of Augsburg, OFM, 177, 185, 196
Decretals, 33, 48, 86, 92, 106–08, 111, 113–14, 166, 208
Denis the Carthusian, 177
"detachment," 201
dice, 114, 155
Diessen (OSA), 170, 176–79, 183
Dietramszell (OSA), 144, 169
discretion, 35–36, 47–48, 76–78, 85–87, 94, 96
"Doctor of Erfurt," 183
Dominicans, reform of, 4, 97, 98, 109, 117–19, 136; and apostolic poverty, 39; statutory legislation of, 46, 53, 57, 62–64, 114; theories of corporate ownership, 109–113
Dominici, Giovanni, OP, 97, 109–11

dominium, 3, 77; and Roman law, 27; and cash stipends, 42, 54; and models of corporate ownership, 42–44, 110, 126–29; and papal power, 52; and mortal sin, 77
drinking, and ritual memory, 28; and charity, 31, 58; and *status*, 49, 57–58; excesses condemned, 114
Dürnstein (OSA), 141

Eberbach (OCist), 72
Ebersberg (OSB), 168
Ebran, Elizabeth, 195
Elliott, Dyan, 148
Elm, Kaspar, 4–5, 11, 13, 21 and n. 52, 217
Ernest, Duke of Bavaria Munich, 141–43
Estate, *see status*

falconry, 52, 187
Fitzralph, Richard, OFM, 68
Fleury (OSB), 31
food, and charity, 31, 58; and *status*, 49, 57–59, 124; and license, 116; critiques of excess, 116; and reforming visitation, 162–63, 170; and reform legislation, 207–9, 211
Fournier, Jacques, *see* Benedict XII
Franciscans, 2, 4, 97, 98, 130; and apostolic poverty, 2, 18, 39, 41, 68, 121, 218; and clerical dominion, 115; statutory legislation of, 48, 55
Freising, 142–43, 168
"friend of God," 196, 198, 199, 201
Fürstenfeld (OCist), 144
Fulda (OSB), 31, 32

gambling, 114
Geisenfeld (OSB), 144
Gerson, Jean, 101
Giotto, 60
Godfrey of Fontaines, 42–44, 75
Godstow, (OSB), 61
Göss (OSB), 147
Göttweig (OSB), 38, 140
Gratian, 116, 166, 193
Graus, František, 10
Great Famine, 11
Great Schism, 11, 71, 72, 89, 100
Gregory IX, 33
Gregory the Great, 25–27, 32, 175, 178, 192, 193, 203
Gregory XII, 91

Groote, Geert, 3, 69, 70
Grünwalder, John, 143–45, 152
Grundmann, Herbert, 2 and n. 6, 4, 19

habit, religious, and material culture, 52–53, 114, 186, 187; and reforming legislation, 209–11; and reform visitation, 162, 170; symbolism of, 32, 56
Hamm, Berndt, 10, 21
Hapsburgs, 139
Heidelberg, University of, 71, 91, 119
Heiligenkreuz (OCist), 45, 186, 187
Heiligenkreuztal (OCist), 38
Henry "the Rich," Duke of Bavaria-Landshut, 168
Henry of Langenstein, 17, 110, 121, 137, 139, 194; sermon to Klosterneuburg, 67–80, 149–50, 151, 183–85, 190, 205, 218
Henry of Segusio, *see* Hostiensis
Herzogenburg (OSA), 141
Hohenwart (OSB), 144
Honorius III, 166
Horst, Ulrich, 2 n. 8
Hostiensis, 34–36, 75, 86, 87, 92
Hugh of Fouilloy, OCist, 186
Hugh of St. Victor, OSA, 178
humanism, 97
Hundred Years' War, 11
hunting, 52
Hus, Jan, 91
Hussites, 100, 102, 130, 193

Imitation of Christ, 4, 179, 195
Indersdorf (OSA), 20, 142, 145, 183–85, 202, 203, 210–11, 213–14
indulgences, 107–108
Innocent III, 25, 32, 34, 44, 52, 92, 106–07, 111, 166, 193, 208
Innocent IV, 45
inquest (inquisitio), 146–48, 156, 166

Jerome, 178
Jesuits, 6
Jews, 93 n. 84, 190, 214
Joan of Arc, 220
John IV of Tülbeck, Bishop of Freising, 210
John of Capistrano, OFM, 4
John of Draschitz (bishop), 3, 141
John of Indersdorf, OSA, 142–43, 145, 175, 184, 192, 194, 217;
Dreierlei Wesen der Menschen of, 194–202, 210–11, 213–14
John of Maulbronn, OSB, 156–60
John of Ochsenhausen, OSB, 143
John XXIII, 89
Judenburg (OFM), 40, 41

Kaminksy, Howard, 11, 33 and n. 24, 49 and n. 84, 115
Kastl, 4, 98
Kastner, Hildebrand, OSB, 144
Kastner, Simon, OSB, 168
Keck, John, OSB, 144
Kempe, Margery, 220
Kerkering, Dietrich, 17, 81–90, 121, 151, 153, 192, 217
Klosterneuburg (OSA), 17, 67, 73–80, 141
Knowles, David, OSB, 217

Lambach (OSB), 161
Lambert, Malcom, 2 n. 8
Langenzenn, (OSA), 206
Leclercq, Jean, 21
Leonard of Gäming, OSB, 139
Lerner, Robert, 2 n. 8
license, 34–36, 42–43, 46–48, 81–82, 84, 86, 94, 116, 121, 202
limitors (*terminarii*), 40, 48, 108
Little, Lester, 2 n. 6
Li Muisis, Gilles, OSB, 53
Lollards, 3, 100, 102, 196, 219
Ludolph of Saxony, 190
Ludowico Barbo, 4
Lübeck, nuns of, 61
Luther, Martin, 4, 221–22

Mahrenberg (OP), 40, 41
Maiselstein, Caspar, 139
Marsili, Luigi, OESA, 97
Marsilius of Inghen, 71
Martin of Leibitz, OSB, 147–48, 175
Martin V, 138, 168
Mary Magdalen, (OSA), 155
Mass stipends, 37–38, 39, 74, 112, 123, 207
"Master of Paris," 185, 192
Matthew Grabow, OP, 93
Mechtild of Magdeburg, 196
Melk (OSB), 4, 8, 118, 139–40, 143–44, 147, 149, 152, 164, 179, 186–187, 192, 194, 206
Merswin, Rulman, 196
Meyer, John, OP, 136, 217

Modern Devotion, 4, 15, 70, 88, 93, 130, 172, 178–79, 196–97, 219, 221
Mondsee (OSB), 185, 211
Montecassino (OSB), 31
Munich, Clares of, 40

Neunkirchen (OSA), 142, 206, 214
Newhauser, Richard, 19
"new piety," 71, 72, 77, 92, 129, 194, 197, 219
Nicholas of Cusa, 101, 146
Nicholas of Dinkelsbühl, 137–41, 153–54, 192, 194; *Reformationis methodus* of, 137–39, 141, 159, 164–65
Nicholas Respitz, OSB, 140, 144
Nider, John, OP, 6, 117–19, 171
nobility, and material culture, 49–50, 56–57; and *status*, 49, 87, 89
Nonnberg (OSB), 185, 192, 193, 194
normative centering, 10
Nott, Oswald, OSB, 183
Nuremberg, 51, 102, 114

obedientiaries, 31, 34, 36–37
Oberalteich (OSB), 183
Observant Movement, and Augustinian canons, 4; and Benedictines, 93–94; and Cistercians, 99; and common life, 7–8, 94–95; and Dominicans, 4, 93–94; and Franciscans, 4, 93–94; historiography of, 3–7, 220–22;
Olomuc, 139
Ozment, Steven, 10

Padua, University of, 91, Benedictines of, 97
Passion of Christ, 190–91, 199
peculium, 30, 32, 34, 47 n. 81, 74
penitence, 16, 197–98
Peraldus, William, 26, 94, 101, 105, 108, 157, 183, 187
Peter of Pulka, 139, 149–50, 152
Peter of Rosenheim, OSB, 140, 144, 152–53, 156, 161
Petershausen, reform chapter of, 98
Petrarch, 178
Peuntner, Thomas, 194
Phrayter, Georg, OSB, 183
Pilgrim IV of Puchheim, 139
pittance (*pictantia*), 30, 31, 37, 57
Pius II, 185, 210
Plank, Andreas, 141
Pomegranate, 195

"Poor Monk" (anonymous Cistercian author), 103–07, 185
possession, 121–23
poverty, 18–19, 25–26, 33, 35, 39, 48, 125, 212, 219
Prague, University of, 71, 81
prebend (*praebenda*), 29, 37–39, 80, 81, 123, 125; at Augustinian canonry of Klosterneuburg, 67, 74; at nunnery of St. Giles, 81–82; at Praemonstratensian canonry of Wilten, 74
priors/prioresses, 73–74, 109, 169–70, 186, 210–11
proprietarii/proprietariae, 8, 17, 18, 26, 47–48, 86, 93, 94, 95, 101–03, 105–08, 127, 147, 152, 169, 182, 190, 203, 212, 218, 220
proprium, proprietas, 1, 27, 32, 36, 46–48; and late-medieval material culture, 7; in legal commentaries, 33–36; 44–45; in Peraldus' *Summa on Vices*, 26, 105, 108
proprium similitudinarium, 120–21
publication, 18, 102–3 and nn. 26, 27, 104
"public intellectuals," 71 and n. 13, 81, 96, 101
"public sins," 93

rapiaria, 178
Raudnitz (OSA), 3, 98, 141, 194; statutes of, 8, 141–43, 145–46, 170, 203, 206
Raymond of Capua, OP, 4, 185
Rebdorf (OSA), 206
Rechentshofen (OSB), 157
Reformatio Sigismundi, 101
resistance to reform, 17, 21, 61–62, 76–77, 85–87, 94–95, 107, 116–19, 135–36, 147–49, 153, 156–60, 165
Richard of St. Victor, OSA, 178
Rigaud, Eudes, 61
Rohr (OSA), 144
Rothuet, John, OSA, *see* John of Indersdorf
Rottenbuch (OSA), 144
Rudolph IV, Duke of Austria, 152
Rule of Augustine, 1, 184, 202, 203, 209
Rule of Benedict, 1, 27, 59, 95–96, 119–30, 192, 208
rusticitas, 50, 58–59
Rutebeuf, 56

Salimbene de Adam, OFM, 58–59
Salutati, Coluccio, 97
Savonarola, OP, 4, 6
Scheyern (OSB), 144
Schlitpacher, John, OSB, 165–66
Schuster, Peter, 11
Scotus, Adam, 177, 182
Seitenstetten (OSB), 169–71
Seligenthal (OCist), 38
sensibility, 14 and n. 37, 31, 63–64, 85, 129, 161, 163, 171–2, 187, 202–3, 205, 209–11
Seyringer, Nicholas, OSB, 139, 141, 144, 164
Sigismund, 89, 91
space, 59, 61–64, 116; critiques of associated with "vice of property," 106, 114; and material culture, 60–64; and reform legislation, 209, 211 and reform visitation, 155, 162, 171–72
St. Anna (OSB), 140
St. Dorothy (OSA), 141
St. Florian (OSA), 59, 141
St. Gall (OSB), 3
St. Giles (OSB), 17, 81–90, 217
St. James (OSA), 154, 155
St. Lawrence (OSA), 155
St. Mary (Irish Benedictines), 140, 144, 175, 194; reform formulary of, 155, 161, 165
St. Matthias (OSB), 93
St. Paul (OSB), 147
St. Peter (OSB), 144, 193, 194
St. Ulrich (OSB), 194
status, 14, 28–9, 31, 32, 33; and clergy, 51–52; and material culture, 28, 48–50, 57–59, 60–64, 68, 73–75, 79–80, 114, 162, 180–82, 197–98; and obedientiaries, 31; and prebends, 30, 67, 74, 81–82, 115; and reform legislation, 209–11; and religious habit, 32, 52–53; and religious life (*status perfectionis*), 39; and satire, 78–80, 84–85; and scholastic models of corporate ownership, 42–44
Steven of Haalsach, 141
Subiaco (OSB), 25, 33, 34, 44, 92, 106–07; and origins of Observant reform, 97, 139–40, 144, 175
sumptuary law, 15, 50–52
Suso, Henry, OP, 63–64, 68, 70, 192, 195, 196, 201

Tancred of Pellavicini, OSB, 58
Tauler, John, OP, 196
Tegernsee (OSB), 8, 54, 144, 170, 180, 183, 185, 187, 194, 206–7
Third Lateran Council, 32, 34, 92
Thomas of Kempen, OSA, 4, 98
tria substantialia, 102, 146, 149, 157
Trier, 98
Trinci, Paolucci, OFM, 3, 97

Urban VI, 71
usus, 47, 121, 123, 129; and cash incomes, 41; and scholastic models of corporate ownership, 42
Utraquists, 114–15

veils, 156
Vener, Job, 17, 90–91, 98, 99, 101, 107, 121; compendium on the "vice of property," 91–96, 104, 106, 157, 183–85, 187, 192, 203, 218
"vice of property," (*vitium proprietatis*), 8, 17, 25, 47, 54, 93, 94–96, 99, 101–8, 121, 147–52, 157, 169, 182, 184, 187, 190, 198, 202, 205, 212. *See also proprium, proprietas*
Vienna, University of, 15, 16, 71, 72, 139, 142, 194
visitation, 135–55, 198–99
vows, 87, 92–94, 116, 157–58, 202

Walsee (OSA), 206
Weihenstephan (OSB), 144, 152–53, 170
Wienhausen (OSA), 61
Westminster (OSB), 36, 59
William of St. Thierry, (OCist), 178
William, Duke of Bavaria Munich, 141–43, 168
Wilten (OPraem), 74, 75
Windesheim (OSA), 4, 135–36, 178–79
Wischler, John, OSB, 119–30, 153, 161, 175, 187, 192
Wittelsbachs, 142–43, 213
Woodford, William, OFM, 115
Wyclif, John, 3 and n. 10, 68, 77, 115, 121
Wyclifites, *see* Lollards

Zenn, Conrad, OESA, 102; *De vita monastica* of, 102–3, 105–7

Studies in the History of Christian Traditions

(formerly Studies in the History of Christian Thought)

Edited by Robert J. Bast

1. McNeill, J. J. *The Blondelian Synthesis.* 1966. Out of print
2. Goertz, H.-J. *Innere und äussere Ordnung in der Theologie Thomas Müntzers.* 1967
3. Bauman, Cl. *Gewaltlosigkeit im Täufertum.* 1968
4. Roldanus, J. *Le Christ et l'Homme dans la Théologie d'Athanase d'Alexandrie.* 2nd ed. 1977
5. Milner, Jr., B. Ch. *Calvin's Doctrine of the Church.* 1970. Out of print
6. Tierney, B. *Origins of Papal Infallibility, 1150-1350.* 2nd ed. 1988
7. Oldfield, J. J. *Tolerance in the Writings of Félicité Lamennais 1809-1831.* 1973
8. Oberman, H. A. (ed.). *Luther and the Dawn of the Modern Era.* 1974. Out of print
9. Holeczek, H. *Humanistische Bibelphilologie bei Erasmus, Thomas More und William Tyndale.* 1975
10. Farr, W. *John Wyclif as Legal Reformer.* 1974
11. Purcell, M. *Papal Crusading Policy 1244-1291.* 1975
12. Ball, B. W. *A Great Expectation.* Eschatological Thought in English Protestantism. 1975
13. Stieber, J. W. *Pope Eugenius IV, the Council of Basel, and the Empire.* 1978. Out of print
14. Partee, Ch. *Calvin and Classical Philosophy.* 1977
15. Misner, P. *Papacy and Development.* Newman and the Primacy of the Pope. 1976
16. Tavard, G. H. *The Seventeenth-Century Tradition.* A Study in Recusant Thought. 1978
17. Quinn, A. *The Confidence of British Philosophers.* An Essay in Historical Narrative. 1977
18. Beck, J. *Le Concil de Basle (1434).* 1979
19. Church, F. F. and George, T. (ed.). *Continuity and Discontinuity in Church History.* 1979
20. Gray, P. T. R. *The Defense of Chalcedon in the East (451-553).* 1979
21. Nijenhuis, W. *Adrianus Saravia (c. 1532-1613).* Dutch Calvinist. 1980
22. Parker, T. H. L. (ed.). *Iohannis Calvini Commentarius in Epistolam Pauli ad Romanos.* 1981
23. Ellis, I. *Seven Against Christ.* A Study of 'Essays and Reviews'. 1980
24. Brann, N. L. *The Abbot Trithemius (1462-1516).* 1981
25. Locher, G. W. *Zwingli's Thought.* New Perspectives. 1981
26. Gogan, B. *The Common Corps of Christendom.* Ecclesiological Themes in Thomas More. 1982
27. Stock, U. *Die Bedeutung der Sakramente in Luthers Sermonen von 1519.* 1982
28. Yardeni, M. (ed.). *Modernité et nonconformisme en France à travers les âges.* 1983
29. Platt, J. *Reformed Thought and Scholasticism.* 1982
30. Watts, P. M. *Nicolaus Cusanus.* A Fifteenth-Century Vision of Man. 1982
31. Sprunger, K. L. *Dutch Puritanism.* 1982
32. Meijering, E. P. *Melanchthon and Patristic Thought.* 1983
33. Stroup, J. *The Struggle for Identity in the Clerical Estate.* 1984
34. 35. Colish, M. L. *The Stoic Tradition from Antiquity to the Early Middle Ages.* 1.2. 2nd ed. 1990
36. Guy, B. *Domestic Correspondence of Dominique-Marie Varlet, Bishop of Babylon, 1678-1742.* 1986
37. 38. Clark, F. *The Pseudo-Gregorian Dialogues.* I. II. 1987
39. Parente, Jr. J. A. *Religious Drama and the Humanist Tradition.* 1987
40. Posthumus Meyjes, G. H. M. *Hugo Grotius, Meletius.* 1988
41. Feld, H. *Der Ikonoklasmus des Westens.* 1990
42. Reeve, A. and Screech, M. A. (eds.). *Erasmus' Annotations on the New Testament.* Acts — Romans — I and II Corinthians. 1990
43. Kirby, W. J. T. *Richard Hooker's Doctrine of the Royal Supremacy.* 1990
44. Gerstner, J. N. *The Thousand Generation Covenant.* Reformed Covenant Theology. 1990
45. Christianson, G. and Izbicki, T. M. (eds.). *Nicholas of Cusa.* 1991
46. Garstein, O. *Rome and the Counter-Reformation in Scandinavia.* 1553-1622. 1992
47. Garstein, O. *Rome and the Counter-Reformation in Scandinavia.* 1622-1656. 1992
48. Perrone Compagni, V. (ed.). *Cornelius Agrippa, De occulta philosophia Libri tres.* 1992

49. Martin, D. D. *Fifteenth-Century Carthusian Reform*. The World of Nicholas Kempf. 1992
50. Hoenen, M. J. F. M. *Marsilius of Inghen*. Divine Knowledge in Late Medieval Thought. 1993
51. O'Malley, J. W., Izbicki, T. M. and Christianson, G. (eds.). *Humanity and Divinity in Renaissance and Reformation*. Essays in Honor of Charles Trinkaus. 1993
52. Reeve, A. (ed.) and Screech, M. A. (introd.). *Erasmus' Annotations on the New Testament*. Galatians to the Apocalypse. 1993
53. Stump, Ph. H. *The Reforms of the Council of Constance (1414-1418)*. 1994
54. Giakalis, A. *Images of the Divine*. The Theology of Icons at the Seventh Ecumenical Council. With a Foreword by Henry Chadwick. 1994
55. Nellen, H. J. M. and Rabbie, E. (eds.). *Hugo Grotius – Theologian*. Essays in Honour of G. H. M. Posthumus Meyjes. 1994
56. Trigg, J. D. *Baptism in the Theology of Martin Luther*. 1994
57. Janse, W. *Albert Hardenberg als Theologe*. Profil eines Bucer-Schülers. 1994
59. Schoor, R. J. M. van de. *The Irenical Theology of Théophile Brachet de La Milletière (1588-1665)*. 1995
60. Strehle, S. *The Catholic Roots of the Protestant Gospel*. Encounter between the Middle Ages and the Reformation. 1995
61. Brown, M. L. *Donne and the Politics of Conscience in Early Modern England*. 1995
62. Screech, M. A. (ed.). *Richard Mocket, Warden of All Souls College, Oxford, Doctrina et Politia Ecclesiae Anglicanae*. An Anglican Summa. Facsimile with Variants of the Text of 1617. Edited with an Introduction. 1995
63. Snoek, G. J. C. *Medieval Piety from Relics to the Eucharist*. A Process of Mutual Interaction. 1995
64. Pixton, P. B. *The German Episcopacy and the Implementation of the Decrees of the Fourth Lateran Council, 1216-1245*. Watchmen on the Tower. 1995
65. Dolnikowski, E. W. *Thomas Bradwardine: A View of Time and a Vision of Eternity in Fourteenth-Century Thought*. 1995
66. Rabbie, E. (ed.). *Hugo Grotius, Ordinum Hollandiae ac Westfrisiae Pietas (1613)*. Critical Edition with Translation and Commentary. 1995
67. Hirsh, J. C. *The Boundaries of Faith*. The Development and Transmission of Medieval Spirituality. 1996
68. Burnett, S. G. *From Christian Hebraism to Jewish Studies*. Johannes Buxtorf (1564-1629) and Hebrew Learning in the Seventeenth Century. 1996
69. Boland O.P., V. *Ideas in God according to Saint Thomas Aquinas*. Sources and Synthesis. 1996
70. Lange, M.E. *Telling Tears in the English Renaissance*. 1996
71. Christianson, G. and Izbicki, T.M. (eds.). *Nicholas of Cusa on Christ and the Church*. Essays in Memory of Chandler McCuskey Brooks for the American Cusanus Society. 1996
72. Mali, A. *Mystic in the New World*. Marie de l'Incarnation (1599-1672). 1996
73. Visser, D. *Apocalypse as Utopian Expectation (800-1500)*. The Apocalypse Commentary of Berengaudus of Ferrières and the Relationship between Exegesis, Liturgy and Iconography. 1996
74. O'Rourke Boyle, M. *Divine Domesticity*. Augustine of Thagaste to Teresa of Avila. 1997
75. Pfizenmaier, T. C. *The Trinitarian Theology of Dr. Samuel Clarke (1675-1729)*. Context, Sources, and Controversy. 1997
76. Berkvens-Stevelinck, C., Israel, J. and Posthumus Meyjes, G. H. M. (eds.). *The Emergence of Tolerance in the Dutch Republic*. 1997
77. Haykin, M. A. G. (ed.). *The Life and Thought of John Gill (1697-1771)*. A Tercentennial Appreciation. 1997
78. Kaiser, C. B. *Creational Theology and the History of Physical Science*. The Creationist Tradition from Basil to Bohr. 1997
79. Lees, J. T. *Anselm of Havelberg*. Deeds into Words in the Twelfth Century. 1997
80. Winter, J. M. van. *Sources Concerning the Hospitallers of St John in the Netherlands, 14th-18th Centuries*. 1998
81. Tierney, B. *Foundations of the Conciliar Theory*. The Contribution of the Medieval Canonists from Gratian to the Great Schism. Enlarged New Edition. 1998
82. Miernowski, J. *Le Dieu Néant*. Théologies négatives à l'aube des temps modernes. 1998
83. Halverson, J. L. *Peter Aureol on Predestination*. A Challenge to Late Medieval Thought. 1998.
84. Houliston, V. (ed.). *Robert Persons, S.J.: The Christian Directory (1582)*. The First Booke of the Christian Exercise, appertayning to Resolution. 1998

85. Grell, O. P. (ed.). *Paracelsus. The Man and His Reputation, His Ideas and Their Transformation.* 1998
86. Mazzola, E. *The Pathology of the English Renaissance.* Sacred Remains and Holy Ghosts. 1998.
87. 88. Marsilius von Inghen. *Quaestiones super quattuor libros sententiarum.* Super Primum. Bearbeitet von M. Santos Noya. 2 Bände. I. Quaestiones 1-7. II. Quaestiones 8-21. 2000
89. Faupel-Drevs, K. *Vom rechten Gebrauch der Bilder im liturgischen Raum.* Mittelalterliche Funktions-bestimmungen bildender Kunst im *Rationale divinorum officiorum* des Durandus von Mende (1230/1-1296). 1999
90. Krey, P. D. W. and Smith, L. (eds.). *Nicholas of Lyra.* the Senses of Scripture. 2000
92. Oakley, F. *Politics and Eternity.* Studies in the History of Medieval and Early-Modern Political Thought. 1999
93. Pryds, D. *The Politics of Preaching.* Robert of Naples (1309-1343) and his Sermons. 2000
94. Posthumus Meyjes, G. H. M. *Jean Gerson – Apostle of Unity.* His Church Politics and Ecclesiology. Translated by J. C. Grayson. 1999
95. Berg, J. van den. *Religious Currents and Cross-Currents.* Essays on Early Modern Protestantism and the Protestant Enlightenment. Edited by J. de Bruijn, P. Holtrop, and E. van der Wall. 1999
96. Izbicki, T. M. and Bellitto, C. M. (eds.). *Reform and Renewal in the Middle Ages and the Renaissance.* Studies in Honor of Louis Pascoe, S. J. 2000
97. Kelly, D. *The Conspiracy of Allusion.* Description, Rewriting, and Authorship from Macrobius to Medieval Romance. 1999
98. Marrone, S. P. *The Light of Thy Countenance.* Science and Knowledge of God in the Thirteenth Century. 2 volumes. 1. A Doctrine of Divine Illumination. 2. God at the Core of Cognition. 2001
99. Howson, B. H. *Erroneous and Schismatical Opinions.* The Question of Orthodoxy regarding the Theology of Hanserd Knollys (c. 1599-169)). 2001
100. Asselt, W. J. van. *The Federal Theology of Johannes Cocceius (1603-1669).* 2001
101. Celenza, C.S. *Piety and Pythagoras in Renaissance Florence* the Symbolum Nesianum. 2001
102. Dam, H.-J. van (ed.), *Hugo Grotius, De imperio summarum potestatum circa sacra.* Critical Edition with Introduction, English translation and Commentary. 2 volumes. 2001
103. Bagge, S. *Kings, Politics, and the Right Order of the World in German Historiography c. 950-1150.* 2002
104. Steiger, J. A. *Fünf Zentralthemen der Theologie Luthers und seiner Erben.* Communicatio – Imago – Figura – Maria – Exempla. Mit Edition zweier christologischer Frühschriften Johann Gerhards. 2002
105. Izbicki, T. M. and Bellitto, C. M. (eds.). *Nicholas of Cusa and his Age: Intellect and Spirituality.* Essays Dedicated to the Memory of F. Edward Cranz, Thomas P. McTighe and Charles Trinkaus. 2002
106. Hascher-Burger, U. *Gesungene Innigkeit.* Studien zu einer Musikhandschrift der Devotio moderna (Utrecht, Universiteitsbibliotheek, MS 16 H 94, olim B 113). Mit einer Edition der Gesänge. 2002
107. Bolliger, D. *Infiniti Contemplatio.* Grundzüge der Scotus- und Scotismusrezeption im Werk Huldrych Zwinglis. 2003
108. Clark, F. *The 'Gregorian' Dialogues and the Origins of Benedictine Monasticism.* 2002
109. Elm, E. *Die Macht der Weisheit.* Das Bild des Bischofs in der *Vita Augustini* des Possidius und andere spätantiken und frühmittelalterlichen Bischofsviten. 2003
110. Bast, R. J. (ed.). *The Reformation of Faith in the Context of Late Medieval Theology and Piety.* Essays by Berndt Hamm. 2004.
111. Heering, J. P. *Hugo Grotius as Apologist for the Christian Religion.* A Study of his Work *De Veritate Religionis Christianae* (1640). Translated by J.C. Grayson. 2004.
112. Lim, P. C.- H. *In Pursuit of Purity, Unity, and Liberty.* Richard Baxter's Puritan Ecclesiology in its Seventeenth-Century Context. 2004.
113. Connors, R. and Gow, A. C. (eds.). *Anglo-American Millennialism, from Milton to the Millerites.* 2004.
114. Zinguer, I. and Yardeni, M. (eds.). *Les Deux Réformes Chrétiennes.* Propagation et Diffusion. 2004.
115. James, F. A. III (ed.). *Peter Martyr Vermigli and the European Reformations*: Semper Reformanda. 2004.
116. Stroll, M. *Calixtus II (1119-1124).* A Pope Born to Rule. 2004.
117. Roest, B. *Franciscan Literature of Religious Instruction before the Council of Trent.* 2004.
118. Wannenmacher, J. E. *Hermeneutik der Heilsgeschichte.* De septem sigillis und die sieben Siegel im Werk Joachims von Fiore. 2004.
119. Thompson, N. *Eucharistic Sacrifice and Patristic Tradition in the Theology of Martin Bucer, 1534-1546.* 2005.
120. Van der Kool, C. *As in a Mirror. John Calvin and Karl Barth on Knowing God.* A Diptych. 2005.
121. Steiger, J. A. *Medizinische Theologie.* Christus medicus und theologia medicinalis bei Martin Luther und im Luthertum der Barockzeit. 2005.

122. Giakalis, A. *Images of the Divine*. The Theology of Icons at the Seventh Ecumenical Council – Revised Edition. With a Foreword by Henry Chadwick. 2005.
123. Heffernan, T. J. and Burman, T. E. (eds.). *Scripture and Pluralism*. Reading the Bible in the Religiously Plural Worlds of the Middle Ages and Renaissance. Papers Presented at the First Annual Symposium of the Marco Institute for Medieval and Renaissance Studies at the University of Tennessee, Knoxville, February 21-22, 2002. 2005.
124. Litz, G., Munzert, H. and Liebenberg, R. (eds.). *Frömmigkeit – Theologie – Frömmigkeitstheologie – Contributions to European Church History*.
125. Ferreiro, A. *Simon Magus in Patristic, Medieval and Early Modern Traditions*. 2005.
126. Goodwin, D. L. *"Take Hold of the Robe of a Jew"*. Herbert of Bosham's Christian Hebraism. 2006.
127. Holder, R. W. *John Calvin and the Grounding of Interpretation*. Calvin's First Commentaries. 2006.
128. Reilly, D. J. *The Art of Reform in Eleventh-Century Flanders*. Gerard of Cambrai, Richard of Saint-Vanne and the Saint-Vaast Bible. 2006.
129. Frassetto, M. (ed.). *Heresy and the Persecuting Society in the Middle Ages*. Essays on the Work of R.I. Moore. 2006.
130. Walters Adams, G. *Visions in Late Medieval England*. Lay Spirituality and Sacred Glimpses of the Hidden Worlds of Faith. 2007.
131. Kirby, T. *The Zurich Connection and Tudor Political Theology*. 2007.
132. Mackay, C.S. *Narrative of the Anabaptist Madness*. The Overthrow of Münster, the Famous Metropolis of Westphalia (2 vols.). 2007.
133. Leroux, N.R. *Martin Luther as Comforter*. Writings on Death. 2007.
134. Tavuzzi, M. *Renaissance Inquisitors*. Dominican Inquisitors and Inquisitorial Districts in Northern Italy, 1474-1527. 2007.
135. Baschera, L. and C. Moser (eds.). *Girolamo Zanchi, De religione christiana fides – Confession of Christian Religion* (2 vols.). 2007.
136. Hurth, E. *Between Faith and Unbelief*. American Transcendentalists and the Challenge of Atheism. 2007.
137. Wilkinson R.J. *Orientalism, Aramaic and Kabbalah in the Catholic Reformation*. The First Printing of the Syriac New Testament. 2007.
138. Wilkinson R.J. *The Kabbalistic Scholars of the Antwerp Polyglot Bible*. 2007.
139. Boreczky E. *John Wyclif's Discourse On Dominion in Community*. 2007.
140. Dowd C. *Rome in Australia: The Papacy and Conflict in the Australian Catholic Missions, 1834-1884* (2 vols.). 2008.
141. Perrone S.T. *Charles V and the Castilian Assembly of the Clergy*. Negotiations for the Ecclesiastical Subsidy. 2008.
142. Smith, K.A. and S. Wells (eds.). *Negotiating Community and Difference in Medieval Europe*. Gender, Power, Patronage and the Authority of Religion in Latin Christendom. 2009
143. Mixson, J.D. *Poverty's Proprietors*. Ownership and Mortal Sin at the Origins of the Observant Movement. 2009

brill.nl/shct